Jerome of Prague
and the Foundations
of the Hussite Movement

Jerome of Prague and the Foundations of the Hussite Movement

THOMAS A. FUDGE

OXFORD

UNIVERSITY PRESS

OXFORD
UNIVERSITY PRESS

Oxford University Press is a department of the University of Oxford. It furthers
the University's objective of excellence in research, scholarship, and education
by publishing worldwide. Oxford is a registered trade mark of Oxford University
Press in the UK and certain other countries.

Published in the United States of America by Oxford University Press
198 Madison Avenue, New York, NY 10016, United States of America.

Library of Congress Cataloging-in-Publication Data
Names: Fudge, Thomas A, author.
Title: Jerome of Prague and the foundations of the Hussite movement / Thomas A. Fudge.
Description: New York: Oxford University Press, 2016. |
Includes bibliographical references and index.
Identifiers: LCCN 2015044384 | ISBN 978-0-19-049884-9 (cloth: alk. paper)
Subjects: LCSH: Jeronym, Prazsky, approximately 1380–1416. | Hussites—History. |
Czechoslovakia—Church history.
Classification: LCC BX4918.J47 F83 2016 | DDC 270.5092—dc23 LC record available
at http://lccn.loc.gov/2015044384

1 3 5 7 9 8 6 4 2
Printed by Sheridan, USA

In honor of Ian Campbell and in memory of Vincent Orange,
former University of Canterbury colleagues,
because they were right.

"Multi famam, conscientiam pauci verentur."
Pliny the Younger, Epistulae, 3.20.9.

Pliny, Letters, vol. 1, Books 1–7, trans. Betty Radice.
Loeb Classical Library, vol. 55.
Cambridge, MA: Harvard University Press, 1969, p. 234.

Contents

List of Illustrations

List of Abbreviations

BRRP	*Bohemian Reformation and Religious Practice*
Castle Archive	Prague Cathedral Chapter Library
CCL	*Corpus Christianorum, Series Latina*
Cerretano	*Liber gestorum*, in Finke, *Acta*, vol. 2, pp. 171–348
CV	*Communio viatorum*
Czech *Acta*	Czech *Acta* of the Council of Constance, in *FRB*, vol. 8, pp. 247–318
De Vita Magistri Ieronomi de Praga	FRB, vol. 8, pp. 335–8
Documenta	František Palacký, ed., *Documenta Mag. Joannis Hus vitam, doctrinam, causam in constantiensi concilio actam et controversias de religione in Bohemia annis 1403–1418 motas illustrantia*
Fillastre	Guillaume Fillastre, *Gesta concilii Constanciensis*, in Finke, *Acta*, vol. 2, pp. 13–170
Finke, *Acta*	Heinrich Finke, ed., *Acta concilii Constanciensis*
FRA	*Fontes rerum austriacarum*
FRB	Jaroslav Goll et al., eds., *Fontes rerum bohemicarum*
Friedberg	Emil Friedberg, ed., *Corpus iuris canonici*
Glorieux	Palémon Glorieux, ed., *Jean Gerson Oeuvres Complètes*
Hardt	Hermann von der Hardt, ed., *Magnum oecumenicum constantiense concilium*
Herold, "Der Streit"	Vilém Herold, "Der Streit zwischen Hieronymus von Prag und Johann Gerson"
Herold, *Pražská univerzita a Wyclif*	Vilém Herold, *Pražská univerzita a Wyclif: Wyclifovo učení o ideách a geneze husitského revolučního myšlení*

HM	Matthias Flacius Illyricus, ed., *Historia et monumenta Ioannis Hus atque Hieronymi Pragensis, confessorum Christi*
Höfler	Konstantin von Höfler, ed., *Geschichtschreiber der Husitischen Bewegung in Böhmen*
Hussite Chronicle	Vavřinec of Březová, *Historia Hussitarum*, in FRB, vol. 5, pp. 329–534.
JWLW	John Wyclif, *John Wyclif's Latin Works*
Kaluza, *Études doctrinales*	Zénon Kaluza, *Études doctrinales sur le XIVe siècle: Théologie, Logique, Philosophie*
Kaluza, *Les querelles doctrinales*	Zénon Kaluza, *Les querelles doctrinales à Paris: Nominalistes et réalistes aux confins du XIVe et XVe siècles*
Klicman	Ladislav Klicman, ed., *Processus iudiciarius contra Jeronimum de Praga habitus Viennae a. 1410–1412*
KNM	National Museum Library, Prague
Lahey, *John Wyclif*	Stephen E. Lahey, *John Wyclif*
Mansi	Giovanni Domenico Mansi, ed., *Sacrorum conciliorum nova, et amplissima collectio . . .*
MC	František Palacký, ed., *Monumenta conciliorum generalium seculi Decimi Quinti*, 2 vols
MIHO	František Ryšánek et al., eds., *Magistri Iohannis Hus, opera omnia*
Narratio de Magistro Hieronymo	FRB, vol. 8, pp. 339–350
NK	National Library, Prague
Notae de concilio Constantiensi	FRB, vol. 8, pp. 319–322
ÖNB	Österreichische Nationalbibliothek, Vienna
Passio	Czech version of the *Narratio*, FRB, vol. 8, pp. 351–367
PL	Jacques Paul Migne, ed., *Patrologia Latina*
Poggio	Poggio Bracciolini, in Helene Harth, ed., *Poggio Bracciolini Lettere*, vol. 2, *Epistolarum familiarium libri*
Relatio	Petr Mladoňovice, *Relatio de Mag. Joannis Hus causa*, in *FRB*, vol. 8, pp. 25–120

Šmahel, *Jeroným Pražsky*	František Šmahel, *Jeroným Pražsky: Život revolučního intelektuála*
Šmahel, *Život a dílo* *Jeronýma*	Šmahel, *Život a dílo Jeronýma Pražského*
Šmahel/Silagi	Šmahel and Gabriel Silagi, eds., *Magistri Hieronymi de Praga. Quaestiones, Polemica, Epistulae*
ST	Jan Sedlák, *Studie a texty k životopisu Husovu*
UB	František Palacký, ed., *Urkundliche Beiträge zur Geschichte des Hussitenkrieges*
WS	Wyclif Society

Jerome of Prague
and the Foundations
of the Hussite Movement

Introduction

JEROME OF PRAGUE has been dead for six hundred years. The Italian humanist Poggio Bracciolini, who witnessed his final hours, referred to him as "a man to remember." It is unfortunate that Jerome has not been as widely remembered as he deserves or that he has been misremembered as something he was not, that is, a mere disciple of Jan Hus or a proto-Protestant. It is sobering to note that this is the first scholarly book on Jerome of Prague written in a major language.[1] That fact only underscores the unfortunate obscurity that continues to largely conceal the fascinating world of late medieval Bohemia. Even noting the work by scholars over the past century and a half in French, German, and English, there are still curious gaps in our knowledge of the foundations of the important Hussite movement and its role on the frontier between the high Middle Ages and the period often called the European Reformations. Hussitica and the wider parameters of Bohemia at the end of the Middle Ages have been illuminated by Czech scholars from Palacký to Šmahel. Regrettably, few Western scholars are able to read Czech, and thus their work is not as widely known as it deserves. Much of the attention on late medieval Bohemia understandably has centered on Hus. Johann Loserth, Peter Hilsch, Ernst Werner, Ferdinand Seibt, Richard Friedenthal, and Thomas Krzenck have written in German. Paul de Vooght and Jean Boulier have contributed in French. Matthew Spinka, David Schaff, Albert H. Wratislaw, František Lützow, Ezra Hall Gillett, Jan Herben, Oscar Kuhns, Paul

---

1. There are two previous but very brief and limited studies. The first, authored by a Lutheran pastor, is Ludwig Heller, *Hieronymus von Prag* (Lübeck: Aschenfeldt, 1835); and the second is Joseph Pilný, *Jérôme de Prague: Un orateur progressiste du Moyen Âge* (Geneva: Perret-Gentil, 1974).

Roubiczek, Joseph Kalmer, and the present author have written books on Hus of uneven quality in English.[2] Some of the aforementioned, along with David R. Holeton, R. R. Betts, Howard Kaminsky, John Klassen, S. Harrison Thomson, Frederick G. Heymann, Jarold K. Zeman, Craig D. Atwood, Émile de Bonnechose, Zdeněk V. David, Otakar Odložilík, Gerald Christianson, Peter Brock, Murray Wagner, Peter Morée, Michael van Dussen, Howard Louthan, Herbert B. Workman, and Olivier Marin, are among the scholars who have made contributions to our understanding of the Hussite period and its legacy in major languages. With the exception of Betts, who produced an important article in 1947, none has made Jerome a direct subject of inquiry, though many have appended to or included in their work some reference or superficial treatment of Jerome. A very small portion of Czech-language historiography on Hussite topics has been translated into Western languages. These include František Šmahel's magnum opus on the Hussite revolution, František Bartoš's second volume on the revolution, Jiří Kejř on the Hus trial, and Rudolf Říčan's study of the Unity of Brethren.

On November 20, 2014, a fatal shooting occurred on the campus of Florida State University in Tallahassee. One student, shot in the back, escaped unharmed. The bullet struck his backpack and was stopped by the "impenetrable dense prose" associated with John Wyclif.[3] The difficulties and challenges of some medieval thinking cannot be exaggerated. Medieval philosophy is not a hurdle easily cleared or mastered. In presenting Jerome and in exploring his contributions to the early Hussite movement and the intellectual world of late medieval Europe, the background to the history of philosophy has been intentionally used sparingly. Instead, a more specific focus on Jerome versus Jean Gerson has been emphasized, especially noting how both thinkers used arguments that suited them to attack each other. Instead of searching for clues within the problematic nexus of nominalism versus realism, it has proven more fruitful to identify of chief importance the central connection between realist metaphysics and Hussite reform, which took its point of departure from the centrality

---

2. A survey of some of this work is in Thomas A. Fudge, "Jan Hus in English Language Historiography," *Journal of Moravian History* 16, no. 2 (2016), forthcoming.

3. Peter Salter, "Hard Words: UNL Prof's Book Slows Bullet, Saves Florida State Student," *Lincoln Journal Star* (November 21, 2014). The book in question is Stephen E. Lahey, *John Wyclif* (New York: Oxford University Press, 2009), and the quotation describing the book is Lahey's.

of morality in the Christian life. I have chosen to focus more on this than on metaphysics, as the latter tends to obfuscate the former and overlook what was the heart of the Hussite reform effort. After all, the question of Christian morality is the harvest of realist thought about divine Ideas. The nature of the debates that occurred between Jerome and Gerson are exemplary of the kinds of arguments that preceded and to some extent characterized the Hussite movement. It has seemed prudent to avoid the increasingly suspect "schools of thought" approach that continues to characterize the work of many intellectual historians. Philosophical schools must be understood as shaped by the formative influences of educational and national politics. It is especially important to understand that Gerson himself bears the greatest burden for creating the rhetorical distinction between the "realists" and the "nominalists." The great value of the work of Zénon Kaluza lies in his delineation of how philosophical debates were conditioned by university politics in the late fourteenth and early fifteenth centuries. It is unfortunate that Kaluza is little known in the Anglo-Saxon world. This is a reflection of a broader lack of awareness of continental work on the history of philosophy in the English-speaking world. In a meaningful sense, Jerome must be understood as standing within the continental legacy of Wyclif as a major mediator of Wyclif's logic and theology, not only in Prague but across Europe. While I am not entirely convinced that the controversy surrounding divine Ideas is essential for understanding Jerome and the early Hussite movement, it is an accessible gateway of interpretation which opens up a means for accessing an altogether compelling chapter in the religious and intellectual history of late medieval Europe.

Jerome of Prague was a passionate fifteenth-century Czech who identified closely with Wyclif in using both philosophy and theology to express dissatisfaction with an evolving theological establishment that in the German lands had become, by the late fourteenth century, closely identified with nominalism. As it was for Wyclif, the idea that scripture does articulate without difficulty the truth of divine Ideas is crucial as a means of criticizing the claims of ecclesiastical authority that Jerome attempted to rebut. The life, thought, and legacy of Jerome are those of a bold outsider who confronted evolving theological and philosophical trends. Jerome took comfort from a restive Bohemia and thoughtfully utilized philosophical and theological discussion to express caution and criticism about dominant educational and theological practice within the empire. While Wyclif retained a modicum of support in England, Jerome was forced to operate

in a much more difficult situation politically. That noted, given his ram-
bunctious peregrinations and propensity for creating discord everywhere
he went, it is doubtful that this factor was either decisive or critical in the
twilight of his career.

In view of the limited use made of the writings of Jerome to date (outside the small purview of a few, mainly Czech scholars), it seems useful
to point out that Jerome cannot be seen either as a spokesman for Hus or
as a faint reflection of the cause of Hus. Interpretations of Jerome must
take into account his independence of Hus and the potential of his own
thought as a separate component in the foundation of the early Hussite
movement. In Jerome, we find a fertile mind, restless inquiry, and deep
theological concern, each characterized by impatience with status quo and
inflexible tradition. If Johan Huizinga sought to delineate the harvest of
the Middle Ages and Heiko Oberman set himself the task of articulating
the harvest of medieval theology, this book hopes to present a compelling
case for why Jerome should be included within that marvelous ingather-
ing. At the core of his dispute with Gerson and central to his conflict with
the church are notions of authority that placed Jerome outside the widely
recognized realm of acceptable Christian doctrine and religious practice.
His judicial conviction on charges of heresy and his theological association with Wyclif, coupled with his wide-ranging and fascinating forays into
the European academic world, are colorful and enlightening and amount
to sufficient justification to echo the verdict of Poggio that Jerome was
indeed a man to remember.

Researching and writing this book have accrued the usual assort-
ment of indebtedness that should never be taken for granted. The scholarly monograph represents incalculable hours and energy, intense labor,
and the contributions of many colleagues. I am especially grateful for
the work of Lubomír Mlčoch and our collaboration during the past fifteen years. I have worked in Prague archives and libraries repeatedly during the past twenty-five years and also in North American repositories.
All have been helpful once again on this project. A research fellowship
at the Kulturwissenschaftliches Kolleg (Institute for Advanced Study) at
the University of Constance in early 2015 allowed me opportunity to write
the first chapters and to think about Jerome in situ within the last year of
his life. I also had the good fortune of stimulating exchanges with Rainer
Behrens, Henry Gerlach, Holger Müller, Dorothea Weltecke, Thomas
Martin Buck, and others while in Germany. At the Institute, Daniela
Göpfrich facilitated my work in many ways. I am grateful to Jürgen

Klöckler and Norbert Fromm for their helpfulness at the Stadtarchiv in Constance and to Walter Liehner at the Stadtarchiv in Überlingen. I am enormously grateful to Gernot Blechner for a comprehensive tour of the Haus zum Delphin, where Jerome spent a night during his first clandestine visit to Constance, and his vast knowledge of local history commensurate with events associated with the Council involving Hus and Jerome. Mathias Trennert-Helwig, dean of the Constance Cathedral (Münster Unserer Lieben Frau), granted permission for me to have opportunity to privately view the sacristy, high altar, and choir in the church where Jerome's trial came to its end and where the defendant heard the sentence of death pronounced. Henry Gerlach proved to be an insightful and valuable guide to the history of Constance, especially on matters relating to the Council. A second research fellowship at Moravian Theological Seminary in the second half of 2015 permitted me ample opportunity to complete revisions and add the last bits and pieces while enjoying the richness of the Moravian Archives and the Moravian Historical Society, together with the fellowship of the college and seminary communities and useful consultation with Craig Atwood, whose work on the Unity of Brethren continues to illuminate other dimensions of the Hussite tradition. An invitation to deliver the Moses Lectures in 2015 made possible a several-months-long stay in Bethlehem.

In 2015, during which the sexcentenary of Hus's death was observed and I had the good fortune of delivering more than three dozen lectures at a number of international venues on several continents, I had occasion to enter into dialogue with a number of colleagues about matters relating to Jerome. These included Stephen Lahey, Martin Dekarli, Ivan Müller, Constant Mews, and many others, in places as far afield as Constance, Prague, Tábor, Leeds, Portland, Oregon, Kalamazoo, Bethlehem, Brisbane, New Brunswick, and the Embassy of the Czech Republic in Washington, D.C. I am particularly indebted to Lahey and Mews for very incisive and useful conversation and to the former for numerous papers that aided me immensely in my journey through the world of medieval philosophy and its occasional "impenetrable dense prose." I must also acknowledge the stimulation of the subtle work of Franz Bibfeldt. The interloans division of the Dixson Library at the University of New England was always accommodating in acquiring materials from around the world in support of the research leading to this book.

I have relied in no small measure on the work of Jerome experts who have preceded me. The footnotes will reveal my dependence on the excellent work of František Šmahel, Zénon Kaluza, the late Vilém Herold, and, to a lesser degree, Ota Pavlíček. The latter's 2014 University of Paris Ph.D. thesis was not available to me, but its expected publication should result in a significant contribution to our knowledge of Jerome, especially with respect to his *Quodlibets* and *Quaestiones*, which doubtless will supplement Šmahel's edition with updates and corrections and should yield a fine textually based study. In addition to specific Jerome scholarship, I have drawn upon the work of specialists who have written on canon law, conciliarism, Wyclif, medieval philosophy, Gerson, and medieval universities, especially those at Oxford, Paris, Vienna, Heidelberg, and Prague. Tom Izbicki's book on the Eucharist appeared too late for me to take into account but his study is germane for understanding the broader dimensions of how the sacrament became at issue in the conflict between Jerome and the Latin church.[4]

My father, the Reverend James G. Fudge, has maintained an active interest in all things Hussite for many years, and his interest in Jerome has been both gratifying and motivational. My University of New England colleague Trish Wright has been extremely supportive, reliable in every way, and dependable at every turn. Her desktop competence is unparalleled, and I have taken advantage of her goodwill more often than defensible. During my extensive travels abroad, she has acted as a research assistant and contributed substantially to the final product, including assisting with the index. At Bethlehem, Ron Szabo saved me from a technological mishap at the eleventh hour thereby relieving me of significant anxiety.

I am grateful to Cynthia Reed, executive editor at OUP, for seeing the potential in this book, to Marcela Maxfield, assistant editor, who looked after the nuts and bolts of the evolving idea, to Alphonsa James, project manager, who kept everything together and on schedule, to Wendy Keebler whose excellent copyediting has once again helped turn my tortured prose into more readable text while saving me from innumerable infelicities, and also to the anonymous referees for the press whose reports were both helpful and insightful. The remaining shortcomings can be attributed to my own contumacious refusal (in the spirit of Jerome) to accept their advice.

This book is dedicated to two former colleagues who, like Jerome, cared less about their reputations and more about conscience and stood

---

4. Thomas M. Izbicki, *The Eucharist in Medieval Canon Law* (Cambridge: Cambridge University Press, 2015).

unflinchingly for principle in the face of mean-spiritedness, professional hostility, moral cowardice, and betrayal. These, too, are men to remember.

Thirty years ago, I became interested in Jan Hus and in the Hussite period of Czech history. Jerome of Prague has always been there, in the back of my mind, lurking in the shadows of other topics, but only now have I found time and opportunity to try to bring him into the light he deserves as an important element in the foundations of the Hussite movement. It is my hope that the verdict expressed six hundred years ago by Poggio will now be shared more widely by those who read this book who might in consequence be inclined to agree that "this was a man to remember."

I

An Emerging Intellectual Knight-Errant

SINCE THE TIME the ashes cooled around the heretic's stake at Constance, Jerome of Prague has remained confined in the shadow of Jan Hus. It is rare to hear of him without reference to Hus. It has frequently been assumed that Jerome was simply a disciple or follower of Hus and that without the latter, he has little independent significance. The intellectual relationship between the two men has generally been assumed but seldom investigated.[1] Jerome is considered a leader of what later became the Hussite movement, yet the nature of that leadership has seldom been explored or disclosed. In Protestant historiography, his name is linked with that of Hus, but any subsequent elaboration often focuses on Hus, while the *scholarus vagans* is quickly forgotten. Who was Jerome of Prague, this "wandering scholar," and what was his role in the religious and intellectual history of the Bohemian province at the end of the Middle Ages?

In the absence of parish registers or other records, we cannot be certain of many details in the life of Jerome. His precise birthdate is unknown. Some consider that it may have been as early as 1365, while others postulate it at sometime after 1370.[2] Still others suggest a more precise probability between 1378 and 1380.[3] It is certain that Jerome was born not later

---

1. I will be raising this question in a conference address, "Was Jerome of Prague a Disciple of Jan Hus?" at the twelfth Bohemian Reformation and Religious Practice biennial symposium, Prague, June 2016.

2. Walter Brandmüller, *Das Konzil von Konstanz 1414–1418*, 2 vols. (Paderborn: Ferdinand Schöningh, 1991–1997), vol. 2, p. 118.

3. Šmahel, *Jeroným Pražsky*, p. 15.

than 1380. The leading expert on Jerome hypothesizes a birthdate in 1378.[4] Judging from his consistent moniker, he was almost certainly born in Prague and more specifically in the New Town.[5] While details are scanty, Jerome may have been awarded a scholarship associated with former university rector Vojtěch Raňkův of Ježov (ca. 1320–1388), which allowed him opportunity for international travel and university education abroad.[6] Vojtěch was associated with the Prague cathedral chapter, received an education at Paris and Oxford, was suspected of being a follower of Richard Fitzralph, and may be regarded as a stimulus for reform. In this important category should also be numbered the Austrian court preacher Konrad Waldhauser (ca.1326–1369); the Moravian cleric Jan Milíč of Kroměříž (d. 1374); theologian and canon Matěj Janov (ca. 1350–1394); the lay scholar Tomáš Štítný (ca.1333–ca. 1401); the brilliant preacher, ex-Cistercian monk, and later Kraków University theology professor Jan Štěkna (ca. 1350– ca. 1410); the archbishop of Prague Jan of Jenštejn (1348–1400); and the Charles University master Štěpán of Kolín (1360–1407). At one time or another, all of these figures were active and influential in Prague and were sympathetic to religious reform.[7]

For the historian, it is regrettable that Jerome seems not to have written much in terms of religious or theological treatises, and his surviving correspondence is scant. Contrary to expectations, Jerome never wrote a *Sentences* commentary. His notebook compendium *Magnum quodam volumen* is lost. There are six university disputation texts chiefly stemming from various Prague *Quodlibeta*. His single theological writing is

---

4. František Šmahel, "Drobné otázky a záhady v studentském životě mistra Jeronýma Pražského," *Český časopis historický* 106, no. 1 (2008): 1–18; and Šmahel, *Život a dílo Jeronýma*, p. 21.

5. Evidence that Jerome came from the New Town of Prague can be found in the *Passio*, in *FRB*, vol. 8, p. 352; and the Czech *Acta*, 318. At house no. 672 Řeznická Street 1, near the corner of Vodičkova, is a bronze relief of Jerome at the stake, suggesting that this is the location of Jerome's birthplace. This reflects a fifteenth-century tradition.

6. In his will, drawn up in 1388, Vojtěch established scholarships for study at either Paris or Oxford for Czech students wishing to work in the faculties of theology or arts. R. R. Betts, *Essays in Czech History* (London: Athlone, 1969), pp. 135–136. There is additional information about him in Vilém Herold, "Vojtěch Raňkův of Ježov (Adalbertus Rankonis de Ericinio) and the Bohemian Reformation," *BRRP* 7 (2009): 72–79. The will is in Johann Loserth, "Nachträgliche Bemerkungen zu dem Magister Adalbertus Ranconis de Ericinio," *Mittheilungen des Vereines für Geschichte der Deutschen in Böhmen* 17 (1879): 198–213, at pp. 210–212.

7. Šmahel, *Život a dílo Jeronýma*, p. 21.

a short treatise known as the "Shield of Faith" (*Scutum fidei christianae*). There are disputation texts around his exchanges with Master Blažej Vlk (Blasius Lupus), subsequent to the 1409 Prague *Quodlibet*. We also possess his objections expressed to Michael of Malenice in the context of the 1411 university *Quodlibet*. Of singular note is his "Eulogy on the Liberal Arts" (*Recommendatio artium liberalium*), which is important on several levels. From the Council of Constance, we have a confession of faith, dated September 11, 1415, and later a formal revocation of error and heresy (September 23, 1415). We also possess four letters from Jerome. The first is addressed to friends living in the college of Jerusalem in Prague (September 6, 1410); the second to Andreas Grillenberg, a canon and official of the Passau Consistory (September 12, 1410), who had been involved in the Vienna legal proceedings; the third to King Sigismund (April 7, 1415); and the fourth, from a Constance prison, to Lord Lacek of Kravář (October 12, 1415), a baron who was in favor of reform, later vice regent of Moravia, and one of the presidents of the Hussite League formed at Prague in September 1415.[8] The letter to Lacek of Kravář is written in Czech; all of the others are in Latin. All of these documents are discussed in some detail here in subsequent later chapters in their historical context.

Unlike Hus, Jerome traveled widely within Europe and even to regions beyond. (See figure 1.1.) His peregrinations took him as far afield as Russia and Jerusalem. He enjoyed significant and sometimes dramatic stints in Prague, Oxford, Paris, Vienna, Heidelberg, Cologne, Hungary, and Poland. In England, he became involved in the increasingly controversial procuring and purveyance of John Wyclif's books to Prague. Much of our knowledge about Jerome comes from two legal procedures against him, the first in Vienna and the second at Constance. His biography can be pieced together chiefly from these two major sets of trial records, from Vienna between 1410 and 1412 and from Constance in 1415 and 1416.[9] Both processes are

---

8. All of these documents have recently been published in a critical edition. See Šmahel/Silagi, pp. 3–259. See appendices 1–3, 5, 8–9.

9. There are no records in the city archives in Überlingen, where Jerome spent several days between his first and second sojourns in Constance. The nearest accounts are those of Jakob Reutlinger (1545–1611), who compiled a sixteen-volume chronicle in eighteen parts. While he mentions the Council of Constance, there are no references to Jerome. Stadtarchiv Überlingen/Reutlinger Chronik, vol. 13, pp. 235–258 and vol. 14, pp. 127–135. The main sources for his life are in Hardt, and the fifteenth-century accounts have been collected in Jaroslav Goll, *Vypsání o Mistru Jeronymovi z Prahy* (Prague: J. Otto, 1878). The best secondary studies are Šmahel, *Jeroným Pražský*; Šmahel, *Život a dílo Jeronýma*; and Betts, *Essays in Czech History*, pp. 195–235.

considered in some detail here in subsequent chapters. During a sermon preached at Constance on May 30, 1416, the Dominican Giacomo Balardi Arrigoni (ca. 1368–1435), bishop of Lodi, described Jerome as "lowborn, base, of unknown origin."[10] It is entirely possible that Bishop Giacomo was influenced on this point by Dietrich Niem.

Niem was born around 1340, and from 1370, he worked as a notary in the *Rota* (the highest church appellate court), where he apparently was involved in modifying the court's procedures.[11] He was at Constance from January 1415.[12] Niem submitted that the two Czech reformers, Hus and Jerome, were unsavory characters with little social standing. They were "born of the lowest common rabble and were squat yokels. However, then becoming unworthy and poverty-stricken young clerics at Charles University in Prague, they were fashioned or instructed with respect to piety by noble masters and graduates—chiefly in sacred theology and the arts—of the German nation."[13] Niem's main work was the 1411 *Viridarium imperatorum et regnum Romanorum*, in which he argued that the spread of heresy in Bohemia and Moravia, which flourished under the influence of Hus and Jerome, was caused indirectly by the incompetence and negligence of King Václav IV, who reigned from 1378 until 1419.[14] It is notable that the flourishing of heresy in the Czech kingdom was connected not simply to Hus but also to Jerome. Niem took an entirely negative view of the Czechs. They were a squalid people possessing barbarian characteristics, they had no business being considered Christian, they consistently exhibited bestial appetites, they were lacking in proper civilization, they were grossly arrogant, and they deserved eternal punishment in hell.[15] Before coming to Constance, Niem wrote his *Avisamenta*, wherein

---

10. Hardt, vol. 3, col. 59. See appendix 10 herein.

11. See Hermann Heimpel, *Dietrich von Niem (c. 1340–1418)* (Münster: Regensbergische Verlagsbuchhandlung, 1932), p. 288.

12. On this latter point, see Heinrich Finke, *Forschungen und Quellen zur Geschichte des Konstanzer Koncils* (Paderborn: F. Schöningh, 1889), pp. 132–149.

13. *De vita ac fatis Constantiensibus Johannis Papae XXIII*, bk. 3, chap. 34, in Hardt, vol. 2, col. 453.

14. The text has been edited in Alphons Lhotsky and Karl Pivec, eds., *Dietrich von Niehem Viridarium imperatorum et regnum Romanorum* (Stuttgart: Hiersemann, 1956), pp. 18–19. For comments about heresy and the king, Jiří Spěváček, *Václav IV. 1361–1419 k předpokladům husitské revoluce* (Prague: Svoboda, 1986), is the definitive study.

15. Lhotsky and Pivec, *Dietrich von Niehem*, pp. 92–93.

FIGURE I.I Jerome in his European context.

1 Jindřichův Hradec
2 Bítov Castle
3 Laa an der Thaya

Pskov

Riga
LATVIA
RUSSIA
BALTIC SEA
LITHUANIA
Vitebsk
Vilnius

Gniezno
WHITE RUSSIA
POLAND
Świdnica
Kraków

3
Bratislava
Vienna
Esztergom
Buda
HUNGARY
TRANSYLVANIA

Constantinople

he reproached Hus for not obeying ecclesiastical authority and claimed that Hus was as antithetical to the church as the Qu'ran.[16] There is little evidence that Niem perceived Jerome as different from an incorrigible heretic. Prior to his arrival at Constance, Niem advocated a total liquidation policy of heretics in Bohemia. He argued that Czech eucharistic doctrines and practices, associated with the type of reformed religious practice occurring in Bohemia, were unacceptable. The authorities were enjoined to suppress heresy, and those who refused to obey proper ecclesiastical authority should simply be expelled. Niem suggested that argument and theological examination were a waste of time and, given the prevailing climate of disobedience, recommended that mere suspicion of heresy was sufficient for the church to act and for suspects to merit condemnation. Niem went on to suggest that a crusade might be assembled as a means by which to achieve conformity in the Bohemian province.[17] Given Niem's activities in the case against Hus, where he may have been influenced to persuade Pope John XXIII against Hus and functioned as a major protagonist, there is no reason to think he softened his approach toward Jerome.[18] So far as Dietrich Niem was concerned, Jan Hus and Jerome of Prague were liabilities to the faith. It is altogether possible that the bishop of Lodi was familiar with the opinions of Niem.

Against this negative point of view, the notary Prokop of Prague, writing much later, said in his chronicle that Jerome was *vir genere nobilis* (a man of nobler birth).[19] Who should be believed? The term *rusticum quadratum* (square hick) was a commonplace of derision.[20] There was a

16. Noted in his *De necessitate reformationis ecclesiae in capite et in membris*, chap. 28, in Hardt, vol. 1, cols. 306–307.

17. *Concilium Theodorici de Niem ad Wicklefistas reprimandos*, in *ST*, vol. 1, pp. 45–55. A relevant date is March 6, 1411, and the text is often referred to as *Contra damnatos Wiclifitas Prage*.

18. For Niem's activities, see the index entries in Thomas A. Fudge, *The Trial of Jan Hus: Medieval Heresy and Criminal Procedure* (New York: Oxford University Press, 2013). There are useful comments in F. M. Bartoš, *Čechy v době Husově 1378–1415* (Prague: Jan Laichter, 1947), p. 351; and Paul de Vooght, "Jean Huss et ses juges," in *Das Konzil von Konstanz*, ed. August Franzen and Wolfgang Müller (Freiburg: Herder, 1964), pp. 172–173.

19. The Chronicle of Prokop the Notary appears in Höfler, vol. 1, p. 70. Palacký accepted this. František Palacký, *Dějiny národu českého v Čechách a v Moravě*, 6 vols. (Prague: Kvasnička a Hampl, 1939), vol. 3, pp. 46–48.

20. Thomas A. Fudge, "Jan Hus at Calvary: The Text of an Early Fifteenth-Century *Passio*," *Journal of Moravian History* 11 (Fall 2011): 52, 55. See also an investigation of the *rusticum quadratum* nomenclature in Anežka Vidmanová, "Sedlák hranatý nebo chlap jak se patří?" *Listý filologické* 123, nos. 1–2 (2000): 52–58.

general cliché that heretics were of poor stock. Again, this later-medieval nomenclature might be contrasted with Augustine's remark that only great men were heretics.[21] Setting aside the discussion about the nature of Jerome's social standing, what is known about his origins has been delineated.[22] The name Jerome, in the Czech context at the end of the Middle Ages, is quite rare. We know nothing of his mother, but it is possible and perhaps even likely that his father's name was Václav, admittedly a common late-medieval Czech name. His father was probably not wealthy but may have been close to the circle of Czech-minded Prague citizens around the Bethlehem Chapel, may have had some connection to a house wherein Hus offended some people, "the house of Václav the goblet-maker," and may have enjoyed some relation with Václav Kříž, who was the cofounder of Bethlehem Chapel.[23] On the question of Jerome's social status or his family's means, it is important to note an entry in the *Book of Attorneys of the English and German Nation* at Paris University from April 7, 1404. The entry provides evidence that Jerome asked to be excused from the so-called bursa, the fee for sitting license exams. Based on the fact that Jerome had previously claimed poverty during his bachelor exams at Prague University, he was exempted from the *dispensatio biennii* bursa, which also meant that he was not obligated to fulfill the duties of a schoolmaster.[24] We have the later testimony of a Camaldolese monk, Jan-Jerome, who claimed to have studied with Jerome at Wenceslas College and also noted that Hus, the later important Hussite preacher and theologian Jakoubek Stříbro (ca. 1373–1429), and Marek of Hradec, later an attorney and university chancellor, were also there at the same time, living in the College of King Wenceslas.[25] The college was established

---

21. Augustine, Enarr. in Ps. 124: 5, in *CCL*, vol. 40, p. 1839.

22. Šmahel, *Život a dílo Jeronýma*, pp. 18–21.

23. Hanuš of Milheim and Václav Kříž were the cofounders. The charter is dated May 24, 1391, and appears in Anton Dittrich, ed., *Monumenta historica universitatis Carolo-Ferdinandeae Pragensis*, vol. 2, *Codex diplomaticus* (Prague: Spurny, 1834), pp. 300–308. On the chapel, see Otakar Odložilík, "The Chapel of Bethlehem in Prague: Remarks on Its Foundation Charter," *Studien zur Älteren Geschichte Osteuropas* 2, no. 1 (1956): 125–141, and Fudge, "'Ansellus dei' and the Bethlehem Chapel in Prague," *CV* 35, no. 2 (1993): 127–61. The goblet-maker's house is referred to in *Documenta*, p. 165, in a series of articles filed against Jan Hus in 1409.

24. Šmahel, *Život a dílo Jeronýma*, p. 159.

25. This note appears in his 1433 work *Contra quattuor articulos bohemorum*, Paris, Bibliothèque Nationale MS Lat. 12532, fol. 78r. On Jan-Jerome, see William P. Hyland,

by King Václav IV in 1380. The comment and reference about Jerome at Wenceslas College cannot be regarded as other than "an intentional distorted recollection."[26]

The first appearance of Jerome of Prague in extant written records dates to September 14, 1398, when he appeared before the four-member examining committee for the bachelor's degree at Prague. That committee consisted of Ludolf Meistermann, Walter Harrasser, Petr Kraft, and Mikuláš Czeyselmaister. Jerome placed second out of twenty-seven students.[27] It is unlikely that he was more than twenty years old, meaning that he had begun university studies by the time he was fourteen, which would not have been unusual for medieval university students. Jerome's promoter was probably Jan of Vysoké Mýto, who delivered a speech on the occasion, *Oportet equa de equis predicari*, a text that has survived in two manuscripts.[28] Jan of Vysoké Mýto had been Hus's promoter in 1393.[29] By 1399, it is possible that Jerome went to Oxford, possibly funded by the scholarship opportunities provided by Vojtěch Raňkův noted above, and he may have resided either in Beam Hall or in White Hall. His sojourn in England was somewhat lengthy.[30] It is possible that Jerome was motivated to go to Oxford on account of the growing interest in Wyclif expressed by Prague university masters.[31] It is likely that he went to Oxford to procure for his Czech teachers in Prague copies of

"John-Jerome of Prague: Portrait of a Fifteenth Century Camaldolese," *American Benedictine Review* 46 (1995): 303–334, with references to other sources.

26. Šmahel, *Život a dílo Jeronýma*, p. 20.

27. Šmahel, *Život a dílo Jeronýma*, p. 16.

28. Bohumil Ryba, ed., *Promoční promluvy mistrů artistické fakulty Mikuláše z Litomyšle a Jana z Mýta na univerzitě Karlově z let 1386 a 1393* (Prague: Česká akademie věd a umění, 1948), pp. 7–8, 24–25.

29. Thomas A. Fudge, *Jan Hus: Religious Reform and Social Revolution in Bohemia* (London: I. B. Tauris, 2010), p. 12.

30. For Beam Hall, see Robert F. Young, "Bohemian Scholars and Students at the English Universities from 1347 to 1750," *English Historical Review* 38 (January 1923): 72; and for White Hall, see Šmahel, *Život a dílo Jeronýma*, p. 26. On his stay in England, see Šmahel, *Jeroným Pražsky*, pp. 49–57.

31. Vilém Herold, *Pražská univerzita a Wyclif: Wyclifovo učení o ideách a geneze husitského revolučního myšlení* (Prague: Univerzita Karlova, 1985), p. 148; and František Šmahel, "Doctor evangelicus super omnes evangelistas: Wyclif's Fortune in Hussite Bohemia," *Bulletin of the Institute of Historical Research* 43 (May 1970): 16–34.

Wyclif's theological works and in this enterprise became a colporter.[32] Some contemporary witnesses later stated that they did not know who should be held responsible for bringing the heretical writings of Wyclif to Bohemia. Nevertheless, Jerome might be nominated as a likely courier.[33] Wyclif's works were readily available in Oxford during Jerome's sojourn, but the policies of Archbishop Thomas Arundel made it such that later visitors from Bohemia, such as Mikuláš Faulfiš (the "rotten fish") and Jiří Kněhnice, had to go to more remote places such as Lutterworth, Braybrook, and Kemerton in order to find copies.[34] Jerome brought from Oxford to Prague, according to his own words, copies of two very important works, *Dialogus* and *Trialogus*, in which Wyclif presented the essence of his teaching about the church and society.[35] By 1401, according to a colophon in a manuscript in the possession of the Austrian National Library in Vienna, we find evidence of Wyclif's tract *De simonia*.[36] Anne Hudson, who drew attention to this fact, presumes also that copies of the next two parts of Wyclif's *Theologica summa*, namely *De eucharistia* and *De Trinitate*, from the year 1403 are of Czech origin.[37] This seems eminently probable. It is likely that Jerome also brought copies of other theological works of Wyclif to Prague.[38]

Jerome may have discovered in England the geometric depiction of the Trinity (discussed at some length here in chapter 2), which later became controversial and which figured into both legal procedures and ongoing theological debate.[39] It is also possible but ultimately unprovable

---

32. František Šmahel, *Die Hussitischen Revolution* (Hannover: Hahnsche, 2002), vol. 1, p. 790; and Hardt, vol. 4, col. 635.

33. Ludolf von Żagan, *Tractatus de longevo schismate*, ed. Johann Loserth, *Archiv für österreichische Geschichte* 60 (1880): 343–561, at p. 425.

34. Anne Hudson, *Studies in the Transmission of Wyclif's Writings* (Aldershot: Ashgate, 2008), II, pp. 642–643; and Michael van Dussen, *From England to Bohemia: Heresy and Communication in the Later Middle Ages* (Cambridge: Cambridge University Press, 2012).

35. Hardt, vol. 4, col. 635.

36. ÖNB, MS 1401.

37. Hudson, *Studies in the Transmission of Wyclif's Writings*, II, p. 648.

38. Šmahel, *Život a dílo Jeronýma*, p. 25.

39. František Šmahel, "Das Scutum fidei christianae magistri Hieronymi Pragensis in der Entwicklung der mittelalterlichen trinitarischen Diagramme," in *Die Bildwelt der Diagramme Joachims von Fiore. Zur Medialität religiös-politischer Programme im Mittelalter*, ed. Alexander Patschovsky (Sigmaringen: J. Thorbecke, 2003), pp. 185–210.

that the Lollard and future Hussite Peter Payne and Jerome had contact in Oxford, but the historical records thus far have yielded no clues to support the assumption.[40] During this same period, Jerome began keeping a notebook, called *Magnum quodam volumen*, with an anonymous scribe who gave it the title, but the source has not survived.[41] Attempts to determine the direct actual influences on Jerome have proven to be unfruitful, but recent work has begun to challenge that counsel of despair.[42] Twenty years ago, his library was ostensibly inventoried.[43] The hypothesis has not found wide acceptance, and indeed there have been convincing arguments mounted against the catalog. It appears that the supposed books of Jerome belonged, in fact, to Jerome of Skutče (also known as Jaroslav of Skutče), a university master who flourished in the Poděbradian era (1452–1471), long after Jerome of Prague had perished.[44]

Following a sojourn in England, Jerome returned to Prague, and we have definite evidence that he testified before a notary on March 12, 1401, which places his return before that date. Unsurprisingly, his return to Prague seems to have coincided with the introduction of copies of Wyclif's books in Bohemia. These included both aforementioned important treatises *Dialogus* and *Trialogus*.[45] Also connected to Oxford and the distribution of Wyclif's books in Bohemia was a certain Mařík, who later became a doctor of theology; he also went to Oxford and personally collected books of the heretic Wyclif.[46] The author of some anonymous fifteenth-century Czech verse compositions was aware of this, as the following text reveals:

---

40. Šmahel, *Život a dílo Jeronýma*, p. 26. There is little current on Payne, who has been egregiously overlooked by scholars. For older work, see F. M. Bartoš, *M. Petr Payne: Diplomat husitské revoluce* (Prague: Kalich, 1956); and William R. Cook, "Peter Payne: Theologian and Diplomat of the Hussite Revolution," unpublished PhD dissertation, Cornell University, 1971.

41. The complete title of the notebook is *De magno quodam volumine, quod agregavit Parisius, Anglie et in aliis studiis, ubi fuit, de materia universalium realium.* See comments in *ST*, vol. 2, p. 211.

42. František Šmahel, *Die Prager Universität im Mittelalter* (Leiden: Brill, 2007), pp. 539–580, is an important contribution on this question.

43. Ivo Kořán, "Knihovna mistra Jeronýma Pražského," *Český časopis historický* 94 (1996): 590–600.

44. Šmahel, *Život a dílo Jeronýma*, pp. 207–212.

45. Šmahel, *University*, p. 261.

46. František M. Bartoš, *Husitství a cizina* (Prague: ČIN, 1931), p. 255; and *Tractatus contra Hussitas*, Nürnberg, Stadtbibliothek, MS Cent. I, 78, fol. 151r.

Everybody should know
and tell it to people in the future,
how Wyclif's books came to Bohemia
and appeared among the masters:
when Master Mařík, the doctor, was in Prague at the Holy Cross,
he knew well that the limping Wyclif,
wrote books against the pope, bishops and priests,
because they did not make him cardinal,
because they knew well that he was a heretic.[47]

The reference is to the theologian Mařík Rvačka, a member of the Augustinian Cyriac Order in the Crosiers with the Red Heart monastery of the Holy Cross the Greater, which had been founded in 1256.[48] Mařík Rvačka served in the role of inquisitor later in Prague, was involved in the interrogation of Hus, and eventually became opposed to the direction of reform spearheaded by Hus. He joined forces with Hus's inveterate enemy Michael de Causis and opposed the introduction of Utraquism, but following the Council of Constance, he disappeared without trace from the historical records.[49]

Major interpreters of Jerome are prepared to state baldly that he was a Wyclifite.[50] However, it is important to note that while Jerome tended to cite word for word from his own work, he mostly "paraphrased, interpreted, shortened, and improved Wyclif's." This is not unlike the manner in which Hus drew on Wyclif. Nevertheless, it must be said that Jerome (or Hus, for that matter) did not simply engage in the indiscriminate parroting of Wyclif. Jerome interpreted and applied Wyclif and his ideas to the university and in the Czech context. "It can even be said that, as was the case with Hus, Jerome was not only interpreting Wyclif's text, but also

---

47. František Svejkovský, ed., *Veršované Skladby doby Husitské* (Prague: Československá akademie věd, 1963), p. 163.

48. Pavel Soukup, "Mařík Rvačka's Defense of Crusading Indulgences from 1412," *BRRP* 8 (2011): 77–97; and Bartoš, *Husitství a cizina*, p. 255.

49. His anti-Utraquist texts are in Hardt, vol. 3, cols. 779–804. See index entries in Fudge, *The Trial of Jan Hus*, for his relation to Hus during the legal procedures. On de Causis, see Thomas A. Fudge, *The Memory and Motivation of Jan Hus, Medieval Priest and Martyr* (Turnhout: Brepols, 2013), pp. 109–133.

50. František Šmahel, "The *Acta* of the Constance Trial of Master Jerome of Prague," in *Text and Controversy from Wyclif to Bale*, ed. Helen Barr and Ann M. Hutchison (Turnhout: Brepols, 2005), p. 324.

bringing it home to the students by expounding those ideas in a more understandable manner. The dependence on Wyclif need not necessarily have led to a loss of individuality in the actual presentation of this."[51] It is possible that Jerome may have gone to England a second time, but the compelling evidence for this assertion is very slender.[52] It has been alleged that he went to Oxford in 1407 but was arrested. The proof for both claims is suspect.[53]

Jerome was not a priest. He was a layman and therefore not formally involved in *cura animarum* (the care of souls). He was significantly more flamboyant than Hus, possessed a more aggressive personality, was a compulsive agitator, and is frequently characterized as being outspoken. He was also permanently associated with the city of his birth. "He is 'Jeronym Pražský,' almost the incarnation of the volatile, restless, zealous, reckless and inconstant city. Though he wandered, led by his *ardor discendi* (enthusiasm for learning), to Oxford, Paris, Heidelberg, Cologne, Jerusalem, Buda, Vienna, Cracow, Vitebsk, and Pskov, he ever returned to the country and city he loved so well."[54] This is a concise, enlightening, and accurate description. He was ordained as an acolyte in the Benedictine monastery of Břevnov just outside Prague on either March 11 or 19, 1402. We find reference to him in the ordination records, noted as the son of Václav, "Jeronimus Wen(ceslai) Pr(agenesis)."[55] Some modern scholars have argued for the later date.[56] Residual ambiguity has been clarified, and the March 11 date has now been convincingly established in a study of ordinands in the diocese of Prague.[57]

While all of these developments were transpiring, other factors coalesced to complicate reform in Prague. The result produced an ethos of religious reform and social revolution that swept Jerome up into its vortex and catapulted him onto an international platform, where he achieved

---

51. Šmahel, *University*, p. 577.

52. Šmahel, "Leben und Werk des Magisters Hieronymus von Prag," *Historica* 13 (1966): 89.

53. *Documenta*, pp. 336–337.

54. Betts, *Essays in Czech History*, p. 92.

55. Antonín Podlaha, ed., *Liber ordinationum cleri 1395–1416*, 2 vols. (Prague: Pražská kapitula, 1910–1922), vol. 2, p. 77.

56. Šmahel, "Drobné otázky a záhady v studentském životě mistra Jeronýma Pražského," pp. 1–18.

57. Eva Doležalová, *Svěcenci pražské diecéze 1395–1416* (Prague: Historický ústav, 2010), p. 97.

both notoriety and renown. "In the year of the Lord 1403, there arose a notable dissension."[58] This comment by a contemporary chronicler refers to the "forty-five articles" against Wyclif which were formally presented to the Prague cathedral chapter for assessment. The submission technically was received and dealt with by cathedral chapter official Jan Kbel and Archdeacon Václav Nos because the recently elected new archbishop, Zbyněk Zajíc of Házmburk, who had been appointed in November 1402 to the see of Prague, did not assume full duties until August 1403. The articles were condemned on May 28, 1403, during a university convocation.[59] These problematic items consisted of twenty-four articles condemned at the Blackfriars synod in London in 1382 and twenty-one further articles selected by Johannes Hübner, a German-Silesian university master at Prague and member of the Dominican order. Hus later claimed some of the articles were doctored or otherwise manufactured by Hübner. University master Mikuláš of Litomyšl confirmed this.[60] At the annual *Quodlibet* that year, on January 3, Hübner declared Wyclif heretical and accused those reading his books as suspected heretics. Hus answered Hübner, saying that the "forty-five articles" had been falsified and should not be relied on. Hübner evidently said the pope ought to be obeyed absolutely. Hus rejected that suggestion.[61] The matter achieved formal notoriety. At Prague in the faculty room at the College of King Charles, there was a full and general convocation of all the masters of the University of Prague. On that occasion, forty-five articles extracted from the books of "John Wyclif of damned memory" were publicly read and condemned by the masters. The rector of the university, Walter Harrasser, commanded that no member of the university should from that time on hold, teach, or defend them.[62] That directive was met with open and sustained disobedience.

---

58. Chronicle of the University of Prague, in *FRB*, vol. 5, p. 569.

59. *Documenta*, pp. 327–331; translated in Norman P. Tanner, ed., *Decrees of the Ecumenical Councils*, 2 vols. (London: Sheed & Ward, 1990), vol. 1, pp. 411–413.

60. *Documenta*, p. 178. This moment appears to be the commencement of events that later produced a five-year legal battle and the condemnation of Hus during the Council of Constance. Fudge, *The Trial of Jan Hus*, p. 116.

61. Hus, letter to Hübner, January 1404, in Václav Novotný, ed., *M. Jana Husi Korespondence a dokumenty* (Prague: Nákladem komise pro vydávání pramenů náboženského hnutí českého, 1920), pp. 11–15.

62. Hardt, vol. 4, col. 652.

Around the same time, there were allegations of irregularity in Vienna. Two professors of theology at Vienna University initiated questions about heresy. These two professors were Peter Pulka (d. 1425), who was university rector in 1407, 1411, and 1421, and Nicholas Prunczlein of Dinkelsbühl (1360–1433), dean of the theology faculty in 1410, university rector in 1405, and canon of All Saints and St. Stephen Cathedral in Vienna. Dinkelsbühl spent almost a half century at Vienna University (1385–1433).[63] Pulka and Dinkelsbühl accused an unnamed colleague of holding heretical views, which upon examination were not unlike those just condemned at Prague. The theological faculty was summoned by the two accusers to judge the cause. Most of the faculty failed to turn up, and so the matter was dropped. It is possible that complacency on the part of the theologians underscored a lack of interest in such matters, and apparently a majority of the theology faculty had no wish to involve themselves in such affairs.[64] Thwarted, the two heresy-hunting professors turned their attention to a priest from Augsburg who had allegedly preached in Vienna and in the course of the homily made favorable mention of "heretical" ideas taught by Wyclif. Pulka and Dinkelsbühl alleged that there were Wyclifites in Vienna. Again, the theology faculty declined to pursue the matter. It seems entirely likely that ongoing philosophical contention and the conservative uses of the so-called *via moderna* were matters that exercised Pulka and Dinkelsbühl and that these considerations were among the factors leading to violence against suspected heretics at that time and thereafter.[65] Two months before Jerome appeared in Vienna, dean of the theology faculty Dinkelsbühl tried to raise some support against three men who had preached publicly, apparently from a pulpit, and in so doing had disseminated errors and made suspicious statements.[66]

---

63. Alois Madre, *Nikolaus von Dinkelsbühl. Leben und Schriften* (Münster: Aschendorff, 1965).

64. Paul P. Bernard, "Jerome of Prague, Austria and the Hussites," *Church History* 27 (1958): 4.

65. Katherine Walsh, "Vom Wegestreit zur Häeresie: Zur Auseinandersetzung um die Lehre John Wyclifs in Wien und Prag an der Wende zum 15. Jahrhundert," *Mittelungen Instituts für Österreichische Geschichtsforschung* 94 (1986): 25–48; and Michael H. Shank, *Unless You Believe, You Shall Not Understand: Logic, University, and Society in Late Medieval Vienna* (Princeton, N.J.: Princeton University Press, 1988), pp. 87–200.

66. Paul Uiblein, ed., *Acta facultatis artium Universitatis Vindobonensis, 1385–1416* (Vienna: Böhlaus, 1968), vol. 1, p. 348; and Paul Uiblein, ed., *Die Akten der Theologischen Fakultät der Universität Wien, 1396–1508* (Vienna: Verbrand der Wissenschaftlichen Gesellschaften Österreichs, 1978), vol. 1, p. 17.

On a technical point, it should be pointed out that the term *via moderna* can only be traced to the period between 1415 and 1425.

While these factors were developing and being investigated by worried authorities in central Europe, between 1404 and 1406, Jerome could be found at Paris, where he succeeded in attracting considerable attention within the university community. Unfortunately for him, most of that scrutiny was negative. We learn that he appeared quite unconcerned about the fact that observers thought he was in danger of falling into heresy. He appears to have taken no note of warnings to avoid continued danger.[67] Just as he was about to be confronted by Jean Gerson, the chancellor of the university, and possibly forced to renounce his errors, he slipped away from Paris under cover of night and was never again seen in the city.[68] Much of Jerome's career might be characterized as a confrontation with Gerson, whom he was destined later to meet in even more dramatic circumstances. After his nocturnal disappearance from Paris, he migrated to another university town and in due course made his appearance in Cologne.[69] The immediate results were no better, and a decade later, he was publicly accused of having spoken and disseminated numerous heresies. Unable to stay away from the halls of academe, Jerome traveled to Heidelberg. Here he encountered even more difficulty and met with strident opposition. Under fire once more for his controversial and, some would say, needlessly provocative views, he was forced to undertake another clandestine getaway to avoid censure and the wrath of university authorities and local theologians.[70] The details of these academic confrontations are examined below. He returned to Prague, where he was more

---

67. Ladislav Klicman, ed., *Processus iudiciarius contra Jeronimum de Praga habitus Viennae a. 1410–1412* (Prague: Česká akademie císaře Františka Josefa pro vědy, slovesnost a umění, 1898), p. 22. This was disclosed in the testimony of Peter Pergoschl during the Vienna trial of 1410.

68. Hardt, vol. 4, col. 681. Vilém Herold, "Der Streit zwischen Hieronymus von Prag und Johann Gerson—eine spätmittelalterliche Diskussion mit tragischen Folgen," in *Société et eglise: Textes et discussions dans les universités d'Europe centrale pendant le moyen âge tardif,* ed. Sophie Włodek (Turnhout: Brepols, 1995), pp. 77–89; and Zénon Kaluza, "Le chancelier Gerson et Jérôme de Prague," in *Études doctrinales sur le XIVe siècle: Théologie, Logique, Philosophie* (Paris: Vrin, 2013), pp. 207–231, are useful discussions of Jerome's time in Paris.

69. Vilém Herold, "Magister Hieronymus von Prag und die Universität Köln," *Miscellanea Medievalia* 20 (1989): 255–73.

70. Klicman, *Processus iudiciarius contra Jeronimum de Praga,* pp. 12, 13; and Hardt, vol. 4, col. 681.

warmly received, but even in his home city, there continued to be some reserve, and ultimately he was compelled to undertake a commitment not to cause any unnecessary unrest in the university. This was certainly a rather baroque response within what was reputed to be a liberal university in terms of free inquiry and discourse and a veritable incubator for heresy.

There is considerable uniformity among his contemporary detractors that Jerome was the "athlete of Antichrist," who stood firmly among the descendants of the "Devil's henchman John Wyclif."[71] The title "athlete of Antichrist" is significant and provides indication of the reputation attached to Jerome, who can be located in various iterations of heresy and heretical progeny throughout the later medieval and early modern period.[72] It is without doubt that Jerome recklessly and without discretion not infrequently expressed his admiration for Wyclif. Among the epitaphs, we find Jerome described as a "genuine philosopher from the dynasty of the ancient Stoics," a "holy man," a "philosopher among theologians," the "fiery and quick-witted debater," and, of course, the "athlete of Antichrist."[73] It was later noted that he taught at Prague, where he received the highest praise and the reputation of a celebrity.[74] Jerome "seems to have openly agitated at every opportunity, rarely retreated from encouraging the implementation of ideas, and seldom shrunk from the implications."[75] Jerome promoted Wyclifite realism and anticlericalism and in the process became both a philosophical and theological outlaw. Though it cannot be traced to him in any way, there is little doubt that Jerome would have approved of the remedy for solving the problems confronting the church at the end of the Middle Ages. Englishman Jore Dorre put forth a prescription aimed at solving once and for all the intransigence of the squabble that seemed to paralyze the Western church. "Recipe for the stomach of St. Peter and its total reform, given at the Council of Constance. Take twenty-four cardinals, a hundred archbishops and prelates, the same number from each nation, and as many priests as it is possible to get. Immerse in Rhine

---

71. Šmahel, *Život a dílo Jeronýma*, p. 15.

72. On this, see Thomas A. Fudge, *Jan Hus Between Time and Eternity: Reconsidering a Medieval Heretic* (Lanham, MD: Lexington, 2016), pp. 187–210.

73. Some of the main sources for his life were initially collected in Goll, *Vypsání o Mistru Jeronymovi z Prahy.*

74. Šmahel/Silagi, p. XXXII.

75. Fudge, *The Memory and Motivation of Jan Hus*, pp. 45–46.

water and keep submerged for three days. It will be good for the stomach of St. Peter and for the removal of all of his afflictions."[76]

By virtue of his involvement in, or active creation of, academic controversy and theological debate, Jerome earned a reputation as a renegade thinker whom some considered not only offensive but fundamentally dangerous. He had made an enemy of Gerson at Paris, but Gerson was only the first of powerful opponents whom Jerome seems to have attracted with ease and regularity. He would come face to face with Gerson again, and the fracas at Paris was recalled to his disadvantage. He gave a highly offensive address in Buda in 1410 before King Sigismund and the Hungarian royal court. It was later reported that he had again disseminated multiple heresies. That may be contestable, but what is irrefutable is that Sigismund was so infuriated with the impertinence of the Prague master that he ordered his immediate arrest on the spot and had Jerome forthwith locked up in an episcopal prison. The matter did not end badly for Jerome, who was shortly thereafter released from his confinement, but he had crossed swords with the most powerful political leader in all of Europe. The two would meet again under even less favorable circumstances for Jerome. Sigismund was a powerful man with considerable clout and influence. Jerome had offended him and as a consequence had needlessly gained another dangerous enemy. Not long after he departed from Hungary, Jerome went to Vienna on his own volition, determined to defend himself against accusations of heresy and theological irregularity. Jerome's behavior at Vienna was unwise both in conduct and in communication. Several of the key figures in the Vienna process were later present during the Council of Constance, when Jerome was once more involved in legal proceedings. Nicholas Dinkelsbühl played a crucial role at Constance, but several years earlier, he, too, had been antagonized by Jerome and was thereafter to be numbered among a coterie of dangerous opponents collected by the restless "athlete of Antichrist." Some of these rather formidable foes, including Gerson, Sigismund, Dinkelsbühl, theologian and Heidelberg University official Johannes Lagenator of Frankfurt, and Mikołaj Trąba, metropolitan/ archbishop of Gniezno, came back later in life to haunt Jerome at the apex of his career. Each of these and others appear in the pages below during the drama of Jerome's meteoric confrontation with the Western church.

---

76. Hardt, vol. 1, p. 499; and ÖNB, MS 5113, fol. 1r.

In the midst of these developments and in the face of ominous storm clouds gathering on the horizons of religious reform in central Europe, the dossier of Jerome's whereabouts and activities is often filled with puzzling and irresolvable lacunae. One of these gaps might be explained by the possibility that he may have undertaken a journey to Jerusalem. Facts and evidence are scarce. This may have occurred somewhere between 1401 and April 1404. The only reference to this pilgrimage to Jerusalem can be found in the first set of accusations lodged against Jerome during the Council of Constance. Jerome said that when the condemnation of the forty-five Wyclifite articles occurred in Prague, "I was in Jerusalem."[77] It is worth pointing out that a second condemnation of the Wyclifite articles also occurred in 1408. The reference to Jerusalem is difficult to establish, and even if it happened, we have no additional details from any source. It is possible that Jerome went to the Near East in April 1408 with the Czech noble Filip Lout of Dědice.[78] Filip was a member of King Václav's royal council between 1406 and 1419. The possibilities and relevant details for dating Jerome's journey to Jerusalem have been outlined to the limits of the extant documents taking into account what seem to be all salient factors. This investigation concludes that it is entirely possible that Jerome went to Jerusalem between early 1407 and the end of 1408.[79] From the fourteenth century onward, the journey from Prague to the Near East usually required between six and eight months, with a sea journey lasting between six and eight weeks. We have no proof that Jerome caused any disturbance either in or along the journey to Jerusalem. History is entirely silent on the question of Jerome in Jerusalem.

In between possible pilgrimages to the Near East, acrimonious intellectual sparring contests, and whispers of heresy, Jerome was also involved in history-making decisions and developments in his native Bohemia. There are persuasive and sound reasons for placing Jerome, rather than Hus, at the forefront of events and developments behind a royal policy that culminated in the establishment of the momentous Decree of Kutná Hora in 1409, which altered the governance of Charles University.[80] The merits

---

77. Hardt, vol. 4, col. 643; and *FRB*, vol. 8, p. 289.

78. F. M. Bartoš, "Několik záhad v životě Prokopa Holého," *Sborník historický* 8 (1961): 167–169.

79. Šmahel, *Život a dílo Jeronýma*, pp. 99–107.

80. In addition to comments from the trial of Jerome in Vienna in 1410, which are examined in chapter 4 below, see František Šmahel, *Idea národa v husitských Čechách* (Prague: Argo, 2000), pp. 40–49.

of that policy, dealt with below in chapter 3, have been subjected to robust debate, but it is undeniable that Kutná Hora changed the course of Czech history and provincialized the university in Prague. Kutná Hora might also be factored among the foundations for the Hussite revolution, which emerged from the ashes of the stake that claimed the lives of Hus and Jerome and subsequently convulsed Bohemia and other parts of Europe for more than two decades.

The story of Jerome's harrowing escape from Vienna is examined below in some detail, but once he had eluded his opponents in hostile territory and reached safety, he returned to Prague. However, the ban of excommunication hung over his head. There is absolutely no indication that Jerome took any note of his infamous status, and there does not appear to have been any effective effort to enforce the penalties of excommunication in Prague. No sooner had Jerome reappeared in the capital than he took charge in alienating even more powerful men. We hear stories of Jerome arranging for defamatory posters to be publicly displayed against Archbishop Zbyněk throughout the city, and there are accounts wherein Jerome publicly subjected the archbishop to ridicule.[81] According to some witnesses, this conduct was evident even in the midst of divine worship. As detailed below, Jerome assumed a leading role in all manner of behavior and protest against the official church and its representatives. By 1412, he had amassed an impressive but troubling curriculum vitae filled with incidents of misbehavior, controversy, notoriety, suspicion, and a reputation as a perennial troublemaker across Europe. That dossier was also crowded with an impressive list of men who may have desired to see Jerome silenced, sanctioned, or worse. By 1413, we find him in Poland and Russia. Controversy dogged his footsteps there, and a variety of incidents in the realm of Eastern Christendom were assiduously reported back in Europe, and in due course, Jerome was called to account for his actions.

After additional travels into eastern Europe, and other rounds of conflict and controversy in various parts of Bohemia, Jerome undertook a final journey. He did not return from this venture, which was marked by an unhappy sojourn on foreign soil, more than a year of harsh imprisonment in a medieval tower, and finally the rigors of an inquisitorial trial under the aegis of the Council of Constance. By that time, Jerome's name was fairly well known in ecclesiastical and intellectual circles throughout Europe.

---

81. Hardt, vol. 4, col. 670.

His philosophical and physical peregrinations ended in a field outside the city walls of Constance on a spring morning after a fifteen-minute walk from the cathedral. His last disputation occurred at a wooden stake he had made little effort to avoid. Defiant and controversial to the end, Jerome must have seemed to many in the fifteenth century to have made a lasting impression on history.

International traveler, highly educated university man, outspoken defender of Czech identity, provocative thinker, possessing notable talents and strength of character, it seems natural that he would have been the subject of numerous studies and evaluations by scholars in several disciplines. In truth, Jerome of Prague has been egregiously overlooked in the history of Christianity and in the study of the later Middle Ages. It is fitting that those interested in understanding better the history of medieval heresy should undertake a "pilgrimage in search of the life and works of a man whose footsteps are worthy of being followed."[82] Poggio Bracciolini, the Italian humanist who witnessed his death, recommended Jerome to the ages with the comment that "this was a man to remember." More puzzling is the fact that Czech history has been relatively uninterested in Jerome (at least compared with Hus), and in the last generation, there has been little increased interest. He is generally unknown in church history, eclipsed by Hus and the Council of Constance and then dwarfed by the movements of Renaissance and Reformation at the end of the Middle Ages. It is unfortunate that Jerome has often been seen as second-rate compared with Hus. It is a serious mistake to characterize Jerome as a cardboard figure with little significance for the history of Christianity.[83] Compared with Hus, Jerome is more human and in some ways a more compelling figure. Hus appears saintly beside the impetuous and outspoken Jerome, and there is something more accessible about Jerome. Perhaps it is his obvious humanity, which is palpable through the surviving sources even after six hundred years. Despite such compelling features, he has been largely ignored in Western historiography. It is not that Jerome has been studied and rejected as unimportant

---

82. Šmahel, *University*, p. 539.

83. David R. Holeton, "Wyclif's Bohemian Fate," *Communio viatorum* 32 (Winter 1989): 218, where it is noted that Jerome is a "cardboard figure whose place in history was derived through his association with Hus rather than for his own personal qualities." A further comment, on p. 222, suggests, "Even though Jerome was also commemorated in the feast of 6 July he never shines through as a personality and is clearly there because of his association with Hus."

but rather that he has been ignored. He was not a priest, he was not a theologian, but he may properly be regarded as a philosopher and an intellectual knight-errant. Jerome has often been characterized as Hus's friend but uncritically assessed somewhat shockingly as Hus's "far less important disciple."[84] Such claims are based mainly on ignorance. In general, it appears that Jerome "has escaped the gaze of the historians of many generations."[85] Thus, his memory has languished in the kingdoms of the dead, and his life and significance have remained shrouded in scholarly indifference.

This point of view is long-standing. We find it expressed indirectly but succinctly three hundred years ago. "Among the MSS. of Basil, there's a Fragment of a sermon of a certain Doctor call'd John of Francfort against Jerome of Prague; which Sermon was preach'd perhaps in the Council, but it's so ill written and so mangled that there's no making any Use of it."[86] The reference is to Johannes Lagenator, who opposed Jerome at Heidelberg. The comment, by the French Protestant divine Jacques Lenfant (1661–1728), is also unintentionally but characteristically representative of the lack of attention paid to Jerome. His name is known well enough, but his thought has been considered too obtuse, his story not sufficiently important, his contribution to medieval religious history too slight, and the records of his life inadequate for research-based evaluation. Thus, scholars have generally been content to note his life in passing with the ill-conceived conviction that the whole matter is too difficult and mangled to bother with. This book brings some attention to a man whose living and whose dying were extraordinary. Some regard his reputation as a Czech reformer to be exaggerated.[87] Others have been content to characterize him in general terms: "Jerome of Prague, the strange, stormy figure of the movement, a layman who was a theological teacher and a heavily committed realist."[88] If it is true that much textual analysis of medieval

---

84. Karl August Fink, "The Significance of the Council of Constance for Secular and Ecclesiastical History," in *Ulrich Richental Das Konzil zu Konstanz*, 2 vols., ed. Otto Feger (Constance: Jan Thorbecke Verlag, 1964), vol. 2, p. 85.

85. Šmahel, "Leben und Werk," p. 82.

86. Jacques Lenfant, *History of the Council of Constance*, 2 vols., trans. Stephen Whatley (London: Rivington, 1730), vol. 1, p. 166.

87. Count [František] Lützow, *The Life and Times of Master John Hus* (London: Dent, 1909), p. 321.

88. Malcolm Lambert, *Medieval Heresy: Popular Movements from the Gregorian Reform to the Reformation*, 3rd ed. (Oxford: Blackwell, 2002), p. 324.

sources proves how little originality there really was in literature and scholastic thinking, then perhaps the whole idea of reform, an intellectual approach to religion and theology, will need to be reconsidered in terms of how originality and intellectual significance are measured.[89] František Šmahel's comment is contextually important, but its implications neither diminish Jerome nor mitigate his role in Czech intellectual and religious history. Even where his presence was evident, he has sometimes been obscured. For example, the eloquent speeches delivered during the 1409 Prague University *Quodlibet* have formerly been ascribed to Hus, when in fact they belong properly to Jerome.[90]

The main scholars to study Jerome and offer solid analyses have been the Polish émigré Zénon Kaluza (working in France) and the Czech scholars František Šmahel, Vilém Herold, and Ota Pavlíček.[91] Recent publications have greatly increased our knowledge of Jerome and his work, but apart from an excellent essay first published in 1947 by R. R. Betts, Jerome has not been scrutinized by Anglo scholars beyond one or two limited appraisals of aspects of his life, and there is little else in major languages.[92] This is all the more surprising when it is pointed out that the bulk of relevant sources exist in Latin as opposed to the often impenetrable screen of the Czech language that attends Hus and so much of Hussite history. The second part of Kaluza's latest publication deals with Jerome and his relation to Wyclif and Hus and the reform movements associated with them.[93] It should be noted that a fully comprehensive interpretation of Jerome's thought has yet to emerge from the extant sources.[94] However, it is expected that Pavlíček's doctoral dissertation will offer the first thorough analytic study of the philosophical and theological dimensions of Jerome's thought based on all extant and known texts. Pavlíček endeavors to address

---

89. Šmahel, *University*, p. 564.

90. Höfler, vol. 2, pp. 112–128, is an example of misattribution.

91. The work of all three is reflected in the pages of this book, but see Pavlíček's forthcoming Ph.D. dissertation, "La dimension philosophique et théologique de la pensée de Jérôme de Prague" (Université Paris-Sorbonne, École doctorale V: Concepts et langages; and Charles University in Prague, Hussite Faculty of Theology, Paris and Prague, 2014), p. 621.

92. Joseph Pilný, *Jérôme de Prague: Un orateur progressiste du Moyen Âge* (Geneva: Perret-Gentil, 1974); and Ludwig Heller, *Hieronymus von Prag* (Lübeck: Aschenfeldt, 1835), are exceptions.

93. Kaluza, *Études doctrinales*, especially pp. 201–332.

94. Šmahel, *Život a dílo Jeronýma*, p. 259.

the various topics of philosophy and theology in the work of Jerome, while explaining his ideas and placing them in their particular context within the history of medieval thought. Šmahel has supplemented his earlier work with two very important contributions. The first is a lively and up-to-date discussion of the life and work of Jerome, and the latter is a critical edition of the works of Jerome.[95] Neither publication should be regarded as definitive nor presenting the final coda on sources or interpretation, but they do offer a solid foundation for additional evaluation and research.

Less than a month before his condemnation and execution as a heretic, Hus remarked that Jerome had warned him that should he travel to Constance, it was unlikely that he would return.[96] Paying no heed to his own counsel, Jerome followed Hus to Constance, arriving there on April 4, 1415. This marked the beginning of the last chapter in the life of Jerome. The story is taken up below, but the ghosts of controversies past all seem to have materialized at Lake Constance. King Sigismund wanted the case against Jerome to proceed as quickly as possible. Gerson assumed the position that under no circumstances could Jerome be released. Things only got worse when agitators such as de Causis succeeded in keeping the case going against Jerome, and in the process, Dinkelsbühl was appointed as one of the prosecutors. The case for the prosecution went to trial in late April 1416, with Jerome confined to his cell. If the Council continued to see the ghost of Wyclif in the proceedings against Hus, then it was the persistent and unmistakable ghost of Hus that seemed to haunt the legal process against Jerome. Observers at the Council consistently referred to Jerome as a follower of Hus of "cursed memory."[97] Guilt by association was a hurdle both Hus and Jerome in turn were summoned to overcome. Neither effort was successful.

At the end, the same bishop who had preached the general sermon against Jan Hus less than a year earlier once more mounted the pulpit. The bishop facetiously told the congregation in the cathedral of Constance that he had no wish to stir the fires by using the sword. Nevertheless, the heinous crimes of heresy which had been committed in the open could not simply be ignored, dismissed, or merely punished in secret.

---

95. Šmahel, *Život a dílo Jeronýma*; and Šmahel/Silagi.

96. Novotný, *M. Jana Husi Korespondence a dokumenty*, pp. 265–266.

97. Fillastre, *Gesta concilii Constanciensis*, in Heinrich Finke, ed., *Acta concilii Constanciensis*, 4 vols. (Münster: Druck und Verlag der Regensbergschen Buchhandlung, 1896–1928), vol. 2, p. 50.

The bishop declared that Jerome was responsible for inciting the entire country of Bohemia to rebellion which had resulted in incalculable damage to the church. It would have been better, the bishop grimly commented, if Jerome had never been born. His unfortunate peregrinations around Europe and his pernicious and dangerous doctrines had resulted in Jerome becoming an even worse offender against the faith than the ancient heretics Sabellius, Arius or Nestorius. More shocking was the fact that Jerome's heresies had spread from one end of Europe to the other.[98] Cardinal Guillaume Fillastre described it as "a fine sermon."[99] When it ended, Jerome stood at the brink of eternity.

The Council of Constance was among the greatest convocations of the entire Middle Ages. It achieved fame and notoriety over the course of four years, in which triumph and tragedy attended its proceedings. Among the tragedies of Constance is the fact that both Hus and Jerome insisted on dying. Some of their followers and admirers, who became known to history as Hussites, later argued that Jerome had been destroyed simply because he refused to give his consent to the condemnation of Wyclif and Hus. While reflecting a simplistic point of view, there is some merit in the observation.[100] Others took the view that there were torments waiting for the doctors of the Council, who had erroneously and perniciously condemned Jerome, while there would be great pleasures and rewards for the Hussites, who adhered fearlessly to the law of God and the purity of Christianity.[101]

The martyrdoms of Hus and Jerome provided the emotional basis for social revolution, continued reform in religious practice, and, ultimately, the establishment of an alternative form of the Christian church in the Bohemian province. The other motivation for these developments was theological and was intimately and organically connected to the Eucharist. The cornerstone in the house of religious reform in medieval Bohemia was eucharistic celebration and the implications of that practice as articulated

---

98. The sermon text is in Hardt, vol. 3, cols. 54–63 and *FRB*, vol. 8, pp. 494–500.

99. Fillastre, *Gesta concilii Constanciensis*, in Finke, vol. 2, p. 61. See appendix 11.

100. An example of this point of view is reflected by Mikuláš of Pelhřimov at the Council of Basel in 1433, according to the *Liber diurnus de gestis Bohemorum in Concilio Basileensi* in František Palacký, ed., *Monumenta conciliorum generalium seculi Decimi Quinti*, 2 vols. (Vienna: Typis C.R. Officinae Typographicae Aulae et Status, 1857–1873), vol. 1, p. 294.

101. Nicholas of Dresden, *Apologia*, in Hardt, vol. 3, cols. 653–657.

by Hussite priests and theologians. The fact that neither Hus nor Jerome played any significant role in that doctrinal, liturgical, or practical development does not diminish their significance for the Hussite revolution or the religious history in the Bohemian province at the end of the Middle Ages. Hus has been given considerable attention in the historiography of medieval history. It is well past time for his colleague Jerome to receive his due attention. He was an intellectual knight-errant and a man who represented what Gerson referred to as "matters still more controversial," whose thinking was disturbing, with far-reaching consequences. Jerome was both the "athlete of Antichrist" and a champion of Christ who independently affirmed that "the truth has never given way and will not yield for a lie, because truth triumphs over everything."[102]

---

102. *Recommendatio artium liberalium*, in Šmahel/Silagi, p. 216. A condensed version of this statement, "truth prevails," would later feature in sermons, manifestos, and in art, as a slogan of the Hussite movement.

2

Jerome as a Wyclifite Thinker

JEROME OF PRAGUE ended his natural life at the stake in Constance. He was not burned alive for no reason. Following a heresy trial, which adhered to inquisitorial procedure, he was convicted of heresy and sentenced accordingly. His heresies were rooted in philosophical concepts and convictions that the later medieval church found objectionable and dangerous. In order to come to terms with his life, his activities, and his reputation as a heretic, it is necessary to look carefully at the intellectual world of the later Middle Ages as the immediate context for Jerome's intellectual odyssey. The Hussites' concern with divine Ideas is a central element in understanding their conception of the law of God and for situating Jerome as a major figure in the genesis of the Hussite movement. In this and the following chapter, the controversy over divine Ideas reappears repeatedly, and the repetition is necessary and useful.

Divine Ideas

A school of thought within the historiography of Hussite studies has argued that the philosophical factor is a better means of understanding the Hussite movement generally and, by extension, Jerome of Prague specifically than simply focusing on the urge to reform church and society.[1] This point of view has gradually come to find increasing acceptance. Against the findings of the eminent medievalist Étienne Gilson, the fourteenth century was not the end of the road or a degenerate, corroded, or

---

1. Vilém Herold, "The University of Paris and the Foundations of the Bohemian Reformation," BRRP 3 (2000): 23.

collapsing form of medieval theology.[2] Instead, it was a time of rich innovation, establishing an important premise for understanding the theological argument that convulsed the fifteenth century and lasted long into the doctrinal disputes of the Reformations. The connection to religious reform and heresy has been more often assumed and stated rather than cogently demonstrated. In some cases, philosophical speculation has more to do with intellectual riddles and puns than with heresy.[3] Many of these disputes seem reducible to logical puzzles woven together in a spiderweb of concepts, principles, and premises. Some scholars have suggested that fourteenth-century thinking around theology was little more than mental games.[4] The merits of that observation are debatable, and while intellectualizing in and of itself never produced religious reform, it is not disagreeable to consider that "One of the glories of the medieval world is the work of philosophers and theologians who tried to develop an integrated and consistent view of God and His universe."[5] One of Jerome's contemporaries opined that "simple people are not able to understand his teachings."[6] It might seem like intellectual arrogance to attempt to articulate the contents of the divine mind, yet that is precisely what many medieval theologians tried to do.[7] In a qualified sense, Jerome must be numbered among those engaged in that breathtaking pursuit.

It does not seem sensible to assume that another obligatory trip across the tired territory of the acrimonious disputes between late medieval realists and nominalists will shed new or further light on what provoked the savage violence at Constance that culminated in two Czech intellectuals being burned at the stake. Nor does it seem prudent to

---

2. Étienne Gilson, *History of Christian Philosophy in the Middle Ages* (New York: Random House, 1955), pp. 528–545. That point of view has been seriously challenged. Heiko Augustinus Oberman, *The Harvest of Medieval Theology: Gabriel Biel and Late Medieval Nominalism* (Grand Rapids, Mich.: Eerdmans, 1967, originally published 1963).

3. Damascus Trapp, "Clm 27034: Unchristened Nominalism and Wycliffite Realism at Prague in 1381," *Recherches de théologie ancienne et médiévale* 24 (1957): 344.

4. Paul de Vooght, *Les sources de la doctrine chrétienne d'après les théologiens du XIVe siècle et du début du XVe* (Paris: Desclée de Brouwer, 1954), pp. 258–263.

5. Allen DuPont Breck, ed., *Johannis Wyclyf Tractatus de Trinitate* (Boulder: University of Colorado Press, 1962), p. vii.

6. Albert (Wojciech Jastrzębiec), bishop of Kraków, letter of April 2, 1413, to Václav Králík of Buřenice, the titular patriarch of Antioch and chancellor of the bishopric of Olomouc, in *Documenta*, pp. 506–507. See appendix 4.

7. Stephen Lahey, *John Wyclif* (New York: Oxford University Press, 2009), p. 88.

follow Richard Fitzralph in his famous characterization of late medieval intellectual debates as the "croaking of frogs and toads in swamps."[8] Traditional categories of realists and nominalists are very artificial divisions which fail to delineate sufficiently philosophical positions. There is little to be gained from exploring once more the burned-out wasteland of fourteenth-century philosophy searching for overlooked clues to help explain why John Wyclif was excoriated as an heresiarch and why Jan Hus and Jerome of Prague were condemned to die. The pitfalls are plentiful, and too many of the pathways are overgrown with thorns and thistles, leading into ravines of irrelevancy or into a morass that does more to obfuscate than illuminate. The furrows of previous excavations are deep and wide, and these have been carefully mined by more capable scholars than I. What is needed is an intellectual biography of Jerome. Failing that objective, it is still necessary to attempt to erect a scaffold on which that goal might later be achieved. Within that elaboration or on that framework, there is an even more urgent brief, and that is to concisely and cogently lay out a convincing identification of the philosophical phantoms that bedeviled theological inquiry which might then provide an explanation for why these phantoms prompted such savage responses to Wyclif, Hus, and Jerome. This appraisal must also illumine the foundations on which the Council of Constance determined that all three of these irascible characters should be destroyed by fire. Such an investigation must shed light on the question of how metaphysical realism led to theological error. It must further illuminate cogently and plainly how philosophical "ideas" influenced the shape of religious practice and produced heresy by considering in what sense the abstract world of speculation about Ideas and universals had any direct influence on religious and social reform in Bohemia.

It seems evident that divine Ideas constitute the bone of contention. Ideas exist in and make up the mind of God. They are created by God, exist eternally with God, but are not equal to God. Since they possess divine

---

8. The phrase is "michi ostendens quomodo cum ranis et buffonibus in paludibus crocitabam," from the autobiographical prayer frequently appended as a last chapter to his *Summa de Questionibus Armenorum,* in L. L. Hammerich, *The Beginning of the Strife between Richard FitzRalph and the Mendicants, with an Edition of His Autobiographical Prayer and His Proposition Unusquisque* (Copenhagen: Levin and Munksgaard, 1938), p. 20. It has been pointed out that the Hammerich edition is based on defective manuscripts. Katherine Walsh, *A Fourteenth-Century Scholar and Primate Richard Fitzralph in Oxford, Avignon and Armagh* (Oxford: Clarendon, 1981), pp. 16–17.

being, they are real.[9] Extreme realism implies the notion of divine Ideas distinct from, or otherwise outside, the divine essence. Wyclif ruled this out. Jerome did not defend that point of view. Wyclif's realism was not extreme, but it worried his contemporaries, because at core it was theological realism. In other words, universals were integrally related to divine Ideas. This is why Jerome based his thought on an elevated regard for ideas, because they were properly understood as being at one with divine essence. The world of ideas was the domain of God. That implied direct and relevant applicability with the faith and with theology. In sum, all truth was grounded in and connected to Ideas in the mind of God.[10] It has been convincingly shown that at the end of the Middle Ages, debates over universals had reemerged as a major controversy.[11] Wyclif and Jerome lived in the storm of that dispute.

By the later fourteenth century, that controversy had become severe. Jerome was expected (as Hus was before him) to submit to the will and authority of the Council of Constance, which the conciliar delegates equated with obedience to God. This was a primary assumption. A secondary assumption was that obedience to the council provided a more secure means for achieving properly constituted and officially sanctioned ecclesiastical renewal. Making an exception of Jerome (or Hus or Wyclif, for that matter) represented the thin end of the wedge from a conciliar point of view. This meant that anyone might bypass obedience to the council by asserting that he was obeying God directly and following the dictates of conscience. During his trial, Hus appealed to conscience, and Pierre d'Ailly countered by pointing out that the court could not be guided by conscience but had to rely on testimony by witnesses.[12] Conceding to Hus's demands, or to similar expectations articulated by Jerome, would have rendered church authority questionable at best and at worst might destroy the claim to mediating divine authority. The only response was to counter direct claims to God with violence predicated on the

---

9. Stephen E. Lahey, trans., *Wyclif: Trialogus* (Cambridge: Cambridge University Press, 2013), pp. 54, 70, 77, 218, et al.

10. See, for example, John Wyclif, *Tractatus de universalibus*, ed. Ivan J. Mueller. (Oxford: Clarendon, 1985), pp. 371–374; and John Wyclif, *De materia et forma*, in *Johannis Wyclif miscellanea philosophica*, ed. Michael H. Dziewicki (London: Trübner/WS, 1902), vol. 1, pp. 170–176. There is a translation of the former: Anthony Kenny, trans., *On Universals (Tractatus de universalibus)* (Oxford: Clarendon, 1985), with an excellent introduction by Paul Vincent Spade, pp. vii–xlvii.

11. Zénon Kaluza, *Les querelles doctrinales à Paris: Nominalistes et réalistes aux confins du XIVe et XVe siècles* (Bergamo: Lubrina, 1988).

12. *Relatio*, in *FRB*, vol. 8, p. 76.

belief that ecclesiastical unity had to trump all considerations of personal conviction, conscience, or mystical insight. Unity was more important than diversity or an appeal to the virtues of toleration.[13] Heresy was a vice, not a virtue. Heretics constituted a marginal group that could not be tolerated.[14] It is fairly obvious that Council delegates either did not or refused to see that the intellectual posture assumed by Wyclif, Hus, and Jerome was not necessarily or intentionally subversive. Or was it? Appeals to God did not necessarily seek to overturn church authority completely, nor did they represent an a priori abrogation of the church as a temporal institution. There is no evidence that Jean Gerson and his colleagues took this factor into account. It may not be plausible to argue that Hus recognized every level of authority (church, tradition, scripture, conscience) when he appealed to God. On the other hand, one cannot assume that he came to Constance because he recognized the authority of the Council absolutely. One might say that Hus and Jerome came to Constance in hopes of persuading the Council to their particular points of view. In this sense, Aeneas Sylvius was right when he suggested that Jerome and Hus were more eager to teach than to be taught (*docendi quippe quam discendi cupidiores*). As Aeneas put it, "both of them arrived, ready not so much to humbly learn about the opinions of others but rather to shamelessly push their opinions, wishing rather to instruct than to learn, and eager for appeal to the people."[15] The summons against the Hussites and their supporters on March 6, 1416, pointed out that these heretics desired to foist their own views on the Council and wished to impose their traditions on the hierarchy of the church.[16] Noncompliance with conciliar authority implied a rejection of divine authority. Jerome's condemnation came down to one proposition that revolved around the concepts of power and obedience. One either obeyed God by submitting to the Council or rejected God and flaunted conciliar authority.

There is persuasive force in identifying divine Ideas as part of the foundation on which the Hussite movement was predicated. That equation is essential for understanding why the law of God was so important to the

---

13. István Bejczy, "*Tolerantia*: A Medieval Concept," *Journal of the History of Ideas* 58, no. 3 (1997): 365–384.

14. František Graus, "Randgruppen der städtischen Gesellschaft im spätmittelalter," *Zeitschrift für historische Forschung* 4 (1981): 399.

15. Aeneae Silvii, *Historia bohemica*, ed. Dana Martínková, Alena Hadravová, and Jiří Matl (Prague: Koniasch Latin, 1998), bk. 2, chap. 36, p. 98.

16. Mansi, vol. 27, cols. 919–922.

Czechs. In Hussite philosophy, the law of God is connected to the mind of God. Ockham and his colleagues were considered *doctores signorum*, or philosophical thinkers, whose work disclosed a great deal about words as signifiers but failed to elaborate on what was signified. Hussites were interested not just in the idea of the law of God but also in the practical application of the idea. One point at issue is whether faith is centered in God or in logic. At the beginning of the fifteenth century, this became controversial in France, England, and Bohemia. The thought of Wyclif stood in opposition to the "doctors of signs." It was Wyclif who eventually wielded the greater intellectual influence in Bohemia. Gerson found Wyclifite thought disturbing. Gerson's suspicions led eventually to a showdown with Jerome.

Despite the towering intellectual presence of Wyclif, it would be folly to assume that the impetus for reform resided solely or even chiefly in the application of philosophy to theology. Wyclifite thought certainly provided a scaffolding on which to develop ideas that had already been in circulation in Bohemia before 1390. For example, Matěj Janov outlined the logic that caused reform thinking to advance into heresy. Writing about the limbs of Antichrist, Matěj launched into an attack on the prelates. This included corruption, unnecessary burdens, requirements falling outside the parameters of scripture or the faith, and the unacceptable tyrannical lording over the laity by churchmen, which, in the words of Matěj, resembled a "circus of roaring lions" intent upon devouring those who failed to perform or conform. Further, the invective targeted clerics who failed to set an example, who engaged in censure and punishment, who arbitrarily pronounced the sentence of ecclesiastical censure, excommunication, and mortal sin and in the end turned the divine order upside down. For example, Matěj claimed that more attention was devoted to proper liturgical form than to the integrity or content of faith. Explicitly, he underscored the preoccupation that appeared to support the argument that it was more important to determine if the priest said Mass properly according to the rubrics than it was to find out if the priest was a manifest sinner. For example, was the cleric a liar, a drunk, or a sodomite? Matěj argued that religious values were subverted by improper words in incorrect order rather than by moral considerations. Matěj alleged that such irregularities were endemic in the church.[17] We find a similar critique in Wyclif, Hus, and Jerome.

17. Matěj Janov, *Regulae veteris et novi testamenti*, 6 vols., ed. Vlastimil Kybal, Otakar Odložilík, and Jana Nechutová (Prague and Innsbruck: Universitního Knihkupectví Wagnerova, 1908–1926; Munich: Oldenbourg, 1993), vol. 3, pp. 113–117 (bk. 3, tractate 5, dist. 8, cap. 1).

Matěj was trained at Prague and Paris, and in his magnum opus, "The Rules of the Old and New Testament" (*Regulae veteris et novi testamenti*), he sought to draw attention to the evils and abuses in the church, which had conspired to seduce people into settling for the status quo of religious faith and practice. In so doing, he argued that the practice of religion ended up evading the true center of Christian devotion and becoming caught up in a plethora of human inventions that veered more toward Antichrist than toward Christ. This had the net result of undermining the purity and integrity of the church.[18] Accordingly, Matěj desired to understand the church not in terms of papal *plenitudo potestatis* or institutional structures but as the community of faith capable of and amenable to reform according to the law of Christ.[19] This was fertile soil into which the seeds of Wyclif were planted and which produced a harvest in thinkers such as Jerome who understood philosophical and metaphysical disputations as foundations for Christian presuppositions about the law of God.

John Wyclif

Wyclif was the only first-rate philosopher at Oxford in the period between 1360 and 1380. His fame was equaled only by his notoriety. He was trenchantly described as the "master of error" by Pope Gregory XI in a bull of May 22, 1377, and dismissed in 1385 by Jan of Jenštejn, archbishop of Prague, as a "very wicked heresiarch."[20] One need not give too much credence to the arguments of Johann Loserth in the nineteenth century to recognize that the influence of Wyclif in the intellectual circles of Bohemia was singularly historic in its impact.[21] Hus was never a Wyclifite in the strict sense, but he imbibed deeply from the well of

---

18. Janov, *Regulae*, vol. 1, pp. 172–177.

19. Vlastimil Kybal, *M. Matěj z Janova. Jeho život, spisy a učení* (Brno: L. Marek, 2000, originally published 1905). See also Howard Kaminsky, "On the Sources of Matthew of Janov's Doctrine," in *Czechoslovakia Past and Present*, 2 vols., ed. Miloslav Rechcigl (The Hague: Mouton, 1968), vol. 2, pp. 1175–1183.

20. Mansi, vol. 26, cols. 565–566. See also Joseph Dahmus, *The Prosecution of John Wyclif* (New Haven, Conn.: Yale University Press, 1952), p. 46. The Jenštejn reference is from his *De consideratione*. The text appears in *ST*, vol. 2, p. 105.

21. Johann Loserth, *Wiclif and Hus*, trans. M. J. Evans (London: Hodder and Stoughton, 1884, 2nd ed. 1925).

Wyclif's writings. On the other hand, Jerome had Wyclif as his model from around 1399 until 1416.[22] He actively drew on Wyclif but with a critical eye.[23]

His pervasive influence aside, Wyclif was known in Prague during his lifetime.[24] "His name was a war cry which resounded from university chairs, from pulpits, in philosophical works, in theological meditations, in private letters, in aggressive polemics, in satirical poems, and in popular songs. Some admired him, others declared that he was the originator of the division in the Czech nation, and the cause of all trouble, and they attacked him violently, and rejected him."[25] The details have been rehearsed elsewhere to make a strong argument for intellectual and religious reform well before the ideas of Wyclif penetrated Bohemia.[26] Revolutions always have roots and antecedents. They do not develop out of thin air. In the haste to ascribe significance to Wyclif, it has been insufficiently noted that the influence of Neoplatonism had reached Prague by the 1370s. Matěj Janov is only one of the conduits by which the influence of the School of Chartres, for example, was introduced in Prague. This factor has only been cursorily addressed.[27] However, it is possible that Jerome was influenced by this perspective along with Augustine, the Platonic tradition, and Wyclif. It is perilous to ascribe too much to the English influence.[28] However, if one is committed to the idea that the philosophical factor is the central key to understanding the history of Hussitism, then it is understandable why Wyclif is given the lion's share of influence at Prague circa 1400, and the common perspective of scholars such as Loserth, Kaminsky, Kalivoda, and Šmahel is understandable. There was no other thinker at Charles

22. František M. Bartoš, "Kostnický proces M. Jeronýma Pražského," *Sborník historický* 4 (1956): 60.

23. *Quaestio de potentia materiae primae*, in Šmahel/ Silagi, pp. 143–146.

24. Trapp, "Clm 27034" pp. 320–360.

25. Otakar Odložilík, "Wyclif and Bohemia," *Věstník královské české společnosti nauk* 1 (1935): 1.

26. Václav Novotný and Vlastimil Kybal, *M. Jan Hus: Život a učení*, 5 vols. (Prague: Laichter, 1919–1931). Novotný wrote the first two volumes of this important work while Kybal wrote the last three.

27. Herold, *Pražská univerzita a Wyclif*, pp. 225–229.

28. Loserth, *Wiclif and Hus*; Howard Kaminsky, *A History of the Hussite Revolution* (Berkeley: University of California Press, 1967), pp. 36–37; Robert Kalivoda, *Husitská ideologie* (Prague: Československá akademie věd, 1961), p. 159; and František Šmahel, *Die Hussitischen Revolution*, trans. Thomas Krzenck, 3 vols. (Hannover: Hahnsche, 2002), vol. 2, pp. 788–832.

University who exerted as powerful or profound an intellectual influence as Wyclif. After his ideas were imported and championed in Prague, Wyclif became the doyen of the intellectual side of the reform movement. Before his name and his works were known at Prague, there was a native reform movement stretching to the 1360s, and significant progress had already been achieved under men such as Jan Milíč of Kroměříž and Matěj Janov. In that paradigm, Wyclif is neither essential nor required. However, what is undeniable is that Wyclif provided a stronger and more sophisticated intellectual framework on which to develop and articulate the reform concepts latent in the Czech province before the dramatic transitions marking the last decade of the fourteenth century and the first decade of the fifteenth. His contribution to the Czech milieu had neither antecedent nor peer. In retrospect, that development was a two-edged sword. Some reformers turned away from the movement, unnerved by the startling, aggressive claims and conclusions advanced by Wyclif, while others found in Wyclif the necessary ammunition to take the Czech reform movement to another level. There were implications for all Christians. The paralysis of analysis would never do. Even members of the laity who detected sin and hypocrisy among the leadership of the church were obliged to take steps to rectify the situation. Priests, prelates, and religious who resisted must either be ignored or removed. Failure to act indicated complicity and commensurate guilt. By extension, dilatory Christians were not members of the true church. Jerome and his colleagues promoted these tenets.

It is natural to wonder why Czechs found realism so appealing. Why did Wyclif become an intellectual superstar at Prague? We must ponder the psychological, sociopolitical, and theological factors that may explain why a number of Czech philosophers were attracted to Wyclifite realism when so many other Christian thinkers throughout Europe were either perplexed or repelled by Oxford doctrine. It is perhaps too simplistic and too facetious to suggest that realism was embraced by the Czechs because nominalism was widely held by the Germans, but the conflict cannot be set aside as playing no role whatever. Context is not determined solely by ideas but is also formed by institutions. Intellectual history is not just a history of ideas but a development shaped by politics, whether these are university, ecclesiastical, or social.[29] The nature of philosophical debate that engulfed Jerome was conditioned by late medieval university politics.

---

29. Kaluza, *Les querelles doctrinales*.

It is certain that the blossoming of realism at Prague was a conscious effort to adapt the content of philosophical method to the intellectual environment. Of course, no thinker at Charles University in the early fifteenth century could possibly admit to adapting philosophy in the service of theology or promoting a particular discourse to conform to political trends. It is true that philosophical and theological disputes and differences in Bohemia were affected and complicated by the linguistic and cultural differences existing between Czechs and Germans.[30] These deepening and sometimes acrimonious social and cultural divisions in Prague resulted in the politicizing of Wyclif. Many of the Germans attacked Wyclif, who was being adopted to some degree by the Czechs. The latter saw this as an excuse to attack them (not just Wyclif), so Wyclif became a rallying point, even though it cannot be argued that all Charles University scholars defended Wyclif's ideas, let alone had read or even understood him. Certainly, many Prague masters had made Wyclif a subject of serious consideration, and some were heavily influenced by the force of argument presented in his voluminous writings. Stanislav of Znojmo and Štěpán Páleč are examples.[31] For others, it was more a case of getting on the dominant bandwagon. The period between 1380 and 1410 marks a watershed in the intellectual history of Charles University, and there is sufficient evidence to sustain the argument that the same period marks the apex of the history of philosophy in the Czech lands.[32] This period, as we have seen, included a keen focus on the controversy about universals, and at the center of that dispute was the thought of Wyclif.[33] Nevertheless, despite its popularity and practice at Charles University, realism was criminalized in

---

30. Ferdinand Seibt, "Die Zeit der Luxemburger und der hussitische Revolution," in *Handbuch der Geschichte der böhmischen Länder*, 4 vols., ed. Karl Bosl (Munich: Hiersemann, 1967–1970), vol. 1, p. 440; Leonard E. Scales, "At the Margins of Community: Germans in Pre-Hussite Bohemia," *Transactions of the Royal Historical Society*, 6th series, 9 (1999): 327–52; and also of some relevance is Scales, *The Shaping of German Identity: Authority and Crisis, 1245–1414* (Cambridge: Cambridge University Press, 2012).

31. On the former, see Gabriel Muchelmans, "Stanislaus of Znaim on Truth and Falsity," in *Mediaeval Semantics and Metaphysics: Studies Dedicated to L. M. de Rijk on the Occasion of His 60th Birthday*, ed. E. P. Bos (Nijmegen: Brepols, 1985), pp. 313–338.

32. Ivan Mueller, ed., *Commentarius in De universalibus Iohannis Wyclif Stephano de Palecz ascriptus* (Prague: Filosofia, 2009), p. 9.

33. František Šmahel, "Verzeichnis der Quellen zum Prager Universalienstreit 1348–1500," *Mediaevalia Philosophica Polonorum* 25 (1980): 1–189, is a useful index of the sources surrounding this controversy. It consists of about 530 sources found in more than 260 manuscripts scattered across three dozen libraries and repositories.

1404 at Prague.[34] This had an additional fertilizing effect as Wyclifite intellectuals at Charles University became ever more determined to utilize the arsenal of Wyclif's thought as a means of achieving independence within an increasingly hostile environment. Contemporary sources suggest that the Czechs were attracted to novelty and utilized Wyclif in an effort to distinguish themselves.[35] The claim cannot simply be dismissed.

On several occasions in the *De universalibus*, Wyclif declared that intellectual errors about universals were the cause of all sin evident in the world.[36] Jerome agreed.[37] The causal connections of this phenomenon must be subjected to scrutiny and elaboration. These positions cast Wyclif in the role of radical thinker. Philosophically, he went beyond the boundaries of reason and in matters of theology exceeded the limits of faith.[38] Of course, neither Wyclif nor Jerome had any particular allegiance to boundaries they considered arbitrary. Therein lay the danger to the church and the basis for the unflinching opposition Wyclif and his followers encountered. Appeals to ecclesiastical authority by some of the nominalists were regarded by Jerome as strategic ruses to discourage inquiry that might lead one beyond the borders of what the medieval church deemed acceptable. It is reasonable to conclude that Wyclif was important for three principal reasons. First, he was a major factor in defining fifteenth-century Czech scholasticism in Prague. By extension, he exerted a formative and fertilizing effect on the mind of Jerome. Second, his condemnation caused others to look his way (perhaps by means of revived Thomism and Scotism) in the winter of their own discontent with Ockham. Third, he stands as an example of philosophy rigorously applied generally to theology and specifically to doctrinal assumptions, claims, and conclusions.[39] In this, Jerome was his eager disciple.

---

34. On the extent to which Platonic works were available in Prague, see Edouard Jeauneau, "Plato apud Bohemos," *Medieval Studies* 41 (1979): 161–214.

35. *Tractatus contra Hussitas*, Nürnberg, Stadtbibliothek, MS Cent. I, 78, fol. 151r; and Ferdinand Seibt, *Hussitica. Zur Struktur einer Revolution* (Cologne: Böhlau, 1965), pp. 61–89.

36. Wyclif, *Tractatus de universalibus*, chap. 3, pp. 70–84.

37. *Quaestio duplex de formis universalibus*, in Šmahel/ Silagi, pp. 47–48.

38. Gordon Leff, "John Wyclif: The Path to Dissent," *Proceedings of the British Academy* 52 (1966): 147.

39. Lahey, *John Wyclif*, p. 225.

Aims of the Bohemian Reform

The history of the Hussite movement was neither accidental nor insignificant. Moreover, it had not developed in random isolation from ideas and theological reflection. What did Hus, Jerome, and the Hussites want to achieve? According to a Hussite poet writing around 1420, they desired to make life better.[40] Life for Jerome and Hus revolved around the Christian faith and was to some extent identified with the church as it had developed by the fifteenth century. The desire to achieve an ideal perfection also motivated these men. This aspiration was rooted in the essential character of the hidden divine world which had applicability for the visible and material human world. That impetus also had a moral component. It is one thing to suggest that the concept of a perfect ideal could be implemented in order to reform both church and society, but it is less clear how that normative ideal was utilized or by what mechanism that might be achieved.[41] The broad thrust of such reform resonated with the clear aims and goals of men such as Milíč and Matěj for a renewal of ecclesiastical and social conditions.[42] The scaffolding of Wyclifite thought allowed these reformers to apply directly into the material world concepts of the world of Ideas, or the archetypal world. For example, the ideal archetypal world was also one of ethical, social, and political implications. Such issues ultimately interested Jerome. Wyclifite philosophy was championed at Prague by Stanislav of Znojmo, Štěpán Páleč, Hus, Jerome, Jakoubek Stříbro, and many others. The first two ultimately backslid from that posture and became strident enemies of Hussite philosophy. The middle two were executed, and their former colleagues Stanislav and Páleč played no mean role in their demise. Jakoubek alone escaped the fracas virtually unscathed, clinging to at least a modified notional commitment to Wyclif. Hus, Jerome, and the Hussites after them wished to inaugurate the ideal world into the present world.

---

40. *Hádání Prahy s Kutnou Horou z r. 1420*, in *Husitské skladby budyšínského rukopisu*, ed. Jiří Daňhelka (Prague: Orbis, 1952), p. 161.

41. See, for example, Vilém Herold, "Wyclif und Hieronymus von Prag: Zum Versuch einer 'praktischen' Umwandlung in der spätmittelalterlichen Ideenlehre," in *Knowledge and the Sciences in Medieval Philosophy*, 3 vols., ed. Simo Knuuttila, Reijo Työrinoja, and Sten Ebbesen (Helsinki: Akateeminen Kirjakauppa, 1990), vol. 3, pp. 212–223, where the assertion is made but the demonstration is missing.

42. Vilém Herold, "Štěpán of Páleč and the Archetypal World of Ideas," *BRRP* 5, no. 1 (2004): 87.

This was the central aim of the Bohemian reformers. The most significant and influential force opposing Jerome was Gerson.

Jerome versus Gerson

Fundamental to understanding Jerome is his notion of the archetypal world (*mundus archetypus*), a view espoused by many Prague masters in the late fourteenth century.[43] This brings into sharp focus the abiding conflict with Gerson. As noted earlier, Jerome conceived of the uncreated world as made up of many Ideas within the divine consciousness. These Ideas can only be described as uncreated, eternal, and unchangeable, and they exist in distinction from one another. Moreover, the Ideas are distinct from God in the divine essence. Ideas are based on divine essence and as such are subordinate to God ontologically. Archetypes are within God's essence. Jerome took the view that these Ideas were the underlying causes of all things in the world that were perceptible by means of the senses. Ideas required a first cause (God), who was responsible for the world of the senses that had been created on the basis of the Ideas that exist in the world of archetypes. Jerome was less concerned with a body of knowledge (as theologians might be in terms of doctrines) but more interested in philosophy and especially in the ideas that inform thinking. In other words, he seems particularly committed to a form of metathinking or a process of thinking about thinking. Eventually, this caused a collision with the church and especially with men such as Gerson.[44] Gerson's approach was via theology, and he rejected realism (based on Platonism), preferring instead the *via moderna* (or nominalism). Gerson attempted to apply a nominalist hermeneutic to theology.[45] The identification of Gerson as a nominalist requires both nuance and an important caveat. For example, Étienne Gilson has advanced the claim that Gerson was not really a nominalist except when it became necessary to adopt that hermeneutic in order to better and more effectively refute forms of realist thought that resulted in the teachings developed by heretics such as Wyclif, Hus, and Jerome. Gerson

---

43. Herold, "Wyclif und Hieronymus von Prag," pp. 212–223.

44. On the important relation between Jerome and Gerson, see especially Zénon Kaluza, "Le chancelier Gerson et Jérôme de Prague," in *Études doctrinales*, pp. 207–231; Herold, "Wyclif und Hieronymus von Prag," pp. 212–223; and Herold, "Der Streit, pp. 77–89.

45. For arguments supporting this idea, see Kaluza, "Le chancelier Gerson et Jérôme de Prague," in *Études doctrinales*, pp. 209–212; and Kaluza, *Les querelles doctrinales*, p. 122.

argued that realism was the basis on which such heresies arose in the first place.[46] So the question remains pertinent: Was Gerson a nominalist? Did he deny the real existence of intellectual categories, or ideas, outside the mind? It may be argued that Gerson was a nominalist only to the extent of rejecting such categories within God.[47] There is much debate about where to place Gerson.[48] What is certain is an important shift in Gerson's intellectual outlook away from philosophical theology to theological spirituality.[49] One of the outcomes is the possibility that Gerson neither appreciated nor understood fully Jerome's point of view.[50] From a methodological perspective, Jerome represented the schools, teaching, reason, logic, and philosophical approaches. By contrast, Gerson represented monasteries, preaching, authority, faith, and theological conviction. Jerome seems to consistently insert Ideas into the mind of God but does not perceive this as violating the unity of divine essence. Obviously, there were thinkers in the early fifteenth century who saw Jerome's approach as containing pitfalls and encouraging exploration along dangerous pathways.[51] Gerson was only one of those who believed that Jerome had to be corrected and, if that failed, had simply to be stopped by all means possible. It is important to note that men like Gerson tended to treat their opponents from an inquisitorial perspective. Opposing ideas were degraded as heresy, major motifs reduced into corruptions of theology, and arguments trivialized. In his hands, Jerome was presented as an intellectual outlaw, a deviant, a heretic. In large measure, Gerson is responsible for creating the rhetorical distinction between realists and nominalists, and this can be observed in his confrontation with Jerome.

---

46. Gilson, *History of Christian Philosophy*, pp. 528–532. For another point of view, see Oberman, *The Harvest of Medieval Theology*, pp. 331–340.

47. Brian Patrick McGuire, *Jean Gerson and the Last Medieval Reformation* (University Park: Pennsylvania State University Press, 2005), p. 382.

48. See D. Catherine Brown, *Pastor and Laity in the Theology of Jean Gerson* (Cambridge: Cambridge University Press, 1987), pp. 79–83.

49. Ably demonstrated in Kaluza, *Les querelles doctrinales*, pp. 13–86.

50. Herold, "Der Streit ," pp. 77–89; and Kaluza, "Le chancelier Gerson et Jérôme de Prague," in *Études doctrinales*, pp. 207–231.

51. Zénon Kaluza, "La question de Jérôme de Prague disputée à Heidelberg," in *Études doctrinales*, pp. 319–320. On Gerson's philosophical leanings, see Kaluza, *Les querelles doctrinales*, pp. 35–86.

In terms of the created world, Jerome believed (possibly having been influenced by Wyclif), that God created first a rational analogical being (*ens analogum*), or a "related being," which was the basis for all created things and contained within itself the possibility for creation and for establishing what was common to all created things within created order in terms of hierarchy, species, and genus.[52] The discussion of analogy was less on linguistics and more on the relation between the nature of concepts and the words used to describe and understand them. In terms of universals, Jerome believed that universals did not exist outside their particular "individuality." In other words, the created universal, for example, a table, is identical with its concrete form, even if they differ in some ways. That is, a table really exists as a table, not just as the idea of a table. What comes into play is essential identities on one hand and formal distinctions on the other. The implications for theology were judged both significant and controversial.

Jerome actively engaged in the polemical interchange with nominalism and the logic employed by the nominalists or by those who chose to utilize the *via moderna* to refute the theological implications of realism (such as Gerson). Universals were not simply signs or mere terms or even abstract ideas. Instead, they functioned in important ways in terms of real propositions (*propositio realis*). In other words, the idea preceded the reality. The idea is the witness of itself and of reality. Each person is a distinct entity, but human nature (which belongs to all) is distinct from personhood. Human nature is not predicated on language. It precedes language and is based on the ontological order of things. The idea causes the reality. Reality precedes signs, and Jerome believed that the truth of proper logic could not be, and was not, based on signs but rather was based on "things" (realities). Thus, "true logic is not in signs but is founded in reality."[53] The concept of universals implied three understandings. First, the universal may have signified essentially nothing. Second, the universal was a synonym for concepts or a mental idea or a construct that was disparate from reality. Third, the universal signified entities or realities that existed

---

52. Kaluza, "Jérôme de Prague et le *Timée* de Platon," in *Études doctrinales*, pp. 253–300.

53. *Utrum veritas generalis sit signanda pro quacunque proposicione vera denominanda*, Basel, Universitätsbibliothek MS VIII A 24, fol. 47v; and in Šmahel/Silagi, p. 11. The point is elaborated in Kaluza, "La question de Jérôme de Prague disputée à Heidelberg," in *Études doctrinales*, pp. 301–32.

outside the mental world or outside any construct, concept, or idea.[54] All of this must be interrogated with respect to the implications for theology. Once again, the centrality over disputes concerning divine Ideas must be underscored.

Generally speaking, it is possible to make some determination about the philosophical convictions espoused by Jerome by examining his surviving university disputations. Recently, Ota Pavlíček has subjected two of these to careful scrutiny. The first, *Utrum veritas generalis sit signanda pro quacunque proposicione vera denominanda*, is a university *quaestio* presented at Heidelberg in 1406.[55] The fuss caused by Jerome at Heidelberg suggested unambiguously that "Jerome was an unscrupulous manipulator."[56] His opponents considered him a perverter of truth whose vexing presence caused sufficient discord to offend even the dead. As a result, he was suspended from all academic activities. The surviving record preserves only the structure of Jerome's address and does not contain the content, and therefore it is evident that it was considerably more elaborate and prolix than the extant outline. The first article of the *quaestio* had to do with Ideas and their relation to God and creation, while the second article dealt with the metaphysical relations between created beings. According to Jerome, ideas are true, eternal, and individual, and they precede creation.[57] Jerome considered that every individual thing had a corresponding idea and that it was specious to suggest otherwise.[58] God was posited as the first cause, and causes are ideas. Ideas are not created, but they do not subsist on their own. Jerome did not conceive of Ideas as separated from the divine mind. In other words, there is an essential connection between God and Ideas and by extension their manifestation in the natural world. These postulations were problematic to men such as Gerson, who became very concerned about the theological implications of Jerome's thought.[59]

---

54. Among those to explore the matter of divine Ideas in the work of Jerome and many of his Czech colleagues is Herold, "Der Streit," pp. 77–89.

55. The text is in Šmahel/Silagi, pp. 5–12.

56. Ota Pavlíček, "Two Philosophical Texts of Jerome of Prague and His Alleged Designation of Opponents of Real Universals as Diabolic Heretics," *BRRP* 8 (2009): 55.

57. *Quaestio de veritatibus generalibus*, in Šmahel/Silagi, pp. 3–12.

58. *Quaestio de veritatibus generalibus*, pp. 7–8; and *Quaestio de mundo archetypo*, p. 167.

59. That acute concern has been noted by a number of scholars, including Zénon Kaluza, "Le 'De universali reali' de Jean De Maisonneuve er les *epicure litterales*," *Freiburger Zeitschrift für Philosophie und Theologie* 33 (1986): 483–485; and Herold, "Der Streit," pp. 77–89.

Jerome is very clearly articulating the conviction that the world of ideas corresponds with the sensory world and that the former is the model for the latter. Universals therefore are not separate from particulars. No sign is the truth, as the two are separate.[60] The implications of that statement follow Wyclif's *De blasphemia*, in which he argued that blasphemy occurred when honor due to God was rendered to something less than God.[61] Examples might include adoration of the host, biblicism, ecclesiastical hierarchy, religious art, and so on. And in a parting shot, Jerome declared that those who claimed that universals were mere signs should be considered dialectical heretics.[62] His entire presentation at Heidelberg, a well-known nominalist stronghold, appears to be an intentional frontal assault and provocative challenge to his detractors. The posture at Heidelberg was not exceptional. It should be noted that practically all of Jerome's writings include a polemical discourse aimed at one aspect or another of nominalist thought. His writings and discourses were building toward an eventual showdown with Gerson.

The second *quaestio* advanced by Jerome, *Utrum a parte rei universalia sit necessarium ponere pro mundi sensibilis armonia*, featured at the 1409 *Quodlibet* in Prague chaired by Matěj Knín.[63] This amounted to a "tournament of the knights of erudition" grappling in an intellectual battle where the combatants undergo a test by the "swords of argument."[64] Once again, we find Jerome actively engaged in the propagation and defense of two articles. The first was devoted to ideas; the second centered its focus on created universals. The repeated themes indicate significance. As we have already seen, ideas and/or universals existed outside the created particulars and were in the divine essence. Jerome argued that this was a necessary condition, according to the will of God, in order to sustain the sensory world in harmony and function.[65] As at Heidelberg, we find Jerome declaring that those who denied this truth were dialectical heretics. As we will see in chapter 4, Jerome was later charged at Vienna with denouncing his enemies, not as

---

60. *Quaestio de veritatibus generalibus*, pp. 9, 10.

61. *Tractatus de blasphemia*, ed. Michael Henry Dziewicki (London: Trübner/WS, 1893), pp. 1–17.

62. *Quaestio de veritatibus generalibus*, p. 11.

63. *Quaestio de universalibus a parte rei*, in Šmahel/Silagi, pp. 83–95.

64. *Recommendatio artium liberalium*, in Šmahel/Silagi, p. 211.

65. *Quaestio de universalibus a parte rei*, p. 88.

dialectical heretics but as diabolic heretics.[66] It might be noted that d'Ailly once asserted that those who believed in real universals "were not worthy of the name of philosophers."[67] The acrimony persisted on both sides of the debate and comes into sharp focus in the confrontation between Jerome and Gerson. It might be noted that such an epithet was hardly new or original but in fact was fairly common.[68] This suggests that the attention paid to Jerome on this point may be overwrought. Part of the controversy revolves around the question of whether Jerome innovated a citation from Anselm or cited it correctly. Pavlíček concludes that Jerome almost certainly never denounced his opponents as "diabolical heretics."[69] Neither of the two witnesses at Jerome's 1410 Vienna trial, Master Nicholas Tell of Tungris (who held a degree from Heidelberg) and Master Konrad Duvel of Hildesheim (who had studied both at Prague and Heidelberg), could remember the exact time of the disputation, but both said it took place "in new schools" or, even more exactly, in the lecture room of ordinary disputations in the school of arts, opposite the monastery of the Augustinian monks in Heidelberg.[70] According to Master Tell, the disputation lasted four days, as five masters argued against Jerome. Jerome's arguments outraged the bachelor of theology Master Konrad of Soest, who asked his junior colleague Konrad Duvel to record some of his statements.[71] The two eyewitnesses claimed that Wilhelm of Eppenbach, Heinrich of Hessen, and Johannes Lagenator of Frankfurt were present during the debate. The latter was in fact nominated as the official opponent.[72] Lagenator (ca. 1380–1440) taught theology at Heidelberg and served as university rector in 1406, 1416, and again in 1428–1429. He was later court preacher to Ludwig III (Palatine elector). Lagenator represented Heidelberg University at the Council of Constance, where he encountered Jerome. On the question of whether Jerome actually denounced his opponents as "diabolic heretics," there is a confusing situation, with manuscript evidence indicating both possibilities based principally on the problems of

---

66. *Quaestio de universalibus a parte rei*, p. 92.

67. Quoted in Francis Oakley, *The Political Thought of Pierre d'Ailly: The Voluntarist Tradition* (New Haven, Conn.: Yale University Press, 1964), p. 25.

68. Trapp, "Clm 27034," pp. 320–321.

69. Pavlíček, "Two Philosophical Texts," p. 76.

70. Klicman, pp. 12, 14.

71. Klicman, p. 14.

72. Klicman, pp. 12–14.

discerning the proper understanding of abbreviations. Pavlíček has gone to the bother of sorting through this challenge and concludes that the issue can be resolved on the basis of paleography, with the outcome that Jerome did not denigrate his opponents as diabolic heretics.[73]

If Jerome's philosophical position was viewed with some disdain by fifteenth-century scholars, this might be understood as a reflection of the rift between competing philosophies jostling for supremacy in the universities. It should be borne in mind that between 1350 and 1500, the idea of the university developed from its older identity as a coterie of scholars into the form that eventually produced the modern university. It was in this context that Jerome flourished. The integration or correlation of philosophy with theology caused outright alarm. It led in Jerome's case to formal charges of heresy. "Heresy was a by-product of the Wycliffite system, a symptom rather than a cause."[74] This may well apply to the case of Jerome in terms of his thought. Heresy was not the cause of his thinking, but it was a result of his philosophical ideas, especially when wedded to issues of theology. Unlike Wyclif or Hus, Jerome wrote sparingly on theological matters. The short exposition "The Shield of the Christian Faith" (*Scutum fidei christianae*) may have been a direct result of Jerome exploring the philosophical dimensions of theology. Advancing his informal theological education and developing specific doctrinal ideas, Jerome believed that there was a common essence in the Trinity in addition to the three persons (an understanding known as quaternitarianism).[75] By analogy, the human soul was made up of three parts nominated as memory, will, and understanding.[76] Humankind are within the created order and both constitute a theatre in which the divine essence (trinity and unity) is revealed.[77] In his "Shield of Faith," Jerome supposed a personal distinction between the

---

73. Pavlíček, "Two Philosophical Texts," pp. 73–76.

74. Michael Wilks, "*Reformatio regni*: Wyclif and Hus as Leaders of Religious Protest Movements," in *Schism, Heresy and Religious Protest*, Studies in Church History, vol. 90, ed. Derek Baker (Cambridge: University Press, 1972), p. 111.

75. The fourth Lateran Council defended Peter Lombard against similar charges leveled by Joachim of Fiore. Clare Monagle, *Orthodoxy and Controversy in Twelfth-Century Discourse: Peter Lombard's Sentences and the Development of Theology* (Turnhout: Brepols, 2013), pp. 139–155.

76. Hardt, vol. 4, col. 645.

77. Jan Hus, *Super IV Sententiarum*, in Václav Flajšhans, ed., *Mag. Jo Hus Opera omnia: Nach neuentdeckten Handschriften*, 3 vols (Osnabrück: Biblio-Verlag, 1966), vol. 2, II, incepcio I, 2–5, pp. 190–2.

persons in the Godhead.[78] Jerome used a drawing in the form of a shield that had four points. (See figure 2.1.) Three of these points were corners, and the fourth was in the middle of the shield. The corners were annotated "Father, Son, and Holy Spirit." Between these words appeared "not" (i.e., the Father is not the Son, etc). Under each of the triune designations, Jerome proposed an analogy to illuminate his thinking. These included words such as "ice, rain, snow = water; memory, reason, will = soul; eagle, lion, calf = animal; and Augustine, Jerome, Ambrose = human being." Jerome explained all of this, but the shield and the annotations hardly require any expansion.[79] The figure of the shield of faith is fairly common in manuscripts, and a number of examples have been identified.[80] Jerome's use of this shield as a pedagogical tool provoked controversy and ultimately came under suspicion of heresy. The analysis was provocative, deceptively simple, yet profoundly revealing. As noted previously, Jerome wrote out an explanation of the shield.[81] Ostensibly, he used the diagram at different universities and during academic disputations to support his understanding of real universals.[82] The "shield of faith" (*scutum fidei*) was a term borrowed from the New Testament (Ephesians 6:16) and implied a defense against improper teaching. Some consider the diagram of the shield a suitable visual teaching device for explaining the doctrine of the Trinity.[83] The *Scutum fidei christianae* is Jerome's sole treatise of a strictly theological or doctrinal nature.[84] It can now be dated fairly accurately to 1406, at precisely the time Jerome was enmeshed in dispute at

78. Ota Pavlíček, "*Scutum fidei christianae*: The Depiction of the Shield of Faith in the Realistic Teaching of Jerome of Prague in the Context of His Interpretation of the Trinity." *BRRP* 9 (2014): 80. This essay is the only study in English and may be commended as reliable.

79. NK, MS V E 28, fols. 130r–v.

80. These include NK, IV A 1, fol. 152v; NK, V E 28, fol. 130r; Castle Archive, C 20 fol. 76v; ÖNB, 4515, fol. 194v; Dessau, Stadtbibliothek, Georg Hs.50, fol. 32r; Rome, Vatican Library, Ottobonianus lat. 2087, fol. 241v; Hamburg, Staats- und Universitätsbibliothek Hist. 31e, fol. 7v; among others.

81. *Scutum fidei christianae* is in Šmahel/Silagi, pp. 194–198.

82. Pavlíček, "*Scutum fidei christianae*," p. 72.

83. *ST*, vol. 1, (1919), pp. 9–10. For details about Jerome at Heidelberg, see especially František Šmahel, "Mag. Hieronymus von Prag und die Heidelberg Universität," in *Die Prager Universität im Mittelalter* (Leiden: Brill, 2007), pp. 526–538.

84. Those who have examined it are Šmahel, *Život a dílo Jeronýma Pražského* (Prague: Argo, 2010), pp. 273–293, Pavlíček, "*Scutum fidei christianae*," pp. 72–97, and Sedlák, "Nauka o sv. Trojici za Husa," pp. 1–23.

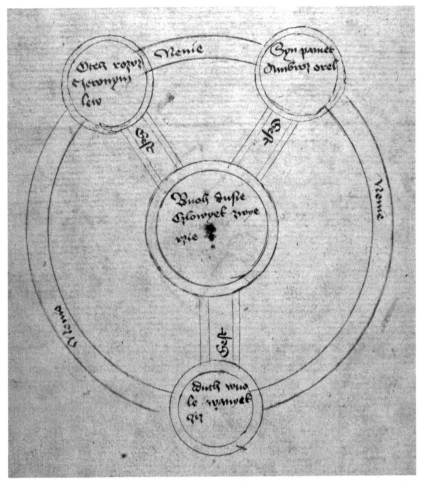

FIGURE 2.1 Czech version of Jerome's *Scutum fidei christianae*. NK, MS IV A1, fol. 152v. Used by permission.

Heidelberg.[85] Pavlíček suggests that it is likely that Jerome's shield of faith was influenced by the doctrinal position assumed by the second Council of Lyons in 1274.[86]

The visual depiction of the "shield of faith" and Jerome's explanation of the idea have been preserved more often than any of Jerome's other writings. The shield might be understood within a tradition of using triangles

---

85. Relevant edition in Šmahel/Silagi, pp. 193–198.

86. Pavlíček, "Two Philosophical Texts of Jerome of Prague," pp. 73–74.

to explain the doctrine of the Trinity.[87] According to Jerome, there are three names yet one thing. There are three persons but one God. The persons within the being and essence of God are distinguished on the basis of relation. In this sense, Jerome could argue that memory, reason, and will make up the human soul, but these distinctions are not identical. Water may be manifested as ice, snow, and rain, but these elements are distinguishable. Further, personalities such as Saints Ambrose, Augustine, and Jerome, while not identical, share a common essence. Jerome of Prague pointed out that the three persons are not three human beings distinguished by essence. Admittedly, there is a common essence; there is a definite distinction in human persons, but there is no distinction in essence, and therefore they do not represent three different human natures. Applied to the doctrine of the Trinity, the three persons in the Godhead do not denote three divine natures. Elevated to the realm of universals, the uncreated Trinity produced the created Trinity.[88] Jerome says that everything in the created order is predicated on an uncreated order. This is the application of Wyclifite thought wherein Ideas in the mind of God are universals that undergird the natural world and everything that exists therein. There is a formal distinction between divine Ideas and God, which, as Jerome argues elsewhere, is fundamental.[89] Once again, disagreement over divine Ideas forced Jerome into an adversarial position with thinkers such as Gerson.

According to the medieval church, the doctrine of the Trinity submits that there are three distinct persons within the Godhead but only one nature.[90] Together with incarnation and the Eucharist, the Trinity was one of the three mysteries of medieval theology. In his disputation with Master Blažej Vlk (Blasius Lupus), subsequent to the 1409 Prague *Quodlibet*, Jerome argued that God is a universal, indeed *the* universal, and as such, God is the basic general cause, the first universal, which means that all things in nature are predicated on God.[91] Heinrich Totting of Oyta

---

87. Several drawings of these shields, from manuscripts in Prague, Vienna, Dessau, Rome, and Hamburg, have been published in Šmahel/Silagi, pp. CLXIX–CLXXV.

88. *Scutum fidei christianae*, p. 195.

89. *Quaestio duplex de formis universalibus*, p. 32, where it is noted "sed forme ydeales non sunt ipse Deus formaliterigitur conclusio vera."

90. See Canon 1 of the fourth Lateran Council, in Norman P. Tanner, ed., *Decrees of the Ecumenical Councils*, 2 vols. (London: Sheed & Ward, 1990), vol. 1, p. 232.

91. *Disputatio Magistri Blasii Lupi* [Blažej Vlk] *contra Magistrum Hieronymus de Praga in material universalium realium cum responsionibus eiusdem*, in Šmahel/Silagi, p. 117.

understood the advantages of realism over nominalism when speaking of the Trinity, and both d'Ailly and Peter Pulka agreed on this point.[92] The conception of God as a universal proved advantageous to Jerome in establishing an integral connection between God and the world. Much later, the shield of faith and its implications were brought up on three separate occasions at Constance, and it is remarkable that Jerome agreed with the accuracy of some of the charges lodged against him on April 27, 1416.[93] The admission is puzzling. Several scholars who have studied the case of Jerome suggest that this agreement might be attributed to his mental state following prolonged harsh imprisonment.[94] What appeared problematic to the church was a nagging suspicion that Jerome was attempting to promote the idea that a Wyclifite perspective on universals was essential for explaining theology and that Jerome believed that universals guaranteed the faith. What is certain is that Jerome's philosophical commitments had clear and intentional application to both philosophy and theology. However, it is not possible to establish absolutely one way or the other if Jerome explicitly attached the faith to philosophy. At the Council of Constance, Jerome formally encountered opposition to any amalgamation of the underlying logic or significance of theology and philosophy and the speculative sciences. The main proponent of maintaining strict lines of demarcation between these realms of inquiry was Gerson.[95]

Gerson emerged as one of Jerome's most strident and dangerous opponents, and by the time the two met formally at the Council of Constance, the divisions between them were firmly entrenched, and neither was amenable to compromise. Jerome was certainly unprepared to succumb to Gerson's persistence and sometimes irresistible force. Gerson consistently opposed any mixing or amalgamation of disciplines and languages, defending especially the traditional Aristotelian way of speaking.[96] Realists argued for a model of unified knowledge and maintained that speculation into philosophy and theology shared the same

92. These are observations noted in Pavlíček, "*Scutum fidei christianae*," p. 85.

93. Mansi, vol. 27, col. 847; and Hardt, vol. 4, cols. 633–647.

94. See, for example, Walter Brandmüller, *Das Konzil von Konstanz 1414–1418*, 2 vols. (Paderborn: Ferdinand Schöningh, 1991–1997), vol. 2, pp. 126–127.

95. Jean Gerson, "Prosperum iter faciet nobis Deus," in Glorieux, vol. 5, pp. 471–480.

96. Kaluza, *Les querelles doctrinales*, pp. 39–40.

principles; this was a Thomist point of view.[97] Gerson could not accommodate that perspective. He was adamant that scripture had a particular form of speaking (logic and grammar), just as other disciplines had their guiding principles. He made this clear at various times throughout his career, but notably the idea was articulated on December 3, 1415.[98] Clearly, Gerson found that line compromised and blurred in Jerome. This caused the defendant at Constance to be viewed with grave and abiding suspicion.[99] Jerome deliberately used philosophy and intellectual argument to promote a particular vision. That vision was scripture as the center of authority; comprehensive reform, which included the church, society, and morality; and, finally, a renewed and robust spirituality. Gerson, too, attempted to transcend the academic categories of philosophy and intellectual discourse and to promote spirituality. On December 7, 1426, a full decade after Jerome's death, Gerson wrote a letter to a Franciscan religious at the Grande Chartreuse pointing out that he, along with Hus, were thinkers who had plunged into insanity on account of their propensity for subtlety and careless inquiry.[100]

In the intellectual world of medieval Christendom, by mere repetition and assertion, ideas and concepts became traditional, they became embedded, and they were sometimes unassailable. The University of Paris in many ways became the unofficial *vox ecclesiae*, and therefore Paris philosophy functioned as a platform for ecclesiastical theology. Gerson perceived the Sorbonne as the protector of Christian faith. Jerome failed to appreciate the priority of Paris. Other university faculties regarded themselves as protecting proper teaching and also understood their role as preparing men to combat heresy.[101] Though separate threads of inquiry and methodology, Aristotelianism, Platonism, Neoplatonism, and Augustinianism had become almost indistinguishable. Alongside this, Thomism, which was maintained perhaps by the sheer force of church authority, "made

---

97. See, for example, Johannes Sharpe, *Quaestio super universalia*, ed. A. D. Conti (Florence: Olschki, 1990), 18.14, 3, pp. 145–150.

98. *Résponse à la consultation des maîtres*, in Glorieux, vol. 10, p. 241.

99. Kaluza, "Le chancelier Gerson et Jérôme de Prague," in *Études doctrinales*, pp. 208–211.

100. "Ignen veni mittere," in Glorieux, vol. 2, pp. 276–280.

101. For example, a 1388 sermon by Heinrich of Oyta (d. 1397) preached before the bishop of Passau. Gustav Sommerfeldt, "Zwei politische Sermone des Heinrich von Oyta und des Nikolaus von Dinkelsbühl (1388 und 1417)," *Historisches Jahrbuch* 26 (1905): 321.

speculation in really new directions veritably impossible."[102] As we shall
see, Jerome resisted that rigidity. While Gerson sought to revitalize the
church, Christian faith, and the practice of religion, Jerome wished to
revolutionize the shape of medieval Christian thinking and the practice
of the faith. The strength of both personalities placed them on a direct
collision course. Their first encounter was at Paris in 1406, their last meeting at Constance ten years later. Each man was convinced of truth and
resisted the other with considerable intransigence, and in the end they
were equally immune to reason.

Gerson's lectures on the curiosity of students, noted in more detail
in chapter 3, amounted to a polemic about vain inquiry in matters of
faith when it was thought preferable simply to submit to the will of God.
Dispositionally, Jerome was disinclined to acquiesce in any stricture. In
1403, Gerson permitted the Dominicans to return to Paris. They had with-
drawn more than a dozen years earlier in the face of opposition to Thomism
spearheaded by d'Ailly. Gerson explained his motivation for allowing the
Dominicans to return in a letter noting that it was not because he agreed
with them but because he felt that Christian charity required it.[103] We shall
consider below why this principle could not be extended and applied in
the case of Jerome. Put pointedly, why could Gerson not perceive toleration of Jerome as an obligation of Christian love? The answer appears
to bring us back to the dispute over divine Ideas. Gerson dismissed the
possibility of subjective ideas. Jerome believed that Ideas were actually
in the mind of God, while Gerson maintained that God's mind simply
was. Jerome took the position that there had to be something in God's
mind in order for everything to be and to happen. Against Jerome, Gerson
regarded it as nonsense to assume that one could know what was in the
mind of God. Jerome represented a school of thought that conceived of
God, for example, having an idea of humanity in the divine mind and
then creating humanity (universal), which existed in the particular, that is,
in individual humans. To put it another way, according to the Johannine
prologue, "in the beginning was the word." This was also a keystone of
Augustinian thought. This ancient tradition had new life breathed into it

102. Samuel Harrison Thomson, "The Philosophical Basis of Wyclif's Theology," *Journal of Religion* 11 (January 1931): 86–87.

103. Heinrich Denifle and Émile Chatelain, eds., *Auctarium Chartularii Universitatis Parisiensis*, 6 vols, (Paris: Didier, 1935–1964), vol. 3, col. 506.

by thinkers such as Giles of Rome and Wyclif. Gerson, however, asserted that Jerome fantasized about things outside the human purview. So far as Gerson was concerned, there was only God and particulars. Ideas and universals were meaningless speculations lacking both substance and significance.[104] Jerome, of course, inherited the intellectual ethos of a Czech tradition that was committed to Wyclifite thought. Matěj Janov had been influenced by the English nation at Paris, and it was he who brought the emphasis to Prague.[105] By the time Jerome came to intellectual maturity, he was a Wyclifite thinker.

Philosophical Discourse and Christian Doctrine

In the preface to his influential examination of Wyclif's philosophical and theological ideas, the Carmelite theologian Thomas Netter (c. 1375–1430) argued that Hussite doctrine was an abominable heresy that caused innumerable rebellions, conflict, murder, and calamity everywhere.[106] We have already seen that Wyclif was one of the major influences on Jerome. Speaking of John Ball, one of the leaders of the 1381 Peasants' Revolt in England, it was noted that the "mad priest of Kent" "taught the perverse doctrine of the perfidious John Wyclif, along with the opinions he held, and the insane lies, and many other things that would take long to recite."[107] The implications suggested by Netter and the English chronicler and Benedictine monk Thomas Walsingham (d. 1422) include the assumption that ideas led to revolt, which resulted in real revolutions disruptive to peace and order both in church and in society. More than fifty years ago, Howard Kaminsky advanced the thesis that the root of Wyclif's thought led to revolution, that Jerome saw and

---

104. Kaluza, *Les querelles doctrinales*, is a solid guide.

105. On the Paris ethos, see William J. Courtenay, *Teaching Careers at the University of Paris in the Thirteenth and Fourteenth Centuries* (Notre Dame, Ind.: US Subcommission for the History of Universities, 1988); William J. Courtenay, *Parisian Scholars in the Early Fourteenth Century: A Social Portrait* (Cambridge: Cambridge University Press, 1999); and Ian P. Wei, *Intellectual Culture in Medieval Paris: Theologians and the University, c. 1100–1330* (Cambridge: Cambridge University Press, 2012).

106. Thomas Netter, *Doctrinale antiquitatum fidei catholicae ecclesiae*, 3 vols. (Venice: Bassanesii, 1757–1759), vol. 1, p. xxviii.

107. Thomas Walsingham, *Historia Anglicana*, 2 vols., ed. Henry Thomas Riley (London: Longman, 1863–1864), vol. 2, p. 32. The "mad priest" reference is from Jean Froissart, *Chroniques*, bk. 2, fol. 70v. The text is available online at http://www.hrionline.ac.uk/onlinefroissart/

seized the broad thrust of these ideas more so than Hus did, and that Jerome had revolutionary intentions with the wedding between philosophy and theology. At the beginning of this chapter, it was noted that the identification of the philosophical phantoms that haunted theological inquiry was essential. That elaboration should also help to explain how metaphysical realism (demonized by men such as Gerson and shaped by university politics) led to theological error and resulted in the condemnation of Jerome as a heretic, with the tragic outcome that he was burned alive at the stake under the aegis of the Council of Constance. That query can be briefly answered by pointing out that it is not realism itself that is at issue but rather the application of that point of view in its Wyclifite dimensions, especially in relation to divine Ideas. For example, the image of a perfect normative ideal of the church in the hands of a realist such as Wyclif, Hus, or Jerome is then understood as a community of the predestined, or the eternally foreknown elect. Members of the community of the predestined have been determined to be saved, and this is known in the mind of God. The divine Idea is then connected to each of the predestined. In practice, subjective decisions and determinations are made. Even though the identities of the blameless cannot be known, except by means of access to the mind of God, those considered blameless are equated with the elect, or part of the true church, and those who fail to meet particular standards are categorized as being outside the true church. Moral issues and simony, which played such a key role in the Czech reform movement, are understood as indications of a community essentially predestined for perdition. The main problem is the claim to knowing the mind of God. Here is where Jerome and Gerson were implacably opposed. Wary of the pitfalls of a doctrine of double predestination (or soteriological determinism), theologians such as Thomas Aquinas and John Duns Scotus introduced an argument against the existence of divine Ideas for each human being. Wyclif advanced the alternative and developed a hitherto unknown level of robust metaphysical reality that simply could not avoid a model of predestination.

Prague masters, including Jerome, considered ideas the highest form of universals. Jerome did, in fact, read not only Wyclif but Platonically influenced texts.[108] There is evidence that Platonic conceptual language appears in his work.[109] Jerome insisted that a philosopher had the right

---

108. *Quaestio de universalibus a parte rei*, p. 92.

109. See, for example, *Quaestio et de universalibus extra signa*, in Šmahel/Silagi, p. 52.

to study and comment on divine Ideas, as this was not simply the purview of theologians, who often insisted on maintaining a monopoly in this area. Jerome argued that a philosopher cannot properly philosophize without delving into a consideration of divine Ideas.[110] In other words, Jerome believed that a correct understanding of the world of ideas was a precondition for being a proper philosopher. Gerson found this objectionable, and this lay at the root of the disquiet with Jerome at Paris in 1406. Jerome attempted to clarify himself a decade later by insisting that he had articulated his understanding of universals in a strictly philosophical sense. Gerson was nonplussed and asserted at Constance that there could be no confusing of the *stylus theologicus* or *logica theologica* with philosophical inquiry. The unique languages had to be distinct. Jerome remained unpersuaded by the force of the argument. Moral concerns in the Bohemian province took on eternal significance. Manuscript glosses note the "authority of Jerome of Prague" in connection with the assertion that "real universals are heresy."[111] By contrast, Jerome considered Plato to be the *rex philosophorum gentilium* ("king of the pagan philosophers"), while Hus regarded Plato as the *divinissimus philosophorum* ("god of philosophers").[112] The implications include the fact that there was a strong ethical, social, and political set of outcomes latent within the concepts advanced by Wyclif, Hus, and Jerome. Put into practice, the Hussites initiated projects aimed at the reform of church and society.[113] These reforms were predicated on a particular understanding of divine Ideas.

Jerome's work at Paris and the controversy it engendered provide a basis for concluding that conflict over universals and ideas created (or was a major component in the creation of) the Hussite reform as it came to shape both philosophy and theology. The reforms facilitated under Hus and those that characterized the early Hussite movement have often been described as moral reforms. The assessment is entirely accurate. The

---

110. *Quaestio duplex de formis universalibus*, p. 17.

111. Castle Archive, MS D 14.2, fol. 223r; but I cite the reference from Pavlíček, "*Scutum fidei christianae*," p. 96.

112. In the *Quaestio utrum a parte rei universalia*, in Šmahel/Silagi, p. 86. Vilém Herold, "Platonic Ideas and 'Hussite' Philosophy," *BRRP* 1 (1996): 16.

113. Vilém Herold, "Die Philosophie des Hussitismus: Zur Rolle der Ideenlehre Platons," in *Verdrängter Humanismus, Verzögerte Aufklärung: Philosophie in Österreich (1400–1650), Vom Konstanzer Konzil zum Auftreten Luthers*, ed. Michael Benedikt (Vienna: Verlag Leben-Kunst-Wissenschaft, 1996), pp. 101–118.

core of reform in Bohemia had to do with sin. Drawing on Wyclif, Czech reformers such as Jerome believed that sin harmed all of creation and was not merely a personal act with limited consequences. This underscored the relation between theology and metaphysics. Sin brings chaos to creation and has long-term and far-reaching consequences. There is an inherent and unavoidable metaphysical butterfly effect of sin. Jerome believed that for every creature in creation, there is a divine Idea. Every act or action of that particular creature is connected to the divine Idea. All of the Ideas on which creation is predicated are related in some fashion in the mind of God. Therefore, given this triangulation, every act or action by one creature has some effect on every other creature. By consequence, every sin has an adverse effect on creation. This being so, it is impossible for an individual to sin without affecting everyone and everything else. In sum, sin is an act against not only neighbor but God and indeed every creature in the entire universe.[114] Sin does damage to everything in Wyclif's ontology.[115] In other words, the fabric of nature and being and all of its associated concepts and categories are affected by sin. Inasmuch as Jerome was deeply influenced by Wyclif, this helps to explain the fundamental premise of moral reform in the Bohemian context. The connection between moral reform, concern with sin, and the philosophical template that prevailed in Prague at the end of the Middle Ages can be explained simply with reference to the idea that sin is caused by a deficient view of universals. In other words, sin consists in choosing an inferior good.[116] The argument has been advanced that Wyclif's understanding of universals transformed the academic theologian into a moral force of considerable strength.[117] The mechanism that triggers the meaningful confluence of abstract thought and movements of reform was not a theoretical concern, nor was it simply a philosophical question. Instead, it was a practical matter.

A generation later, it was considered insufficient to limit reform to amending outward appearances or obvious abuses. At session 40 of

---

114. John Wyclif, *De mandatis divinis*, chap. 5, p. 39.

115. Stephen Lahey, "Wyclif, the 'Hussite Philosophy,' and the Law of Christ," *BRRP* 9 (2014): 58.

116. John Wyclif, *On Universals*, trans. Anthony Kenny (Oxford: Oxford University Press, 1985), pp. 145–150.

117. Jeremy I. Catto, "Wyclif and Wycliffism at Oxford 1356–1430," in *The History of the University of Oxford*, ed. J.I. Catto and T.A.R. Evans (Oxford: Oxford University Press, 1992), vol. 2, p. 193.

the Council of Constance, which sat on October 30, 1417, the delegates nominated pluralism, absenteeism, simony, indulgences, tithing, the jurisdiction of the Curia, matters pertaining to the papal chancery and the penitentiary, dispensations, papal provisions, absolution, annates, and a variety of other superficial initiatives associated with irregularities or abuses within the ecclesiastical structure.[118] What was essential was to examine and reform the structure itself, the basis on which the abuses occurred and were able to flourish. What was necessary was to flesh out the root causes that undergirded abuses that produced consequential effects throughout the faith and religious practice. Men such as Gerson and d'Ailly perceived that the ideas and reform initiatives associated with Jerome and Hus were the natural result of their philosophical convictions. They were convinced that the theologies of church reform advanced by the Czechs were the direct consequences of their faith in *realia ante rem*, that is, in the independent existence of universals that precede the existence of individual objects. Can Gerson's dismissal of abuses around the practice of simony be regarded as an example of Jean Buridan's belief that morality is relative?[119] While Jerome and his predecessors argued that the priesthood was invalidated by simony and immorality, by contrast, Gerson said that the offense of simony was not heretical and preferred to minimize it by calling it the "simonian slip," as though it were an error of omission or an inadvertent mistake.[120] Jerome believed that simony indicated that neither the individual in question nor the church he represented constituted the true church.

Men such as Wyclif, Hus, and Jerome forged ahead and called into question not only abuses but structures. For example, Hus considered religious practice to be equally concerned with doctrine and morals.[121] The undercurrent has to do with authority. Jerome perceived authority as rooted in God but mediated through the church exclusively. On the other hand, Gerson wanted the church to be less centralized so that ecclesiastical

---

118. Mansi, vol. 27, col. 1164.

119. Jean Buridan, *Quaestiones in decem libros in Ethicorum Aristotelis ad Nicomachum* (Oxford: Cripps, 1637).

120. *De simonia*, in Glorieux, vol. 6, pp. 169–173, which was written at the Council of Constance.

121. See his *De sex erroribus*, in *Betlemské texty*, ed. Bohumil Byba (Prague: Orbis, 1951), pp. 41–63.

power could be transferred from the pope to a general council. This resulted in the obedience formerly demanded by the papacy simply being transferred to the general council, which also expected unqualified submission. Neither Hus nor Jerome acquiesced in that perspective. Shifting ultimate authority from a pope to a council, from an office to a synod, from an individual man to a group of men, did not solve the problem. By contrast, Gerson adamantly supported conciliar theory. The council had the authority to condemn ideas and the individuals who promoted them even if the ideas might be true in one sense or another. This was certainly the case in the legal procedures involving Wyclif, Hus, and Jerome. But the crucial difference between theology and the "speculative sciences" must be maintained. The Sorbonne had successfully avoided error and heresy by forcing academics to adhere to certain rules of faith. Gerson also argued that the council had every right (indeed a solemn duty) to damn deviations in thought and theology, even if there were no scriptural basis for the judgment, and offenders might also be legitimately and lawfully exterminated. This included both ideas and individuals. With allusion to the Constance heretics, Gerson maintained that they would only conditionally agree to recant their errors, demanding, in the case of Hus, to be corrected on the basis of scripture. The dictates of law, the fathers, and papal decretals were irrelevant. Gerson declared that everyone could plainly see how such attitudes produced heresy.[122] Jerome demanded to be proven incorrect by means of argument. He was amendable to neither papal nor conciliar claims to power and authority. Gerson had earlier opined that the best response to such behavior was to abandon reason, take up the "axe of the secular arm," a "sharp scythe," and deal with the "desperate pestilence" by "cutting out heresies along with their authors and sending them into the fire."[123]

It has been argued that the understanding of ideas played a major role in the condemnation of Jerome at Constance.[124] This is certainly true but not for ideas in and of themselves. The condemnation of ideas lay squarely in the perceived implication of ideas if put into practice. Jerome wanted

---

122. "Prosperum iter faciet nobis Deus," in Glorieux, vol. 5, pp. 476–477.

123. In his letter to Konrad, archbishop of Prague, dated May 27, 1414, *Documenta*, pp. 523–526.

124. Herold, "Der Streit," pp. 77–89. This article focuses on the reasons for Jerome's conviction.

to interrogate the foundations of faith apart from the strictures of ecclesiastical dogma and church authority. Between Constance and Kraków,
and from Paris to Pskov, theologians and prelates were profoundly disturbed by the agenda Jerome defended and promoted. Once more, we
must ask why this posture was so threatening. Did the men at Constance,
like Gerson, perceive the implications of revolution latent in the thought
of Jerome? Hus had proven intractable and troublesome. Jerome's vehe-
mence prompted alarm, and behind the Czech reform initiative lay the
sinister spirit of Wyclif. "Refusal to recant Wycliffite beliefs meant excommunication and opprobrium, virtual suicide for any medieval scholar."[125]
Jerome appeared unconcerned, and for a period of more than fifteen years,
he hardly slackened in his campaign to advance reform under the guiding principles of philosophical reflection fashioned largely by the works
of Wyclif.

It has been suggested that Wyclifism was an ideology of revolution.
In the hands of men such as Jerome, at least in the mind of Gerson, that
threat appeared on the verge of implementation. In what ways did Wyclif
present a threat to the church, and how specifically could his thought be
conceived of as revolutionary? In brief, the ideas of Wyclif implied that
the mystical body of Christ could not be restricted to an institution or a
human group. By extension, that idea yielded a correlate that naturally and
logically concluded that there was no need for popes, priests, or prelates.
If that conclusion was valid, then the predestined laity could be priests.[126]
Should that premise be adopted, this theoretically discounted the priesthood as a legitimate order. If the structure of the late medieval church
could be thus renovated, then every Christian possessed spiritual authority, which implied a rejection of church hierarchy. In practice, the laity
could remove unjust, wicked, or sinful leaders. There were implications
for the principle of papacy and property. The papal bull *Clericos laicos*
prohibited priests from surrendering property without papal consent.[127]

---

125. Lahey, *John Wyclif*, p. 27.

126. Wyclif imagined that one day the church might be made up solely of laity ("Nec video
quin dicta navis Petri possit pure per tempus stare in laycis"). John Wyclif, *Tractatus de civili
domini*, ed. Reginald Lane Poole (London: Trübner/WS, 1885), vol. 1, p. 392.

127. Sext. 3.23.3 *Clericos laicos* (1296), in Friedberg, vol. 2, cols. 1062–1063. See also Thomas
M. Izbicki, "Clericis laicos and the Canonists," in *Popes, Teachers, and Canon Law in the
Middle Ages*, ed. J. R. Sweeney and S. Chodorow (Ithaca, N.Y.: Cornell University Press,
1989), pp. 179–190.

The Hussite program took little note of such injunctions. By divesting the church of its visible structure, this meant that canon law, papal decretals, and formal statements of theology might be set aside and an argument mounted defending the rule for church and society being the law of God (*lex Dei*). It may be argued that these ideas were designed to produce reform. Political and social order had always been impenetrable to reform, save for abuses. Wyclif wanted to change the order and the structure itself. Hus and Jerome appeared prepared to take those ideas some distance, and the history of the Hussite movement reveals experiments aimed at achieving just that.[128] Hussites such as Peter Payne argued before the Council of Basel in 1433 that clerics should lead lives of poverty and not possess political power. Even though Payne cited Richard Fitzralph, the concept was also Wyclifite: grace is the necessary prerequisite for exercising lordship or dominion.[129] The implications were staggering. Sin disqualified one from membership in the true church. When Hus asserted at the Council of Constance that neither kings nor popes living in sin possessed any legitimate authority, King Sigismund adroitly replied: "Jan Hus, no one lives without crime (sin)" (*Iohannes Hus, nemo sine crimine vivit*).[130]

By the dawn of the fifteenth century, the work of Peter Lombard and Thomas Aquinas had provided the medieval church with an exacting schedule of orthodox doctrinal limits which also served as a theological coat of armor generally impenetrable to challenge. Wielding an intellectual mace, Jerome assailed that armor. Jerome seems to have been unimpressed and called for new ways of addressing old problems. Perhaps the main problem that lurked below the academic sophistication and eloquence of the debate was the nature of the church itself and its claims to authority. Men such as Hus and Jerome argued that the visible church had failed to conform to the law of God. This marked out the subversiveness of positions defended by Wyclif, Hus, and Jerome. In sum, there was an appeal beyond the church to scripture, and the "law of God," which implied a definite rejection of the church as it had evolved. The church

---

128. Howard Kaminsky, "Wyclifism as Ideology of Revolution," *Church History* 32 (March 1963): 57–74.

129. František M. Bartoš, ed., *Petri Payne Anglici positio, replica et propositio in concilio Basiliensi a. 1433 atque oratio ad Sigismundum regem a. 1429 Bratislaviae pronunciatae* (Tábor: Českobratrský evangelický sbor, 1949), pp. 38–39; and Wyclif, *De civili dominio*, vol. 1, p. 22.

130. *Relatio*, in *FRB*, vol. 8, p. 95.

feared that Wyclifite doctrine led inevitably to heresy. In specific terms, for Hus this was the Eucharist, and for Jerome it was suspect Trinitarianism. The Wyclifite critique when applied to medieval Christendom canceled the efficacy of the sacramental functions, subverted institutional teaching authority, and undermined the social structure of the church. Dinkelsbühl, who took an uncompromising stand against Jerome, first at Vienna and later at Constance, argued in his *Commentary on Matthew* that when the common good was imperiled, evil might legitimately be used to counter the threat.[131] Neither Hus nor Jerome countenanced that principle as consistent with the law of God. The type of realism adopted by Jerome was also applied as a foundation for understanding concepts of authority and order in both church and society. This exposed cracks in the structures of medieval religious practice, and Gerson was only one who perceived it posed a clear and present danger to the Latin church.

More frightening was that the sacerdotal function of the church was potentially imperiled by the application of Wyclifite-realist philosophy. Applied to the Eucharist, the underlying theme of Wyclif's thought was the idea of two substances and the necessity of combining them in theology, while being aware that each substance was independent but that a conversion from one to the other could occur without either denying or destroying one or the other substance. For example, God and humankind, the universal and the accident, divine and natural, scripture and tradition, faith and reason, Augustine and Aristotle, church and society, popes and princes, the body of Christ and eucharistic bread, and so on.[132] Realism led Wyclif to deny transubstantiation on the grounds that the Eucharistic bread could not be annihilated, since it participated in the being of God, and for it to be annihilated implied the destruction of creation and of God. Thus, Wyclif could not conceive of annihilation, and this together with his commitment to spatiotemporal atomism resulted in the conclusion that transubstantiation was impossible.[133] As a nominalist, d'Ailly took the

---

131. Michael H. Shank, *Unless You Believe, You Shall Not Understand: Logic, University, and Society in Late Medieval Vienna* (Princeton, N.J.: Princeton University Press, 1988), p. 204, relying on Melk, Stiftsbibliothek, codex 504.

132. There is a good discussion of this in Lahey, *John Wyclif,* pp. 102–134, especially pp. 112–113.

133. Lahey, *John Wyclif,* p. 101. But see Wyclif, *Tractatus de universalibus,* pp. 307–314. On the relation between realism and the sacrament, see J. J. M. Paul Bakker, "Réalisme et rémanence. La doctrine eucharistique de Jean Wyclif," in *John Wyclif: Logica, politica, teologia,* ed. Mariateresa Fumagalli Beonio Brocchieri and Stefano Simonetta (Florence: Sismel Edizioni del Galluzzo, 2003), pp. 87–112.

view that realism required its adherents to deny eucharistic orthodoxy and by natural and logical consequences embrace remanentism. The denials of Hus and Jerome made no impression. If Jerome was an inconsistent realist, this only underscores the limitations of Wyclifite philosophy in the Bohemian reform movement. However, we know that Stanislav of Znojmo, though at one time firmly committed to Wyclifite thought, fought against an unacceptable conclusion and avoided Eucharistic heresy by performing an exegetical gymnastic wherein he argued that God, as the first cause, did not necessarily require bread as requisite property in order to support the existence of another property, in this case, the flesh of the son of God.[134] If the idea of annihilation was generally repugnant to a realist philosopher, an exception might be made when it came to eucharistic doctrine for the sake of theological expediency. This suggests that at least on occasion, philosophical concepts were adopted and adapted to serve theological convictions and a priori assumptions.

Hus had taken the position that the true faith by which the faithful were defined was concerned not with visible things but with that which was invisible.[135] Moreover, he argued that the church was the bride of Christ and not a structure of wood or stone.[136] Jerome agreed. This implied that the papal schism had nothing to do with the integrity of the church. It hardly mattered how many popes there were, because the church was neither identified with popes nor ultimately subject to them. The church was one, and it was identified neither by institutions nor by claims to authority but by faith, hope, and love. Its visible hierarchy was not significant.[137] Gerson opposed this and consistently argued that church hierarchy was divinely ordained.[138] The allegation that Jerome once preached that there was a common or universal ass (*communem asinum*) implied that he believed in a universal church and a universal truth, and this constituted the fundamental heresy of Jerome. Ultimately, neither Jerome nor Hus could believe

---

134. See his commentary on Wyclif's *De universalibus* in *Johannis Wyclif Miscellaea philosophica II*, ed. Michael Henry Dziewicki (London: Trübner/WS, 1905), pp. 71–79. The work has been falsely ascribed to Wyclif.

135. *De corpore Christi*, in *Mag. Jo. Hus Opera Omnia: Nach neuentdeckten Handschriften*, 3 vols., ed. Václav Flajšhans (Osnabrück: Biblio-Verlag, 1966), vol. 1, part 2, p. 18.

136. *Výklad na vieru*, in *MIHO*, vol. 1, chap. 18, pp. 85–86.

137. *Contra Palecz*, in *MIHO*, vol. 22, pp. 254–256.

138. *Propositio facta coram Anglicis*, Glorieux, vol. 6, pp. 125–135, is an example.

that an archbishop who burned books, or a pope who demanded the cessation of preaching, or a Council that forbade Utraquism and urged the revocation of heresies never held, could possibly represent the true universal church.[139] Worse still, from the medieval church's point of view, was the clear conviction expressed by Jerome that the idea of conditional authority applied even to the church hierarchy. In terms of authority, all rights and claims thereto were conditionally related to the incumbent or claimant being in a state of grace. Sin imperiled spiritual authority. The posture assumed by Jerome was an undeniable manifestation of the tyranny of the righteous and an example wherein Jerome is strikingly revealed as a Wyclifite thinker. The implications of this doctrine included antipapalism, dismissal of the episcopate, rendering the religious irrelevant, and fueling revolution on virtually every level. It also sanctioned disobedience. Receiving the sacraments from the hand of a simoniac cleric was worthless, and obeying the directive of a craven sinner in holy orders was offensive. Both should be rejected as activities outside the church. The great irony is that men such as Gerson and d'Ailly opposed this perspective but agreed with the conciliar decisions concerning the pope at the Council of Constance. John XXIII was removed from office on May 29, 1415, and the deposition decree said he was a "simoniac, a notorious destroyer of the church, and on account of his wicked life was a scandal to the church."[140] These same men balked at the ideas presented by Jerome.

Hus argued that the law of God was sufficient for life, theology, and religious practice. The Council of Constance disagreed. This constituted another angle of authority posited by Hussites generally and Jerome specifically. The mind of God was equivalent to the eternal word of God, which was Christ, who was also the ultimate meaning to which scripture pointed. However, scripture did not contain the whole of the mind of God. Jerome could argue that point effortlessly. The idea of scripture was eternal and therefore could not logically be a book. The Bible is simply an iteration of the eternal divine Idea (or word of God). The real issue was the eternal word of God or the law of God. The question remains: Did Jerome make connections between scripture and divine Ideas? Why would such connection be problematic? What were its implications as perceived

---

139. Lectures on *Epistolas apostolorum canonicas septem commentarii*, in *HM*, vol. 2, p. 254 (comments on I Peter 2).

140. Hardt, vol. 4, pp. 185–186.

by the later medieval church and those who were forced to deal directly with Jerome? We know that Gerson opposed vernacular translations of scripture on the grounds that this would destroy the idea of ecclesiastical unity.[141] Following Wyclif, Jerome saw no correlation between a book and the unity of the faith.

Faith and Philosophy

It is too extreme and ultimately indefensible to argue that the theology present in the early Hussite movement and latent in the thought of Jerome was required by abstract philosophy. Instead, it is more reasonable to posit that reason and revelation both led to universal truth. Some perspectives destroyed the union of faith and reason but remained an intellectual force in the thought of Jerome. Following Wyclif once again, Jerome believed that correct theology or religious practice could only be achieved by connecting reason to faith.[142] For Jerome, faith was beyond reason, but many of his opponents were prepared to accept dogma unquestioningly on the basis of ecclesiastical authority. Wyclif's great detractor Thomas Netter summed things up rather adroitly when he wrote that "in matters of faith, trained spiritual men are considered expert, and the rest of the people need only believe."[143] Jerome trenchantly disagreed. He took his disagreement across Europe and did not falter in his defense of the principle that faith and reason were not mutually exclusive and that theology need not be kept separate from philosophy. By the fourteenth century, medieval thought had almost been entirely altered. "After a brief honeymoon [one might almost have said, before the wedding breakfast was over] theology and philosophy think they see that their marriage was a mistake. While waiting for the decree of divorce, which is not long in coming, they proceed to divide their effects. Each resumes possession of its own problems, and warns the other against interference."[144] Jerome resisted that breakdown and refused to acquiesce in a retrograde or fossilized version of either. His

---

141. *Contra vanam curiositatem studentium*, in Glorieux, vol. 3, pp. 248–249.

142. John Wyclif, *De veritate Sacrae Scripturae*, ed. Rudolf Buddensieg, 3 vols. (London: Trübner/WS, 1905–1907), vol. 1, p. 249.

143. Netter, *Doctrinale antiquitatem fidei ecclesiae catholicae*, vol. 2, chap. 44, col. 277.

144. Gilson's summation of the aftermath of Aristotle and the medieval synthesis is quoted in David Knowles, *The Evolution of Medieval Thought* (New York: Vintage, 1962), p. 300.

position, expressed during sustained peregrinations, encountered solid and unyielding opposition. His search for a synthesis of conflicting views was unsuccessful.

Wyclif provided theory that served as a scaffold on which to articulate more cogently, but not necessarily consistently, a preexisting impulse for reform. Wyclifite realism did not burst upon the intellectual landscape of Czech academia without warning or in some unexpectedly capricious manner. It is more accurate to say that the Wyclifite explosion had been building up for more than two decades and may ultimately have forced itself upon the initially reluctant thinking of scholars at Charles University. Matěj Janov had already provided the model for transitioning from the philosophically true understanding of scripture to addressing the need for religious reform. Both Hus and Jakoubek Stříbro thoroughly mined this fertile soil, and there they discovered the foundations for what became the Hussite revolution. The ideology of the Hussite movement codified in the 1420 "Four Articles of Prague" requires neither particular metaphysical foundation nor causal connection to the world of abstract ideas. Stripped of the trappings of abstract philosophical discourse, and tortured Wyclifite intellectualizing, the ideas of men such as Jerome were exposed to the full glare of the later medieval church, revealing the practical horrors of a reform agenda that ultimately threatened the raison d'être of Christendom itself. The only theological connection between philosophy and reform was a notional conception of grace. Men such as Jerome do not appear to have grasped the possibility of grace. Here he must be distinguished from Gerson, who possessed a theology of grace.[145] Making assumptions about the absence of divine grace propelled Jerome to conclude that any Christian, especially priests, prelates, and popes, who appeared sinful or wicked neither exercised legitimate authority nor was a member of the true church. It is little wonder Gerson and his supporters regarded Jerome as a merchant of self-righteousness.

Theology and philosophy were disciplines that thrived on truth claims, assumed an academic vita that appeared impervious to challenge, and exhibited stout resistance to all efforts to change its essential content or structure. Jerome proposed that such mentalities could neither be

---

145. *De consolatione theologiae*, in Glorieux, vol. 9, pp. 185–245. See also Mark S. Burrows, *Jean Gerson and De Consolatione Theologiae: The Consolation of a Biblical and Reforming Theology for a Disordered Age* (Tübingen: J. C. B. Mohr, 1991); with some modifying comment in McGuire, *Jean Gerson*, pp. 300–304.

tolerated nor sustained. Gerson was only one of his enemies. It has already been pointed out that Gerson allowed the Dominicans he disagreed with theologically to return to the Sorbonne while he was university chancellor, on the grounds that such toleration was a duty imposed on him by the faith. No similar consideration was extended to the wandering scholar from Prague. The merciless execution of Jerome was a tragic consequence of the debates about divine Ideas.[146] Why could Gerson not perceive toleration of Jerome as an obligation of Christian love? The answer is twofold. First, Gerson objected to the presumption that men such as Jerome might actually believe they had access to the mind of God and could therefore be certain about divine grace and know the nature of divine election. Second, the impertinence of that perceived intellectual and theological arrogance produced numerous confrontations that were dangerous to the faith. These disruptive intellectual tournaments involved Jerome over the course of more than a decade, in which his name, and his reputation as a Wyclifite thinker, came to the forefront of academic discourse all over Europe.

---

146. Herold, "Der Streit," p. 89.

3

Disputation and Discord

THE FUGITIVE AND THE ESTABLISHMENT

IN A VERY real sense, Jerome of Prague represents the antithesis of Heiko Oberman's portrait of Gabriel Biel (ca. 1422–1495) and the harvest of medieval theology.[1] Jerome is a philosophical anti-Biel. According to Oberman, nominalism was not a schismatic fracture within academic discourse but instead was a vital part of the intellectual life of late medieval Christianity. Jerome, of course, militated against that idea, taking, as we have seen, the opposite point of view. Oberman's *The Harvest of Medieval Theology* concludes that the medieval theological tradition was vibrant, robust, filled with the richness of Christian faith, and loyal to the spirit of its task, featuring a coherent solution to the major problems it sought to resolve. The life and thought of Jerome again presents a striking dissent. The summation of Biel's thought is also a harvest of earlier theological reflection, which includes thinkers such as William Ockham, Robert Holcot, Gregory of Rimini, Pierre d'Ailly, and Jean Gerson.

Jerome and the Harvest of Medieval Thought

It has been argued that nominalists fostered theological doubt and exploited distinctions between *potentia absoluta* and *potentia ordinata* (absolute and established orders) in order to conceal bona fide skepticism and that they also deliberately utilized those categories to shield themselves from suspicion of heresy, to wit, that church dogma was true according to the latter

---

1. Heiko Augustinus Oberman, *The Harvest of Medieval Theology: Gabriel Biel and Late Medieval Nominalism* (Grand Rapids, Mich.: Eerdmans, 1967).

but in terms of the former could be false.[2] Oberman rejected that reading by illuminating later medieval thought mediated through the prism
of Biel. However, Jerome is revealed as a fifteenth-century anti-Biel when
investigating the relation between faith and reason. For example, nominalists in the Biel tradition held that matters of faith could neither be resolved
nor established by logic alone. Again, Jerome presents an alternative point
of view. The tradition that Biel represented rejected the privileging of
scripture over tradition. The former was maintained by Bradwardine and
Wyclif, while the latter was championed by Ockham and Gerson (among
others).[3] Once again, we encounter the important dichotomy between
Jerome and Gerson. Oberman understood Biel as unarguably demonstrat-
ing that nominalism did not reflect a disintegration of medieval thought.
Biel was without doubt a follower of Ockham, but at the same time, he
was also influenced by Gerson. That triangulation illuminates the artificial
"schools of thought" approach and underscores that so-called nominalists ranged widely across the spectrum of questions that are important for
understanding Jerome. Despite its obvious strengths, one of the shortcomings of Oberman's *Harvest* is that by maintaining an unswerving focus on
theology, Oberman tended to underestimate the role philosophy played in
the shaping of late medieval theology. Our Czech anti-Biel is a towering
corrective. It is unavoidably true that the politics of the universities contributed mightily to the context of theology and philosophical considerations
that came to bear on dogma. That reality is starkly revealed in not only the
divide existing between the fractious philosophical disputes that created a
division running through the University of Paris and German universities
during the entire later medieval period but also evident in the confrontations between Jerome and Gerson. If the latter reflected the evolving synthesis of medieval theology, then the former consistently and persistently
emerges as the anti-Biel and therefore militates against a presumptive
conclusion that the Moderni movement was undeniably a fait accompli by
1420. The Hussite movement in general and Jerome specifically present a
largely overlooked challenge to that assumption. In his university debates
and in his running battle with established institutions, it seems eminently
clear that Jerome is actively fighting against the perceived domination of

---

2. This is an underlying theme in Carl Feckes, *Die Rechtfertigungslehre des Gabriel Biel und
ihre Stellung innerhalb der nominalistischen Schule* (Münster: Aschendorff, 1925).

3. Oberman, *The Harvest of Medieval Theology*, pp. 365–412.

the Moderni movement, especially in his disputes with Gerson. With the evolving conflict with Gerson gaining momentum, and against the important backdrop of disputes over divine Ideas, we are in the best position to understand Jerome's activity as a Wyclifite thinker.

Provocation in Paris

As noted above, there are puzzling lacunae in Jerome's curriculum vitae. While it has proven impossible to pinpoint when he was in Jerusalem, it is considerably easier to determine when he was in Paris, where we first catch a glimpse of his controversial nature and the acrimonious disputes about divine Ideas. On April 7, 1404, Jerome began in the faculty of arts, where he was listed eighth out of fourteen. This decision was accepted by the English nation during a convocation in the Church of Saint Julian the Poor, meaning that Jerome was considered a member of the English nation.[4] This is the same affiliation Matěj Janov had twenty-five years earlier. Jerome obtained an M.A. degree (master in *artibus*) on September 21, 1405.[5] It is curious that Jerome is the only one of nine masters not assigned regular lectures. This may be on account of the provocations he aroused in various disputations.[6] However, he may have taught less formally while in Paris as *magister regens in artibus*.[7] His formal inception occurred on January 27, 1405, during a university convocation in the Church of St. Mathurin.[8] While in Paris, he studied the works and thought of John Wyclif, especially on logic, and during this time, he dispatched even more Wyclifite books to Prague, thus indicating that his dalliance with the Oxford professor was no passing fancy.[9] Some of Jerome's presentations before the Sorbonne were memorable and were remarked on years later with the recollection that he

---

4. Anton Denifle and Émile Chatelain, eds., *Auctarium Chartularii Universitatis Parisiensis*, 6 vols. (Paris: Didier, 1935–1964), vol. 1, cols. 879, 880, 894, 906. See also Vilém Herold, "The University of Paris and the Foundations of the Bohemian Reformation," *BRRP* 3 (2000): 15–24.

5. Šmahel, *Jeroným Pražsky*, p. 66; and František Šmahel, "Leben und Werk des Magisters Hieronymus von Prag," *Historica* 13 (1966): 85–86.

6. Šmahel, *Život a dílo Jeronýma*, p. 28.

7. Herold, "The University of Paris," p. 22.

8. Denifle and Chatelain, *Auctarium Chartularii Universitatis Parisiensis*, vol. 2, col. 883.

9. Klicman reveals references to this.

consistently inserted provocative comments or suggestive notions into his disputation texts. This practice became characteristic.

In Paris, a noteworthy three-day university disputation was convened in the Church of St. Bernard in 1406. The event was conducted by Jerome. The debate revolved around the matter of universals, and in the course of argumentation, Jerome ostensibly endorsed Wyclifite categories and conclusions with such provocation that he succeeded in arousing enormous opposition and engendering serious outrage.[10] The disputation caused an intellectual uproar and created such scandal that Jerome was formally summoned to appear before Gerson, the chancellor of the university. The confrontation never occurred. "At length, once he had become well known to the masters of Paris, who were zealots for the faith, and had been determined by them to be suspected of heresy, they, and particularly the honorable man Jean Gerson, who was chancellor of the university, planned to compel him to retract his errors. But Jerome was warned by some unknown person and he secretly fled from the city and the university."[11]

Prior to this, in 1403, Gerson had written a tract "Against the meddlesome curiosity of students," based on university lectures delivered on November 8 and 9, 1402.[12] Gerson declared that curiosity was among the most serious threats to the proper study of theology. He defined curiosity as a corruption or disturbance that prompted the student to devote more attention to useless trivialities than to what is really important. Prior to this, in question 167 of the Secunda Secundae in his *Summa theologiae*, Thomas Aquinas addressed the sin of *curiositas* (curiosity), which he considered quite separate from *studiositas* (study or scholarship).[13] According to Gerson, this vice manifested itself especially in the preoccupation with logic or dialectic rather than with the faith or taking an inordinate interest in strange and unusual ideas.[14] For Gerson, such curiosity amounted

---

10. Zénon Kaluza, "Le chancelier Gerson et Jérôme de Prague," in *Études doctrinales sur le XIVe siècle: Théologie, Logique, Philosophie* (Paris: Vrin, 2013), pp. 207–209; and Šmahel/Silagi, pp. XXII–XXIII.

11. Hardt, vol. 4, col. 681.

12. *Contra vanam curiositatem studentium*, in Glorieux, vol. 3, pp. 224–249; and see also Zénon Kaluza, *Les querelles doctrinales à Paris: Nominalistes et réalistes aux confins du XIVe et du XVe siècles* (Bergamo: Lubrina, 1988), pp. 13–34.

13. *Summa theologiae*, II, II, 9.167.

14. Steven Ozment, ed., *Jean Gerson: Selections from A Deo Exivit, Contra curiositatem studentium and De mystica theologia speculativa* (Leiden: Brill, 1969), pp. 27–45.

to sin.[15] Gerson rejected foreign, new, and unaccustomed ideas within the realm of theology. When it came to theological issues, Gerson assumed the position that reason possessed strictly circumscribed competence. It is not surprising, Gerson wrote, that philosophical reasoning always fails when it tackles theological concerns. When philosophy trespasses onto the territory of faith, it always leads to the "stone of error," and when it contumaciously persists in attempting to satisfy its curiosity, it encounters only death. According to Gerson, it was more than enough to simply believe the gospel.[16] Could Gerson have had the likes of Jerome in mind?

Gerson's point of view constitutes a very important component in understanding his opposition to Jerome both at Paris and later in Constance. Gerson was concerned about the development of theories of abstract knowledge and "formal distinctions" and was also alarmed by the intermingling of theology and philosophy. Fundamentally, Gerson held a very different understanding of theology from Jerome. Šmahel has drawn attention to the warning issued by the poet Eustache Deschamps, who said that the Sorbonne was "the mother of faith but the wicked stepmother of heresy." From an official point of view of the Western church culminating at the Council of Constance, Gerson signified the former, while men such as Jerome represented the latter.[17] Gerson was on the side of truth. Jerome promulgated a monstrous misrepresentation of Christian theology.

While in Paris, Jerome discovered more about the Platonic tradition, which, as has been noted, performed for him a similar function to what the Bible did for Wyclif, and it is certain that he also discovered there Pseudo-Dionysius in the Dominican library.[18] Many years later, the dean of Cambrai,

---

15. For an analysis of the medieval idea of curiosity as sin, see Heiko Augustinus Oberman, *Contra vanam curiositatem: Ein Kapitel der Theologie zwischen Seelenwinkel und Weltall* (Zurich: Theologischer Verlag, 1974).

16. *Contra curiositatem studentium*, in Glorieux, vol. 3, pp. 229–234.

17. The same observation has been made in Šmahel, *Život a dílo Jeronýma*, p. 28.

18. Zénon Kaluza, *Études doctrinales sur le XIVe siècle: Théologie, Logique, Philosophie* (Paris: Vrin, 2013), p. 251; and Šmahel, *Život a dílo Jeronýma*, p. 30. Paris, Bibliothèque nationale de France, MS lat. 17341 contains a thirteenth-century collection of Dionysius. Jackie Luss, "Some Examples of the Use Made of the Pseudo-Dionysius by University Teachers in the Later Middle Ages," in *The Universities in the Late Middle Ages*, ed. Josef Ijsewijn and Jacques Paquet (Louvain: Leuven University Press, 1978), pp. 228–241. We also know that Hus utilized Pseudo-Dionysius. *Tractatus de ecclesia*, ed. S. Harrison Thomson (Boulder: University of Colorado Press, 1956), pp. 64–66, 120–22; *Passio Domini nostri Iesu Cristi*, in *MIHO*, vol. 8, p. 224; *Výklad na páteř*, in *MIHO*, vol. 1, p. 367; *Postilla adumbrata*, in *MIHO*, vol. 13, pp. 401, 617; and *Super IV Sententiarum*, in MIHO, pp. 108, 125, 227, 233–238.

Giles Charlier, noted that he personally witnessed how the Paris doctors and masters were made to endure for three days Jerome's endless speech to everyone and about everything ("ad omne quare et omnibus").[19] The comment was made in Charlier's response to Hussite speeches at the Council of Basel during the week of February 13–17, 1433. The assertion is suspect, as Charlier would only have been about fifteen years of age when Jerome was in Paris.[20]

Conflict in Cologne

Following his exodus from Paris, Jerome appeared in Cologne around March 1406. Here he matriculated as a "respected master," somewhere after March 24, being listed first out of seventeen.[21] His academic qualifications and acumen may have been apparent, but ostensibly there were concerns about him at Cologne. Men such as theologian Dietrich Kerkering was surely familiar with the controversy created by Jerome, and Kerkering later attended the Council of Constance. These comments were related much later and so should be taken with some reserve. Nevertheless, representatives at the Council of Constance reflected on events a decade earlier: "Sitting there another master of the University in Cologne am Rhein, rose and said: 'Jerome, in our place too, in Cologne you have presented in this position many heresies and it is still remembered.' To this Master Jerome said: 'Tell me here, please, one heresy publicly'—And he, feeling ashamed, said: 'I do not remember just now, but later they will be presented against you.'"[22] There is doubtless a grain of truth in the reflection made at Constance, for in due course disputes arising at Cologne caused Jerome to leave. As late as 1425, the Cologne masters condemned his teaching at the behest of the electors of the empire. This occurred on Christmas Eve, 1425. Cologne representatives were at Constance in 1416, where they accused Jerome of heresy. While specific details are lacking, it seems obvious that his sojourn in Cologne was stormy.[23] We know the content of

---

19. Mansi, vol. 29, col. 964.

20. Šmahel, *Život a dílo Jeronýma*, p. 29.

21. R. R. Betts, *Essays in Czech History* (London: Athlone, 1969), p. 199. The university had been established in 1388. See also Šmahel, "Leben und Werk," pp. 91–92.

22. *Passio, FRB*, vol. 8, p. 355.

23. Vilém Herold, "Magister Hieronymus von Prag und die Universität Köln," *Miscellanea Medievalia* 20 (1989): 255–273.

his disputes at Cologne only by means of anecdotal evidence presented years later during the Council of Constance.[24] There must have been sufficient cause, for the University of Cologne later became a force opposing Hussite theology. This was a point made by Dietrich of Moers, archbishop of Cologne, in a letter dated May 10, 1425, to Pope Martin V.[25] By the time of the Council of Basel, and perhaps with the still-vivid recollection of the ruckus caused by Jerome, the university continued to be committed to containing the *contagiosa haeresis* of the Hussite tradition.[26] That relentless commitment to opposing the contagious Czech heresy appears to stem in part from the lasting impression left in that German university town by Jerome almost two decades earlier.

Heresy in Heidelberg

Forced out of Cologne, Jerome fled to Heidelberg, another university center which traced its foundation to 1385. He matriculated also as a master on April 7, 1406, and he appears in the records listed fourteenth out of thirty-six, having been received as a master of arts, but "shortly thereafter he was excluded from the faculty."[27] Another acrimonious disputation created further unrest when it was reported that Jerome was both inappropriate and offensive. Sometime in April, a several-day-long disputation occurred at Heidelberg. We know of this event mainly from inquisitorial records relating to the legal procedures at Vienna and Constance. In this disputation, Jerome apparently argued about the nature of universals, stating that universals in the human mind approximated to realities both in creation and in God's mind. In one sense, Jerome was reflecting the earlier ideas of John Duns Scotus and others. But apparently, he intruded onto dangerous territory by defiantly concluding that those who disagreed with him were *heretici diabolice*. By implication, this

---

24. Hardt, vol. 4, col. 645; and *Relatio*, p. 342; and especially from the May 23, 1416, interrogation during his trial in Constance.

25. Hermann Keussen, "Regesten und Auszüge zur Geschichte der Universität Köln 1388–1559," *Mitteilungen aus dem Stadtarchiv von Köln* 15 (1918): 62.

26. Franz Joseph von Bianco, *Die alte Universität Köln und die späteren Gelehrten-Schulen dieser Stadt nach archivarischen und anderen Quellen*, 2 vols. (Cologne: C. Genly, 1850–1855), vol. 2, pp. 169–170.

27. Noted in Karl Wundt, *Programma memorabilia nonnulla ordinis philosophici Heidelbergensis exhibens* (Heidelberg: Wiesen, 1779), vol. 1, p. 5.

condemned men such as Marsiglio of Padua, William Ockham, and others, because these thinkers did not allow for the possibility of the existence of universals outside the mind. Those later submitting evidence on the Heidelberg disputation included Nicholas Tell of Tungris and Konrad Duvel of Hildesheim.[28] Ostensibly, Jerome had advanced similar arguments in Cologne and possibly also at Paris and was now notorious on account of those disagreements.

Jerome's performance at Heidelberg stirred up considerable controversy. Engaging in academic debates, as was his custom, Jerome drew the ire of the German scholars. After several days of cantankerous debate and heated disputation, many of the faculty had grown so irritated they refused to listen further to Jerome. He paid no attention to the faculty suspension or to the accusations submitted to the bishop of Worms, the former Prague professor Matouš of Kraków.[29] Jerome was suspended (*ab omni actu scolastico*) from all functions of the arts faculty. None of this derailed Jerome, who responded to the complaint and censures by announcing, through public notices posted on the gates of university buildings, that he nevertheless intended to submit a response to the objections of his opponent. The dean, Ysebrandus de Wyringia, tried to prevent this by publishing another prohibition under the threat and punishment of permanent expulsion from the faculty of arts.[30] Once again, Jerome took no note of this action. The following day, he realized his intention at the cemetery of the Church of St. Peter. However, it was later alleged that when he arrived to take up a continuation of his disputation perspective, he found in the cemetery only peasants and old women (*rusticos et vetulas*), because the university students had been forbidden to attend under oath by the chancellor himself.[31] As an upshot of these developments, we learn further that

---

28. Klicman, pp. 13–15, on the depositions of Nicholas Tell and Konrad Duvel of Hildesheim (from Heidelberg), who testified during the Vienna trial. The testimony of Tell is taken up in Götz-Rüdiger Tewes, *Die Bursen der Kölner Artisten-Fakultät bis zur Mitte des 16. Jahrhunderts* (Cologne: Böhlau, 1993), pp. 304–306.

29. On the bishop, see Matthias Nuding, *Matthäus von Krakau: Theologe, Politiker, Kirchenreformer in Krakau, Prag und Heidelberg zur Zeit des Großen Abendländischen Schismas* (Tübingen: Mohr Siebeck, 2007); and more superficially in Miroslav Danys, *Master Matthew of Cracow* (Warsaw: Wydawnictwa Naukowego Semper, 1995).

30. Klicman, p. 12.

31. Johann Friedrich Hautz, *Geschichte der Universität Heidelberg* (Mannheim: J. Schneider, 1862), p. 232.

Jerome was twice referred to in records as heretical.[32] The so-called "students war," which broke out on June 11 and 12, must have involved Jerome to some extent, but this has been inadequately considered.[33]

What outraged the Heidelberg professors most? The complaint filed with the bishop of Worms (Matouš of Kraków) allegedly contained four heretical or at least four scandalous articles. One of them undoubtedly was the Wyclifite-sounding formulation "quod in mente divina plures essent formalitates formaliter et realiter distincte," suggesting that in the mind of God there were numerous real and formal distinctions.[34] Both witnesses during the Vienna process remembered it, but they did not see anything in it at the time that they personally considered improper. The prosecutions of Constance are in this respect more complete but less reliable, because they do not distinguish what Jerome proclaimed or defended at individual universities.[35] The separate point of prosecution about his scandalous work in Heidelberg then refers to exactly this list of heretical articles.[36] It is possible that Jerome, even in Heidelberg, used his explanation of the Holy Trinity utilizing the illustration of the so-called shield of faith and in so doing provoked the German scholars to indignation. At Constance on May 23, 1415, an unnamed theologian said to Jerome: "When you were in Heidelberg, you claimed a lot of heretical things about the Trinity and in the same place you had drawn some kind of shield, comparing the divine Trinity of persons to water, snow and all kinds of other things." Jerome did not deny the allegation but promised to recant anything that could be proven to him as amounting to heresy.[37] The Heidelberg nominalists were particularly infuriated by the fact that Jerome had offended William Ockham (d. ca. 1349), Jean Buridan (d. after 1358), and Marsilius of Inghen (d. 1396), whom he allegedly called heretics of the true dialectics and who evidently were considered to have nothing in common with "real" logic. Even if, as we already know, Jerome defended himself saying that it was in

---

32. Heidelberg, University Archives, MS. H IV 101/1, fol. 8r, which I have not seen, relying on Ota Pavlíček, "Two Philosophical Texts of Jerome of Prague and His Alleged Designation of Opponents of Real Universals as Diabolic Heretics," *BRRP* 8 (2009): 56.

33. Šmahel/Silagi, p. XXVII.

34. Klicman, pp. 5, 12–15.

35. Hardt, vol. 4, cols. 645–646.

36. Hardt, vol. 4, col. 681.

37. *FRB*, vol. 8, p. 342.

Cologne where he committed impertinence toward the leading nominalists, it is not only the eyewitnesses at the Vienna process who incriminate him but also the written record of his quaestio *Utrum veritas generalis sit signanda pro quacunque proposicione vere deniminanda.*[38] "Those, who consider universals to be mere hallmarks, are not dialecticians, but heretics of the true dialectics."[39] Thus alarmed by such ideas and scandalized by the impertinence with which Jerome evidently noised about his perspectives, during the tenure of Ysebrandus de Wyringia as dean, the faculty of arts inaugurated a statute that restricted the conditions for accepting bachelors and masters from other universities by a carefully designed preliminary censorship of predetermined quaestiones. It was evident that the university wanted no repeat performance of such impertinence and outrageous behavior as that displayed by the rogue Jerome.

Meanwhile, Johannes Lagenator of Frankfurt offered a rebuttal immediately after Jerome delivered his *Quaestio utrum veritas generalis sit signanda pro quacunque proposicione vere deniminanda.* A fragment of that riposte survives at the end of Jerome's *quaestio.*[40] In this fragment (which has been analyzed by Pavlíček), we find the following points. Lagenator issued a warning about useless philosophizing, perhaps with a nod to Fitzralph's critique of croaking frogs in the swamps. Truth was to be protected by learned men who ward off the deceptions introduced by heretics. False doctrine and dangerous ideas were thwarted by the keepers of orthodoxy. Jerome was indirectly dismissed as "a crazy, mischievous, and reprehensible perverter of the ancient wisdom of the Greeks," and Jerome was really an "unscrupulous manipulator."[41] Jerome's ideas were considered either, at best, convenient fictions or, at worst, a series of unverifiable hypotheses amounting to heresy. The posture assumed by Lagenator is an example of a prevailing tendency in the later Middle Ages for academics to involve themselves in matters pertaining to heresy and to appoint themselves as

38. *Quaestio de veritatibus generalibus*, in Šmahel/Silagi, pp. 3–12.

39. "Non dialectici, sed vere dialectice heretici sunt, qui dicuntur universalia esse signa." Basel, Universitätsbibliothek, MS A VIII 24, fol. 47v.

40. Basel, Universitätsbibliothek, MS VIII A 24, fols. 45v–48r. There is a critical edition: Angelika Häse, "Johannes de Franckfordia: Videte, ne quis vos decipiat. Angriffsrede gegen die Quaestio Utrum veritas generalis sit significanda des Hieronymus von Prag (1406)," in *Johannes von Frankfurt, Zwölf Werke des Heidelberger Theologen und Inquisitors*, ed. Dorothea von Walz (Heidelberg: C. Winter Universitätsverlag, 2000), pp. 99–100.

41. Pavlíček, "Two Philosophical Texts," pp. 55, 58.

special prosecutors or defined authorities on what constituted truth and heresy and moreover to judge what was acceptable within the Christian faith. Gerson's stance against Hus and Jerome in the days leading up to the Council of Constance and during the legal proceedings involving both men is a definite example. Be that as it may, a ban was later passed, on November 8, 1412, against all "perverse and damned teaching about the real existence of universals."[42] The furor involving Jerome meant that Heidelberg had taken a prominent stand against Wyclifite doctrine, just as surely as the University of Cologne had assumed an adversarial posture toward Hussite heresy in the wake of Jerome's acrimonious appearance there. In the aftermath of the intellectual bellicosity in Heidelberg, Jerome was called on to recant; he refused and was therefore suspended, and in the process, his university membership was revoked. As noted, Matouš of Kraków, the bishop of Worms, a confirmed nominalist and intellectual colleague of Heinrich Totting of Oyta, received accusations summarized in four articles of heresy lodged against Jerome. Refusing either to recant or to submit to ecclesiastical authority, Jerome once again fled. It is at Heidelberg where we have evidence of the first known instance wherein a diagram of a shield was used to explain the Trinity.[43] It was explicitly noted, as we have seen above, that three points on the shield were the words "water," "ice," and "snow."[44] It is not clear if Jerome created the shield or adapted it from elsewhere, but from the time of his appearance at Heidelberg until the Council of Constance, the shield is linked to Jerome, his suspected intellectual irregularities, and the growing suspicion of heresy.[45]

Medieval university disputations have rarely survived the ravages of time. This means that much of Jerome's literary work is not extant, for it was in the university forum of debate where he flourished. Apart from the university debates and disputations, Jerome wrote little, but by several accounts, he was a tremendous orator. His surviving works have been noted in chapter 1. Collections of references to the literary works of Hus

---

42. Eduard Winkelmann, ed., *Urkundenbuch der Universität Heidelberg* (Heidelberg: C. Winter Universitätsverlag, 1886), vol. 2, p. 106.

43. *FRB*, vol. 8, p. 342.

44. For comments on Jerome at Heidelberg, see Hardt, vol. 4, p. 218, col. 681; and also Šmahel, *Jeroným Pražsky*, pp. 69–76.

45. František Šmahel, *Die Prager Universität im Mittelalter* (Leiden: Brill, 2007), p. 542.

and Jerome note a wide disparity. There are 353 titles for Hus and Jerome based mainly on incipits, but only twenty-four of these are by Jerome.[46] In sum, university polemics and disputation *quaestiones* are mostly what survive from Jerome's pen and mind.[47] This is most unfortunate and prompts the question: How wise is it to say so much about so little?

During the time Jerome was away from Prague, interest in Wyclif continued apace at Charles University, but this preoccupation with such matters also generated sustained opposition. Perhaps the most significant of these controversies surrounded Wyclif's eucharistic doctrine. While Hus did not follow Wyclif, suspicions and accusations of eucharistic heresy continued to dog Hus up to the Council of Constance. In Prague, in the aftermath of the condemnation of Wyclifite ideas, the Cistercian monk and theologian Jan Štěkna accused Stanislav of Znojmo of holding such errors. Archbishop Zbyněk investigated the matter at the urging of a papal bull. By February 6, 1406, Stanislav had recanted. This marked the beginning of the eucharistic controversy in Prague.[48] It would persist into the 1440s.

Prevarication in Prague

Having successively fled from Paris, Cologne, and Heidelberg, by the end of 1406, the fugitive Jerome had arrived back in Prague. He passed university requirements and was admitted as a master in the faculty of arts in January 1407. He must have asked Prague to recognize his Paris, Cologne, and Heidelberg master's degrees. Perhaps as an extraordinary step and in light of the turmoil at Paris, Cologne, and Heidelberg, Jerome apparently was required to take an oath pledging not to cause unnecessary conflict or engender needless provocation at Charles University.[49] The four-member board of examiners chaired by Ondřej Brod placed Jerome

---

46. František M. Bartoš and Pavel Spunar, *Soupis pramenů k literární činnosti M. Jana Husa a M. Jeronyma Pražského* (Prague: Historický ústav ČSAV, 1965), pp. 277–289. Numbers 1–329 are to Hus and 330–353 to Jerome.

47. Šmahel, *University*, p. 578.

48. Jan Sedlák, "Eucharistické trakáty Stanislava ze Znojma," in *Miscellanea husitica Iohannis Sedlák*, ed. Pavel Klener (Prague: Katolická teologická fakulta university Karlovy, 1996), pp. 103–110.

49. This was noted during the Vienna trial; Klicman, p. 23.

first out of thirteen candidates.[50] Jerome was then received in Prague as a scholar in good standing. He never indicated any interest in proceeding to holy orders but remained a layman and never studied theology formally.[51] We have essentially no information about Jerome's lectures at Prague, with the exception of his tract *De probationibus propositionum*, which he was asked about on May 23, 1416, at Constance.[52] On the strength of holding four master of arts degrees, Jerome must be regarded as principally a highly trained philosopher. He was mainly interested in the philosophical aspects of theology.[53] His views can be extracted primarily from the various philosophical *quaestiones* that were prepared at Paris, Cologne, Heidelberg, and Prague. Later evidence suggests that Jerome aggressively promoted a radical form of realism wherein he rashly asserted the doctrines of Wyclif "openly, publicly, and notoriously."[54] Other interpretations have characterized Jerome as inclining toward an "excessive realism."[55] Jerome's lost notebook, the *Magnum quodam volumen*, must have been a dossier of authorities and arguments and something of a reference compendium. Jerome often cited the Bible, Augustine, Seneca, Boethius, Wyclif, and other authorities.[56] Points of departure frequently include Platonic sources, the works of Augustine, or the writings of Wyclif.[57] It is of some interest that Jerome does not refer to Aquinas.[58] The surviving fragments

---

50. *Liber decanorum Facultatis philosophicae Universitatis Pragensis* in *Monumenta historica Universitatis Carolo-Ferdinandeae Pragensis* (Prague: Joan. Nep. Gerzabek, 1830), vol. 1, pt. 1, p. 391; and Šmahel, *Život a dílo Jeronýma*, p. 35.

51. Šmahel, *Jeroným Pražsky*, pp. 59–77.

52. Hardt, vol. 4, col. 751.

53. Šmahel, "Leben und Werk," p. 94.

54. Klicman, pp. 12–13; but see also Kaluza, "La question de Jérôme de Prague disputée à Heidelberg," in *Études doctrinales*, p. 316.

55. M. Hoenen, "Academics and Intellectual Life in the Low Countries: The University Career of Heymeric de Campo (†1460)," *Recherches de théologie ancienne et médiévale* 61 (1994): 192.

56. Vilém Herold, *Pražská univerzita a Wyclif: Wyclifovo učení o ideách a geneze husitského revolučního myšlení* (Prague: Univerzita Karlova, 1985), pp. 204–219.

57. See *Quaestio de mundo archetypo*, in Šmahel/Silagi, p. 177; and *Recommendatio artium liberalium*, in Šmahel/Silagi, pp. 214–215, 217; and *Quaestio de potentia materiae primae*, in Šmahel/Silagi, p. 143.

58. An observation noted by Herold, "Magister Hieronymus von Prag und die Universität Köln," pp. 255–273.

of his work confirm his stature as a philosopher and his reputation as an original, if not reckless, thinker.[59] During his stay in Paris, Jerome imbibed deeply of sources and fundamental texts that shaped his thought about ideas and universals. There can now no longer be any doubt that Jerome became familiar not only with Wyclif but also with John Scotus Erigena, a ninth-century Irish thinker, and with Pseudo-Dionysius the Areopagite.[60] During this stint in Prague, Jerome seems to have enjoyed privilege from King Václav IV in terms of appointment to Charles College. It is likely that Jerome resided here from 1409 onward when he was in Prague.[61] Charles College (or the Carolinum) was founded in 1366 by Emperor Charles for twelve masters of arts. It played no mean role in the early years of the Hussite movement.

As early as 1403, formal concerns were lodged in Prague over the ideas of Wyclif, and some of these concerns were predicated on the combative interchange involving divine Ideas. The matter continued to simmer, and by early 1408, renewed charges were lodged at the Papal Curia by the Saxon university master Ludolf Meistermann, who was a radical nominalist. Pope Gregory XII referred the matter to Cardinal François of Bordeaux. A ruling was made in the spring. On April 20, it was determined that teaching the ideas and doctrines of Wyclif was forbidden, debating Wyclifite tenets was outlawed, and even owning Wyclif books was adjudicated illegal.[62] Many of the scholars and thinkers in Prague were unsettled by this judgment. On May 24, 1408, an assembly of Czech university masters convened at the house of the "Black Rose" in Příkopě Street. This group included Stanislav of Znojmo, Jan Hus, Štěpán Páleč, Jan Eliášův, Ondřej Brod, Jakoubek Stříbro, and Jan Příbram. The whereabouts of Jerome cannot be determined with any degree of precision, and it is possible that he was not in Europe at all but may have been on a pilgrimage to Jerusalem

59. Šmahel, *University*, p. 579.

60. These identifications have been articulated in František Šmahel, "Prolegomena zum Prager Universalienstreit: Zwischenbilanz einer Quellenanalyse," in *The Universities in the Late Middle Ages*, ed. Josef Ijsewijn and Jacques Paquet (Louvain: Leuven University Press, 1978), pp. 242–255; Kaluza, "Le chancelier Gerson et Jérôme de Prague," in *Études doctrinales*, pp. 218–230; and Stanislaw Sousedík, "M. Hieronymi Pragensis ex Iohanne Scoto Eriugena excerpta," *Listy filologické* 98 (1975): 4–7.

61. On Jerome's appointment to the college, see Charles University Archives, sig. A 17 1, 1, p. 732. On this point, I rely on Šmahel, *Život a dílo Jeronýma*, p. 46.

62. Decision text in F. M. Bartoš, "V předvečer Kutnohorského dekretu," *Časopis českého musea* 102 (1928): 107–108.

or otherwise outside of Bohemia. Despite his absence and the decree of disapprobation, these men nevertheless passed a resolution effectively refusing to submit to the anti-Wyclifite climate fostered by the Germans and facilitated by Archbishop Zbyněk, who at this stage appears to have turned his back rather decisively on the reform movement.[63] A few years later, it was alleged that Jerome had been present in Prague during this confrontation.[64] If true, we can only imagine his vociferous opposition to the anti-Wyclif mandate. On the other hand, if Jerome had been in Prague, why did he later deny it? If he had been present, why has none of the sources recorded his contributions to the debate, which must surely have been obstreperous?

As a result of this anti-Wyclifite mandate, the first order to hand over copies of Wyclif's books occurred either in late 1408 or early 1409.[65] Inasmuch as the text is not extant, the date must remain uncertain. It has been noted that both Jerome and Hus were among the ringleaders in resisting the mandate of the archbishop. Hus's role in the matter has been reviewed and explicated. Jerome's involvement has been less clear. Nevertheless, fault lines of conflict began to be exposed, and these patterns of splintering ran along nationalistic and theological lines. Demographic shifts began to appear in terms of power differential, and in 1408, Czechs were able to gain a majority on the Old Town council.[66] Recalcitrant "Wyclifites" were attacked on account of the fact that they had poisoned elements of the nobility and the university and were exerting strong influence over many Czechs. The seeds of this growing discontent yielded a harvest of conflict in which Jerome played a leading role.[67] Before that major division became reality, the issue of heresy once again came to the forefront. In the spring

---

63. Václav Novotný and Vlastimil Kybal, *M. Jan Hus: Život a učení*, 5 vols. (Prague: Laichter, 1919–1931), vol. 1, pp. 221–222.

64. Hardt, vol. 4, col. 652.

65. On the order to surrender copies of Wyclif's writings, see Jiří Kejř, *Husův proces* (Prague: Vyšehrad, 2000), p. 23; Höfler, vol. 2, pp. 123–124; and testimony given at the heresy trial of Jerome in Vienna in 1410 by Butzbach, Vohburg, Czungl, Tesser, Chenczl (also Keutzel), and Weinstein, in Klicman, pp. 15–16, 20, 23, 25, 27, 28, 30, 32, 33.

66. Jaroslav Mezník, *Praha před husitskou revolucí* (Prague: Academia, 1990), pp. 119–123.

67. Štěpán Dolany, "Medula tritici seu Antiwiclef," in *Thesaurus anecdotorum novissimus seu veterum monumentorum*, 6 vols., ed. Bernard Pez (Augsburg: Philippi, Martini, & Joannis Veith fratrum, 1721–1729), vol. 4, pp. 157–158. See Jana Nechutová, "Dialogus volatilis Štěpána z Dolan," *Listý filologické* 107 (1984): 11–18.

of 1408, Czech university master Matěj Knín was arrested and arraigned on suspicion of heresy. He stood trial before the archbishop on May 14. There were legal irregularities, and the matter was not dealt with effectively or legally. Refusing to demonstrate the guilt of Knín according to legal procedure, the examiner Jan Kbel demanded unqualified recantation. Either in ignorance or by willful neglect, Archbishop Zbyněk supported Kbel on this procedural point. By consequence, Knín was forced to accept the humiliation and was compelled to withdraw heresies he claimed not to hold.[68] This incident would have consequences for the reform movement in Prague and would bring notoriety to Jerome. The latter later remarked that Knín was an honorable man who had been subjected to vile slander.[69]

The Quodlibet of 1409

By January 1409, disaster had struck, yielding dire consequences for Jerome.[70] There were two defining events. The first was the annual university Quodlibet. The other was the momentous Decree of Kutná Hora. Both events were accomplished in the first month of 1409. The Quodlibet of January 1409 became a fully developed political agenda.[71] The leader for the 1409 Quodlibet was advertised as the aforementioned master and heresy suspect Matěj Knín.[72] This announcement was received with consternation. Already agitated by nationalistic controversy and disputes over Wyclifism and divine Ideas, and worried about the implications of potential heresy, the Germans threatened a boycott citing a prevailing reluctance to sit under the direction of one suspected of heresy. In an effort to prevent further conflict, King Václav ordered the Germans to participate

---

68. *Documenta*, p. 338.

69. *Recommendatio artium liberalium*, p. 221.

70. Ladislaus Klicman, "Der Wiener Process gegen Hieronymus von Prag, 1410–1412," *Mitteilungen des Instituts für Oesterreichische Geschichtsforschung* 21 (1900): 447.

71. For a description of the debates at Prague, see Jiří Kejř, "Struktura a průběh disputace de quodlibet na pražské universitě," *Acta universitatis carolinae, Historia universitatis carolinae Pragensis* 1 (1960): 17–42; and Vilém Herold and Pavel Spunar, "L'Université de Prague et les rôle des disputations *de quolibet* à sa faculté des Arts à la fin du XIVe et au début du XVe siècle," in *Compte rendu de la 69e Session annuelle du Comité de l'Union Académique Internationale* (Brussels: Secretariat administratif de L'U A.I., Palais des Académies, 1996), pp. 27–39.

72. Herold, *Pražská univerzita a Wyclif*, pp. 187–93.

and forbade further resistance. Records shortly thereafter summarized the atmosphere in Prague on the eve of the *Quodlibet*. "Because Knín was willing to dispute, there were many masters, especially Walter Harrasser, Master Peter Storch, and Master Johann Hofman and others who did not want to attend the *Quodlibet*. They publicly said they preferred to leave Prague than attend the *actus* of one suspected of heresy. However, the king ordered the three nations by means of a letter to attend on Master Matěj."[73] Harrasser was Bavarian, Storch was Saxon, and Hofman was from Svídnice. Storch and Hofman ultimately did attend out of fear of the king's mandate. Nevertheless, a number of students, masters, and bachelors boycotted the *Quodlibet*, effectively flaunting the king's circumscription.[74] Jerome denounced them as "cowardly knights."[75]

The university *Quodlibet* in Prague occurred annually on January 3 and normally lasted several days. The process was subject to very strict regulations. The leader of the debate was chosen six months prior to the event to allow for careful and comprehensive preparation. All participants were notified of the specific questions several days in advance. All masters were obligated to attend under penalty of sanction and fine. The proceedings were divided into several parts. The leader of the debate opened with a speech and then presented his solution to the principal question (*quaestio*). The opening *quaestio* was always divided into three parts. A debate followed, and the leader had the last word, usually defending his thesis. The second part of the *Quodlibet* allowed all participating masters opportunity to solve the *quaestio* originally set. The leader of the debate had to be prepared to deal with all of the submissions. Handbooks are extant containing a list of arguments on each *quaestio* and providing positive and negative answers. Depending on how a specific master answered the question, the leader took up the other option. There are four of these *Quodlibet* handbooks known. These belonged to Matěj Knín from the 1409 *Quodlibet*, to Jan Hus from the 1411 disputation, to Šimon of Tišnov from the 1416 event, and to Prokop of Kladruby, who chaired the debates in 1417. In addition to the *quaestio*, each master was obliged to deal with a *probleum*, meaning he had to find a suitable answer to the question at hand with a humorous

---

73. Klicman, pp. 16–17.

74. Jiří Kejř, *Kvodlibetní disputace na Pražské Universitě* (Prague: Universita Karlova, 1971), pp. 88–90, 116–136.

75. *Recommendatio artium liberalium*, p. 211.

character. Once all participants had spoken, the leader closed the *Quodlibet* debate with a speech. In 1409, the Prague *Quodlibet* featured the general question of whether or not God, as the immutable highest good in all creation, was the creator of the sum parts of the universe. The clear underpinnings of Wyclifite thought were evident. As was soon apparent, Jerome played a major role in the deliberations and outcomes of the *Quodlibet*.[76]

Whereas Jerome's whereabouts cannot be determined with respect to the furor over the "forty-five" articles of Wyclif in 1403 or 1408, he can be placed in Prague during January 1409. There is no argument that Jerome was a participant in the *Quodlibet* of Matěj Knín. His *quaestio* amounted to a defense of Wyclif's metaphysical realism. In fact, he delivered a lecture outside the regular *Quodlibet* proceedings. The *Recommendatio artium liberalium* ("A Eulogy on the Liberal Arts"; see figure 3.1) was an impassioned discourse wherein Jerome publicly sided with King Václav in defending the Czech nation.[77] Given the divisive and acrimonious climate at the university, Jerome elected to target his remarks at a particular group of people. He subjected them to ridicule, calling them uneducated and wicked clerics; criticized the Germans, masters, and priests for failing to attend, praised Knín (the master *Quodlibetarius*); denounced those who suggested the Czech nation was fraught with heresy; openly advocated the study of Wyclif's books; and congratulated the city councilors who had been commissioned by the king to protect Prague. He praised many others, especially those of Czech origin, including Václav, the university, the liberal arts faculty, the city of Prague ("sacrosancta civitas Pragensia"), and the holy Czech nation. Jerome's use of the concept *nacio bohemica* is original and is a clear departure from prior concepts embedded in Czech sources. Jerome's nationalism may be considered extreme, and he appears to determine Czech identity based on both language and blood, articulating the idea of the *purus Bohemus* (pure Czech). It might also be stressed that to these two requirements Jerome added a third, not inconsequential requirement, that a true Czech had an obligation to the faith.[78] This is an echo from antiquity, when a Greek rhetorician said he preferred to think of

---

76. On the careful preparations for this *Quodlibet*, see Jiří Kejř, "Sporné otázky v bádání o Dekretu kutnohorském," *Acta universitatis carolinae, Historia universitatis carolinae Pragensis* 3, no. 1 (1962): 83–95. This essay also notes the themes of the thirty-four proposed questions.

77. The text appears in Höfler, vol. 2, pp. 112–128, containing many errors, not least among them a false attribution to Hus. A better version is in Šmahel/Silagi, pp. 199–222.

78. František Šmahel, *Idea národa v husitských Čechách* (Prague: Argo, 2000), pp. 45–46.

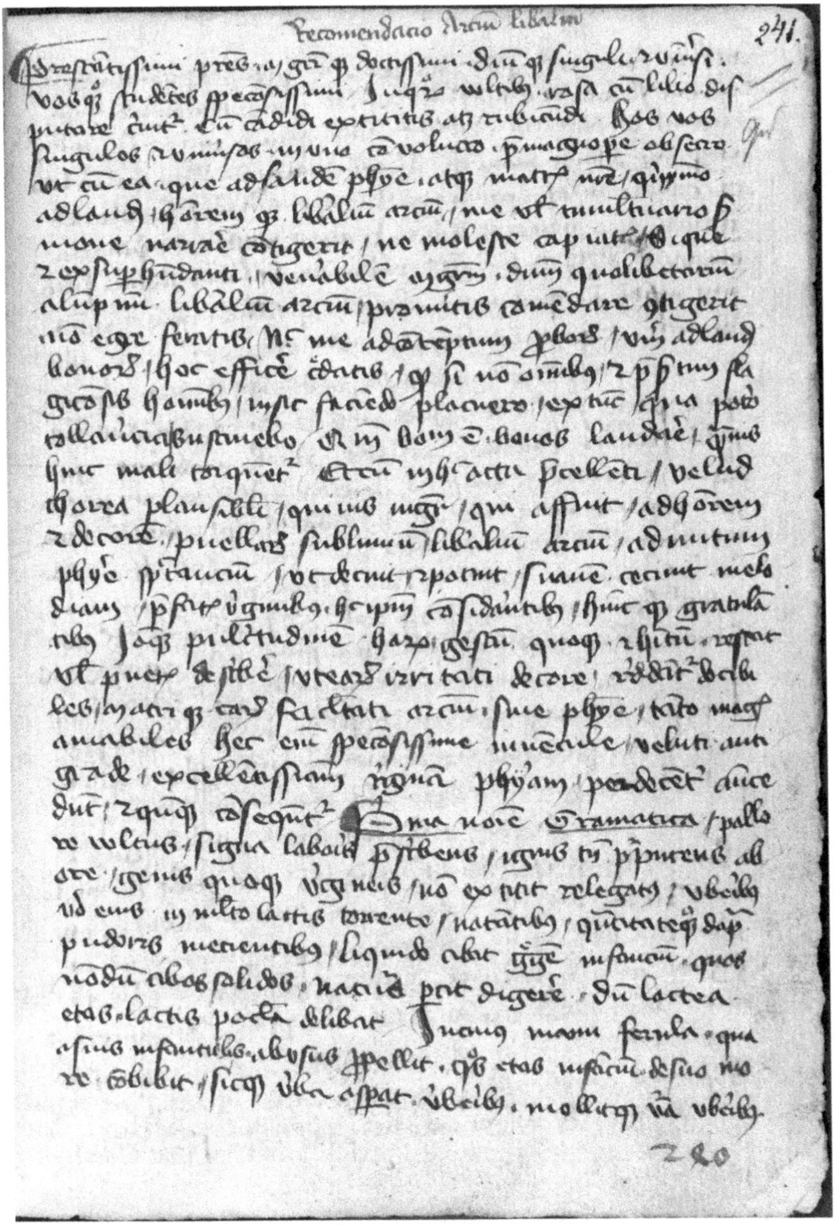

FIGURE 3.1 Jerome, *Recommendatio artium liberalium*. NK, MS X E 24, fol. 241r. Used by permission.

true Greeks not simply as those who shared birth and nation but as those who engaged in the Greek discipline or education.[79] In the *Recommendatio*, Jerome described the debate in terms of scholars jousting in a tournament.[80] There have been efforts to link the authorship of the song "Slyšte, rytieři boží, připravte se již k boji" ("Hear, knights of God, prepare yourselves for the fight") to Jerome, but these remain conjecture and cannot be proven.[81] The song ridicules Archbishop Zbyněk, warns of the advent of Antichrist, champions Václav, and reiterates the idea that no proper Czech could be a heretic. It was during the 1409 *Quodlibet* that Jerome began to speak of a *nacio bohemica* (Czech nation), defined as a collective of individual Czechs who, as a community, were possessed of rights.[82] It is also at this time that Jerome began to lobby for the Czechs against the Germans in view of majority vote and ultimately control in the university.

In this context, on the eve of the dramatic events of January 1409, it is possible to locate Jerome's *quaestio*, which reveals in no small measure the depth and dimensions of the conflict brewing in Prague. In this *quaestio, Utrum unum terminorum inter se convertibilium*, Jerome underscored the argument of Matěj Knín.[83] A single sentence is sufficient to reveal that perspective. "The fanatical adversaries obsessed by obstinate superciliousness or for other reasons do not understand or do not want to comprehend the sense, or the verbal expression of these [Wyclif] truths, in spite of the fact that my colleague Matěj Knín, called Pater, excellently explained them."[84] One must wonder why Knín is referred to as father. He does beget Jerome as the "athlete of Antichrist" in the Wyclifite Mass.[85] Nejedlý thinks he

---

79. George Norlin, trans., *Isocrates I*, Loeb Classical Library, 209 (Cambridge, MA: Harvard University Press, 1928), *Panegyricus*, 50, p. 149.

80. *Recommendatio artium liberalium*, p. 211.

81. The text is in Zdeněk Nejedlý, *Dějiny husitského zpěvu*, 6 vols. (Prague: Československá akademie věd, 1954–1956), vol. 3, pp. 442–443. There is a translation in Thomas A. Fudge, *The Memory and Motivation of Jan Hus, Medieval Priest and Martyr* (Turnhout: Brepols, 2013), pp. 178–179.

82. Šmahel, *Idea národa v husitských Čechách*, pp. 44–48.

83. The *quaestio* is known in a single copy. NK, MS X E 24, where the colophon reads: "Expliciunt dicta reverendi magistri Jeronimi de Praga ano domini 1409 in quodlibet reverendi magistri Matye de Knin enunciata . . ."

84. Šmahel/Silagi, pp. 75–76.

85. Discussed in Thomas A. Fudge, *Jan Hus Between Time and Eternity: Reconsidering a Medieval Heretic* (Lanham, MD: Lexington, 2016), pp. 187–210.

is called father because he was considered the father of all iniquity on account of his public questioning in 1408, which brought the religious controversy to a head.[86] This, however, is an explanation that makes sense only after the *Quodlibet* and does not shed light on why Jerome uses the term in the midst of his own speech. It may be resolved simply as a reference to Knín as the leader or chair of the *Quodlibet* whom Jerome now lauded as the leader of the *Quodlibet* presiding like a prince over the formation of intellectual combat.[87]

The occasion of the *Quodlibet* was seized on by Jerome to invite a visiting French embassy, including Master Jacques de Nouvion of Paris University and others, who had been commissioned by the king, Charles VI, along with a delegation from Brabant, which included the bishop of Chalons-sur-Saône, who were in Prague hoping to persuade Václav to help end the papal schism. And so it came to pass, that on the last day of the annual university disputation, Old Town councilors, leading figures from Brabant, and the bishop of Chalons were in attendance at the *Quodlibet*, having been invited by Jerome. It is certain that Jerome's invitation was designed to exploit his own speech, which he had already planned as a public provocation.

The Knín *Quodlibet* focused on the validity of realism but soon progressed (perhaps by design) into a debate about Wyclif. Jerome was unrestrained in his defense of Wyclif and divine Ideas.[88] His speech became a key factor in legal proceedings both at Vienna and later at Constance. The speech (noted above) incorporated the "shield of faith" and an apparent blatant denunciation of nominalism. Jerome allegedly argued that "they are not logicians but diabolical heretics who say that universals are mere names." Jerome's provocation did not pass unnoticed. Master Blažej Vlk (Blasius Lupus), a ranking member of the faculty, former dean of the faculty of arts, and university chancellor, objected but Jerome thundered on. Jerome castigated the masters who refused to attend the *Quodlibet* or came only because they were ordered to by the king. These men were an insult to the university. Their renown was merely outward, because within they were filled with "foulness, lasciviousness, simony, error, and faithlessness." They were robbers and sacrilegious. Such men were heretics

---

86. Nejedlý, *Dějiny husitského zpěvu*, vol. 3, p. 372.

87. *Recommendatio artium liberalium*, p. 221.

88. *ST*, vol. 2, pp. 197–262.

both in their lives and in conduct. Jerome's national commitment was evident when he asserted that these same individuals falsely accused the holy Czech nation (*nostrum conmunitatem sacrosanctam Boemicam*) of heresy when in fact there had never been a heretic among the pure Czechs. "Such idiots, these priests," Jerome fumed, "should be embarrassed because of such shameless lies."[89] Popular songs, possibly written or inspired by Jerome, proclaimed the same refrain.[90] Jerome called upon all those loyal to King Václav, the Czech land, and the holy city of Prague to withstand such "treacherous liars who seek to corrupt the good name and shame the members of our holy Czech nation." He went on to say that it was a mark of gross impertinence and great ignorance for worthless priests to preach sermons filled with lies claiming that many in Prague were heretics and labeling them Wyclifites. Jerome asserted that he had studied the works of Wyclif and declared that there was much of value to be gained therein. However, he offered the caveat that he was not so benighted as to think that everything Wyclif had to say was right any more than any other doctrine or theology. Jerome said no other writings could be placed on the same level of authority as scripture. It is true, Jerome said, that gold, silver, and other precious stones are buried in the mud and must be extracted. He challenged his hearers, wishing to know who among them would forbid harvesting the treasures ("wealth of truth") from the books of Wyclif. Jerome then launched into a recommendation of Wyclif: "For my part, I urge all of you to often read and study hard his books, especially the philosophical ones, and to do so often and with diligence. Should you find something therein which you cannot understand, on account of your youth, set it aside until you are more mature. If you find anything which appears to contradict the faith, do not hide it and do not adhere to it but instead be obedient to the faith."[91] In other words, the speech urged the usefulness of Wyclif for intellectual training. Jerome used the university debate as an opportunity to deliver an impassioned speech that clearly defended Wyclif, openly criticized the Germans, railed on the wickedness of simoniacal clerics, and promoted the interests of the Czechs. It has previously been noted that Jerome ostensibly went so far as to assert

89. *Recommendatio artium liberalium*, pp. 212, 213, 217, 218.

90. Bohuslav Havránek, ed., *Výbor z český literatury husitské doby*, 2 vols. (Prague: Československá akademie věd, 1963–1964), vol. 1, p. 268.

91. *Recommendatio artium liberalium*, p. 215.

that whoever denied the basic premises of realism ought to be considered a "devilish heretic."[92] The reference is controversial. Johannes Vohburg later testified that Walter Harrasser and Henning of Baltenhagen (university chancellor) were present during Jerome's disputation, while Achatius Chenczl (or Käutzl) of Salzburg (d. 1431) said later that a messenger from the Prague archbishop interrupted Jerome, objecting to his effrontery, but to little avail.[93]

Perhaps carried away by the emotion and the drama of the moment, at one stage during his speech, Jerome left his place and "went up to where Master Knín was sitting and stroked him by the beard, and said in the vulgar tongue [German]: 'Behold, my good boy, they are after your life and they want to have you out of the way on account of that Wyclif, and you are guiltless of that. Where are the ones who are after you?' "[94] The last sentence apparently was spoken in Latin. Then (according to Heinrich de Aurus, a bachelor) Jerome placed a beret on the head of the reader of the *Quodlibet* and said: "Behold, you deserve to be crowned."[95] This dramatic showmanship was intended by Jerome to underscore his support for the controversial ideas already outlawed and formally criminalized in Prague. At the conclusion of the *Quodlibet*, Jerome turned his attention specifically to Wyclif. "See, my dearest children, I will tell you news of Master John Wyclif, who some say was burned and condemned by the church." He then produced a letter from Oxford University, handed to him at that moment by an unnamed colleague, which refuted the allegations. Jerome then said: "Would that God would grant that my soul were where Wyclif's is."[96] The statement was reckless, and several years later, Jerome would be made to hear his declaration again, this time in a formal court proceeding. The letter brandished by Jerome had been brought to Bohemia by the Wyclifite book hunters Mikuláš Faulfiš and Jiří of Kněhnice. Some

92. Šmahel/Silagi, pp. 199–222. See also comments in František Šmahel, "Mistr Jeroným Pražský na soudu dějin," *Husitský tábor*, supp. 1 (2001): 313–323.

93. Klicman, pp. 20, 26.

94. Klicman, p. 28, on the basis of evidence presented by Kaspar Weinstein of Eichstädt, who at the time was a Prague student.

95. Klicman, p. 33.

96. Klicman, p. 33, on the evidence of Henrich von Aura. The text of the letter is in Konstantin von Höfler, *Concilia Pragensia 1353–1413* (Vienna: Geyer, 1972), p. 53, with a date of October 5, 1406, and preserved in NK, MS XI E 3, fol. 1r.

scholars have defended its authenticity, but during the proceedings of the Council of Constance, it was represented as a spurious document.[97] The issue of the faked document arose at Constance, but Jerome said on that occasion that he had no previous knowledge that the document was falsified or otherwise under question.[98] It has long been suspected that Peter Payne may have been involved in procuring the letter for the Czechs, whether through legitimate channels or by means of illicit purveyance. The question cannot be satisfactorily resolved.

Jerome's approach at the 1409 *Quodlibet* appears to contravene the principle championed by Heinrich Langenstein at Vienna, who challenged heretics (and others) with the counsel "unless you believe you will not understand"[99] That admonition drew on various statements in Anselm, especially the conviction "nor do I seek to understand that I may believe, but I believe that I may understand. For this, too, I believe, that, unless I first believe, I shall not understand."[100] Intellectually, Jerome seems more attuned to Peter Abelard's point of view, when the latter claimed that "by doubting we come to inquiry, by inquiry we perceive truth," and elsewhere declared that "nothing can be believed unless it is first understood."[101] This promoted the idea that one must first understand in order to believe. Abelard even went so far as to declare that he did not believe anyone could completely understand theological matters unless he had stayed up all night studying philosophy, paying particular attention to dialectic.[102]

---

97. Novotný and Kybal, *M. Jan Hus*, vol. 1, p. 313, say the letter is genuine, but detractors at Constance claimed it was false. Hardt, vol. 4, col. 644.

98. *FRB*, vol. 8, p. 290. See also Ferdinand Seibt, *Hussitica. Zur Struktur einer Revolution* (Cologne: Böhlau, 1965), pp. 78–79.

99. Anselm, "credo, ut intelligam," *Proslogium*, ch. 1, in *PL*, vol. 158, col. 227.

100. "Rectus ordo exigit ut profunda Christianae fidei credamus, priusquam ea praesumamus ratione discutere, ita negligentiae mihi videtur, si, postquam confirmati sumus in fide, non studemus quod credimus intelligere." Anselm, *Libri duo Cum Deus Homo*, bk. 1, 1–2, in *PL*, vol. 158, col. 362. "Neque enim quaero intelligere, ut credam; sed credo, ut intelligam. Nam et hoc credo quia nisi credidero, non intelligam." Anselm, *Proslogeum*, chap. 1, in *PL*, vol. 158, col. 227.

101. Blanche Boyer and Richard McKeon, eds., *Peter Abailard Sic et Non: A Critical Edition* (Chicago: University of Chicago Press, 1976), p. 103; and Jacques Monfrin, ed., *Historia Calamitatum: Texte critique, avec une introduction* (Paris: J. Vrin, 1978), pp. 62–109, lines 692, 695–700.

102. Paraphrase of a core idea in the Prologue of *Sic et Non*, pp. 89–104, and Ralph Norman, "Abelard's Legacy: Why Theology Is Not Faith Seeking Understanding," *Australian eJournal of Theology* 10 (May 2007): 1–10.

It seems evident that Jerome's *quaestio* was strictly philosophical. That is to say, his delineation of universals did not specifically or intentionally enter into theological considerations.[103] This was not always perceived as such, and there were powerful voices later alleging that Jerome had violated the special and unique *modus loquendi* (method of speaking) that Gerson insisted scripture and theology had. According to Gerson, logic was better suited to matters of philosophy, while rhetoric was better suited to theology and theological discourse. Gerson denounced Wyclif, Hus, and Jerome in part because he was convinced they did not appreciate the role and function of metaphor in scripture and misunderstood the essential *modus loquendi*.[104] So far as Gerson was concerned, Jerome fatally confused logic with rhetoric. The dispute was partly over the language of ideas which allowed for certain assertions. The idiom is considered trustworthy. The discourse puts something into words that invokes a form of security or certainty allowing those words or ideas to be something more than mere words or ideas. Gerson believed there needed to be strict rules circumscribing the special and unique *modus loquendi* reserved for the sacred discourses around scripture and theology. Jerome recognized no such distinctions, declining the priority of Paris, and instead presented a Wyclifite understanding of divine Ideas.

In contrast to the admonition of Gerson, Jerome appeared to be attempting to find new ways of approaching old problems. If Jerome was the intellectual stepson of Peter Abelard, then it was expected that he would positively ignore and actively rebut Anselm's rule on thinking, which advised that no Christian should question or enter into dispute about anything the church has internalized as truth and publicly declared.[105] This placed Jerome in a situation where he had to resolve hermeneutical quagmires, and in so doing, he ran the risk of violating the kinds of parameters the medieval church had established and which men such as Anselm and Gerson guarded with assiduous care. If Abelard ran afoul of ecclesiastical

---

103. Zénon Kaluza, "Jérôme de Prague et le *Timée* de Platon," in *Études doctrinales sur le XIVe siècle: Théologie, Logique, Philosophie* (Paris: Vrin, 2013), pp. 253–256.

104. Kaluza, "Jérôme de Prague et le *Timée* de Platon," *Études doctrinales*, pp. 266–287; and Michael H. Shank, *Unless You Believe, You Shall Not Understand: Logic, University, and Society in Late Medieval Vienna* (Princeton, N.J.: Princeton University Press, 1988), pp. 176–185.

105. *Epistola de incarnatione verbi*, in Franciscus Salesius Schmitt, ed., *S. Anselmi Cantuariensis archiepiscopi Opera Omnia*, 6 vols. (Stuttgart-Bad Cannstatt: Frommann, 1968), vol. 2, pp. 6–7.

authority in the twelfth century, it is no wonder that Jerome suffered a similar fate in the fifteenth. It is worth considering a comparison between the two men. It has been suggested that Abelard was, within the limits of the twelfth century, possibly the first significant forerunner of the modern intellectual.[106] It seems somewhat apparent that both men were constantly provoking new ideas and stimulating passionate discussion and even arguments. They were iconoclasts with respect to established ideas and traditions, resisting with some vigor anything that appeared to restrict thought or intellectual pursuits. They relentlessly challenged old ideas by proposing new solutions.[107] Intellectual martyrdom overtook Jerome at the height of his powers. His fame increased because of his relentless challenge to entrenched ideas and certain medieval religious practices but equally, it seems, as a result of growing opposition from established thinkers and other critics. Fame gave way to infamy, and notoriety replaced intellectual genius. He was rapidly transformed from university master and philosopher into heretic and the "athlete of Antichrist."

After the bellicose *Quodlibet* of 1409, Jerome seems to have emerged more prominently as a recognized leader among the reform party. This may be attributed to his stirring and one might even say strident performance during the disputation and his apparent disregard for who might be offended by his arguments. As we have seen, it was also at this event that he declared that no Czech had ever been a heretic and that truth could not be overcome with a lie and ultimately truth would prevail.[108] This became a Hussite motif and was noted even in hostile sources.[109] We find evidence that the opposite argument was sometimes mounted, and ethnic and nationalist bias is certainly reflected in statements such as that the Czechs are the "sons of heretical wickedness." In other words, being Czech implied also being heretical.[110] It might usefully be noted again that

106. Jacques LeGoff, *Les intellectuels au moyen âge* (Paris: Seuil, 1972), p. 40.

107. Wim Verbaal, "Trapping the Future: Abelard's Multi-Layered Image-Building," in *Rethinking Abelard: A Collection of Critical Essays*, ed. Babette S. Hellemans, (Leiden: Brill, 2014), p. 187.

108. *Recommendatio artium liberalium*, pp. 217–219. See also p. LXVII.

109. For example, Andreas von Regensburg, *Sämtliche Werke*, ed. Georg Leidinger (Munich: Rieger, 1903), p. 121.

110. Ludolf of Żagan, *Tractatus de longevo schismate* in *Archiv für österreichische Geschichte*, ed. Johann Loserth (Vienna: Carl Gerold's Solin, 1880), vol. 60, p. 433.

at Jerome's baccalaureate in 1398, his promoter Jan of Vysoké Mýto placed emphasis on an individual, noting where that person was born and the national identity in question.[111]

The aforementioned attempt by Master Blažej Vlk to engage in debate with Jerome during the *Quodlibet* was not successful, as Jerome had no intention of surrendering the momentum of his speech, particularly in front of the special guests he had invited. Nevertheless, by Easter, Jerome did take up the opportunity to dispute with Vlk over universals. The debate really centered on Wyclif. However, the private disputation did not conclude, as Archbishop Zbyněk intervened and once again issued a writ prohibiting further debate. This intervention was revealed at the Vienna trial, based on evidence provided by Achacius Chenczl from Salzburg. Chenczl had been a student first at Prague and later at Vienna. He testified that he had heard Jerome praising Wyclif and spoke of Vlk's opposition to Jerome. This must have been subsequent to April 11. Chenczl also pointed out that Jerome had referred to the shield of faith during his debate with Vlk.[112] The interaction between Jerome and Vlk is not easily untangled from the fragmentary sources that survive from 1409. According to one line of interpretation, Jerome spoke at the *Quodlibet*. This has been established without serious dispute. Sometime thereafter, following the end of the *Quodlibet*, Vlk objected in a text known as *Deinde procedam sic*. At some further indeterminate time, Jerome replied to Vlk, and the latter subsequently offered an additional response in a fragment bearing the incipit *Item secundo sic arguitur contra idem*.[113] The disagreement focused on Wyclif's concept of universals, and Vlk's counterblast to Jerome consisted of fourteen arguments carefully mounted *contra universalia realia*.[114] For a long time, it has been thought that only fragmentary glimpses of this debate were extant. This conjecture can now be refuted and set aside. It is now possible to defend the proposition that the entire exchange has been preserved and

111. Bohumil Ryba, ed., *Promoční promluvy mistrů artistické fakulty Mikuláše z Litomyšle a Jana z Mýta na univerzitě Karlově z let 1386 a 1393* (Prague: Česká akademie věd a umění, 1948), p. 24.

112. Klicman, p. 26.

113. Jan Sedlák, "Filosofické spory pražské v době Husově," *Studie a texty* 2 (1915): 209–211. Vlk's *Deinde procedam sic* in on pp. 224–229; his *Item secundo sic arguitur contra idem* is on pp. 258–262.

114. See the discussion in Šmahel, *University*, pp. 544–564.

that part of this text is one of the copies that was displayed on the master's college gate with a challenge for debate.[115]

By the time academic controversy erupted in Prague, Jerome had run afoul of authorities in several locations, including Paris, Cologne, and Heidelberg. He had earned a reputation as an insane master committed to the contagious plague of Wyclifism, bringing chaos to Bohemia and Moravia, invading the courts of princes, the seats of higher learning, and the cathedrals of priests, infecting the faith, corrupting both men and women, causing great disturbance and tumult.[116] That reputation would accompany Jerome and precede his appearance at the Council of Constance. The same reputation would dog the judicial procedures brought to bear on him, and a steadfast conviction in the veracity of the reputation would inform and dictate the thinking of the men at Constance who ultimately determined his fate. Of course, Jerome's propensity for effrontery and intellectual aggravation did absolutely nothing to dent the impact of that reputation and indeed only added to it. Some would say it was certain that Jerome was addicted to needless provocation. It is equally certain that he took no note of such concerns.

The Decree of Kutná Hora

Some of the same trends that swirled around Jerome and the university disputation of 1409 resulted shortly thereafter in the Decree of Kutná Hora. Jerome played a major role in these affairs, both at the university *Quodlibet* in Prague, as we have seen, and also in the developments resulting in the decree, which irrevocably changed the nature of Charles University. It is doubtful that Jerome was aware of the storms he helped unleash. All of this came back to haunt him, and he was soon to learn difficult lessons during ecclesiastical court trials at Vienna and Constance.[117]

---

115. The relevant texts have been preserved in Castle Archive, MS N 12; and a useful analysis appears in Šmahel, *University*, pp. 547–553.

116. Štěpán Dolany, "Antiwikleffus," in *Thesaurus anecdotorum novissimus seu veterum monumentorum*, 6 vols., ed. Bernard Pez (Augsburg: Philippi, Martini, & Joannis Veith fratrum, 1721–1729), vol. 4, cols. 157–158. "Quidam insani magistri et homines pestiferi Wiklefitici odinis et schismatic—post discursum peregrinarum nobis terrarium et districtuum, etiam in terris nostris Bohemiae et Moraviae aulus principum, collegia et cathedras sacerdotum, scholas studentium, promiscui sexus popularem tumultum fidelium—tuba ipsorum ululans et pestifera—replevit."

117. Šmahel, *Život a dílo Jeronýma*, p. 44.

Prior to those events, Jerome acted not only to secure a new approach to thinking in the Czech lands but also to ensure Czech ascendancy. "When he [Jerome] realized how things were in the university, Jerome, along with Master Jan Hus, and other noble men of Bohemia ... desiring to take a stand, approached the king of Bohemia and told him how things were. He argued that these things were a poor example, and were contributing to the degradation of the Czech language. He also persuaded Master Jan Hus that in his Czech sermons he should inform the people of Bohemia that they should no longer tolerate being treated in this manner by the Germans."[118] At the Vienna trial, we learn from several witnesses— Johannes Schwab von Butzbach, Konrad Kreutzer of Nürnberg, Johannes Vohburg, Nicholas Czungl (d. 1452), and Johannes Tesser—that it was Jerome who was the instigator and the distinguished provocateur of these affairs.[119] Indeed, Schwab said that on account of Jerome's agitation, much discord and division arose at Prague among the nations.[120] The reference has both the 1409 *Quodlibet* and the Decree of Kutná Hora in mind. Along with professional jealousy and wounded national pride, philosophy played a central role in the Vienna trial.[121]

Before the court case at Vienna unfolded, Jerome's persistent intervention and lobbying were so aggressive that he even created annoyance at the royal court. At length, the king became quite agitated when pressed by Jerome and Hus at Kutná Hora and in barely concealed rage addressed Hus: "You are always disturbing me, you and your companion Jerome; and if those whose duty it is do not see to it, I myself will see that you suffer in the fire."[122] Despite a variety of objections, the king ultimately seemed predisposed to the ideas later codified in the decree. At one stage, when hesitation on the part of Václav became evident and the king appeared to be on the verge of buckling under a sustained and powerful German lobby, Hus and Jerome sprang into renewed action. We catch glimpses of them riding in a wagon back and forth from the royal court. Their efforts eventually

---

118. Hardt, vol. 4, col. 758.

119. Klicman, pp. 16, 18, 20, 23–24, 25.

120. Klicman, p. 16.

121. Klicman, "Der Wiener Process," pp. 446–447.

122. *Relatio*, on the testimony of the Czech lawyer and diplomat Jan Náz at the Hus trial, p. 80; and Hardt, vol. 4, p. 312.

prevailed, and the Decree of Kutná Hora was issued on January 18, 1409.[123] The royal declaration reversed the controlling governance of the university by taking the three votes currently possessed by the Germans and assigning them to the Czechs, while reassigning the single Czech vote to the Germans. The proclamation declared that since the Czechs possessed the inheritance rights of the kingdom and the Germans had no citizenship rights, the change was necessary. Majority voting rights applied to all councils, courts, examinations, and official acts of the university. Overnight, control of the university in Prague was radically altered. Hus was pleased with the outcome at Kutná Hora and ostensibly announced his pleasure from the pulpit of Bethlehem Chapel: "Children, let us praise almighty God that we have expelled the Germans and achieved our goal. We are the victors."[124] The lawyer and reformer Jan Jesenice defended the king's decision with respect to the Decree of Kutná Hora.[125] There is some evidence that the king, having signed the decree, was then dilatory in implementing the new policy. By late April, Jerome and Hus were again in contact with Václav, who was spending time at the castles of Žebrák and Točník.[126] Immediately after this, the king forced the handing over of the university's insignia. This occurred during a formal meeting and was achieved by the king's representative Mikuláš Bohatý of Lobkovice, together with Old Town councilors and armed men. By May, the German dean Albrecht Varentrapp and rector Henning of Baltenhagen were unceremoniously deposed, the university insignia forcibly removed from their hands by royal police. The king's decree was read, and the deposed Germans were replaced by Czechs. Master Zdeněk of Labouň was appointed chancellor, and Master Šimon Tišnov was made dean of arts.[127] The latter was an advocate of Wyclifite thinking. In the autumn of that year, Hus was elected rector of the university, and we know he preached at Bethlehem Chapel,

---

123. *Documenta*, pp. 347–348. See also František Šmahel and Martin Nodl, "Kutnohorský dekret po 600 letech," *Český časopis historický* 107 (2009): 1–45; and a critical edition of the decree edited by Gustav Friedrich, "Dekret Kutnohorský. Poměr jeho rukopisných textů," *Český časopis historický* 15 (1909): I–XII.

124. *Documenta*, p. 183.

125. In his *Defensio mandatum*, in *Documenta*, pp. 355–363. See Jiří Kejř, *Husitský pravník: M. Jan z Jesenice* (Prague: ČSAV, 1965), pp. 15–19.

126. Klicman, p. 20.

127. Novotný and Kybal, *M. Jan Hus*, vol. 1, pt. 1, pp. 338–345.

referring to the Decree of Kutná Hora and calling it a great victory, urging his hearers to be thankful to Mikuláš for the triumph.[128] The flush of victory orchestrated by Hus and Jerome may have made them oblivious to the ominous dark clouds gathering above Prague. The Decree of Kutná Hora yielded serious consequences. Between six hundred and eight hundred students and faculty left Prague as a result of the decree.[129] Václav appointed both Hus and Jerome to fill vacancies at Charles College created by the exodus. The order has not survived.[130] There can be little doubt that Jerome played a central and crucial role in the events culminating in the proclamation of the historic decree signed at Kutná Hora. Indeed, it is fundamentally correct to argue that "it was during his stay in Prague from 1408 to 1409, in which the decisive attack was carried forward against the three nations, where he [Jerome] seems to hold the reins in his hand."[131] It is furthermore possible to argue that Jerome's advocacy of Czech interests and his defense of the royal house were instrumental in securing at least passive support for the Czech masters and by extension the reform efforts.

Mikuláš Bohatý of Lobkovice was a royal councilor and manager of the royal mines at Kutná Hora. He was one of the main players in the development of events resulting in the promulgation of the Decree of Kutná Hora. The other main influences were Hus, Jesenice, and Jerome. These men constituted the main force behind the formation of a new intellectual climate at the university.[132] By 1409, Jerome must be reckoned among the vanguard of voices and influences within the movement for religious reform in the Bohemian province. The events of January 1409 left no doubt about the nature and significance of his role, and from this stage on through 1416, Jerome is numbered with Wyclif and Hus as the preeminent influences in the religious reforms in Bohemia.

---

128. His inaugural speech has been published in Havránek, *Výbor z českÿ literatury husitské doby*, vol. 1, pp. 105–110.

129. František Šmahel, "The Kuttenberg Decree and the Withdrawal of the German Students from Prague in 1409: A Discussion," *History of Universities* 4 (1984): 153–166.

130. I rely entirely on Šmahel, who cites Archives of Charles University, A 17 I, 1, p. 732, which I have not seen. Also pertinent is Šmahel, *Život a dílo Jeronýma*, p. 45.

131. Seibt, *Hussitica*, p. 79.

132. Some scholars have attributed the Decree of Kutná Hora to the influence of Mikuláš; F. M. Bartoš, "Kdo vymohl Čechům dekret kutnohorský," *Jihočeský sborník historický* 18 (1939): 66–68. Others take the position that Jerome, Hus, and Jesenice constituted the main force behind the formation; Kejř, *Husitský pravník*, p. 23.

After 1409

Following these momentous events in Prague and triumphs in the kingdom of Bohemia, Jerome resumed his frenetic travels throughout Europe. He made a deep impression in Hungary when he appeared practically without notice at the royal court in Buda and proceeded to deliver an address before King Sigismund and an assembly of secular and ecclesiastical dignitaries. As we have already seen, he provoked such wrath and indignation that he was soon ensconced in an episcopal penitentiary. After gaining his freedom, he journeyed to Vienna, where he became the defendant in a heresy trial. The story of Jerome's time in Hungary and Austria is taken up in some detail in chapter 4. Meanwhile, ongoing political and cultural contacts between the governments and universities in Bohemia and Poland, edged between more academic disputations and theological controversies, resulted in Jerome making his way into eastern Europe and beyond in the years after 1409. He continued those journeys as late as Christmas, 1414.

On June 21, 1410, Hus was elected leader for the next university *Quodlibet*, scheduled for January 1411.[133] At the *Quodlibet*, Hus arranged questions for sixty-seven masters, but the fallout from the Kutná Hora policy caused twelve of these to decline participation.[134] Ongoing theological disputes, national conflict, and suspicion of heresy continued to roil affairs in Prague and within the university. Hus attempted to lighten the atmosphere by introducing the participants by associating each with one of the classical thinkers, likely drawn from Walter Burley's *De vita et moribus philosophorum*.[135] Matěj Knín did not attend Hus's *Quodlibet*, and we must assume that he was by that time deceased. Jerome was number thirty-nine on the list of fifty-five university masters participating in the event, and Hus aligned him with the philosopher Chrysippus (ca. 279 BCE–ca. 206 BCE), a Greek Stoic who excelled in logic and was noted for bracing intellectual audacity. The aligning of Jerome with Chrysippus seems rather apropos. The arguments in Hus's *Quodlibet* teem with quotations and allusions to the classical period, especially from Seneca, Aristotle, Boethius, Averroës,

---

133. Bohumil Ryba, ed., *Magistri Iohannis Hus Quodlibet* (Turnhout: Brepols, 2006), p. 2.

134. Kejř, *Kvodlibetní disputace*, pp. 90–94, 137–148.

135. Hermann Knust, ed., *Gualteri Burlaei Liber de vita et moribus philosophorum* (Tübingen: Gedruckt für den litterarischen verein in Stuttgart, 1886). It is now thought by some to have been written by an anonymous author.

Avicenna, and Cato. It is regrettable that Jerome's *quaestio*, identified as *Utrum omne dependens sit ens per participacionem prime cause*, is not extant, but we know that Hus took a favorable view of it, and we know this title from Hus's handbook for the *Quodlibet*.[136] In addition to the main *quaestio*, Hus assigned a secondary "problem" to each participant and jokingly underscored a weakness of each of the masters. It is interesting that women were nominated as Jerome's weakness, and Hus made the somewhat risqué comment that the closed bud of a lily can burst into bloom more quickly in the hands of a virgin.[137] We are not informed how Jerome received this introduction. It would be quite misleading to make more of this than an academic joke, and that assumption can be sustained inasmuch as no opponent of Jerome's thereafter, especially during the legal proceedings at Constance, ever suggested that he had been inappropriately involved with women. It is doubtful that his enemies would have allowed such an opportunity to slip away had there been the slightest evidence to excoriate their opponent further.

Not long after the *Quodlibet*, in the late winter or early spring of 1411, Hus wrote a letter to King Władysław Jagiełło of Poland, congratulating him on the victory at Grünwald over the Teutonic Knights, which had been achieved on July 15, 1410. Hus urged the king to take steps to come to terms of peace with Sigismund.[138] This overture to Władysław did not elicit any reply, but there is some possibility that Jerome later went to the Polish kingdom as an ambassador on behalf of the Czech king. In the meantime, developments on a European scale brought Jerome, Hus, and their colleagues into renewed conflict with the church. Pope John XXIII announced a crusade against King Ladislas of Naples on September 9, 1411.[139] The initiative was actively resisted by Hus in Prague, and there was also opposition in Vienna. The dean of Passau, Wenceslas Tiem, and a papal notary, Johannes Pace (or representative of the Curia Pax de Fantuciis), had been commissioned with implementing the fund-raising bull in Vienna. They

136. Ryba, *Magistri Iohannis Hus Quodlibet*, pp. 201–204; and Kejř, *Kvodlibetní disputace*, pp. 143–144.

137. "Probleuma: Quare, ut ait Solinus in Libro rerum, lilium clausum nondumque apertum in manu virginis cicius aperitur?" Ryba, *Magistri Iohannis Hus Quodlibet*, p. 203.

138. Václav Novotný, ed., *M. Jana Husi Korespondence a dokumenty* (Prague: Nákladem komise pro vydávání pramenů náboženského hnutí českého, 1920), pp. 86–87.

139. *HM*, vol. 1, pp. 212–213.

accused the university of taking a caviler attitude toward church affairs and being sympathetic to heretics. It should be noted that Tiem and Pace included in their complaint that Hus came to Vienna, spread heretical views, and had been welcomed by the university. There is no record that Hus was ever in Vienna. This is doubtless an uninformed reference to Jerome, who had been there the previous year and had been the subject of a heresy procedure. The sale of indulgences in Austrian territory had been strictly forbidden by Duke Albrecht on the recommendation of the university in Vienna. Tiem and Pace complained about the negligence of Vienna University in implementing the sale of indulgences. Their efforts met with great frustration, and the matter was not resolved until the Council of Constance convened.[140] The precise role played by Jerome in the indulgences controversy at Vienna is indefinite, but it cannot be doubted that he contributed to the resistance encountered by Tiem and Pace. While it is always challenging to try to determine where Jerome was at many times during these years and what exactly he was up to, by late 1411, he was clearly back in Prague, and we find him involved as a participant in the *Quodlibet* of Michael of Malenice (also known as Čížek). Thirty-seven masters participated, including Jerome.[141]

On June 11, 1412, Hus wrote a second letter to Władysław of Poland, expressing joy at the agreement reached with Sigismund. This is a reference to the Peace of Thorn, signed in February 1411, which ended the conflict between the Knights of the Teutonic Order and Poland-Lithuania. Sigismund had supported the knights against the Poles. Hus urged Władysław to deal with simony (which Hus called a heresy) in his realm, along with other irregularities of the priesthood.[142] This letter to the Polish king may be understood within the context of Hus's reform efforts and against the papal initiatives that added fuel to the fires around issues such as indulgences and relics. Despite active attempts of the theological faculty to prevent the event, Hus conducted a university debate condemning the crusade bull of Pope John XXIII on June 17, after posting public notices

---

140. Karl Joseph von Hefele and Henri Leclercq, *Histoire des Conciles d'apres les Documents Originaux*, 10 vols. (Paris: Letouzey and Ané, 1907–1952), vol. 7, pt. 1, pp. 171–172.

141. František Šmahel, "Kvodlibetní diskuse ke kvestii principalis mistra Michala z Malenic roku 1412," *Acta universitatis carolinae, Historia universitatis carolinae Pragensis* 21, no. 1 (1981): 27–52; and Kejř, *Kvodlibetní disputace*, pp. 94–97.

142. Novotný, *M. Jana Husi Korespondence a dokumenty*, pp. 122–123.

challenging his detractors.[143] Challenges notwithstanding, the university disputation took place as scheduled and announced, with Hus opening the discussion by posing a direct query: "According to the law of Christ is it lawful and expedient to the honor of God and the salvation of people and the well-being of the realm, for the faithful to approve the papal bulls concerning raising the cross against King Ladislas."[144] The redoubtable Jerome took the podium to conclude the debate. Once again, it is of some regret that the speech delivered by Jerome is no longer extant. One can only imagine the rhetoric and the reckless abandon with which Jerome probably assailed the cult of relics and the trafficking in indulgences. We have sufficient evidence elsewhere for his attitude and activities around these issues to suspect on firm ground that Jerome would have launched a frontal assault on these religious practices. We do have a summary note about the reaction to his speech, which has been recorded in one of the old Czech chronicles.[145] That account succinctly reveals that at the height of the debate, Jerome nearly succeeded in causing a public riot and in encouraging a student-driven demonstration at the town hall, which was only barely averted. The matter is taken up in context in chapter 5.

By 1413, Hus was in exile in southern Bohemia, and Jerome could be found in Poland. He appeared in Kraków at the court of Władysław in March and thereafter was known to have visited the court of the Lithuanian duke Witołd in White Russia. We are told that he was distinguished on account of his long beard. Notwithstanding the beard, he was favorably received by the king. Regrettably, there are no known records of what was said, but the next day, Jerome inexplicably appeared clean-shaven, wearing a red gown with a gray fur-lined hood. A letter dated April 2, written by Albert (Wojciech Jastrzębiec), bishop of Kraków, to Václav Králík of Bařenice, the titular patriarch of Antioch and chancellor of the bishopric of Olomouc, provides some information about Jerome's activities.[146] According to the letter, Jerome, who was incorrectly identified as being

---

143. "Utrum secundum legem Jesu Christi licet et expedit pro honore dei et salute populi ac pro commodo regni bullas pape de ereccione crucis contra Ladislaum regem Apulie et suos complices Christi fidelibus approbare," in *HM*, vol. 1 (1558), fols. 174r–189r.

144. Text of Hus's speech in *HM*, vol. 1, pp. 174–189.

145. František Šimek, ed., *Staré letopisy české z vratislavského rukopisu novočeským pravopisem* (Prague: Historické spolku a společnosti Husova Musea, 1937), p. 10.

146. *Documenta*, pp. 506–507. See appendix 4 herein.

from Prachatice, remained only a few days in the realm but during that time "created more disturbance among the clergy and the people than had ever occurred within that diocese within human memory." Bishop Wojciech interviewed Jerome and questioned him about the condemned Wyclifite articles. The bishop reported that in the course of discussing these matters, Jerome denounced them as errors and professed an ortho-dox view of the faith on every point. The bishop acknowledged that while Jerome had come to Poland at the invitation of King Władysław and Duke Witołd, it was quite apparent that the king was ignorant of who and what Jerome really was. Apparently, his public preaching included a searing cri-tique of the abuses of priests, and he used the opportunity to disseminate the aims and emphases of the Czech reform movement. He took part in several disputations wherein canon lawyers, theologians, the papal nuncio Bernard (bishop of Castello), and Mikołaj Trąba (metropolitan/archbishop of Gniezno) were present. Trąba also appeared at Constance during the Council and might be considered another adversary Jerome acquired well before he arrived in Constance. According to Bishop Wojciech's letter, Jerome was sent back to Bohemia because the Polish land was too arid for the seeds planted to flourish and bear fruit, and the Poles were so simple-minded that they were unable to grasp the teachings of such a great phi-losopher, and even less capable were the Lithuanians and Russians. All of this represented the views of the bishop of Kraków, and from his letter we learn a fair amount about Jerome's stay in Poland.

Theologians at Vienna were doubtless aware of this letter and on this basis made allegations that Jerome had shamelessly attempted to seduce King Władysław and Duke Witołd into heresy. It is most likely that the information about the letter was facilitated by Jan Náz (former Prague uni-versity professor of law and vicar of the bishop of Olomouc), who appeared on April 24 to urge assistance in combating heresy. Doubtless, Náz had Wyclif, Hus, and Jerome in mind as the promoters of theological devi-ance.[147] During the Council of Constance, the Polish clergy alleged that Jerome had secretly escaped from Kraków (in much the same manner as he had from Paris, Cologne, Heidelberg, Vienna, and even Constance itself initially), but the charge is not based on any known fact.[148]

---

147. Šmahel, *Život a dílo Jeronýma*, p. 62.

148. Mansi, vol. 27, col. 846; but see Paweł Kras, *Husyci w piętnastowiecznej Polsce* (Lublin: Towarzystwo naukowe katolickiego uniwersytetu Lubelskiego, 1998), pp. 40–44.

Jerome went also to White Russia and allegedly seemed to support the "Ruthenian schismatics" or the Orthodox church.[149] At Constance, Jerome was accused of declaring that the schismatic Ruthenians were good Christians.[150] Polish theologians were concerned with the *rebaptisatio Ruthenorum*. One of the questions in the Russian church was whether Orthodox converts to the Roman church had to be rebaptized. Jerome took the view that it was unnecessary. This may have pleased Duke Witołd more than the bishop of Vilnius, Mikołaj Gorzkowski.[151] Nevertheless, in April, Jerome arrived in Vitebsk with Witołd.[152] Jerome's activities attracted attention in Austria, Poland, Moravia, and Bohemia.[153] These peregrinations in eastern Europe and Russia have been called "one of the mysterious chapters of his life."[154] It is impossible to say whether Jerome undertook this trip on his own initiative, whether he was traveling as an ambassador of the Hussite movement, or whether he was representing the Czech government. Compounding the mystery is the fact that there are no chronicles or other documents mentioning Jerome in Lithuania, and thus the only surviving witness to this chapter in his life are the accusations at Constance. The Polish visit by Jerome can be considered one of the truly obscure chapters of his peripatetic life. It is of some note that writings by Hus, Jakoubek, Jerome, and other leaders of the Hussite movement were later found in the personal libraries of Polish professors, thereby lending direct information about Czech reform ideas to the Polish context.[155]

The connections between Bohemia, Vienna, and Poland are also underscored in correspondence between Hus and the Carthusian Johannes Sywort, or Siwart. Originally from Transylvania, Siwart was a Carthusian

---

149. Hardt, vol. 4, cols. 677–680.

150. Hardt, vol. 4, col. 679.

151. Hardt, vol. 4, col. 643. A modern rumor alleges that Jerome actually received baptism in the Eastern rite and that the baptismal certificate has been discovered at Riga, Latvia, and is now in the possession of the Czech Orthodox Church. No concrete evidence has appeared, and I have been unable to confirm the rumor. Liturgical historian David Holeton does not believe baptismal registers were kept in the early fifteenth century.

152. The chronology has challenges, as noted in Šmahel, *Život a dílo Jeronýma*, pp. 65–66.

153. Hardt, vol. 4, col. 680.

154. Šmahel, *Život a dílo Jeronýma*, p. 63; and Šmahel, *Jeroným Pražský*, pp. 137–139.

155. Paweł Kras, "Polish-Czech Relations in the Hussite Period—Religious Aspects," *BRRP* 4 (2002): 192.

member of the theology faculty at Vienna. He took a bachelor's degree from Vienna in 1408 and from 1412 had served as the dean of the faculty of theology.[156] The contact between Hus and Siwart began when the latter wrote a letter to the bishop of Zagreb, complaining that some Croatian students openly adhered to the teachings of Wyclif in Vienna, were attacking the priesthood, and were actively proselytizing in an attempt to win converts to their cause.[157] Siwart likewise wrote another letter to the Zagreb chapter, alleging that Czech students were championing Wyclifite ideas in Vienna and noting especially Jerome's activities in Kraków. He warned the chapter that Wyclifite heresy was spreading from Bohemia into neighboring countries. He argued that the main cause of this dissemination was Jerome. He called for the elimination of Wyclifism in Zagreb, Austria, and Prague, asserting that while Hussite preachers appeared to have honey in their mouths, their hearts were filled with deadly venom.[158] These letters came to Hus's attention, and on July 1, 1413, he replied, denouncing Siwart and defending Jerome in a very forceful and indignant missive.[159] One week later, the university in Prague, via its chancellor Michael Čížek of Malenice, sent a letter to the rector and the professors at Vienna, protesting accusations against Czech scholars and specifically those directed at Jerome. Prague asked Vienna to stop Siwart; otherwise, they would ask Duke Albrecht to intervene.[160] As though in an effort to defend their actions and to provide proof that heresy was a clear and present danger in Austria, Vienna replied in a long letter, mentioning that Dominic of Zagreb (Agram), who had formerly studied at Prague, was later found guilty of adhering to sixteen points of Wyclifite heresy in Vienna but when confronted and pressured recanted his heretical allegiances.[161] The matter seems to have fizzled out at that stage, but it reveals another perspective on the role Jerome seems to have played in the anxieties surrounding

---

156. See Katherine Walsh, "Magister Johannes [Siwart] de Septemcastris an der Universität Wien. Versuch eines Gelehrtenprofils aus der Hussitenzeit," in *Ex ipsis rerum Documentis. Beiträge zue Mediävistik: Festschrift für Harald Zimmermann zum 65. Geburtstag*, ed. Klaus Herbers, Hans-Henning Kortüm, and Carol Servatius (Sigmaringen: Thorbecke, 1991), pp. 557–569.

157. The activity was allegedly centered in (Agram) Zagreb. ÖNB, MS 4299, fol. 230.

158. ÖNB, MS 4299, fols. 230b–231a.

159. Novotný, *M. Jana Husi Korespondence a dokumenty*, pp. 173–175.

160. *Documenta*, pp. 63–64.

161. ÖNB, MS 4299, fols. 232b–235b.

heresy in central and eastern Europe. It is of some note that on May 24, the University of Kraków requested a copy of the trial proceedings against Jerome from Vienna.[162] Whether he remained for an extended period of time in Poland or Russia or whether he made more than one trip to that area cannot be determined with any degree of certainty. However, there are Polish records that indicate that on December 21, 1414, Jerome appeared in Poland with letters from King Václav and Lord Lacek of Kravář. It is possible to understand this evidence as providing a vital clue to support the assumption that Jerome was, from time to time, employed as an unofficial diplomat of the Czech government. This may also help to explain his apparent immunity in Poland and Lithuania from heresy prosecution.[163]

Officials at Vienna wrote letters to Prague University and to the law faculty and also to city councilors of the Old Town. In this correspondence, Chancellor Dietrich Rudolf of Hammelburg included a copy of the summons for Jerome to appear before the officials of the Passau diocese. These documents were sent to Prague via university representative Antonín of Silesia. On April 27, Rudolf sent a separate missive to Kraków University, which included a note about the anathema of Jerome, who was described as the apostle of Hus.[164] All of this activity, from England to Vienna, from Paris to Lithuania, must be regarded as the stage on which the life of Jerome was played out. In distinction to Hus, Jerome was a great traveler, and his life was lived in near-constant activity across Europe.[165] It seems likely that Jerome of Prague was "driven by curiosity and *Wanderlust.*"[166] He was the quintessential *scholarus vagans* (wandering scholar), who as much as anyone promoted Wyclifite thought across the European continent. His detractors considered his travels ruinous to the faith, and it is from these frequent travels and regular controversies that he earned the moniker "athlete of Antichrist." Jerome was an intellectual renegade and a fugitive who challenged the establishments of his world. In some ways, it is the heresy trial in Vienna that constitutes the most important event of those years, and that topic is taken up in some detail in the next chapter.

---

162. Shank, *Unless You Believe*, p. 178.

163. Šmahel, *Život a dílo Jeronýma*, p. 70.

164. *Acta universitatis et rectoratus 1382–1422*, fol. 53r. Cited in Šmahel, *Život a dílo Jeronýma*, p. 62, on whom I rely.

165. Šmahel, *Život a dílo Jeronýma*, p. 15.

166. Bernard, "Jerome of Prague, Austria and the Hussites," p. 5.

4

Heresy and Intrigue in Vienna

IT IS QUITE possible that Jerome of Prague engaged in what might be described as diplomatic trips abroad to various destinations on behalf of developments occurring in Bohemia. Be that as it may, by 1410, he arrived in Hungary. Jerome's intemperate outbursts in mainly academic settings elsewhere in Europe had often provoked the wrath of local officials and incurred hostility among his detractors. None of this seemed to make much of an impact of Jerome, as he simply left town when the noose began to tighten around him. Things were less smooth in Hungary, and events there are prescient of how Jerome's career would proceed in the years ahead. One or more letters from Archbishop Zbyněk preceded Jerome to Hungary. These missives denounced Jerome as a dangerous heretic. The language is careless and derogatory. This set the stage for Jerome's stormy reception. In Buda (the German name for Buda is Ofen), Jerome spoke in the presence of Sigismund, and his speech might arguably be characterized as full of "indiscreet zeal."[1] His appearance on Maundy Thursday was both sudden and unannounced.

Preaching and Prison in Buda

On March 20, 1410, he addressed King Sigismund along with many Hungarian bishops and prelates in the royal chapel in the castle at Buda.[2]

---

1. R. R. Betts, *Essays in Czech History* (London: Athlone, 1969), p. 208. The essay first appeared as "Jerome of Prague," *University of Birmingham Historical Journal* 1 (1947): 51–91; and it also appeared in a Czech version as "Jeroným Pražský," *Československý časopis historický* 5 (1957): 199–226.

2. Hardt, vol. 4, col. 673.

The speech has been described by some sources as a sermon. This is precisely how it was characterized shortly thereafter in the testimony of Berthold Puchhauser of Regensburg during legal proceedings in Vienna.[3] Puchhauser was a professor of theology whom Jerome had met possibly ten years earlier in Oxford. In contrast to Puchhauser, Jerome simply referred to his speech as a *collacio* (address).[4] The distinction is crucial, because Jerome would have needed official approbation in order to preach, and the fact that he was not a priest may have made such a request difficult and any resulting permission irregular. However the address should be understood, Jerome did nominate a text on which his remarks were predicated. Jerome launched into an impassioned speech based on John 13:15, which has Christ telling his disciples, "I have given you an example to do to others as I have done to you." Dressed in lay clothes and wearing a long beard, Jerome made an immediate and lasting impression on the audience. He argued that inasmuch as the state of irregularity and immorality among the priesthood was so great, the political powers should intervene and effect reform and restoration in order to bring the church back to a state of virtue. The address resonated with themes articulated by John Wyclif, which appeared to favor the intervention of royal power in matters of church reform. This may have appealed to Sigismund's ego, but the political implications of the idea were rather thorny.

The reaction to the address was probably not what Jerome anticipated. The bearded speaker was alleged to have uttered many suspect remarks in the presence of the king and before the large gathering of priests, bishops, and prelates. These controversial remarks included apparent endorsement of the errors of Wyclif, which amounted to "numerous scandalous and erroneous matters." It did not end there. Jerome went on to enumerate "heresies about the sacrament of the altar." Wyclif had been particularly outspoken on the sacrament. This was considered acutely inappropriate and offensive. Wyclif was expelled from Oxford in 1381 and lost the support of his principal patron, John of Gaunt, not when he spoke negatively of the pope but when he commented critically about the Eucharist. Even during the lifetime of Jerome, the Eucharist became a flashpoint of controversy in Bohemia. Jerome's speech before Sigismund also contained offensive comments about the priesthood, which were thought to inspire

---

3. Klicman, p. 21.

4. Hearing at Constance, May 23, 1416. Hardt, vol. 4, col. 753.

sedition and outrage against the church.[5] Sigismund was unimpressed with comments about clerical corruption and church privilege. The king may have been amenable to the idea that, as king, he had authority over the church, but on account of the hostility of the bishops toward Jerome, he would have been in a politically delicate and difficult situation. There is no evidence to refute the general conclusion that Jerome's comments were received with great offense as being scandalous and heretical. The authorities felt compelled to have the guest speaker arrested, and this was accomplished on the spot at the order of Sigismund. At the conclusion of his address, Jerome was promptly arrested and imprisoned by Jan of Kanisza, bishop of Esztergom.[6] We have Jerome's own brief account of his detention, and we learn that he was locked up for fourteen days but despite the confinement was treated well.[7] There is no evidence that a trial of any sort took place at Buda or that there was any further censure of Jerome after he was handed over to the bishop of Esztergom. More puzzling is that we possess no information on the circumstances that resulted in Jerome gaining his freedom. Evidently, Archbishop Zbyněk sent a letter to Sigismund that caused the king to issue an order that the prisoner be released into the custody of a certain unnamed knight with orders to escort Jerome to Prague.[8] Jerome later testified that once this exchange took place, he was remanded into the care of a "certain baron," who then released him without restriction.[9] Half a dozen years later, at Constance, Jerome admitted that he had published a *querela* (complaint) against Archbishop Zbyněk sometime prior to his journey to Buda. According to Jerome, this was the basis for the prejudice evident against him at the Hungarian royal court. In other words, it was not so much the substance of his remarks that engendered his censure and detention as it was the trumped-up mischief caused by the embarrassed archbishop, who felt obliged to defend the dignity of his cloth. If Jerome is to be believed, this is why Zbyněk dispatched

---

5. All of these points appear in the articles of accusation against Jerome at Constance on April 27, 1416. Hardt, vol. 4, col. 673.

6. We learn these details from the evidence submitted by Johannes Stückler during the Vienna process. Klicman, p. 30.

7. Hardt, vol. 4, col. 636.

8. Once again, our knowledge on his point comes from the evidence of Johannes Stückler at Vienna. Klicman, p. 30.

9. Hardt, vol. 4, col. 636.

a letter to Hungary, and it was on account of this hostile missive that he was arrested.[10] Obvious questions arise around the motives for Zbyněk to send the first letter, only later to request that the prisoner be released. It is possible that jurisdictional authority claims were at issue and that the see of Prague did not wish for Jerome to be prosecuted and punished outside the archdiocese of Prague. It is also possible that pressure from the archbishop's opponents in Prague was sufficient to cause the prelate to make the request. It may have simply been a political move at the behest of King Václav, who at the same time was beginning to become embroiled in acrimonious disagreements with the archbishop of Prague. There is no conclusive evidence on which to formulate a definitive explanation. There is much that remains unaccounted for and inexplicable about Jerome's activities in Buda. The only thing we can be certain of is that not long after he was released, he suddenly appeared in Vienna, and what happened next was clear indication that a Hungarian jail had done nothing to dent Jerome's spirit or willingness to engage in disputation.

Controversy and Court in Vienna

If the conditions of his release included a return to Prague, this was never fulfilled. There is no evidence that he went to Prague after release from the Esztergom episcopal prison. Instead, and on his own volition, by August, he appeared in Vienna.[11] Ostensibly, Jerome voluntarily went to Vienna to face accusations. His announcement was blunt: "I have come twenty-four miles to the venerable doctors and masters of this kindly university of Vienna because I heard that I was defamed amongst them."[12] We cannot know how this information came to his attention. Jerome refers to the fact that in that same month (August), Peter Pulka, his "venerable teacher" Nicholas Dinkelsbühl, Lambert Sluter of Gelderen (d. 1419), and others formally charged him with heresy. Given previous, though largely unsuccessful, efforts to prosecute heretics at Vienna, it is notable that the faculty of arts offered to financially contribute to the prosecution of Jerome.[13]

---

10. Hardt, vol. 4, cols. 640–641.

11. This corrects a dating error that occurred in later articles of accusation. Hardt, vol. 4, col. 638.

12. Klicman, pp. 1, 4.

13. Michael H. Shank, *Unless You Believe, You Shall Not Understand: Logic, University, and Society in Late Medieval Vienna* (Princeton, N.J.: Princeton University Press, 1988), p. 190.

There must have been some satisfaction that the suspect had appeared in Vienna on his own volition.

The University of Vienna had been founded on March 12, 1365. Prague academics went to Austria in 1411 to teach in the relatively newly founded university. These included Pavel of Prague and an unnamed master of arts.[14] The *via moderna* came to Vienna even earlier from Paris by means of Heinrich Langenstein (d. 1397), Heinrich Totting of Oyta, a German scholar from Oldenburg, and others.[15] Oyta had been at Prague. From Vienna, a doctor of theology named Lambert Sluter of Gelderen obtained information about Jerome's speech delivered at Buda from one of his students and also from an anonymous Hungarian prelate. This same Lambert was present on August 29, 1410, when Jerome was investigated for heresy at Vienna.[16] The most dramatic aspect of Jerome's stay in Vienna was a formal trial based on allegations of heresy.

The trial protocol is extant in Rome. The codex of 305 folios contains a number of sources relating to later Hussite history and to fifteenth-century councils. The Vatican manuscript consists of a detailed notarial protocol, with the articles of prosecution, witness depositions, court rulings, and so on. The Latin is deplorable, with excessively long sentences, grammatical peculiarities, and confused narratives, and in some places the text degenerates almost to the point of incomprehensibility.[17] The existence of the trial protocols has elicited different comments from scholars acquainted with its content. According to one opinion, the edited records provide "great value for the chronology of Jerome's life and for his international reputation." The protocols are also a fine "example of an examination for heresy in a court which was a curious mixture of an archbishop's consistory and a university court of discipline."[18] Others say the data are not reliable, are

---

The reference to Dinkelsbühl is in Friedrich Firnhaber, "Petrus de Pulka, Abgesabdter der Wiener universität am Concilium zu Constanz," *Archiv für österreichische Geschichte* 15 (1856): 20.

14. Elemér Mályusz, *Kaiser Sigismund in Ungarn 1387–1437*, trans. Anikó Sznodits (Budapest: Akadémiai Kiadó, 1990), pp. 293–294.

15. Shank, *Unless You Believe*.

16. Šmahel, *Život a dílo Jeronýma*, p. 47.

17. Rome, Vatican Library, MS Ottobonianus 348, fols. 260–280. The text has been edited and published as Klicman. See p. x for comments and observations about the nature of the manuscript source.

18. Betts, *Essays in Czech History*, p. 211.

contradictory, and are also biased against Jerome.[19] It does constitute our fullest and therefore most significant source for the events in Vienna.

Toward the end of the month (either August 29 or 31) in the town palace of the canon and official of the Passau consistory, Andreas Grillenberg (d. 1418 or 1419; also known as Pottenstein, Grippenperk, or Grippenberg), the trial began. It was well attended. Among those present were the professors of theology Nicholas Dinkelsbühl, Peter Pulka, Lambert Sluter of Gelderen, and Michael Suchenschatz (d. 1424), along with the canon lawyers Heinrich von Kitzbühl (d. 1437), Kaspar von Maiselstein (d. 1432), and Johannes Sindram of Heiligenstadt (d. 1425).[20] The trial assessors consisted of four professors, four canon lawyers, and "other masters, bachelors, and scholars of the university." The legal proceeding did not mince words and described Jerome as one "defamed in regard to particular articles which are contrary to the Catholic faith and others which have been condemned in holy general councils and to which John Wyclif had adhered." This was to be from the outset another example of Wyclif on trial. Johannes Gwerleich, a bachelor of laws, was appointed *procurator fiscalis* and assumed the role of prosecutor. Jerome was given the opportunity to have legal representation, but he declined to have a lawyer and took an oath on the gospels to tell the truth.[21] Gwerleich submitted a recommendation for the excommunication of Jerome. Grillenberg preferred a new citation wherein Jerome was required to answer the charge of suspicion of heresy.[22] As prosecutor, Gwerleich called upon witnesses with knowledge about Jerome and broadened the scope of his prosecutorial inquiry to include the defendant's activities in Oxford, Paris, Heidelberg, and Prague. There is scant evidence that the theology faculty took much interest in the hearings.[23]

The opportunity for Jerome to have an attorney in a heresy trial is unusual but not unprecedented. This question is a vexed one in the history of law, medieval legal procedure, and heresy trials. Defense lawyers

---

19. Šmahel, *Život a dílo Jeronýma*, p. 53; and František Šmahel, "Leben und Werk des Magisters Hieronymus von Prag," *Historica* 13 (1966): 82–83.

20. Klicman, p. v.

21. Klicman, pp. vi, 2.

22. Klicman, p. 40.

23. Paul Uiblein, ed., *Die Akten der Theologischen Fakultät der Universität Wien, 1396–1508* (Vienna: Verbrand der Wissenschaftlichen Gesellschaften Österreichs, 1978), vol. 1, pp. 17–20.

were almost always excluded from cases that involved heretics. A technical but important distinction was drawn between suspected heretics and convicted or condemned heretics, including those excommunicated for heresy. This is a significant difference from criminal procedures in modern Western societies. We have medieval legal commentary that makes clear that lawyers should not assist heretics at all, under the threat and penalty of *infamia* and being disbarred from the legal profession.[24] There is also a certain measure of allowance, developed later, reflected in a decretal ruling that lawyers were not ordinarily permitted to take part in heresy proceedings.[25] That decretal appeared to imply that there were legal exceptions to the rule. This may have created a distinction that became incorporated into law. Accused heretics might have legal counsel, but convicted heretics were not allowed the advice of counsel in court. Lawyers who may have been amenable to representing heretics were warned in a papal decretal: "we strictly forbid lawyers and notaries from assisting in any way by counsel or support any heretic or those who adhere to them or believe in them or giving them any assistance or defense in any manner."[26] There is, of course, always the manner in which legal rulings and distinctions may have been applied in practice, but it appears that the right of a defendant to have an attorney in heresy trials diminished after the mid-thirteenth century. We know that the Council of Albi prohibited advocates in heresy proceedings in 1254, while in 1256, the Council of Béziers handed down an opposite ruling declaring that defendants should be allowed adequate defense.[27] We also find evidence somewhat later where inquisitors suggested that lawyers taking part in heresy trials were liable to the suspicion of heresy if they represented a defendant accused of heresy.[28] Despite exclusive claims on both sides of this issue, it is possible to locate cases in which accused heretics did have legal counsel. In 1323, an imprisoned defendant was denied an attorney and imprisoned by the inquisitor in

---

24. X 5.7.10 *Vergentis in senium* (1199), in Friedberg, vol. 2, cols. 782–783.

25. X 5.1.15 *Veniens* (1202), in Friedberg, vol. 2, col. 737.

26. X 5.7.11 *Si adversus* (1205), in Friedberg, vol. 2, cols. 783–784. On lawyers, see James A. Brundage, "The Medieval Advocate's Profession," *Law and History Review* 6, no. 2 (1988): 439–464.

27. Mansi, vol. 22, col. 838; and vol. 23, cols. 689–702.

28. Nicholas Eymeric, *Directorium inquisitorum* (Venice: Simeonis Vasalini, 1595), p. 565. Originally written around 1376.

Tours. An appellate process overturned the court's decision.[29] There are other situations in which similar cases were not challenged or verdicts vacated, and in still other proceedings, such as the case involving Jerome in Vienna, a defendant refused legal counsel. Other chapters in medieval legal history reveal that requests for counsel were denied with an appeal to existing legal statute.[30] By the fifteenth century, Pope Martin V adjudicated that even suspected heretics could not have lawyers.[31] There is only slight indication, even in early inquisitorial records and registers, that accused heretics were permitted lawyers in legal proceedings.[32] There are exceptions to that general practice and scholars who have argued for opposite interpretations of law and procedure on this point.[33] Medieval statutes in canon law can be found that can also be read as excluding attorneys for heretical defendants. "We grant in matters concerning heretical depravity, one may go about that business without the noise of qualifications and the appearance of lawyers and judgments."[34]

Witnesses in heresy trials and within the inquisitorial procedure might be anonymous and the depositions of unidentified testimonies not necessarily revealed to the defendant, and there was no prevailing legal statute that required it to be otherwise. Such practices reflect a legal ethos from a different place and time, and while representative of another departure from modern court proceedings, this fact cannot be taken to imply unfairness or irregularity. This factor is not relevant in the Jerome case at Vienna. The medieval court ordinarily did attempt to preclude known enemies of

---

29. Jean-Marie Vidal, ed., *Bullaire de l'inquisition française au xiv siècle et jusqu'à la fin du grand schisme* (Paris: Letouzey et Ané, 1913), pp. 77–83.

30. The case of Jan Hus at the Council of Constance is an example. Václav Novotný, ed., *M. Jana Husi Korespondence a dokumenty* (Prague: Nákladem komise pro vydávání pramenů náboženského hnutí českého, 1920), p. 246. In a letter written by Hus sometime after January 19, 1415, he notes that in the presence of witnesses and notaries, his request for a "procurator and advocate" was refused.

31. *Inter cunctas*, 1418, in Mansi, vol. 27, col. 1213.

32. Louis Tanon, *Histoire des Tribunaux de l'Inquisition en France* (Paris: Larose & Forcel, 1893), p. 401.

33. Examples include Walter Ullmann, "The Defense of the Accused in the Medieval Inquisition," in *The Irish Ecclesiastical Record* 73, (1950): 481–489; and Henry Ansgar Kelly, "Inquisition and the Prosecution of Heresy: Misconceptions and Abuses," *Church History* 58 (1989): 445; and Kelly, "Inquisitorial Due Process and the Status of Secret Crimes," *Monumenta iuris canonici*, series C, subsidia 9 (1992): 408.

34. Sext. 5.2.20, *Statuta quaedam*, in Friedberg, vol. 2, col. 1078.

the suspect from giving testimony or otherwise prejudicially influencing or perverting the natural course of justice.[35] Ultimately, the judgment of the court (*sententia*) could only be determined and upheld on the basis of confession by the defendant, the *regina probationum* (the queen of proofs), or if the charges were sustained by means of due process or through the stages of the *ordo iudiciarius* of prevailing standard procedure and medieval equivalents of due process. If successful, at this stage the accused was considered *infamis* (infamous). Jerome may have been thought to be controversial, heretical, or indeed infamous, but he had not hitherto been so determined in a court of law. The importance of this requirement cannot be overstated.

The Charges

The charges against Jerome consisted of two parts. The first accusations, the *articuli primo loco positi*, consisted precisely of the forty-five Wyclifite articles previously condemned in Prague in 1403 and then again in 1408, pronouncements Jerome later claimed were published during his absence. In addition, there were twelve other articles that related more specifically to the person and opinions of the defendant.[36] Jerome answered issues involving the forty-five articles chiefly with denials. As a result, they were subsequently dropped from the proceedings and thereafter were not part of the trial. His answers have been noted as generally "evasive."[37] However, the willingness of the court to drop charges after simple denials by the defendant raises the question of whether these long-standing pro forma Wyclifite accusations were simply part of the repertoire of heresy hunting in central Europe at this time. There were no efforts to prove that Jerome held or was implicated in these troubling theses, and the court simply dismissed those concerns on a basic asked-and-answered premise and made no effort to sustain those charges.

Once Jerome had spoken to these accusations and provided answers to the charges, the aforementioned additional ten articles were introduced by Gwerleich. These focused on statements and heretical activities

---

35. Bernard Gui, *Practica inquisitionis heretice pravitatis*, ed. Célestin Douais (Paris: Picard, 1886), pp. 214–215.

36. Klicman, pp. 6, 7.

37. Klicman, p. vi.

perpetrated by the defendant in Prague, at Heidelberg, and elsewhere.[38] Questions of alleged excommunication in Prague churches by Archbishop Zbyněk were raised. Troubling declarations about Wyclif's holiness, ostensibly promoted by the defendant, entered the legal proceedings. Jerome would have to answer to allegations that he had previously declared that Wyclif's teachings were preferable to Augustine's. Accusations of teaching realism at Heidelberg were now at issue. Beyond this, Jerome was charged with willfully violating his oath not to cause discord at Prague but then promptly participating in the developments that resulted in the acrimonious and divisive Kutná Hora decree, which then cast the defendant into a perjurious dilemma. The records appear to indicate that Jerome seemed a bit surprised at the introduction of these articles.[39]

The second set of charges were considerably more entrenched in the case against Jerome. The *articuli secundo loco positi* consisted of an additional ten articles lodged against the defendant. These charges constituted the actual indictment. First, the articles included claims that Jerome had glorified Wyclif, declaring that he was a saint or representing him as the "evangelical doctor and destined for eternal life." Ostensibly, Jerome had asserted that he would defend Wyclif even to the stake. Second, Jerome was alleged to have opined that Wyclif's teaching was preferable even to that of the venerable Augustine. Third, "in the mind of God there are several formal entities, which are both formally and really distinct." Fourth, Jerome was indicted as a notorious teacher of realism. This charge appears to have been based on his performance at Heidelberg. Fifth, there were charges around the assumption that Jerome was an excommunicate. Sixth, Jerome was accused of perjury. This accusation appeared to find its evidential foundation on the fact that he had taken an oath at Prague not to disturb the nations of the Prague university. Having undertaken that solemn oath, the defendant had summarily violated it by disseminating disunity, hostility, and division. Ostensibly, this charge took as its point of departure the acrimonious university *Quodlibet* eighteen months earlier and the events that produced the Decree of Kutná Hora. Seventh, Jerome was accused of denying biblical authority when he was in Buda (specifically, the gospels of Mark and Luke) and also arraigned on charges of illicit preaching. Eighth, the defendant was alleged to have attacked the priesthood on two counts

---

38. Klicman, pp. 9–10.

39. Šmahel, *Život a dílo Jeronýma*, pp. 50–51.

of morals and immunity, while at the same time openly commending the lives of heresy suspects, namely, Stanislav of Znojmo, Štěpán Páleč, Jan Hus, Marek of Hradec Králové, and others not specifically named in the indictment. Ninth, Jerome was alleged to have taught that secular authorities had both the right and the duty to supervise the activities of priests, to the extent that he apparently taught that every secular lord should have jurisdiction over the priesthood. Tenth, the defendant had been arrested by the archbishop of Esztergom and released only on the insistence of Archbishop Zbyněk of Prague, who had sent a knight to escort Jerome back to Prague.[40] These charges constituted the heart of the real complaint against Jerome. In response, Jerome denied articles one through eight, and there are no recorded replies to articles nine or ten. Notably, there is no reply on the charge of perjury. If there were responses to these parts of the indictment, these either have not been recorded or have been lost.

If Jerome summarily denied the first set of accusations, he was no less reticent to dismiss the second set also. Even in the absence of specific documentation, it is without doubt that Jerome essentially and categorically also denied these articles.[41] It has been observed that "Jerome's defense was extremely evasive and equivocal."[42] The brushes Jerome had with authority during his academic tenure at several European universities now came back to haunt him. The Vienna process incorporated both questions of authority and considerations of theology. Peter Bergochsel (or Pergochsl or Pergexel) testified in September, noting that at Paris, Jerome dealt with a *quaestio* concerning the notion of "idea" in the thought of God.[43] Obviously, Jerome's handling of the *quaestio* signaled alarm. We find corroboration of this in the writings of both Jean Gerson and Gilles Charlier.[44] It is worth pointing out that Charlier's testimony is very suspect and almost certainly based on second-hand information. Moreover,

---

40. Klicman, p. 286, wherein the latter consists of a comment made by Jerome during the Council of Constance. In fact, Jerome makes this point twice.

41. Klicman, "Der Wiener Process gegen Hieronymus von Prag, 1410–1412," *Mitteilungen des Instituts für Oesterreichische Geschichtsforschung* 21, no. 3 (1900): 450.

42. Paul B. Bernard, "Jerome of Prague, Austria and the Hussites," *Church History* 27 (1958): 8.

43. Klicman, p. 22.

44. Glorieux, vol. 2, p. 278. This is in a letter to an anonymous Minorite dated December 7, 1426; and Gilles Charlier in Mansi, vol. 29, col. 964.

both testimonies come twenty to thirty years after the fact and have been mediated through the trial of Jerome during the Council of Constance, the execution of the defendant at the conclusion of that process, the bellicosity of the Hussite uprising, the failed crusade initiatives, the ascendancy of Hussite theology, and the virtual institutionalizing of heresy in Bohemia. Bergochsel's September testimony noted that at Paris, Jerome was warned to be more careful with his reckless comments, and the masters went so far as to order him to cease and desist, with a very specific admonition: "Master, stop that, or else you will be led into saying something even less becoming." Apparently, according to the witness, Jerome is alleged to have replied, "willingly."[45] The broad thrust of the testimony appears to get at one of the basic anxieties over Jerome, which included the defendant's propensity for scandal, needless provocation, defiance of authority, and willingness to push out the boundaries of convention and tradition. Such behavior often excited the medieval mind and is not infrequently found among the foundations of heresy charges throughout the later Middle Ages.

With respect to Heidelberg, one of the witnesses testified: "He was arraigned on four articles before the bishop of Worms, but certain difficulties prevented his recantation ... and during a lengthy disputation spanning four days Jerome attempted to argue for a realist logic, and to prove that universals ought to be predicated in propositions, and therefore he maintained that masters [William] Ockam, [Johann of] Maulfeld, [Jean] Buridan, Marsilius of Inghen (1340–1396) and their followers were not dialecticians, but diabolical heretics."[46] It has been pointed out previously that the accusation is ambiguous. Did Jerome mean that realism was the guarantor of orthodoxy? This is something Wyclif would say. Alternatively, did Jerome mean to argue that realism was the guarantor of proper philosophical and logical thinking?[47] It remains patently unclear, but what is definite is that Jerome's thought, his thinking about thinking, his approach to questions of philosophy directly, and his theological ruminations indirectly were cause for concern and significant enough to be raised in a formal judicial proceeding.

---

45. Klicman, p. 32. There are Czech extracts from the Vienna process in Šmahel, *Jeroným Pražský*, pp. 219–220.

46. Klicman, pp. 12–13, 22.

47. Ota Pavlíček, "Two Philosophical Texts of Jerome of Prague and His Alleged Designation of Opponents of Real Universals as Diabolic Heretics," *BRRP* 8 (2009): 96.

The Vienna trial reveals that suspicion of eucharistic irregularity or heresy persisted. This became a hallmark of Hussite history from the time of Hus right on through the age of the Táborites and even beyond. We learn from the depositions of Johannes Schwab von Butzbach and Konrad Kreuzer during the Vienna trial that at Prague, Matěj Knín was forced to "purge himself" of suspicions that he favored Wyclif and did not believe in transubstantiation, holding instead to the idea that bread and wine remained following consecration.[48] Hus was similarly attacked over the course of many years, even in the absence of unimpeachable evidence. At Vienna, Jerome affirmed that he held to the validity of the doctrine of transubstantiation. Master Johannes Vohburg said he attended the Knín *Quodlibet* in Prague the previous year and testified that both Knín and Blažej Vlk opposed Jerome.[49] The testimony is arguable, but it does reveal the nature and depth of theological disagreement at Prague and the lack of consensus among university masters on questions of philosophy.

Jerome testified that he knew of no evil in Hus or in any of the others who had been nominated in article eight as heresy suspects, and he rather testily said that it was not within his purview to determine whether an individual was saved or lost. This forces a clear line of demarcation between men such as Jerome and his detractors such as Gerson and, later, the bishop of Lodi, Michael de Causis, Jan Železný, and others, who presumed to know truth and maintained their claim to possessing insight into eternal matters. Jerome would not entertain speculation on such matters as it pertained to others and deferred the line of questioning entirely, insisting to his examiners that the aforementioned suspects, such as Stanislav, Páleč, and Hus, should answer for themselves.[50] Jerome referred to indignities forced upon him by his accusers and mentioned Johannes Schwab von Butzbach. In a heated discussion, Jerome evidently had pointed his finger at Butzbach, who had pointed back at him, and the two had quarreled over what was compatible with the faith.[51]

There was critical discussion about whether Jerome had previously been excommunicated. There was testimony on this point by Czungl.[52]

---

48. Klicman, pp. 16–17.

49. Klicman, p. 20.

50. Klicman, p. 8.

51. Testimony of Konrad Kreutzer, in Klicman, p. 16.

52. Klicman, p. 23.

Jerome denied having been subjected to such censure.[53] There is no evidence to support a claim that he had been thus censured at any time prior to his arrival in Vienna. Kaspar Weinstein said that he had heard it rumored that Jerome, Hus, and Štěpán Páleč had been excommunicated along with some of their associates. When pressed on who the others were, Weinstein said he could not recall. However, he did submit more precise testimony that in the house of a furrier in the Old Town of Prague where he had previously lodged, there was an incident that caused him to believe that the defendant in the Vienna case had been previously under the censure of the church. According to Weinstein, "I had just returned from the disputation when my landlord said to me: 'Why have the judges and sheriffs [*scabini*] paid a visit to your schools today? Have you heard any news?' I replied that I knew nothing, and they said: 'We have heard that Páleč, Jan Jesenice, Marek, and in particular Jerome and Hus and others have been excommunicated, because they have been saying that the bread is not with the body of Christ, and that there is a common (universal?) ass.'"[54] The latter suggestion was repeated by a student in the course of the trial, to the effect that Jerome had indeed insisted on a peculiar universal. "We heard him say in a sermon ... that there is a universal ass and similar things." Once again, it is significant that Jerome is alleged to have engaged in preaching.

There are three separate issues in the Weinstein testimony that must be taken up. First, there are some difficulties with the allegation of excommunication. The easiest case to address among the several alleged excommunicates noted in the Vienna trial is Hus. Hus was subjected to the censure of excommunication four times between 1410 and 1412. Archbishop Zbyněk excommunicated Hus on July 18 and September 24, 1410. Hus was again excommunicated by Cardinal Odo Colonna in February 1411 and lastly by Cardinal Peter Stephaneschi in September 1412.[55] Jesenice was sanctioned in March 1412.[56] The only incident that precedes the Vienna trial is the action taken by Zbyněk the month before Jerome appeared in Austria. If the chronology does not mitigate against including Jerome in the Prague sanctions, it certainly calls into serious question the probability of it. In the second half of March, we can reliably place Jerome at Buda and account for

---

53. Klicman, p. 10.

54. Klicman, 28–29.

55. *Documenta*, pp. 397–399, 202, 461–464.

56. Jiří Kejř, *Husitský právník: M. Jan z Jesenice* (Prague: ČSAV, 1965), p. 61.

his whereabouts after his controversial address at the royal court. We have already determined that he spent a fortnight in the episcopal prison at Esztergom northwest of Buda. The distance between the two cities is forty kilometers, or twenty-five miles. We can be fairly certain that Jerome was released from the episcopal accommodations on or about April 3. Bishop Jan of Kanisza remanded his prisoner into the safekeeping of an anonymous knight who was supposed to escort Jerome to Prague. It is highly questionable that this occurred. Indeed, we have already heard Jerome's testimony that the knight released him on his own recognizance. Jerome's whereabouts and activities over the next four months are shrouded in obscurity. If he returned to Prague, the surviving historical records provide no indication. Where was he?

Given his propensity for wanderlust, it seems unlikely that he lingered in Esztergom or even anywhere within the kingdom of Hungary. Having agitated Sigismund to the point of being remanded to a prison cell, it is likely Jerome wanted to put some distance between himself and the wrath of the king. As for events in Prague concerning the burning of Wyclif's books, Hus's defiance of the archbishop, the inauguration of a legal battle, and other events leading up to Hus's excommunication, we hear not a word of Jerome in Prague. It is therefore highly unlikely that Jerome was in Prague in June or July and therefore could not have been included in the excommunication of Hus by Archbishop Zbyněk.

It is about 200 kilometers (or 120 miles) between Esztergom and Vienna. Jerome very precisely says that he traveled a distance of twenty-four miles in order to face his accusers. We cannot be certain from which location this distance implies, but it is suggestive that the distance is so precisely given and hardly a throwaway number. He may have traveled from Bratislava, but this is conjecture, and no sources have confirmed it.

Second, there is the suggestion of theological eucharistic irregularity in Prague. The matter was apparently so acute that a number of Prague masters were sanctioned, "because they have been saying that the bread is not the Body of Christ." This is a direct reference to the doctrine of remanence promulgated by Wyclif. Once again, the figure of Hus is the best one to examine on this charge. It can be summarily dismissed on the grounds that Hus did not at that time or at any time thereafter hold to the Wyclifite doctrine of the Eucharist. This was a persistent false allegation advanced against Hus from this time until the Council of Constance. It is baseless and lacks any foundation. Hus's sermons, letters, university disputations, and theological writing exhibit no sympathy for any other understanding of the sacrament save that elaborated in the dogma of the fourth Lateran Council.[57] It is worthless on such a question to assert that in his heart, Hus denied transubstantiation.[58]

Third, the allegation of a student reflecting a wider recollection that "we heard him [Jerome] say in a sermon that there is a universal ass" is largely dismissed by scholars studying Jerome and the question of universals.[59] It may be doubted that Jerome actually preached formal sermons, but we have already encountered the problem of nomenclature with respect to his address before the prelates and King Sigismund in the royal chapel at Buda. Perhaps the presumed sermon was a lecture or some other academic speech. Did Jerome say there was a universal ass? There is no way to establish the comment one way or the other. On one level, there should be no hesitation in assuming that Jerome would make such a comment, if for no other reason than to provoke or stimulate his hearers. There is plenty of evidence to support his characterization as a provocateur. But would Jerome say such a thing from an intellectual or philosophical point of view? It is unlikely, as he would have scarcely countenanced the notion of an ass in the realm of pure ideas. An ass is something of a lower order, associated with elemental nature and unworthy of pure ideas, much in the same manner as dirt and dung. The notion of a clear diversity of ideas precludes similarity between a pure idea and an ass. Logically, universals and pure ideas have no relation to a hypothetical universal ass.[60] Nevertheless, it is possible that Jerome may have made such a quip to amuse or entertain, and the testimony of the student, though incorrect and inapplicable, may reflect a throwaway comment.

Having virtually excluded Jerome from Prague and the tumultuous events of the summer of 1410, we now find the testimony of Nicholas Czungl, providing evidence that Jerome must have been in Prague,

---

57. See Thomas A. Fudge, *Jan Hus: Religious Reform and Social Revolution in Bohemia* (London: I. B. Tauris, 2010), pp. 49–54.

58. Walter Brandmüller, while admitting a lack of evidence, claims that "in his heart Hus was a remanentist." Brandmüller has made this comment in private conversation and during symposia proceedings.

59. Katherine Walsh, "Wyclif's Legacy in Central Europe in the Late Fourteenth and Early Fifteenth Centuries," in *From Ockham to Wyclif*, Studies in Church History, Subsidia 5, ed. Anne Hudson and Michael Wilks (Oxford: Blackwell, 1987), p. 397, says that R. R. Betts mistranslated the phrase "esse unum communem asinum."

60. On this, there may be some value in considering Jerome's *quaestio* and his comments in *Utrum a parte rei universalia sit necessarium ponere pro mundi sensibilis harmonia*, in *ST*, p. 218.

although the witness is ambiguous. The mandate of Archbishop Zbyněk against all things Wyclifite was proclaimed in the capital, and all who refused to surrender the books of the heretic were to be censured. Following this proclamation and during a Sunday sermon, a Dominican friar named Peter preached at St. Clement's and announced that on the authority of the archbishop, he was proactively excommunicating all those who refused to obey the archiepiscopal order and furthermore was denouncing those same recalcitrant characters as heretics. Friar Peter went on to make mention of ideas about universals. He said he wanted to name the suspects but had been forbidden to do so by the authorities. Czungl testified that he was not absolutely certain who Friar Peter had in mind, but he believed that Peter did, in fact, name Hus, Jerome, Jesenice, and Stanislav of Znojmo as among the offenders. It was rumored that Jerome became so incensed with the declarations of the Dominican that he wanted to drag Peter from St. Clement's but was prevented from doing so by a crowd that had gathered outside the church.[61] From fairly reliable information we have elsewhere, Jerome's response to the incendiary sermon in the Dominican church is very much in keeping with his temperament. However, it seems odd that none of the Czech sources notes Jerome's presence in Prague at the time. The matter remains a puzzle.

Witnesses against Jerome

With the initial charges asked and answered, the prosecutor, Gwerleich, called for an adjournment until September 2, at which time it was announced that witnesses would be summoned by the prosecution to rebut Jerome's plea of innocence on several of the articles of indictment.[62] On that date, fifteen witnesses were called and sworn in, and they gave sworn testimony. On September 5, an additional witness, the theologian Berthold Puchhauser of Regensburg, was heard. These testimonies went to some length in establishing Jerome's Wyclifite position expressed at Paris, Heidelberg, and Cologne. His role in the Knín *Quodlibet* at Prague in January 1409 was also a major component of the evidence submitted. The witnesses also entered sworn testimony into the record concerning the alleged excommunication of Jerome dating to 1409. Pursuant to

---

61. Klicman, p. 23.

62. Klicman, p. 10.

these events, developments leading to the Decree of Kutná Hora were also entered into the proceedings. Additional "evidence" about Jerome's opinions on Wyclif and his notorious acts in Hungary, including preaching and subsequent imprisonment, were also considered germane, and witnesses spoke to all of this.[63] Members of the tribunal included Lambert Sluter of Gelderen, Nicholas Dinkelsbühl, Michael Suchenschatz, Kaspar Maiselstein, and Johannes Sindram of Heiligenstadt. Sindram had previously been dean of the law faculty.[64] It is quite unclear whether Jerome was brought to the hearing in chains or whether he came of his own free will. The records are either silent or ambivalent. Nevertheless, Jerome was present.

The witnesses who appeared in September and provided testimonial evidence against Jerome included a number of academics, clerics, and students: Nicholas Tell of Tungris, who held a degree from Heidelberg; Konrad Duvel of Hildesheim, who had studied in Prague and Heidelberg; Johannes Schwab von Butzbach, who had studied at Prague and Vienna; Konrad Kreuzer of Nürnberg, who had studied at Prague; Johannes Vohburg, who had taken studies at Prague and Vienna; Peter Bergochsel, who had studied at Prague and Paris; and Berthold Puchhauser of Regensburg. These were all professors at the University of Vienna. Nicholas Czungl was a curate or parish priest in Bernsdorf, Johannes Tesser held a bachelor's degree and was a priest from Würzburg, Achatius Chenczl of Salzburg had been a student in Vienna, Kaspar Weinstein was a priest from the diocese of Eichstädt, Johannes Stückler of Passau had taken a bachelor's degree from Prague, Berthold of Munich held a bachelor's degree from Prague, Heinrich von Aura was a priest from the diocese of Würzburg and held a bachelor's degree from Prague but had also studied at Vienna, and the other witness was Johannes of Korutany (also known as Johannes von Kärnthen or Johannes de Korinthia).[65] These individuals were summoned by Thomas, the representative of the statutory official. It is noteworthy that at least eight of these deponents had studied in Prague. Two of them had

---

63. Klicman, pp. 12–24.

64. Šmahel, *Život a dílo Jeronýma*, p. 49.

65. Alfred A. Strnad, "Die Zeugen im Wiener Prozess gegen Hieronymus von Prag: Prosopographische Anmerkungen zu einem Inquisitionsverfahren im Vorfelde des Hussitismus," in *Husitství—reformace—renesance: Sborník k 60. narozeninám Františka Šmahela*, 3 vols, ed. Jaroslav Pánek, Miloslav Polívka, and Noemi Rejchrtová (Prague: Historický ústav, 1994), vol. 1, pp. 331–367, is a fine analysis of the witnesses in the Vienna trial.

studied at Heidelberg, one had been at Paris, none had any known formal connection to Cologne, and most of them were German. One other bachelor of arts, Heinrich Stoll von Hammelburg, and two other students previously unnamed, Nicholas Züngel of Gmünd and Daniel Hochenkircher, are also noted in relation to events at Vienna.[66]

It might be pointed out that the depositions of these witnesses do not relate to the forty-five articles of Wyclif but only to the additional articles appended to the *articuli primo loco positi* (the forty-five articles) and to the *articuli secundo loco positi* (articles 13 to 22). The witnesses appear only to have provided testimony on those articles of which they claimed personal knowledge. For example, there does not appear to be any evidence submitted on charges twenty-one or twenty-two. The most verbose of the deponents (Kaspar Weinstein and Heinrich von Aura) do not proceed beyond article twenty. Other witnesses reach only to article eighteen, while most are silent after article fifteen or sixteen. This may present a difficulty for the prosecution if charges that had been laid had no prima facie evidence or testimonial witness. We find recurring and corroborative testimony by both Chenczl and Johannes of Korutany, who said that Jerome used the shield of faith in Prague during and after the *Quodlibet* in 1409, with the suggestion that this activity was either improper or otherwise problematic, with the abiding insinuation of heresy.[67]

While all of this was going on, Prague university officials, especially acting chancellor Jan Ondřejův, also known as Šindel, wrote to the magistrates at Vienna on September 3, on behalf of Charles College, protesting Jerome's treatment.[68] Acting chancellor Šindel's letter came straight to the point: "This unforeseen misfortune which has befallen the honourable man, Master Jerome of Prague, master of the universities of Paris, Cologne, Heidelberg and our own, has brought sadness to our hearts and affliction to our minds. Wherefore we humbly ask of your prudence that you deign to look graciously on the innocence of Master Jerome and protect him from the insults of his enemies, believing us that he has conducted himself from his youth in those universities praiseworthily in his acts, learning and morals."[69] The letter is a platitude, for it was widely

66. Strnad, "Die Zeugen im Wiener Prozess," pp. 341–342, 363.

67. Klicman, pp. 26, 31.

68. *Documenta*, p. 407.

69. The translation is from Betts, *Essays in Czech History*, p. 212.

known and incontrovertible that Jerome had hardly been a model of deco-
rum. There was no reply to Šindel's letter. It is possible to consider that
the correspondence was a rhetorical exercise and therefore not authen-
tic.[70] The missive blatantly tends to overlook the controversial aspects of
Jerome's thought and peregrinations.

Fourteen witnesses gave testimony about Jerome on September 2. After
a brief recess, the hearings resumed on September 5. The Augustinian
theologian Berthold Puchhauser of Regensburg, who belonged to the
Order of the Augustinian Hermits, testified that Jerome had once told
him that he had addressed the issue of secular and church power while in
Buda and that he also had information that the archbishop of Canterbury
had exhumed Wyclif's body on account of heresy.[71] The latter comment
was specious but probably based on misinformation, as opposed to an
outright lie. After all, it was demonstrable that Wyclif's remains were not
disinterred and lay undisturbed in consecrated soil at Lutterworth until
1428.[72] There was much hearsay evidence and a strong focus on the recent
appearance of Jerome in Hungary and also on events in Prague, especially those between Germans and Czechs. As noted previously, most of
the witnesses were Germans or Austrians who had left Prague in 1409 as
a result of the controversial Decree of Kutná Hora.[73] We hear testimony
affirming Jerome's significant role in this from Johannes Swab, Johannes
Vohburg, Nicholas Czungl, and Johannes Tesser.[74] It seems both apparent

---

70. Šmahel, *Život a dílo Jeronýma*, p. 52. The existence of such rhetorical documents during
this time has been well attested. Examples are the letters addressed to ecclesiastical authorities and attributed to royal officials and institutions in Prague and eleven manuscript folios
of documents relating to Hus. Božena Kopičková and Anežka Vidmanová, *Listy na Husovu
obrana z let 1410–1412: Konec jedné legendy?* (Prague: Karolinum, 1999).

71. Klicman, p. 21.

72. While Wyclif had been long condemned and an order formulated at session 8 of the
Council of Constance for his removal from consecrated ground (May 4, 1415), it was not until
December 9, 1427, that Pope Martin V renewed that order and instructed Richard Fleming,
bishop of Lincoln, to proceed against the mortal remains of Wyclif. Odoricus Raynaldi, ed.,
Annales ecclesiastici (Bar-le-Duc: Guerin, 1874), vol. 28, p. 55. Acting on that directive in the
spring of 1428, Wyclif was disinterred from the church cemetery in Lutterworth, his remains
were burned, and the ashes were afterward thrown into the River Swift. All of this was in
strict accordance with canon law statutes. See X 3.40.7, *De homine*, in Friedberg, vol. 2,
col. 640. For the Council of Constance decision, see Norman P. Tanner, ed., *Decrees of the
Ecumenical Councils*, 2 vols. (London: Sheed & Ward, 1990), vol. 1, pp. 415–416.

73. Klicman, pp. 12–34.

74. Klicman, pp. 16 (Swab), 20 (Vohburg), 23–24 (Czungl), 25 (Tesser).

and important that the prosecutors at Vienna were more focused on their previous dispute with Jerome than on any concern over theological irregularity. This suggests the politics of heresy. One deponent testified that he would be satisfied if Jerome were prosecuted alone on his contribution to the damage inflicted on the university in Prague.[75] This further underscores the political nature of heresy trials. Following these events, the court scheduled a fifteen-day adjournment. Gwerleich wanted Jerome kept in custody but yielded to Jerome's vehement protests that the process was too protracted and was preventing him from attending to other commitments. Jerome promised not to leave Vienna, on pain of excommunication and conviction of perjury. It may be important to point out that Jerome did not take a formal oath on the matter. The promise was requested by Gwerleich.[76] Elsewhere we encounter the caveat that Jerome had undertaken not to depart without special permission.[77]

Having narrowly escaped another prison confinement, Jerome was doubtless aware that the net was closing in on him and that he was likely to be condemned. The scope of testimony against him in Vienna did not provide in any one point sufficient evidence to secure a conviction, but the sum and substance presented were enough to raise the very real possibility that the court might return a verdict of guilt. Once the court adjourned, on September 6, Jerome wrote a letter to some of his friends who were living in the college of Jerusalem in Prague.[78] The letter provides some indirect reflection on his own struggle and offers encouragement to his colleagues to remain steadfast against the enemies of God who appeared intent on the subversion of the truth and purity of Christianity. The concept and location of the college of Jerusalem in Prague has a history prior to the time of Jerome and one that is important for the early period of reform in Bohemia. This house with a chapel in what is now Bartolomějská Street was originally a brothel. Later it became the center founded by Jan Milíč of Kroměříž in the early 1370s. The Jerusalem experiment of Milíč was the earliest scene of frequent communion among the laity, a strong emphasis on moral reform, and a clear application of the social implications of

75. Klicman, p. 24; and Klicman, "Der Wiener Process," p. 453.

76. Klicman, p. 11.

77. Letter of Andreas Grillenberg to Archbishop Zbyněk, September 30, 1410, in *Documenta*, p. 418.

78. Šmahel/Silagi, pp. 243–246.

the gospel. A second chapel, known as Božieho Tela, "Chapel of the Body of God," likewise practiced lay communion and renewed religious practice, which may be traced from the 1340s, but the circumstances around this initiative are not as well known. At the college of Jerusalem, Milíč strove to apply the gospel within the culture of Prague prostitution, and the increased frequency of communion found impetus in a deepening eschatological awareness. There is no evidence from elsewhere in later medieval Europe that a community of Christians communed daily. This renewed religious practice became part of the foundation for widespread church reform and social revolution. The idea of frequent communion was advocated by a number of well-respected academics, and this, too, reveals the contours of the uniqueness in the later medieval Bohemian religious world.[79] After Milíč's death in 1374, Emperor Charles IV handed the house over to the Cistercian Order for establishing the theological college of St. Bernard. It seems that the college became a place of residence for foreign bachelors and students. In the aftermath of the Decree of Kutná Hora, it was largely abandoned during the secession in the spring of 1409. In this vacated college, a number of bachelors and students immediately took up residence. They were generally known as enthusiastic followers of Hus and his reforms. It is to these people that Jerome addressed his letter from Vienna.

Jerome Escapes

Despite previous undertakings to remain in Vienna until the end of the legal proceedings, at some point, Jerome decided it was no longer in his best interests to stay in Austria. He had made a verbal commitment to prosecutor Gwerleich to remain in Vienna as part of his plea to avoid being confined. We cannot be certain if Jerome's next move was calculated or compulsive. The precise date is unknown, but once the court adjourned,

---

79. David R. Holeton, "The Bohemian Eucharistic Movement in Its European Context," *BRRP* 1 (1996): 31–32; and Olivier Marin, *L'archevêque, le maître et le dévot: Genèses du mouvement réformateur pragois années 1360–1419* (Paris: Honoré Champion Éditeur, 2005), pp. 457–575, for an up-to-date analysis. On the subject and problems associated with prostitution in Prague, there are two important studies: Wojciech Iwańczak, "Prostytucja w późnośredniowiecznej Pradze," in *Biedni i Bogaci: studia z dziejów społeczeństwa i Kultury ofiarowane Bronisławowi Geremkowi w sześćdziesiątą rocznicę urodzin*, ed. Maurice Aymand (Warsaw: PWN, 1992), pp. 95–104; and David C. Mengel, "From Venice to Jerusalem and Beyond: Milíč of Kroměříž and the Topography of Prostitution in Fourteenth-Century Prague," *Speculum* 79 (April 2004): 407–442.

Jerome surreptitiously absconded. It might have been immediately after the announcement of the recess following September 5, or it may have been as late as just before the trial was to resume (after mid-September). We can postulate that Jerome left Vienna somewhere after the sixth and before the tenth of September. His movements and activities in this period have once again been lost to history, but what is certain is that Jerome left Vienna, never to return. His failure to remain in the city was legally problematic.

Having escaped from Vienna, Jerome went first to Laa an der Thaya in Lower Austria, a distance of about seventy kilometers or forty-four miles almost directly north of Vienna. The town is situated in what is now the northern Weinviertel region on the south Moravian border and was a benefice of Andreas Grillenberg, the canon and official of the Passau consistory who had been involved in the Vienna process. Here Jerome characteristically involved himself in a lively discussion with a schoolmaster and a notary. From Laa an der Thaya, he then went on in a northwesterly direction to Bítov Castle, about sixty kilometers, or thirty-six miles, away. The castle sits above the Želetavska River in southern Moravia a few miles inside the safety of what is today Czech territory. In 1410, it was still Austrian land, but it was controlled by those sympathetic to Hus, especially Johannes of Lichtenberg, who was a friend and admirer of Hus. Jerome would have been aware of this fact and in consequence would have felt reasonably secure in the castle and safe in friendly territory. It is likely that he was hosted by Jan Bítovský (ca.1360–1420) during his sojourn at Bítov Castle.[80] If he were traveling on foot, it probably took him two days to reach Laa an der Thaya and another two days to arrive at Bítov Castle. If he rode a horse, he may have reached Bítov Castle within two days. We are not informed about the details of his travel.

It is not known exactly when the authorities were made aware of Jerome's desertion, but they were certainly apprised shortly after September 12, for on that date, Jerome alerted them to the precise location of his hideout. He wrote a mocking letter from Bítov, addressed facetiously "to my venerable father and lord master, the official master of the church of Passau

---

80. Jan Urban, "Kdo vlastně hostil Jeronýma Pražského v září 1410?," in *Zrození mýtu: dva životy husitské epochy. K poctě Petra Čorneje*, eds., Robert Novotný and Petr Šámal (Prague: Paseka, 2011), pp. 50–59.

and parish priest in Laa."[81] The letter virtually dripped with biting sarcasm and boldness. Jerome stated his view that he was not inclined to remain on trial in the midst of hundreds of enemies but perhaps somewhat daringly invited Grillenberg to send his accusers to Prague, where discussions might continue and the trial be more properly conducted. Jerome also suggested that the matter might be referred to the Curia, where he assumed (whether earnestly or facetiously) that fairness could be expected. Five years later, during the Council of Constance, Jerome refuted the jurisdictional authority of the Passau diocese and insisted that he was threatened with violence and was under no obligation to remain, inasmuch as he had gone to Vienna of his own accord. "I did not flee contumaciously, but I was unwilling to remain to suffer violent treatment, nor was I bound to do so."[82] Jerome also claimed that since he was from another bishopric, the prosecutor lacked authority to subject him to legal procedure and judicial punishment.[83] There is little doubt that Jerome's flight from Vienna, his mockery of the trial proceedings there, and his belittling of Grillenberg did not serve him well thereafter. A number of Vienna academics later crossed paths with Jerome. These included Dinkelsbühl, Pulka, Heinrich von Kitzbühl, Nicholas von Höbersdorf, Lambert Sluter of Gelderen, Peter Deckinger, Puchhauser, Johannes Sindram of Heiligenstadt, and Kaspar Maiselstein, who were present during the Vienna process and later appeared at Constance. Pulka officially represented Vienna University at the Council between November 1414 and April 1418.[84] It is unlikely that they forgot any of these details.

The aggrieved Canon Grillenberg wrote to Archbishop Zbyněk, alleging that Jerome, already implicated in serious errors, had endeavored to

---

81. The text appears in Klicman, pp. 34–5; Hardt, vol. 4, col. 683; and *Documenta*, p. 416. See appendix 3.

82. "Respondeo, quod violenter arrestatus fui, nec quicquam mecum juridice sed violenter actum est, nec habebant quicquam jurisdictionis super me, quia de alia eram diocesi.... Nec furtive, nec contumaciter recessi, sed violentiam mihi ab eis infligendam expectare non volui, prout nec tenebar, nec debui." Hardt, vol. 4, col. 638.

83. *FRB*, vol. 8, p. 287.

84. Uiblein, ed., *Acta facultatis artium Universitatis Vindobonensis 1385–1416* (Vienna: Böhlaus, 1968), vol. 1, p. 456; and Firnhaber, "Petrus de Pulka," pp. 29–30, which notes that a large number of delegates traveled to Constance. Maiselstein, however, left Constance in April 1415 and thus did not see Jerome. Pulka, letter of April 27, 1415, in Firnhaber, "Petrus de Pulka," pp. 19–12. For Pulka's brief, see Dieter Girgensohn, *Peter von Pulka und die Wiedereinführung des Laienkelches* (Göttingen: Vandenhoek & Ruprecht, 1964), p. 53.

promote the teachings of Wyclif, which had been "condemned by the Apostolic see," and in his work had imperiled *fragilium corda* (weak souls). Having no regard for his own salvation, this same Jerome had boldly disseminated heresy in Heidelberg, Prague, and Hungary. Following these forays, he had appeared in Vienna at the "glorious university," described by Grillenberg as "our beloved mother in whom there is no duplicity," and came to spread even further his "perverse teachings" and to publish more broadly his errors. By September 20, Grillenberg issued a formal citation for Jerome to appear within eight days, or if he were unable to present himself, he was admonished to send a representative in his stead, in order to answer charges of contumacy and rectify his absconding. The notice was posted on the main doors of St. Stephen's Cathedral in Vienna.[85] Predictably, Jerome neither acknowledged the citation nor appeared. A summary judgment thereafter was handed down. The writ specified that Jerome was guilty of perjury and suspected of heresy on account of his apparent adherence to Wyclifite opinions. He was therefore excommunicated. There are two quite different versions of the edict. The first is a general citation dated October 22, 1410, but there is also a second version, addressed to Archbishop Zbyněk, with the earlier date of September 30.[86] In the latter version, the officials of the diocese of Passau sent a letter to the archbishop of Prague with notification of the Vienna trial and its outcome. Jerome was characterized as excommunicate and, until he absolved himself of the charges, should be so considered. The archbishop was implored "by the bowels of mercy of Jesus Christ" to publish and enforce the decree of sanction against Jerome. All bishops were asked to have the condemnation read in every church in their diocese. The writ was read and proclaimed in Vienna at St. Stephen's Cathedral and also in Prague and Kraków, where it was nailed to church doors and publicized in many other places. Zbyněk circulated the letter to the Prague churches and cathedral chapters. Eighteen parish priests ratified the document, with their seals confirming that they had publicized the announcement in their parishes. The original document wound up at Vyšehrad.[87] Jerome would later admit

---

85. See Klicman, pp. 5–6, for the text, which has also been noted in Hardt, vol. 4, cols. 638–639.

86. Klicman, pp. 36–9, dated October 22, 1410; and *Documenta*, pp. 417–420, dated September 30, 1410.

87. *Documenta*, pp. 417–420.

that he knew of these actions but went on to argue that he took no note, since Zbyněk had not actually summoned him to his court.[88] There were dissenters who declined to follow the instructions of the archbishop. One of the Prague priests who refused to obey the edict against Jerome was Křišťan of Prachatice, who administered the Eucharist to Jerome even though the latter was under the ban of excommunication. Křišťan was a close personal friend of Hus.[89]

During his second trial at Constance, Jerome admitted that he knew of the sentence (as published in Prague) but had taken no note of it.[90] During the Council of Constance, it was declared that Jerome became "odious" on account of his stubbornness over the course of five years and because of his ignominious and obdurate thinking had vilified the keys of the church and had persisted in doing so up to the present time.[91] He was now both an intellectual outlaw and a heretic.

The October 22, 1410, documents form the first of two formal notarial papers of the legal process against Jerome. The second version dates to August 31, 1412. Both documents originated with Heinrich of Mühldorf, who was a cleric from the diocese of Salzburg.[92] There are irregularities. From the session of the trial of August 29, 1410, among the *articuli primo loco positi*, we find the forty-five articles of Wyclif and the twelve articles lodged against Jerome personally. There are only fifty-five replies from Jerome, not the fifty-seven one might expect. Klicman has attempted to resolve this by suggesting that more than one of the fifty-seven articles were considered redundant, and therefore separate answers had been collated.[93] The second set of charges (*articuli secundo loco positi*) consists of the accusations read by the prosecutor after Jerome had replied to the first set. These are numbered thirteen through twenty-two, following on from the former twelve appended to the original forty-five articles. The first notarial collection includes several components. We find, first, the transcript of the August 29 hearing; second, the transcript of the September 2 session and

88. Hardt, vol. 4, col. 640.

89. Hardt, vol. 4, col. 640; see also Jiří Kejř, *Husův proces* (Prague: Vyšehrad, 2000), pp. 62–63.

90. Hardt, vol. 4, col. 639.

91. *FRB*, vol. 8, p. 287.

92. Klicman, p. x.

93. Klicman, p. ix.

the oath of the witnesses; third, the transcript of the September 5 session, along with the oath of Puchhauser; fourth, the undated transcripts of the depositions of the several witnesses; fifth, an undated transcript of a session wherein Jerome did not appear but where his letter from Bítov, dated September 12, was read; sixth, the public citation for the fugitive (dated September 20), which was posted publicly; and seventh, the transcript of yet another meeting wherein the sentence of excommunication was announced against the absent suspect and dated October 22. The second notarial collection includes the aforementioned seven components along with a new notarial clause, and this is from the year 1412.

In defense of Jerome's actions to flee from Vienna (contrary to his vow), it was apparent that the proceedings for heresy were tainted. The depositions of the witnesses suggested that his theological opinions were very much subservient to the role he had played in the disputes at Prague leading up to the Decree of Kutná Hora and its strident bellicosity. There were grounds for questioning the impartiality of the court when it appeared that many of the witnesses felt personally aggrieved by the developments in Prague and had been adversely affected. The court was prejudicially disposed in favor of the prosecution. The verdict seemed obvious, and Jerome has had his modern defenders over his decision to flee from Vienna without waiting for the court trial to conclude. "Jerome would be condemned as a heretic in revenge for Kutná Hora . . . only a madman or a fool would have failed to make use of the opportunity to escape certain condemnation given these circumstances."[94]

Meanwhile, Jerome must have had some effect in Vienna, because Grillenberg later asked secular authorities in the city to arrest a number of citizens on suspicion of being Wyclifite heretics having been adversely influenced by Jerome. We do not know how many were suspected, and we have only a single name connected with these proceedings, which has come down to us from the following year. Hans Griesser (or der Griezze), a layman from Ybbs an der Donau (on the Danube), was tried before the *Stadtrath*, the superior court of Vienna but declared he would recant. The superior court therefore declined to press the matter further. Having been deprived of the satisfaction of a guilty verdict against Jerome, and doubtless embarrassed by the letter he had received from Bítov Castle, Grillenberg was unhappy with this decision and appealed the matter to the university,

---

94. Bernard, "Jerome of Prague, Austria and the Hussites," p. 9.

which had jurisdiction. Rebuffing the canon, the university agreed with the court. Grillenberg ignored this advice, went ahead with the trial on his own, and proceeded to a guilty verdict for heresy. The defendant was executed at the stake on September 9, 1411.[95] Doubtless moved by anger and burning indignation, Grillenberg then accused the university of favoring heresy and threatened to excommunicate it. This was by almost any calibration heavy-handed, and the rector Peter Deckinger, a theologian and professor of canon law, who had served as rector in 1399, 1404, 1410, and 1414, interceded with Georg von Hohenlohe (1389–1423), the ordinary of Passau, and the matter was ended without ecclesiastical sanctions lodged against the university.

The fallout from the trial of Jerome in Vienna continued to smolder for two full years after Jerome escaped. On August 31, 1412, Gwerleich issued yet another demand for Jerome to appear at Vienna to explain his illegal departure and to address the canonical issue of excommunication or to at least make an effort to have the ban lifted. Jerome was warned that nonappearance would result in a formal declaration of heresy. According to law, excommunication was automatic after one year for nonappearance and thereby made a suspect guilty of heresy.[96] Even though two years had elapsed, Jerome paid no heed to the demand. The penalties of canon law automatically and naturally took effect. With this final citation, the Vienna trial was formally closed on August 31, 1412, with Jerome in absentia and nonresponsive to the citation.[97] Suspicions of heresy persisted in Vienna. In March 1413, three members of the university faculty were censured during the deanship of Pulka for having spoken in a manner considered problematic. Reprimands, retractions, and legal challenges followed.[98]

Shortly thereafter, either in October or November 1412, a German text appeared referring to Jerome's escape from Vienna and also to one of Jerome's enemies, the German Duke Ernest of Carinthia. Ernest was reported in this text to be attending the Týn Church in Prague, where,

---

95. The Anonymous Chronicle of Vienna (1411) notes: "Item an Mitichn nach unser Frawn Tag Navitatis ward Hans der Griezzer verprant umb etleich Artikel, di wider Christum glawben waren, und wolt die nicht abtreten, alss ainer was umb das opfer." There is a summary of the Griesser process in Bernard, "Jerome of Prague, Austria and the Hussites," pp. 10–11.

96. Sext 5.2.7 Quum contumacia, in Friedberg, vol. 2, col. 1071.

97. Klicman, p, viii.

98. Uiblein, *Die Akten der Theologischen Fakultät*, vol. 1, p. 24.

during the German services, the lies of Antichrist were proclaimed and Ernest was denounced as spending time with whores and thereby offending the people of God. The reference is to Ernest the Iron, Duke of Austria (1377–1424), though it should be noted that the moniker was applied only posthumously. The manifesto concludes with a call to battle: "Let us stand in the battle line with our head, Master Hus, and our leader, Master Jerome."[99] The reference to Jerome is significant, inasmuch as it placed him at the forefront of the reform movement, presumably reflecting a more common understanding. The reference to Ernest and the propaganda aimed at him is supported by Jerome's later statements at Constance.[100] Twice in the 1412 manifesto, Jerome is referred to as *unser furraer* ("our leader"), who was able to escape the punishment of the stake devised for him by his enemies at Vienna, ostensibly via divine intervention. That was one perspective. The theologians and scholars who stood against Jerome and had sought to silence and sanction him at Vienna had failed to capture and suppress the wandering intellectual knight-errant. Bitter at the outcome of the trial proceedings in Austria, they would have to wait for another opportunity to confront their nemesis. But there would be another encounter, and some of the same men who had frequented the courtrooms of Vienna in the heresy trial of Jerome would appear once more at a similar setting in Germany five years later. The outcome there would be much different. But in the intervening five years, Jerome covered considerable geographical and intellectual ground. Nevertheless, the heresy and intrigue in Vienna were an important stepping stone in Jerome's career, a stepping stone that led to the cornerstone we encounter at Constance.

---

99. Vyšší Brod MS 123, fols. 278r–279v. German text published in F. M. Bartoš, "Hus a jeho strana v osvětlení nepřátelského pamfletu z r. 1412," *Reformační sborník* 4 (1931): 5–7.

100. Mansi, vol. 27, col. 845.

5

Iconoclasm

ATTACKING MEDIEVAL RELIGIOUS PRACTICE

ONE OF THE trajectories that reformed religious practice in Bohemia followed in the aftermath of the Council of Constance was radically iconoclastic and hostile to the ethos of the official church. This chapter examines the nature of Hussite iconoclasm and seeks to understand its possible relation to Jerome of Prague. Radical Christians in Bohemia, who regarded Jerome as one of their leaders, soon unleashed a reign of terror across the religious landscape.

[They] went throughout the kingdom destroying, pillaging and burning churches, monasteries, church halls, chapels, altars and baptisteries. They likewise destroyed images of Christ and of the blessed Virgin and other saints. Wherever they went they tore up and burned sacred vestments, ecclesiastical paraphernalia and robes. They took and destroyed chalices and items pertaining to confirmation with the sacred chrism. They assaulted people and took some prisoner, killing and burning priests. . . . This [group] had within its ranks some priests. Some of them had been parish priests, others had been vicars, who now put aside their holy orders, grew unkempt beards, wore no tonsure and walked together with the others. They said Mass everywhere without wearing vestments, but having on ordinary clothes, outside any consecrated place such as churches, chapels and oratories. They neglected the missal and the offices indicated therein and ignored altogether the canonical hours. Beyond this, the [group] had no respect for confirmation, extreme unction, auricular confession and other sacraments. . . .

For these and other similar reasons the university in Prague was much hindered in its ability to carry out its academic activity and had to be closed. Furthermore [another group] made up of a bunch of poor and dirty fellows [soon followed this pattern].[1]

This account was written sometime after 1453 by Jan Papoušek of Soběslav. He had originally been a Hussite priest who understood his own movement as essentially Waldensian in nature. He supplied Aeneas Sylvius with material for the latter's *Historia Bohemica*, which appeared in 1458 and which devoted a number of chapters to a vivid description of the Czech heretics. The two men had met in 1451 in Jindřichův Hradec. Papoušek was rector of Charles University twice. When Jan Rokycana was expelled from the Church of Our Lady before Týn in 1437, Papoušek was installed. In due course, he converted to the Roman church. When Jiří Poděbrady, the future Hussite king, took Prague in 1448, Papoušek fled to Jindřichův Hradec. He returned to Prague in 1453 and assumed a position in the cathedral chapter of St. Vitus. Later he became provost in Litoměřice. One might reasonably expect a narrative account from this point of view to be biased, hostile, and unreliable. In order to evaluate Papoušek's perspective and his historical summary, it is necessary to return to Prague in 1416, just after the execution of Jerome.

Violence against Images in Hussite Bohemia

Several events took place toward the end of 1416 in Prague that appeared to create a more favorable environment for those who chose to remain faithful to the Roman church in the aftermath of the executions of Jan Hus and Jerome. On January 25, 1417, yielding to pressure exerted by Archbishop Konrad, the university in Prague published a manifesto condemning all doctrinal innovations that were rapidly gaining ground, especially in the rural areas. In reply to this manifesto, on the following Sunday, in the Týn Church in the square of the Old Town, Jakoubek Stříbro either preached a sermon or delivered an address following a typical university *quaestio*, which presented a decisive stand against the adoration of images.[2] We do

---

1. *FRA*, vol. 1, pt. 7, pp. 158–162.

2. *Posicio de imaginibus*, NK, MS IV G 14, fols. 254v–262v. See also Kristína Sedláčková, "Jakoubek of Stříbro and the So-Called 'Sermon in Týn Church' of 31 January 1417," *BRRP*

not know why Jakoubek spoke in the Týn Church, but his position on images had been enumerated publicly for at least a half dozen years prior to his appearance there. His address caused a great stir, less by its content, which rather lacked originality, than because, being a master in the faculty of theology, he appeared to be opposing his university's point of view and also offering encouragement to radical Hussites to persist with their opinions and activities.[3] Jakoubek put to use practically everything that had been previously written on this subject. The fourteenth-century thinker and reformer Matěj Janov was his principal source. However, Jakoubek introduced into his sermon the notion of a hierarchy of images, starting from a divine archetype and descending to creations of human art. The address on January 31, 1417, in the Týn Church included the question "are the faithful bound by evangelical law to adore images in churches, or to adore and venerate them in any manner whatsoever?"[4] This address brought to an end the protracted and somewhat bellicose debate over the place of images in religious practice.[5] Controversies that persisted beyond this point were simply reiterations of arguments already presented by the Prague masters. Here we find some intellectual basis for some of the behavior enumerated by Papoušek more than thirty-five years later.

The conservative Hussite chronicle of Vavřinec of Březová details the continuation of iconoclasm and the assault on medieval religious practice in Hussite Bohemia. This suggests similarity with the perspective Papoušek wrote about almost a generation later. For example, Vavřinec noted that on August 17, 1419, common people "were running around the churches and were breaking organs and pictures especially in those churches where people were not permitted to take the Utraquist communion. Parish priests and monks ran away and hid out of fear." The authorities were either unwilling or unable to prevent this type of overt iconoclastic

6 (2007): 77–85; and Jan Bělohlávková, "Die Ansichten über Bilder in Werke der tschechischen Reformprediger" *Studie o rukopisech* 29 (1992): 53–64.

3. The reaction is disputed. Some scholars consider it provocative, while others are more reserved. On the former, see František M. Bartoš, "Do čtyř pražský artikulů. Z myšlenkových i ústavních zápasům let 1415–1420," *Sborník příspěvků k dejinám hlavního města Prahy* 5 (1932): 494; while another view is noted by František Šmahel, *Husitská revoluce*, 4 vols. (Prague: Historický ústav, 1994), vol. 2, pp. 295–296.

4. *Posicio de imaginibus*, NK, MS IV G 14, fol. 255ʳ.

5. See also William R. Cook, "The Question of Images and the Hussite Movement in Prague," *Christianesimo nella storia* 3 (1982): 329–342.

outrage. On August 18, the carnage continued. Mincing none of his words, Vavřinec wrote, "they burned down the monastery of Kartouzy. Then they entered the Church of the Mother of God at Luže, and destroyed, ruined, wrecked, damaged, and broke open the grave of Master Albík, the provost of Vyšehrad and Archbishop of Caesaria in the chapel of the same church founded by him, and also [desecrated] pictures." These mobs of radicals appeared on August 20 in Písek, about 110 kilometers, or seventy miles, south of Prague, and before they were finished, the Dominican monastery had been destroyed and burned down. Some of the monks living there were captured. Their fate is unknown.[6]

The iconoclasm was not restricted. In 1420, some Hussites proceeded to demolish the monastery of the Knights of the Cross in Zderaz and the monastery of St. Clement at the Bridge, and they also ransacked the monastery of Zbraslav. Priests of the radical communities, together with armed men and ordinary people, destroyed pictures, smashed altars, broke monstrances, and desecrated the wine of these religious houses.[7] Vavřinec linked the violence against the visual reminders of religious practice to the ideas communicated by the radical priests to their congregations. For example, the preachers of these communities delivered daily sermons wherein they spoke vehemently against many things related to traditional religious practice. This included "the sign of the passion of Christ," holy pictures, and religious architecture. The radical preachers "encouraged people to crush them with sledgehammers or burn them down." As a result of this sort of preaching, many of those influenced by the radicals "crushed and chopped and burned down pictures in all churches wherever they could find them or poked out their eyes and cut off their noses like ugly sods. Thus they pierced pictures painted on walls with spears and halberds ... or hideously threw dirt at them." At the same time, some rather lovely altar pieces in front of the town hall were crushed, and others were completely destroyed at the Church of St. Ambrose. The chronicler lamented that there was hardly an image that survived in any church.[8] Hyperbole notwithstanding, the details recorded by Vavřinec fully support the allegations contained in the narrative later prepared by Papoušek, which purported to detail radical practices within the Hussite tradition.

---

6. Hussite Chronicle, in *FRB*, vol. 5, p. 347.

7. Hussite Chronicle, in *FRB*, vol. 5, p. 399.

8. Hussite Chronicle, in *FRB*, vol. 5, p. 411.

An anonymous anti-Hussite rhymed chronicle, which can be reliably dated to the period around 1419 and 1420, adds additional support to the Papoušek depiction.[9]

> A terrible beast has come . . .
> Many soon gathered together in Prague
> They destroyed churches and monasteries
> Images and chairs were smashed
> Not even organs were spared

The reference in the anonymous rhymed chronicle appears to support events that transpired on August 10, 1420, when a large group of people from the southern Bohemian city of Tábor joined with likeminded sympathizers from the New Town of Prague. Led by the radical priest Václav Koranda of Plzeň, they arrived at Zbraslav and entered the undefended Cistercian monastery. Many of this group broke into the wine cellars and got drunk. They disinterred the body of King Václav and poured wine over him, enjoining him to drink with them. Eventually, they set fire to all of the buildings and burned them down.[10] The author of the rhymed chronicle went on to detail further atrocities:

> Not being satisfied with this
> They disinterred sacred bones
> Defamed altars and vestments as well.
> They burned down the Carthusian monastery
> Dragged the monks out saying:
> Look at these silent ones
> Lying like pigs in the sty

Once again, while the chronology is imprecise, it is possible to link these allegations to actual events, which once more have been grimly recorded within the pages of the Hussite Chronicle. The chapter house of the Carthusian order at Smíchov, southwest of Prague, was destroyed on August 17, 1419. Most of the monks were German, and these religious were expelled under the direction of the military commander and fervent

---

9. Třeboň, State Archives, MS A 16 fol. 223r–v.

10. Hussite Chronicle, in *FRB*, vol. 5, p. 399.

Hussite devotee Jan Žižka, and the monastery was subsequently burned down.[11] Again, the revelations of Papoušek concerning the nature of Hussite religious practice are corroborated by more than one contemporary source.

By 1421, outspoken preachers declared in sermons that "monasteries were dens of villains" and had been founded inappropriately in violation of the law of Christ. Therefore, these preachers said that all monasteries should be uprooted by the faithful. Encouraged by such teaching, the followers of radical religion demolished within a little more than one year many monasteries and religious houses belonging to both male and female orders. The chronicler included in his grim, unedifying list Kartouzy in Prague, Strahov, Břevnov, the Mother of God at the end of the Bridge, Saints Peter and Paul at Zderaz, St. Ambrose, Zbraslav, Koruna, Milevsko, Nepomuk, Ostrov, the Apostolic Gate, Želev, Gredy of the monks, Kladruby, Cedlic, Opatovice, Vilémov, Hradiště, Osek, and Tůšen. Numerous houses of the mendicant orders were also destroyed. These included St. Thomas, St. Clement, Botice on Zelená Hora (Green Mountain), two in the northwestern Czech town of Žatec, two at Hradec Králové in eastern Bohemia, two in Úštek, one in Písek, one in Klatovy, one in Čáslav, one in Nymburk, and one near the important mining town of Kutná Hora. Convents were also destroyed, including those in Lúnevice, between Louny and Žatec, St. Katherine in Prague, St. Anne in the Lesser Town, St. Mary Magdalene, Chotěšov, Doksany, and in Týnice.[12] In other words, a very limited survey of theologically inspired popular uprisings over a five-year period following the death of Jerome provides unassailable support for the thesis advanced by Papoušek. That thesis submitted in narrative outline that radical preachers in Bohemia inspired popular communities to amalgamate, organize, commit serious acts of iconoclasm, and thereby confront, undermine, attack, and destroy aspects of well-established medieval religious practice. Inasmuch as this portrait can be supported by reliable sources, it is now necessary to see how, and to what extent, the activities and influence of Jerome can be related to this emerging culture of radical religion and its violent responses to traditional practices.

Before considering Jerome's role in the early history of Czech iconoclasm, it is important to identify the nature of the act and of those who

---

11. Hussite Chronicle, in *FRB*, vol. 5, p. 591

12. Hussite Chronicle, in *FRB*, vol. 5, p. 409.

perpetrated the breaking of images. The iconoclast is one who challenges beliefs or institutions. This may be done abstractly (theoretically) or concretely (literally). Reform, by nature, is iconoclastic to some extent, because it seeks to subvert, overthrow, and replace a status quo. Concretely, iconoclasm seeks to destroy what icons signify and is an expression of overt hostility to the visual forms and evidence of religion. These forms may include religious art, sacred objects, books, bones, relics, altars, vestments, candles, lamps, organs, and other religious paraphernalia. Iconoclasm may also be symbolic to the extent of expressing disregard or challenge to that which is signified. The rejection of visible symbols, their violent removal, is a necessary component of movements or ideas of reform. In the Middle Ages, iconoclasm was often illegal, technically speaking, and its commission was considered blasphemous or sacrilegious. This was certainly the case in late medieval Bohemia. Expressions of discontent, indicative of religious crisis, might be prompted by social grievances or theological disagreement. Again, this is certainly true to some extent in Bohemia at the end of the Middle Ages.

Iconoclasm is revolutionary. It is an act of violence. It is a rejection of that which is attacked. Further, it is a repudiation of either the symbol itself or those that sponsor the symbolic code. Literal acts of iconoclasm sometimes involved throwing snowballs at crucifixes; ears, noses, hands, feet, and heads chopped from statues; pictures defaced or destroyed; eyes gouged out of images of saints; the burning of sacred objects; throwing these same objects into lakes or rivers; burying them; depositing them into sewers or latrines; or feeding consecrated hosts to animals. And sometimes it suited the iconoclast merely to deface or ridicule the object, as opposed to undertaking its complete destruction. Chalices and monstrances were sometimes emptied onto the ground and the host trampled underfoot. Books, manuscripts, relics, reliquaries, cemeteries, burial monuments, or altars might likewise be damaged or destroyed as a protest against the practice of medieval religion. Can any of this savagery be linked to Jerome? Can his influence be linked to the iconoclastic tirades evident in Bohemia between 1410 and the 1430s?

During the course of 1410 and 1411, as pressure began to be applied to the nascent reform movements in Prague, we have very little evidence of Jerome's whereabouts or activities, but there is no good reason not to assume that once he fled from Vienna, he did not return to Prague. On the eve of his trial in Vienna, the archbishop of Prague took active steps to curb the influence of John Wyclif in the capital but also to assert

church authority over the reformers and to enforce policy with respect
to heresy. With the active assistance of Zdeněk of Chrást, archdeacon
of Žatec, Archbishop Zbyněk conducted the burning of Wyclifite books
on July 16, 1410, destroying approximately two hundred volumes.[13]
Chroniclers recorded the ensuing uproar in Prague over the book burning.[14] This uproar consisted of both peaceful protests and public hooli-
ganism, which sometimes turned violent. For example, a mob invaded
St. Vitus's Cathedral in the castle and chased the priest from the altar,
while six men with drawn swords entered St. Stephen's Church in the
New Town and threatened the priest with death. These acts occurred on
July 22.[15]

  Though ultimately unprovable, it is likely that if Jerome was in Prague
at the time, he must have been involved, as the activities around the book-
burning episode mirror to some extent other allegations of his behavior,
personality, and disposition. The conundrum is that none of the contemporary sources mentions his presence or involvement. Two days after the
book burning, the archbishop excommunicated Hus. A few weeks after
this incident, Kaspar Weinstein testified in court during the Vienna process against Jerome that he understood that Jerome had also been rumored
to have been sanctioned alongside Hus, Štěpán Páleč, and some of their
associates.[16] The claim is controversial, and the rumor leading to the
excommunication focused on interpretations of the Eucharist and philosophical ideas. Zbyněk excommunicated Hus as a corrupter of the faith,
with the caveat that Hus's legal appeal, filed three and a half weeks earlier,
was frivolous, and therefore the appellants were disobedient.[17] On June 25,
1410, Hus and seven of his associates, namely, Master Zdislav of Zvířetice,
Jan of Brandýs, Beneš of Lysa, Petr of Sepekov, Peter of Valencia, Michael

---

13. Chronicle of the University of Prague, in *FRB*, vol. 5, pp. 571–571; song text in NK, MS.
III G 16, fol. 18r.

14. František Palacký, ed., "Staři letopisové češti od r. 1378 do 1527," in *Scriptores rerum bohemicarum* (Prague: J.S.P., 1829), vol. 3, pp. 12–13; and Count [František] Lützow, *The Life and
Times of Master John Hus* (London: Dent, 1909), p. 126.

15. Chronicle of the University of Prague, in *FRB*, vol. 5, p. 572.

16. Cited in R. R. Betts, "The University of Prague: The First Sixty Years," in *Prague Essays*,
ed. R.W. Seton-Watson (Oxford: Clarendon , 1949), p. 61.

17. *Documenta*, pp. 397–399.

of Drnovice, and Jan of Lanstein, filed an appeal against the prohibition by Pope Alexander V to stop preaching.[18] In this appeal, Hus also protested the seizure of Wyclif's books and the threat of burning them. Jerome was not among those who appealed to the pope, and he is not mentioned in the writ of excommunication. It is inconceivable that had he been in Prague, he would not have lent his name and voice to the appeal and to the protests. His whereabouts remain a mystery.

Once the books had been destroyed, a number of university faculty members protested the immolation by holding a two-week-long disputation defending Wyclif's works. This would have run from late July into early August 1410. Those involved in the disputation included Hus, Jakoubek Stříbro, Prokop of Plzeň, Zdislav of Zvířetice, Šimon Tišnov, and Jan Jičín.[19] It is once again inconceivable that Jerome would have passed on an opportunity to engage in a disputation defending Wyclif and one also aimed at protesting the apparent arbitrary uses of ecclesiastical power. Hus went on record stating his disagreement with the book burning. Jerome would have been an equally strong voice.[20] We can only conclude that by this time, he had departed for Vienna.

Five years later, prosecutors in Constance put the blame on Jerome for putting up defamatory "books" against the Prague archbishop, which he was not ashamed to sign.[21] Once again, at his trial during the Council of Constance, Jerome was accused of abusing the deceased Archbishop Zbyněk while Hus was in the pulpit preaching to a congregation in Bethlehem Chapel. He allegedly also posted a libel against the archbishop, which excited common people to inappropriate activities. "Jerome wrote and posted in many places a notorious libel against the archbishop of Prague, Lord Zbyněk. [While] Hus was preaching, Jerome thrust his head out of a window in the Bethlehem Chapel and abused Zbyněk of happy memory in a serious manner in the presence of a large crowd of people. In this way he incited the people against him."[22] It is quite impossible to date these events, and our knowledge of them comes from legal indictments several years after their alleged commission.

---

18. *Documenta*, pp. 387–396.

19. *Documenta*, pp. 399–400.

20. Jan Hus, "Defensio libri de trinitate," in *MIHO*, vol. 22, pp. 41–56, esp. pp. 49–50.

21. Hardt, vol. 4, cols. 640–641.

22. Hardt, vol. 4, cols. 640–641, 670.

Jerome as Instigator

By 1412, with the trials and imprisonments of Buda and Vienna behind him, Jerome was in Prague, and here we have some definite evidence of his activities. At the June 17 disputation, Jerome supported Hus in the latter's definite stand against the abuses of indulgences. This occurred during a disputation in the university. It is reported that Jerome launched into a long, impassioned speech, which unfortunately is no longer extant, and then "jumped from his place" and insisted that the congregation go directly to the city magistrates and inform them that the indulgences were false and demand that action be taken forthwith to prevent further abuse in the city. Jerome evidently announced that he and Hus would proceed immediately to the civil authorities and boldly declare that the papal bull and the indulgences were wicked. Jerome then invited all who agreed with him to follow. This was a clear and definite attempt to lead a group of students directly to the town hall and stage a public demonstration and protest against indulgences. Incited by these words, many students rose to follow Jerome. The university chancellor, Marek of Hradec, was hard pressed to restrain Jerome from galvanizing students in a public protest, and he had great difficulty in persuading the students against this course of action. It was alleged that Jerome objected to this intervention and shouted at Marek in Czech: "listen to me, Master Marek, you will not risk your neck for me but I will give my neck for you." Even across six hundred years, the tensions exhibited in this confrontation remain palpable. Jerome then referred to II Timothy 1:12, where Saint Paul noted that God had the power to protect. When the *actum* had concluded, the chronicler pointed out that even though the impromptu protest had been averted, many more students accompanied Jerome to his house than those who stayed with Hus. This was on account of the fact that the students were pleased with Jerome's discourse.[23] This incident provides indication of Jerome's popular appeal and the scope of his leadership. It also forms a fascinating portrait of the differences in personality between Hus and

---

23. František Šimek, ed., *Staré letopisy české z vratislavského rukopisu novočeským pravopisem* (Prague: Historické spolku a společnosti Husova Musea, 1937), p. 10; and František Šimek and Miloslav Kaňák, eds., *Staré letopisy české z rukopisu křižovnického* (Prague: Státní nakladatelství Krásné Literatury, Hudby a Umění, 1939), p. 45. The entire incident is discussed in Václav Novotný and Vlastimil Kybal, *M. Jan Hus: Život a učení,* 5 vols. (Prague: Laichter, 1919–1931), vol. 2, pp. 93–97. See also František Šmahel, "Leben und Werk des Magisters Hieronymus von Prag," *Historica* 13 (1966): 98–100.

Jerome. The former was cautious, less impulsive, while the latter was prepared to instigate social revolution and, if taken literally at his word, go so far as to risk his own neck. One can only surmise the nature of the discourse that transpired between Jerome and the group of students who accompanied him to his lodgings following the disputation. These actions do not correspond to the initiatives later taken up within the Táborite tradition, but they do indicate a turning point in the formation of a new community.

Less than a month later, on July 11, three young men were executed for lodging a vehement protest against indulgences. Had they been with Jerome at his house? We will never know. The bodies of the slain were retrieved and carried in procession, led by Master Jan Jičín, along with a great congregation of people. Pious women wrapped the bodies in white linen. The next day, they were buried in Bethlehem Chapel with the rites of martyrs. Jerome was later accused of being among the prime instigators of the original protests.[24] This is in contrast to the narrative in a Czech chronicle that has unnamed women and Jan Jičín as central characters.[25] In the records from Constance, Jerome has been assigned the leading role in the procession, and it is he who arranged for the sung Mass at the funeral. Witnesses claim that Jerome began the Mass himself by singing the *Gaudeamus* and following the requiem persisted in militating against the sale of indulgences. The truth lies somewhere between the two accounts, but it cannot be refuted that Jerome was one of the leaders in the Prague reform movement actively encouraging a reconsideration of medieval religious practice. Some of the protests against indulgences that circulated in Prague may be associated with Jerome, and some of these went so far as to denounce the promoters of indulgences as "disciples of Asmodeus, Belial, and Mammon."[26] We find no evidence for the days that followed that either Jerome or Hus was active or visible in Prague. The executions of Martin, Jan, and Stašek must have been sobering, and the atmosphere in the city was more reflective than revolutionary.[27]

24. Hardt, vol. 4, cols. 642, 676–677.

25. Šimek and Kaňák, *Staré letopisy české z rukopisu*, pp. 10–11.

26. Paul de Vooght, *L'Hérésie de Jean Huss*, 2nd ed. (Louvain: Publications universitaires de Louvain, 1975), pp. 198–199.

27. Jaroslav Mezník, *Praha před husitskou revolucí* (Prague: Academia, 1990), p. 164.

At some stage, Jerome took into his service Peter of Valencia. This man had been one of those who appealed to the pope from Zbyněk in 1409.[28] Five university students at Prague—Přibík of Húžné, Hroch of Podvek, Peter of Valencia, Michael of Drnovice, and Jan of Lanstein—filed an appeal with the Pisan Curia against Archbishop Zbyněk's order to surrender Wyclifite books. The date is uncertain, but it must have been either in late 1408 or early 1409. The text is not extant.[29] The attorney for the students was Marek of Hradec, who was forced later to restrain Jerome from leading a student protest to the city hall. The association of Jerome with Peter of Valencia creates a further, if tenuous, link between protests and radical reforms.

As noted earlier, Jerome was said to have preached a sermon before King Sigismund at Buda in 1410. There is further evidence to suggest that even though he was a layman, Jerome was in the habit of preaching regularly.[30] Ostensibly, Jerome was charged with preaching the errors of Wyclif and Hus and wickedly declaring that neither popes nor bishops had the authority to offer indulgences. Jerome apparently went further and often asserted that it was entirely permissible for any literate layperson or intelligent individual who possessed understanding to preach the word of God. Jerome was alleged to have asserted that it was licit to have lay preaching both inside and outside the church. It was unnecessary to have either papal or episcopal permission to preach, and the idea of requiring a license to preach was equally, according to Jerome, quite indefensible. Apparently, this was a regular theme of Jerome's in public discourse. At his trial in Constance, he was charged with making such statements frequently in many places, throughout various ecclesiastical jurisdictions, and in many kingdoms and with publicizing these opinions both in Bohemia and later in Moravia. If the accusation against him is accurate, it appears that Jerome seems to be promoting the idea that all people are priests in the sense of proclaiming the gospel. The idea was controversial, and the charge against Jerome included three additional points. First, Jerome himself was but a layman. Second, his representations of the subject were notorious. Third, he disseminated such errors while wearing a long beard.[31]

---

28. Hardt, vol. 4, col. 642.

29. Referred to in the *Ordo procedendi* and in the Chronicle of the University of Prague, in *FRB*, vol. 5, pp. 570–571.

30. Hardt, vol. 4, col. 670. See also the claim that Jerome frequently preached in Prague and in rural areas. Novotný and Kybal, *M. Jan Hus*, vol. 1, pp. 240–241.

31. Hardt, vol. 4, col. 673.

An apocryphal saying attributed to Plutarch asserted that "the beard does not define a philosopher" (*philosophum non facit barba*). The reference to Jerome's beard becomes a perennial one, and indeed the beard of Jerome is one of the abiding images from this chapter of religious history. It is difficult to assign any particular relevance to the repeated references to Jerome's beard. The only one that makes any sense at all would be that its presence indicated a further disqualification of Jerome as a preacher. Medieval priests were normally clean-shaven, and a beard was a visible sign that the one assuming typically priestly functions was neither viable nor acceptable. Popes Julius II and Clement VII were the first prominent churchmen in the West to wear beards.[32] It was not until 1531 that a formal *apologia* appeared, arguing that the appeal for clean-shaven priests was based on corrupt sources, which were then dismantled by means of historical criticism and philological analyses.[33] In the early fifteenth century, these arguments were unknown, and Jerome's beard remained a contentious matter.

Among the iconoclastic activities involving Jerome is the likelihood that he wrote songs in the vernacular Czech that were used to promote his ideas.[34] This was a feature of the Hussite movement, and we find evidence of songs both in liturgy and also in popular manifestations that were intentionally didactic.[35] Hus used the medium of song also to convey theological or religious ideas.[36] Jerome composed Czech-language songs and commissioned others to be composed, which tradesmen and common people learned and sang. According to his detractors, Jerome

---

32. On the subject of beards, see Thomas A. Fudge, "Picturing the Death and Life of Jan Hus in the Iconography of Early Modern Europe," *Kosmas: Czechoslovak and Central European Journal* 23, no. 1 (2009): 3–4, with references to pertinent sources.

33. Giovanni Pierio Valeriano, *Pro sacerdotum barbis* (Rome: Apud Caluum, 1531), with important passages on A2, B3–B3v. I have also used the more accessible *Pro sacerdotum barbis Ad clarissimum Cardinalem Hippolytus Medicem, Declamatio* (Frankfurt: Erasmus Kämpffer, 1613), pp. 1–16.

34. Hardt, vol. 4, col. 669.

35. The relation between popular songs and promoting particular messages has been examined in Thomas A. Fudge, *The Magnificent Ride: The First Reformation in Hussite Bohemia* (Aldershot: Ashgate, 1998), pp. 186–216; and more recently by Marcela K. Perett, "Vernacular Songs as 'Oral Pamphlets': The Hussites and Their Propaganda Campaign," *Viator* 42, no. 2 (2011: 371–391. On liturgy, see the source texts and references in Jana Fojtíková, "Hudební doklady Husova kultu z 15. a 16. století: Příspěvek ke studiu husitské tradice v době předbělohorské," *Miscellanea Musicologica* 29 (1981): 51–142.

36. MIHO, vol. 4, pp. 533–78.

composed many songs that were sung day and night in the streets of Prague vilifying the Holy Church. The same Jerome taught many lay-people the words of consecration and songs of this kind. Evidently, Jerome taught that common people could celebrate the body of Christ. This created considerable commotion and from an official church point of view constituted a serious heresy, as it corroded the authority of the sacerdotal ministry of the church. As a result, considerable turmoil was stirred up against the clergy in the Czech lands and the surrounding areas.[37] There was nothing random about iconoclasm in the early stages of reform and revolt inspired by men such as Jerome. In Prague and throughout Hussite Bohemia, there was outrage about the old practices of religion, which had been revealed by men such as Jerome to be fraud-ulent and which common people had been devoted to. Once those reli-gious practices were discredited or accepted as no longer legitimate, it became impossible to maintain that iconoclasm was merely a side effect of reform. Instead, under the influence of men such as Jerome, icono-clasm in its many dimensions evolved into a necessary and important element in the establishment of reformed religious practice. Jerome was conscious that public disputations, popular songs, and hymnody, along with preaching, were the main tools at his disposal, by which he could influence and facilitate a new Christian community. He took advantage of all three.

During the height of the dispute between the Prague reformers and their ordinary, books were burned, and the archbishop was ridiculed pub-licly. We have already noted the allegation that Jerome castigated Zbyněk through an open window in Bethlehem Chapel while Hus was preach-ing. Did Jerome write the defamatory verses against the archbishop, who was mocked for his insufficient education and was given the nick-name ABCD, or the alphabetizer in the Czech "alphabet"?[38] Probably not, but the sentiment of the song would certainly have resonated with Jerome. Some of the verses of the song *Musí býti ohlášeno* ("It Has to Be Announced") are distinguished by the same nationalistic tenor as Jerome's speech during the 1409 *Quodlibet* conducted by Matěj Knín. It applies, for example, to the hexastich that emerged from the outrage over the book-burning exercise:

37. *FRB*, vol. 8, p. 297.

38. Prague, National Library MS III G 16, fol. 18r.

Zbyněk burned books,
Zdeněk ignited them.
They did an injustice to the Czechs,
Woe to all those popes!
Behold, Czechs!
Behold, Czechs![39]

Even if Jerome was not the author of these verses, they provide proof of resonance with his appeals, which certainly were not voiced only in university lecture rooms. The actions of Archbishop Zbyněk and Canon Zdeněk of Chrást were certainly intolerable to Jerome. Eighteen months before the destruction of heretical books, Jerome had publicly enjoined people, "never in the future hand over books" to those who do not understand them and to those who ridicule the truth.[40]

It is impossible to untangle reality and truth from inflated or exaggerated claims used to demonize and facilitate political agendas. That said, there is sufficient corroborated testimony and circumstantial evidence to posit an argument that Jerome was an iconoclast on several levels and may have resorted to various forms of violence in his campaign of protest against certain features of late medieval religious practice. Almost all of the evidence for these actions must be accessed from the records of his trial at Constance, and therefore they must be used with caution. Nevertheless, it is important to point out that in many cases, Jerome admitted to at least a kernel of truth contained in the allegations. It is fair to conclude that acts of violence and iconoclasm were within the practice and purview of Jerome. There is at least circumstantial evidence to suspect that he played a role in an escalation of unrest in Prague, which resulted in public demonstrations that took to the streets.[41]

A number of isolated instances were brought together in a legal proceeding that aimed to demonstrate the unorthodox behavior of Jerome and his apparent contempt for aspects of religious culture. For example, during a confrontation with his opponents in Prague, he slapped the Dominican Beneš of Mladá Boleslav across the face. The confrontation

---

39. Bohuslav Havránek, ed., *Výbor z český literatury husitské doby*, 2 vols. (Prague: Československá akademie věd, 1963–1964), vol. 1, p. 268.

40. *Recommendatio artium liberalium*, in Šmahel/Silagi, p. 216.

41. See, for example, the *Anonymi invective contra husitas*, in Höfler, vol. 1, p. 624.

quickly escalated, and Jerome is reported to have pulled a knife on the monk. It is not possible from the reports to determine whether Jerome meant to harm the monk or whether he simply intended to intimidate him, though the implication is that he probably would have killed or seriously wounded him. The outcome of the hostility was altered when Master Zdislav of Zvířetice, a Prague academic and later chancellor of the university, intervened, and Jerome was prevented from using the weapon.[42]

One of the more notorious acts of iconoclasm was a well-organized procession featuring a sharp critique of the by now thoroughly politicized practice of indulgence sales in Prague. Probably in August 1412, Voksa of Valdštejn, the commander of the castle guard, possibly with the collusion of Jerome, organized the public event.[43] This incident featured an allegorical float, escorted by "armed Wyclifites," imitation papal bulls, and indulgences. Two "public whores," or students dressed as whores, with papal bulls hanging from their breasts, were the centerpiece of the blasphemous cart. Leering at the crowd, the loose women enticed the onlookers with lewd words and gestures. The procession wound its way from the Lesser Town, across the bridge spanning the Vltava River, past major ecclesiastical buildings in Prague, including the palace of the archbishop, through the Old Town, and past the king's palace, with much fanfare of enthusiastic crowds who shouted approval. Once the procession reached the New Town square outside the city hall, the papal bulls and indulgences were burned "around the time of vespers." All the while, the pope was characterized as a heretic and the "pimp of whores." Jerome's presence and participation are rather shadowy. It is doubtful that Hus would have either encouraged or approved of such behavior, but there can scarcely be any doubt that Jerome would not only have enjoyed the affair but would have actively promoted it.

In the same month (August), Jerome can be found in southern Bohemia at Jindřichův Hradec, where he once again came into physical conflict with religious figures. We are not told why Jerome was there, but whether by design or coincidence, there was another confrontation. We are informed that Jerome drove the priests Jan of Vysoké Mýto and Beneš of St. Michael's Church in Prague-Opatovice out of town. The two

---

42. Hardt, vol. 4, cols. 641–642.

43. Hardt, vol. 4, cols. 671–672; and *Documenta*, p. 640. Martin Lupáč took part in the affair and wrote about it. See Šmahel/Silagi, pp. LXXIII–LXXIV, with references to sources.

clerics had come to Jindřichův Hradec to publish the indulgences granted by Pope John XXIII. Jerome was alleged to have been "inspired by the devil" and under such malevolent inspiration accosted the religious with a group of armed men, hailing the indulgence preachers as "liars" who had come to represent a pope who was likewise a "liar, a heretic, and a usurer." Thus inflamed, the men with Jerome rushed at the two hapless clerics and chased them from their house to the parish church, where the two sought to gain sanctuary. The sanctuary of the church was temporary, and the men with Jerome took no note of the normal rules governing churches and shortly thereafter drove the two priests out of Jindřichův Hradec altogether.[44] Anticlericalism often went hand in hand with iconoclasm.[45]

Having thwarted the preaching and sale of indulgences at Jindřichův Hradec, Jerome returned to Prague. Allegations of continued iconoclasm persisted. This time, it seems that relics were the object of Jerome's indignation, and a near-fatal incident transpired. On either September 28 or 29, Jerome assailed the commerce and veneration of relics at the Carmelite Church of St. Mary's of the Snows. In the melee, Jerome either seized or produced a sword and subdued three friars. He turned two of them over to the authorities of the New Town, and they were remanded to the town jail in the company of "thieves and robbers." Jerome effectively kidnapped, or took into personal custody, a third friar named Mikuláš. Evidently, the fracas began when a friar insisted on payment for showing the relics. A citizen of Prague replied that in his view, the whole business was nonsense, and seizing the relic from the friar, he trampled the holy object underfoot.[46] It is not difficult to hold the opinion that Jerome incited the Praguer to trample the relics at St. Mary's of the Snows, and articles of accusation at Constance asserted that he had commanded the relics to be thrown to the ground. After all, indulgences were also part of the controversy over relics, and we have already established Jerome as a main player in the disputes. Iconoclasm and violence went hand in hand,

---

44. Hardt, vol. 4, cols. 642, 671.

45. For a brief sketch, see František Šmahel, "The Hussite Critique of the Clergy's Civil Dominion," in *Anticlericalism in Late Medieval and Early Modern Europe*, ed. Peter A. Dykema and Heiko A. Oberman (Leiden: Brill, 1993), pp. 83–90.

46. Hardt, vol. 4, cols. 641, 666–667, and 751–752. See Novotný and Kybal, *M. Jan Hus*, vol. 2, pp. 160–161; Štěpán Dolany, "Antihus," in *Thesaurus anecdotorum novissimus seu veterum monumentorum*, ed. Bernard Pez, 6 vols. (Augsburg: Philippi, Martini, & Joannis Veith fratrum, 1721–1729), vol. 4, cols. 380–382; and Šmahel, *Život a dílo Jeronýma*, p. 54.

and Jerome did not shrink from leadership in this area. On another occasion, a Dominican from St. Clement's was seduced into apostasy, apparently at sword point, by Jerome but was later drowned in the river. Jerome was accused of murder in connection with the incident, which he denied, saying the monk had accidentally drowned while bathing.[47] Other similar allegations against Jerome included the accusation that he personally took the Dominican monk Mikuláš into a boat on the Vltava River at Prague. Ostensibly, Jerome tied the monk to the end of a long rope and threw him overboard. He then endeavored to bully Mikuláš into retracting his previous opinions wherein he had spoken against Wyclif, by taunting the hapless man with words such as "now tell me monk, was Master John Wyclif a holy man or not?" It was later alleged that Jerome would have drowned the Dominican had he not been prevented by some others who happened by and saved Mikuláš from grave peril.[48]

In the autumn of 1412, Hus went into exile after being sanctioned with his fourth excommunication. Hus agreed to vacate Prague in order to spare the city the rather severe implications of interdict. With Hus in exile and Jerome back in Prague, the latter may have come even more to the forefront in the sense of leading a reform movement.[49] Unlike Hus, Jerome appears to have preferred to take the message and initiative of reform to the people, in public places, and to do so in shocking and offensive ways. On March 31, 1414, there was an incident at the Monastery of St. James wherein a crucifix was smeared with excrement. Usual suspects were rounded up, and the arrested perpetrator turned out to be a blacksmith from Poříčí in the New Town. He claimed that Jerome had put him up to undertake the desecration of the icon. On April 6, a similar occurrence was repeated at the Servite cloister of the Blessed Virgin Mary on the Sand in the New Town. Once again, the incident was put down to the incitement of Jerome, and the act had been carried out by a member of the "Wyclifite sect." In April, a picture of a cross was desecrated in the New Town at the Church of Mary of the Snows, once again at the apparent instigation of Jerome. In May, at the Monastery of St. James, another similar attack was made against a crucifix on the grounds that Jerome had insisted

---

47. Hardt, vol. 4, cols. 642, 671–672.

48. Hardt, vol. 4, col. 667.

49. Ferdinand Seibt, *Hussitica. Zur Struktur einer Revolution* (Cologne: Böhlau, 1965), p. 79.

that depicting the crucified Christ was heretical.[50] These incidents must be seen as parallel to those mentioned by Vavřinec of Březova a scant three years after Jerome met his end at Constance, and these are also very much consistent with the later descriptions provided by Papoušek.

Jerome did not believe that the images in question had legitimacy and therefore might be desecrated. Iconoclasm in Bohemia was, at the center, a result of theological controversy. Jerome clearly saw relevance in abusing images in situ rather than taking them away for private destruction. Which came first in the early history of iconoclasm, indication of a process already complete or an agent of change ramping up to effect change? An evaluation of the causes and effects of iconoclasm with any degree of precision is a difficult if not impossible task. Some scholars believe it is impossible to correlate theological debate with iconoclastic activities.[51] I do not subscribe to that thesis. A combination of social, religious, and historical factors precipitated the climate of iconoclasm. The ideas coming out of the reform movement in Prague possess specific social and political dimensions, as the writings of Hus, Jakoubek, Mikuláš Pelhřimov, and Petr Chelčický reveal.

It is entirely possible that Jerome, and some of the Hussites who followed him, recognized that the cult of images within late medieval religious practice tended to obscure the spiritual reality that these images physically reflected. In response, Jerome's philosophical leanings caused him to believe that the physical replacement of spiritual reality was theologically indefensible and markedly inferior to the purity of Christian religion. Jerome would have understood that an overreliance on images and the externalization of religion presented the possibility for undermining the rational and minimizing the need for a reasoned faith or intellectual proofs to buttress the integrity of the faith. It can be argued that iconoclasm eliminated the danger that images may have overshadowed the realities they sought to represent.

More specifically, it seems fruitful to consider the connection between relics and indulgences.[52] The two were very closely related. Iconoclasm was a decisive rejection of both elements, and in 1412 Prague, this was both a political and a theological statement against external piety and abuses

---

50. Hardt, vol. 4, cols. 674–675; and *FRB*, vol. 8, p. 300.

51. Milena Bartlová, "Understanding Hussite Iconoclasm," *BRRP* 7 (2009): 126.

52. Etienne Delaruelle, *L'Eglise au temps du Grand Schisme et de la Crise Conciliaire (1378–1449)*, vol. 14 of *Histoire de l'Eglise*, ed. A. Fliche and V. Martin (Paris: Bloud & Gay, 1964), pp. 810–820.

associated with relics and indulgences. Jerome was on public record in opposition to both aspects of late medieval religion. Progressing to acts of iconoclasm presented a natural step in the critique. The Hussites presented the first major challenge to the visual culture of medieval religious practice in the Latin West. The theological and philosophical ideas developed by Wyclif, Hus, and Jerome, when popularized, created expressions and incidents of popular iconoclasm.[53] Men such as Wyclif and Hus were concerned with theological and ethical issues, but those concerns could easily be translated into physical violence and attacks on religious practice. Men such as Jerome went further than Wyclif and Hus and inflamed the populace to iconoclastic tirades, and as later Hussite history shows in myriad examples, iconoclasm became a distinguishing feature of reformed religious practice, especially among the Táborites.[54]

It may be noted that there are no particular iconoclastic tendencies reflected in Jerome's writings. One might naturally have expected to encounter some opinion or justification for violence against religious objects or a reasoned discourse enumerating why these objects were offensive or in some way inconsistent with the truth of pure Christianity. In that hope or expectation, one may scour the pages of Jerome's extant writings in vain for evidence of iconoclastic tendencies. The absence of rhetoric or suggestion in support of iconoclasm in his writings does not exclude the possibility that in his speeches he may have encouraged it.[55] History is also silent on what sort of advice or encouragement Jerome may have given to his hearers outside of formal settings. Jerome was popular with students, and we have already encountered evidence of groups of students accompanying him from disputations. It is highly unlikely that following his impassioned comments at the June 17, 1412, university disputation, wherein he nearly succeeded in organizing a public rally against indulgences and a demonstration march on the town hall, the conversation thereafter did not involve discussion of additional acts of protest. We have no way of knowing. Similarly, one cannot often make definite correlations between sermons and acts of iconoclasm. The sermon by Jakoubek Stříbro

---

53. For Wyclif's views of images, see his *Tractatus de mandatis divinis*, ed., F. D. Matthew (London: C.K. Paul & Co./WS, 1922), pp. 153–166.

54. For an important but often ignored study of this subject, see Horst Bredekamp, *Kunst als Medium sozialer Konflikte. Bilderkämpfe von der Spätantike bis zur Hussitenrevolution* (Frankfurt am Main: Suhrkamp, 1975), pp. 231–333, an analysis from a Marxist perspective.

55. Šmahel, *Život a dílo Jeronýma*, p. 69.

in the Týn Church in January 1417 is an example. Nevertheless, Jakoubek was quite clear on the matter. Images that were inordinately revered ought to be thrown out with all haste, for they could be an impediment to true religion and may distract people from what is truly significant.[56] Indeed, in an earlier sermon (1415 or 1416), he pointed out that while the early church had no images, the late medieval church featured so many that it was quite impossible to distinguish which ones possessed divine significance or legitimacy and which were merely human institutions.[57]

It is interesting that similar elements of iconoclasm took place at Kozí Hrádek and Sezimovo Ústí. These acts included a rejection of the veneration of the cross and relics and the blasphemous naming of nonconsecrated objects after saints.[58] We cannot definitively place Jerome in those locations, but it is possible to point out that Hus was accommodated in these two places for almost two years. Hus was at Kozí Hrádek from October 1412 until the spring of 1414. From then until July, he was at Sezimovo Ústí. Did Jerome visit Hus in exile? Did he undertake or inspire acts of iconoclasm and protest against aspects of religious practice? It is impossible to say for certain. What can be asserted is that in southern Bohemia, radical communities emerged following the deaths of Hus and Jerome, and their approach to religious practice was radical and iconoclastic. We can also point to numerous testimonies that Jerome advocated a reconsideration of particular aspects of medieval religion. It would be imprudent to speculate further, but the possibility exists that Jerome spearheaded a more radical approach to reform and religious practice.

Jerome also lodged peaceful protests against those elements of religious practice that he found objectionable. On one occasion, Jerome apparently dressed up as a beggar, with his usual long beard and barefoot, and rode on a donkey to Žebrák Castle, where King Václav was staying, a distance of about forty-five kilometers, or twenty-eight miles, southwest of Prague. The name of the castle means "beggar," and the king evidently took the stunt against indulgences in good humor.[59] At Constance, Jerome was

---

56. *Littera de ymaginibus*, NK, MS III G 28, fols. 225v–227v.

57. Noted in Paul de Vooght, *Jacobellus de Stříbro (†1429), premier théologien du hussitisme* (Louvain: Publications universitaires de Louvain, 1972), pp. 143–144.

58. František Šmahel, *Dějiny Tábora* (České Budějovice: Jihočeské nakladatelství, 1988), vol. 1, pp. 212–213.

59. Novotný and Kybal, *M. Jan Hus*, vol. 2, p. 130.

characterized as assuming a consistent and persistent, and also strident, stand against indulgences. If he could not be present to thwart the sale of indulgences, he evidently sent others to carry out his bidding. The same might be said with respect to other seeming random acts of iconoclasm.

Jerome maintained sustained criticism of the use of indulgences, the legitimacy of papal or episcopal censure, and the abuses perpetrated by priests. He did not call for the eradication of indulgences or the elimination of clerical powers of discipline, but he did advocate the cessation of abuses associated with them. It is possible that Jerome was influenced on these three matters by the work of his colleague Hus, but it is only with respect to the third point where Jerome acknowledges indebtedness to Hus. It is not possible to prove similar dependence or influence for the first two.

It seems crucial to maintain a distinction between religiously or theologically inspired iconoclasm and those occurrences that were primarily a result of militaristic acts. The theory around iconoclasm is difficult, but the reality of those deeds has often been clearly recorded. In those cases associated with Jerome, these were public, not private, acts. Once again, the distinction is critical. The acts attributed to Jerome were inspired by theological conviction and a logical approach to criticizing religious practice. It is specious to argue that iconoclasm, even in the context of the Hussite wars, was fueled mainly by military considerations.[60] Destroying a monastery or church might be considered strategically important, but taking the time to attack the representations of religious practice served no military purpose. It is impossible to dismiss Papoušek's account as a simplistic effort at trying to prove that Hussites were heretics. Certainly, he took that equation as self-evident. His account, and those of other chroniclers such as Vavřinec of Březová, also engaged in reflecting history. Iconoclasm was part of the fabric of the faith that emerged in Bohemia within the reform efforts of men from Jan Milíč of Kroměříž to Hus. Jerome was an important component of that evolution.

It is not possible to conclude that Jerome inspired common people to commit iconoclastic acts because he despised images that represented

---

60. Both Norbert Schnitzler and Karel Stejskal have done this. See Norbert Schnitzler, *Ikonoklasmus—Bildersturm: Theologischer Bilderstreit und Ikonoklastisches Handlen wäherend des 15. a und 16. Jahrhundert* (Munich: Fink, 1996), pp. 51–60; and Karel Stejskal, "Ikonoklasmus českého středověku a jeho limity," *Umění* 48 (2000): 206–217.

power. Instead, Jerome practiced what later Hussite thinkers succinctly expressed when they declared that iconoclasm was an act of justice intended to warn a sinful church.[61] The emphases that Jerome inserted into the nascent reform movement contributed to the radicalization of religion in Bohemia. Jakoubek Stříbro later remarked that there were many truths, some of which should not be revealed until hearts were ready to receive them.[62] Jerome preferred bombshells over caution, and the fragments of his life that survive are witness to his belief that all of truth was required to transform hearts and therefore ought not to be suppressed. On his deathbed, Jakoubek told Jan Rokycana that he ought to keep two sets of books. One set should be used for his own consideration, while the other might be used to instruct the common people.[63] Jerome appears to have thought the two sets should be amalgamated into one and the common book should be used to pursue the law of God, attacking and destroying where necessary all impediments to that goal. Unlike Jakoubek, Jerome did not live long enough to cultivate the caution of old men. There are no grounds for advancing reasonable doubt in the consideration of whether Jerome was an influence on the trajectories of iconoclasm in Hussite Bohemia, which, in sum, in many respects, was intentionally conceived as a theologically inspired attack on aspects of medieval religious practice.

---

61. This was the view of Jan Rokycana, pointed out in Josef Krása, "Studie o rukopiesch husitské," *Umění* 22, no. 1 (1974): 19, 44.

62. Noted in František M. Bartoš, "Táboři a duchovní jejich otec," *Jihočeský sborník historický* 2 (1929): 81.

63. *Liber diurnus de gestis bohemorum in concilio basileensi*, in *MC*, vol. 1, p. 298.

6

Trial at the Council of Constance

THE PERIPATETIC CAREER of Jerome of Prague included one final dramatic chapter before its epic climax. The case of Jan Hus, especially at the Council of Constance, is a fairly well-known, if often misunderstood, episode in the history of late medieval Christianity, and its details have been well rehearsed.[1] Prior to Hus's removal to Constance, he spent two years in exile outside of Prague. Jerome took the view that if Hus could obtain a *salvus conductus*, then he ought to go to the Council of Constance. Perhaps Jerome imagined that Hus might have a more successful appearance there than he had in Vienna. The synod in southern Germany has been characterized as "one of the most magnificent church assemblies known to history."[2] Jerome visited Hus at Krakovec Castle and supported Hus in his decision to go to Constance. It was during this visit that Jerome's fate became inextricably linked with that of Hus. Jerome promised to join Hus in Constance and help out if needed. "Dear Master, be firm, maintain courageously what you have written and preached concerning the pride, avarice, and other vices of the churchmen based upon Holy Scripture. If the task becomes too difficult for you, or I hear that you have come into any danger, I will come to your assistance at once."[3] Of course, Hus did come

---

1. Matthew Spinka, *John Hus at the Council of Constance* (New York: Columbia University Press, 1965), includes a reliable translation of the chronicle of Petr Mladoňovice. See also analyses of the trial in Jiří Kejř, *Husův proces* (Prague: Vyšehrad, 2000), and Thomas A. Fudge, *The Trial of Jan Hus: Medieval Heresy and Criminal Procedure* (New York: Oxford University Press, 2013).

2. Franz Xaver von Funk, *Lehrbuch der Kirchengeschichte*, 4th ed. (Paderborn: Schöningh, 1902), p. 470.

3. František Šmahel, *Jeroným Pražský: Život revolučního intelektuála* (Prague: Svobodné slovo, 1966), pp. 152–153.

into grave danger and within weeks of his arrival in Germany was imprisoned. Thereafter, he was incarcerated in at least five different locations. In due course, Jerome fulfilled his commitment and made the dangerous journey to Constance. Before turning our attention to the particulars of the trial at Constance, it will be necessary to look briefly at the nature of the records that exist for the Council and especially those that come to bear directly on Jerome of Prague.

The Problem of the Acta

The *Acta* of the Council of Constance remain something of an unsolved mystery. Two decades after its sessions, we learn the records were never included in the Vatican archives, but one manuscript belonging to Guillaume Fillastre, Cardinal-Priest of St. Mark's, was brought to the Council of Basel, where it was used.[4] It is quite uncertain if there is in existence or ever was a "single collection of *Acta* compiled by the central secretariat of the Council."[5] We do have records stating expenses and referring specifically to expenditures associated with copying the acts of the Council (*pro actis concilii copiandis*).[6] Elsewhere we find manuscript reference to records from Constance that might seem to suggest that a proper recording procedure was in place: "This book contains the ordinances, statutes, decrees and other acts and deeds [that were enacted] of the general Council of Constance, with our most holy father in Christ, the lord Pope John XXIII, presiding by divine providence. They [the ordinances] have been collected, examined and drawn up in order by us, the protonotaries, notaries, and scribes listed below in writing, who were instructed to do this by our Lord the Pope, with the approval of the Council."[7]

---

4. Juan of Segovia, "Historia gestorum generalis synodi basiliensis," in *Monumenta conciliorum*, ed. Ernest Birk (Vienna: Typis C.R. Officinae typographicae aulae et status, 1873), vol. 2, pp. 75–76.

5. František Šmahel, "The *Acta* of the Constance Trial of Master Jerome of Prague," in *Text and Controversy from Wyclif to Bale*, ed. Helen Barr and Ann M. Hutchison (Turnhout: Brepols, 2005), p. 324.

6. Friedrich Firnhaber, "Petrus de Pulka, Abgesabdter der Wiener universität am Concilium zu Constanz," *Archiv für österreichische Geschichte* 15 (1856): 1–70. On Pulka, see especially Dieter Girgensohn, *Peter von Pulka und die Wiedereinführung des Laienkelches* (Göttingen: Vandenhoek & Ruprecht, 1964).

7. Rome, Biblioteca Apostolica Vaticana, Vat Lat, 1335, was completed in 1423. Its opening lines seem relevant, forming as they do, in effect, the incipit preceding an invocation to the

While it is has thus far proven impossible to locate or identify a single collection of *Acta*, there are various *Acta* existing parallel, and there are still a considerable number of manuscripts that have yet to be properly examined and subjected to a serious analysis. Some scholars remain pessimistic that much that is currently unknown is likely to emerge from the fragmentary sources that do remain.[8] Among the puzzles in the case of Jerome is that if further collections of sources exist on the Council of Constance, why is there no additional information on the trial of Jerome in the German sources?[9] The earliest printed edition of the *Acta* is as late as 1500 and appeared in Hagenau under the publishing imprint of Johannes Rynman.[10] This edition appears to have been based on a summary of the official *Acta* compiled between 1437 and 1442 by a special commission of the Council of Basel directed by Cardinals Ludwig Aleman and Giovanni de Casanova.[11] This collection featured the major decisions and decrees of the forty-five general sessions, along with major pronouncements such as bulls like the *Inter cunctus* of Martin V, which confirmed the conciliar decisions concerning John Wyclif, Hus and Jerome.[12] The earliest effort at sorting through the voluminous *Acta* and related documents was undertaken by Hermann von der Hardt (1660–1746). One of the indispensable source collections for the Council of Constance is Hardt's great work, but its usefulness is vitiated by its appalling confusion. In his first volume, Hardt included tracts by Czech polemicists such as Štěpán Páleč and Mařík Rvačka. In the second and third volumes, one encounters a series of texts relating to the trials of Hus and Jerome. The fourth volume contains a version or semblance of the *Acta* and excerpts from sources such as the diary of Guillaume Fillastre (cardinal of St. Mark)

Trinity. See C. M. D. Crowder, "Le Concile de Constance et l'edition de von der Hardt," *Revue d'histoire ecclésiastique* 57 (1962): 435.

8. Šmahel, "The *Acta* of the Constance Trial," p. 334.

9. Šmahel, "The *Acta* of the Constance Trial," p. 324. The *Acta* of the Council, insofar as it exists, is contained in Mansi, vols. 27, 28. Mansi is essentially a reprint of an older collection by the French Jesuit Jean Hardouin, *Conciliorum collectio regia maxima* (Paris: Ex Tipogr. Regia, 1714–1715), vol. 8. Another standard edition is that of Hardt, vol. 4 (1699). The most comprehensive secondary source is Walter Brandmüller, *Das Konzil von Konstanz 1414–1418*, 2 vols. (Paderborn: Ferdinand Schöningh, 1991–1997).

10. See Šmahel, "The *Acta* of the Constance Trial," p. 324 for publication details.

11. See Finke, *Acta*, vol. 4, pp. viii–ix.

12. Šmahel, *Život a dílo Jeronýma*, p. 324.

and the *Liber gestorum* of the papal notary Giacomo Cerretano. The fifth volume is made up chiefly of many documents relating to the organization and composition of the Council. The sixth volume details the relationship between pope and Council underscored in an assorted collection of documents. Volume seven contains indices. Despite the challenges presented by the absence of sources or the glaring lacunae in those that do exist or the confused nature of the editions produced by Hardt, there is considerable anecdotal detail about Jerome, and indeed Hardt is often the sole source for details of Jerome's earlier life and activities prior to his appearance before the synod at Constance. I use both Hardt and the collection of the Italian prelate and scholar Giovanni Domenico Mansi (1692–1769).[13] The latter should not be dismissed or considered simply an inferior reproduction of the former. While Hardt has often been preferred as a source basis for the trial of Jerome in this book, the value of the Mansi collection should neither be dismissed nor minimized. More recent collections supplement Hardt and Mansi, especially in areas where they are most deficient. This is mainly in terms of personal accounts such as the journals of Cardinal Fillastre, the notary Cerretano, and Guillaume de la Tour. There are also plenty of other writings of varying value, including speeches, pamphlets, letters, memoranda, and ephemeral literature.[14]

It has been suggested that it may be defensible to assume the existence of a single protocol of the *Acta* provided by the central secretariat.[15] C. M. D. Crowder has argued that logically speaking, it was necessary for the Council to have a record of its own proceedings and decisions. He also points out (perhaps tellingly) that the earliest manuscripts do not seem to reflect particular national bias.[16] While this may be true, it is prudent to keep in mind that the observation may be premature.[17] Almost a century ago, we find quite a different reading of the texts. "The more we read of the records of Constance, the more we find national feeling obstruding itself at every turn."[18] The Council of Constance operated on

---

13. Mansi, vols. 27, 28.

14. Finke, *Acta*, is a valuable resource.

15. Crowder, "Le Concile de Constance," p. 433.

16. Crowder, "Le Concile de Constance," pp. 429–433.

17. Šmahel, "The *Acta* of the Constance Trial," p. 328.

18. Louise R. Loomis, "The Organization by Nations at Constance," *Church History* 1 (December 1932): 210.

a different basis from what was usual or expected by ecclesiastical synods in the Middle Ages. The Council was convened by Pope John XXIII,
one of the three rival pontiffs at the time. John represented the Pisan
line. The synod was actively supported by Emperor-elect Sigismund. The
formal business of the Council commenced on November 5, 1414, in the
cathedral of Constance. The synod was represented by numerous bishops who had gathered from all over Europe. What was different about
the business transactions conducted at Constance was that voting was
done according to nations, not by individuals. It is uncertain how this
came about. Some believed that the arrangement had been proposed by
Robert Hallum, bishop of Salisbury, who had just arrived from England,
while the pope believed this was a strategy devised by Sigismund.[19] There
were four "nations" at Constance: Italian, French, German, and English.
Prelates often served as presidents of the four nations. For example, at
one stage, Bartolomeo de la Capra, archbishop of Milan, presided over
the Italian nation. Jean Mauroux, patriarch of Antioch, convened the
French nation. Johann Wallenrode, archbishop of Riga, had responsibil-
ity for the German nation. Robert Hallum, bishop of Salisbury, chaired
the English nation. This bred contempt. Guillaume Fillastre, the cardinal of St. Mark, complained that the Council appeared to be controlled
by "MARS" and that this was openly expressed. This was an allusion to
the acronym formed by the first letters of the respective sees, that is,
Milan, Antioch, Riga, and Salisbury.[20] Evidently, King Sigismund suggested that the Hungarians might form a fifth nation, but the idea was
never pursued.[21]

As delineated elsewhere, it is regrettable that the official court
Acta from the trials of Hus and Jerome appear to have been lost.[22]
Commenting specifically on the Hus process, Jiří Kejř has advanced the
argument that the records were retained at Constance. However, once
the heresy trials concluded and following the end of the Council itself,

---

19. Heinrich Finke, *Forschungen und Quellen zur Geschichte des Konstanzer Koncils*
(Paderborn: F. Schöningh, 1889), p. 29 (on the Hallum initiative); and Hermann Georg
Peter, *Die Information Papst Johannes XXIII. und dessen Flucht aus Konstanz bis Schaffhausen*
(Freiburg: Joseph Waibel, 1926), pp. 77–80, for John's views.

20. Fillastre, pp. 114–115.

21. This detail can be found in the diary of Guillaume de la Tour, in Finke, *Acta*, vol. 2, p. 351.

22. Fudge, *The Trial of Jan Hus*, pp. 23–25.

the records were possibly left behind. As time passed, these records were lost.[23] With respect to the court case involving Jerome, it is impossible to maintain that detailed records of the trial proceedings were not kept. It was customary and conventional to keep meticulous documentation. This was a standard feature of late medieval courts. From a procedural point of view, it was a firm requirement that such *Acta* be maintained. There is no basis for supposing that this requirement was not upheld during the trial of Jerome. It is possible that the *Acta* were taken from Constance to the Papal Curia by the new administration of Martin V. However, no trace of these records has been found by scholars who have worked in the several Vatican repositories. Alternatively, there is neither proof nor convincing argument to make any claim that the Curia of Martin V removed the *Acta* or made any effort to preserve them. It may be necessary simply to assume that the records of the trial of Jerome were left in Constance, perhaps in the episcopal library. The diocese of Constance dates to the late sixth century. The prince-bishopric was dissolved in 1803 and became part of the margraviate of Baden. The diocese itself was dissolved in 1821. Parts of it thereafter were incorporated into the archdiocese of Freiburg. Otto III of Hachberg was bishop of Constance during the Hus trial from 1410 until 1434, when he was deposed. There is no convincing argument to sustain a conclusion that *Acta* in the Jerome case were not kept. Their loss depreciates our knowledge and understanding of many issues within that trial proceeding. The unavailability of the official *Acta* means there are unavoidable gaps in the sources. These problems can be alleviated to some extent by consulting other existing documents.

With respect to the trial of Jerome and related topics, we have the so-called Freiburg Manuscript.[24] This Czech-language collection of texts in all likelihood was assembled and provided by Petr Mladoňovice, who wrote an eyewitness account of the death of Hus and was also in Constance for part of the time that Jerome's case was under consideration. This source is a transcription, meaning the translation itself is older and could be assigned to the period as early as 1416–1417.[25]

---

23. Kejř, *Husův proces*, p. 17.

24. *FRB*, vol. 8, no 13, pp. 247–318. For additional information on this collection, see pp. lxxiv–lxxvii.

25. Šmahel, "The *Acta* of the Constance Trial," p. 327.

The Freiburg Manuscript consists of the following documents: (1) a Czech translation of the *Acta* of the Council as it relates to Hus and Jerome; (2) letters written by Hus from the Dominican and Franciscan prisons; (3) a Czech translation of the last part of the *Relatio* written by Mladoňovice, which graphically details the last aspect of the Hus trial and his execution; (4) a Czech text about Jerome; (5) a Czech translation of the lengthy and important letter written by the Italian humanist Poggio Bracciolini, who witnessed the latter stages of the trial and the death of Jerome; (6) a version of a letter sent by members of the Czech nobility to Sigismund supporting Hus; (7) several letters by Sigismund; (8) a chronicle about the famous Hussite military personality Jan Žižka; and (9) an overview of the Hussite wars. The Prague professor of history Václav Novotný (1869–1932), editor of texts from the Hussite period, has argued that Mladoňovice was responsible for the collection.[26]

In terms of the accounts of Jerome at the Council of Constance, it is possible to identify more than a dozen sources. These include Gobelinus Persona,[27] Dietrich Niem,[28] Erdwinus Erdmannus,[29] the Magdeburg Chronicle,[30] the diary of Guillaume Fillastre,[31] the chronicle of the Council prepared by Ulrich Richental,[32] and an account by Mladoňovice.[33] There are also two anonymous accounts.[34] Additionally, the Hussite Chronicle, written by Vavřinec of Březová, has information about Jerome.[35] Poggio's

---

26. The claim is controversial. Zdeněk Fiala, *Zpráva o mistru Janu Husovi v Kostnici* (Prague: Universita Karlova, 1965), p. 45, with notes on p. 30 from the Czech version, disputes this with the argument that the Novotný thesis is highly unlikely.

27. Hardt, vol. 4, p. 772.

28. *De vita ac fatis Constantiensibus Johannis Papae XXIII*, bk. 3, chap. 34, vol. 2, cols. 449–454.

29. Hardt, vol. 4, p. 772.

30. Hardt, vol. 4, p. 772.

31. *Gesta concilii Constanciensis*, in Finke, *Acta*, vol. 2, pp. 13–170.

32. New edition by Thomas Martin Buck, ed., *Chronik des Konstanzer Konzils 1414–1418 von Ulrich Richental* (Ostfildern: Jan Thorbecke Verlag, 2010).

33. *FRB*, vol. 8, pp. 339–350.

34. The first is a composite text reflecting several hands, one of whom is a certain Franciscus de Tachovia, of whom nothing is known. *Notae de Concilio Constantiensis*, *FRB*, vol. 8, pp. 319–322. The other is *De Vita Magistri Ieronomi*, in *FRB*, vol. 8, pp. 335–338.

35. *FRB*, vol. 5, pp. 337, 340–341, 343–345.

aforementioned letter to Leonardo Bruni of May 30, 1416, is a useful historical document.[36] Beyond these, there are the *Acta* of the Council.[37] One other source might be mentioned. While the printed edition of the *Fasciculi zizaniorum* omits them, the collection does include texts on the trials of Hus and Jerome at Constance that remain in manuscript form.[38] There are so many differences from other versions with respect to the final hearing and judgment against Jerome, pronounced on May 30, 1416, that it is entirely reasonable to consider the Bodleian manuscript a separate and independent record.[39]

The anonymous *De vita Magistri Ieronomi* is really a narrative about the last trial and the fate of Jerome. The author was present at the events, was probably a Czech himself, and exhibits a clear and definite sympathy for Jerome. The anonymous *Narratio de Magistro Hieronymo Pragensi, pro Christi nomine Constantiae exusto* has unfortunately not survived in manuscript form and was first printed in the sixteenth century.[40] An imperial councilor in Vienna, Caspar von Nidbruck, and the Croatian Lutheran Matija Vlačić Ilirik (Matthias Flacius Illyricus) collaborated on producing these two volumes of sources relating to Hus and Jerome. There is nothing in the text or the publication making any connection to Flacius or to editorship of the collection. However, a letter of July 26, 1555, from Nidbruck to Flacius connects the latter to the source collection.[41] The Czech text of this source (ascribed by Novotný to Mladoňovice) survives in manuscript form in the Freiburg collection from the former Gymnasium Library in Freiburg. It was also published as an appendix to the Jena Codex in 1495. Two other accounts survive. One bears the title "The life and death of the famous Master Jerome who was burned to death for the truth of God on

---

36. Poggio, vol. 2, pp. 157–163. See appendix 12.

37. Hardt, vol. 4, cols. 629–691; Mansi, vol. 27, cols. 794–795; and acts of the trial of Jerome, Mansi, vol. 27, cols. 842–864.

38. W. W. Shirley, ed., *Fasciculi Zizaniorum Magistri Johannis Wyclif cum Tritico: Ascribed to Thomas Netter of Walden* (London: Longman, 1858). The manuscript is Oxford, Bodleian Library, MS e Musaeo 86, fols. 129ra–130ra.

39. Comments on this in Šmahel, "The *Acta* of the Constance Trial," p. 332.

40. *HM*, vol. 2, fols. 349a–354a. Modern text in *FRB*, vol. 8, pp. 339–350.

41. Viktor Bibl, "Der Briefwechsel zwischen Flacius und Nidbruck. Aus den Handschriften 9737b, i und k der k.u.k. Hofbibliothek in Wien," *Jahrbuch der Gesellschaft für der Geschichte des Protestantismus in Österreich* 20 (1899): 95–101.

account of the argument and creed of Master Jan Hus."[42] The other bears
the incipit "Here begins the life and death of the famous Jerome who was
burned to death in Constance for the truth of God who died because of the
argument of Master Jan Hus."[43]

The *Narratio de Magistro Hieronymo* is similar in design to the *Relatio*
of Mladoňovice. This consists of official documents, addresses by Jerome,
and, most important, the entire text of the latter's revocation of September
23, 1415. The author, almost certainly Mladoňovice, was present for some
of the legal process against Jerome but was not in Constance when Jerome
was executed. His whereabouts cannot be determined with any certainty,
but it was both characteristic and unfortunate of Mladoňovice to be absent
at important moments.[44] It is entirely likely that anonymous texts by eyewitnesses of Jerome's death came to his attention and he relied on these to
round out his account to the extent of essential verbatim copying.[45] The last
portions of the text were rendered into Czech but with some alterations.[46]
It is possible that by the beginning of the sixteenth century, the text was
then translated back into Latin. At the outset of the text, the author noted
that he had decided to write it in order to preserve the memory of Jerome
from oblivion, into which his subject had already begun to succumb. The
narrative is important, the author insists, for the benefit of those professing the faith and as a model of perseverance and fidelity to the truth. What
is self-evident from this brief survey of the state of the surviving sources
around the *Acta* of the Council of Constance, as they relate to Jerome, is
that a new, and critical, edition is desperately needed.

Jerome and the Council of Constance

At the beginning of the Council proceedings, Jerome's old foe from
Vienna, Nicholas Dinkelsbühl, preached a sermon before Sigismund on
the text of Genesis 47:25, wherein he instructed the king to take particular

---

42. KNM, MS 25 E 17.

43. KNM, MS 36 F 19.

44. In terms of the three hearings in the Hus case, Fudge, *The Trial of Jan Hus*, pp. 265–
269, notes that Mladoňovice missed the first hearing altogether and was late arriving for the
second and third.

45. *FRB*, vol. 8, pp. 335–338, 346–350.

46. *FRB*, vol. 8, pp. 351–367.

note that his relation to the convocation was significant. As Dinkelsbühl put it, "our fate is in your hands."[47] The statement was a distortion of reality and a trivializing of the underpinnings of the synod. Nevertheless, the king was probably pleased to hear this assessment of his importance. At the Christmas Eve Mass, 1414, Pope John XXIII presented the king with a dagger symbolic of his role as an advocate for the church (*advocatus ecclesiae*). The pope implored the monarch to fulfill his duty for the benefit of the church. Pierre d'Ailly urged Sigismund to act as a defender of the faith and to bring aid to the church as Constantine *redivivus*, just as his imperial predecessor had done more than a millennium earlier. Somewhat later, Robert Hallum, bishop of Salisbury, said as much to Sigismund in an address, when he affirmed that the king had been given a glorious opportunity in which he might serve the house of God and argued that the church hierarchy had to be reformed in head and in members.[48] We also find where the bishop of Lodi, Giacomo Balardi, in his sermon against Jan Hus, identified Sigismund as the most important figure in the church's war on heresy.[49]

We have previously seen that Jerome made a commitment to Hus that he would hasten to Constance, if needed, to support the latter. Hus arrived in Constance on November 3. Exactly two months later, on January 3, 1415, he warned Jerome not to come to Constance.[50] The events over those two months must have plunged Hus into despair and also brought him to an acute realization that grave danger lurked in Constance, not only for him but also for those who supported his cause. But before that preexisting danger had been fully appreciated, Hus departed from Bohemia. Thus, it came to pass that on November 3, Hus arrived in Constance and took up residence in St. Paul Street in the Pfister house with the young widow Fida.[51] The Pfister house is today located at 22 Hussenstraße.[52] Three and

---

47. Hardt, vol. 2, cols. 182–187.

48. Finke, *Acta*, vol. 2, pp. 394–395.

49. FRB, vol. 8, pp. 489–493.

50. Václav Novotný, ed., *M. Jana Husi Korespondence a dokumenty* (Prague: Nákladem komise pro vydávání pramenů náboženského hnutí českého, 1920), p. 236.

51. Buck, *Chronik des Konstanzer Konzils*, p. 60.

52. This has been established in an altogether impressive essay, based on archival sources, in Gernot Blechner, "Wo in Konstanz war die Herberge des Jan Hus?—Eine Hauslokalisierung

a half weeks later, he was arrested on the orders of Pope John XXIII and held under armed guard for eight days in the custody of William Challant, bishop of Lausanne, in the cathedral precentor's house just north of the cathedral.[53] Though the comment is ambiguous, sources note that the pope would not countenance having Hus spend a single night in the papal palace.[54] After eight days, Hus was transferred to a dungeon at the Dominican monastery.[55] It was here, after more than four weeks in "a dark and dank dungeon near the latrines," that Hus wrote warning Jerome to stay away from Constance. His own situation was precarious, and his harsh imprisonment did not bode well. Moreover, the city teemed with "women and young girls of ill repute, whores."[56]

The headstrong and impetuous Jerome took little note of Hus's letter. He wanted to help his friend and also desired to demonstrate the purity and orthodoxy of his faith publicly before the Council.[57] On the day of St. Ambrose, April 4, 1415, he arrived in Constance, accompanied by one unnamed associate, and took up residence in St. Paul Street at a house belonging to the Gutjar family.[58] That house has traditionally been thought to have been located at 14 Hussenstraße.[59] Richental says that Jerome arrived in Constance on April 1. It should be pointed out that Richental was writing sometime after these events, whereas Mladoňovice, who was writing at the time, says that Jerome did not arrive before April 4. The latter witness is preferred, because Mladoňovice was frequently in the company of Jerome and wrote his account shortly thereafter. Jerome did not linger long in Constance. After spending a single night in the city and upon learning of the imminent danger to himself, he retired to Überlingen the following day, some twenty-five miles from Constance on the north side

---

anhand zeitgenössischen Quellenmaterials," *Schriften des Vereins für Geschichte des Bodensees und seiner Umgebung* 101 (1983): pp. 49–71.

53. *Relatio*, p. 40.

54. *Liber gestorum* of the papal notary Giacomo Cerretano, in Finke, *Acta*, vol. 2, p. 189.

55. *Relatio*, p. 41.

56. Czech *Acta*, p. 317.

57. Hardt, vol. 4, col. 684.

58. Buck, *Chronik des Konstanzer Konzils*, p. 62; and Hardt, vol. 4, p. 93.

59. Gernot Blechner, ed., *1313–2013: 700 Jahre Haus Zum Delphin* (Constance: Werner C. Schupp, 2013).

of the lake. On April 7, he demanded a safe conduct.[60] Mladoňovice must have accompanied Jerome to Überlingen, for we know that he assisted Jerome with his request and that he brought the request back to Constance and saw that it got to Sigismund. In his haste (or panic) to depart from Constance, Jerome left behind his sword in the Gutjar house as he made his way to Überlingen and thereafter back to the Bohemian Forest, where he intended to hide.[61] During his brief stay in Constance, Jerome was in the company of Mladoňovice.

Hus had set out from Bohemia for Constance six months earlier. He had the promise of an imperial safe conduct. The commitment of protection had not shielded Hus from arrest and incarceration. Jerome had no such guarantee. The text of his request for protection reads in part like a challenge. Jerome had already come to Constance, entered the city, and spent a night within its walls. His boldness, after the night in the Gutjar house, however, seems to have failed him. Perhaps he discovered imminent danger. Possibly, he felt threatened. Whatever the particulars, he decided to seek imperial protection. There was absolutely no chance that Jerome would be granted a safe conduct. The one held by Hus generated considerable controversy, and by April 8, Sigismund had revoked all safe conducts held by anyone in Constance.[62] The request for protection was effectively denied. By April 7, the same day on which he asked for a safe conduct, Jerome arranged for the posting of public placards in Constance defending Hus.[63] Does this mean that Jerome actually returned to Constance to post the placards, or did he commission Mladoňovice or some others to do it? The placards were affixed to the doors of churches and places where Council dignitaries were lodged. Jerome was not likely in Constance long enough to have learned these details. The advertisements declared that Hus was innocent of the charges and allegations leveled against him and went on to announce that his incarceration was illegal.[64] We do know that

---

60. Hardt, vol. 4, pp. 103–104. See appendix 5.

61. Buck, *Chronik des Konstanzer Konzils*, p. 62.

62. *Documenta*, pp. 543–544.

63. One of the anonymous scribes of the *Notae de Concilio Constantiensis, FRB*, vol. 8, pp. 319–320, says he copied Jerome's letter and the application for safe conduct.

64. Hardt, vol. 4, col. 103.

Mladoňovice assisted Jerome in rendering the original Czech texts into German and Latin.[65] The *Passio* notes that the letters or advertisements were written in Latin, German, and Czech.[66] This means either that Mladoňovice must have returned to Überlingen, that the notices were prepared during his first visit to the town, or that Jerome came to Constance a second time. The latter seems improbable. Having come all the way to Constance from Prague, spending only one night, departing in such haste as to forget his sword, and removing himself a distance of twenty-five miles from Constance amount to sufficient circumstantial evidence to conclude that Jerome did not return to the scene of the Council. On May 26, 1416, Jerome told the Council that he had sent letters to Constance with the intent that they be posted on his behalf.[67] Nevertheless, Jerome's actions contravened Sigismund's official orders given on January 1 concerning the public posting of placards about Hus. Such activities were prohibited. Even if Jerome were aware of that decree, it is certain he would not have paid any attention to it whatsoever.

There is very dubious testimony that somehow during his short stay in Constance, Jerome managed to see Hus in prison.[68] This seems highly unlikely. Hus had been transferred from the Dominican prison to the west tower of the Gottlieben Castle on March 24, a distance of about five kilometers, or three miles, west of the city along the Rhine River. Inasmuch as only two letters from Hus's pen survives from the Gottlieben incarceration (presumably, incoming and outgoing mail was intercepted), it seems unlikely that Hus would have been granted visitors, especially one such as Jerome.[69] The suggestion that Hus and Jerome were able to visit in the prison at Gottlieben Castle is another of those misrepresentations that attend events from the time of the Council of Constance. "The very fine chronicle" says that Jerome went to Constance with Hus and the two were thereafter burned. The second statement is true, but the first is not

---

65. *FRB*, vol. 8, p. 340.

66. *FRB*, vol. 8, p. 353.

67. Hardt, vol. 4, col. 755.

68. Hardt, vol. 4, p. 103.

69. Both letters are in Bohumil Ryba, ed., *Sto Listů M. Jana Husi* (Prague: Laichter, 1949), pp. 184–187.

accurate, as the journeys of the two men to Constance are fairly well documented and occurred several months apart.[70]

Jerome's hasty departure from Constance and his retreat to Überlingen constituted a tactical move on his part to avoid hostile recriminations.[71] Jerome's abrupt relocation is reminiscent of his clandestine departure from Vienna several years earlier. His actions at Constance have been appropriately characterized as "the Vienna maneuver."[72] It is noteworthy that if Jerome was so intent on gaining the safe haven of Bohemia, he seems to have taken a rather curious circuitous route to gain that safety.[73] That decision would present its own perils.

Meanwhile, on April 9, six Czech lords attempted to secure a guarantee of a public hearing at an upcoming session of the Council. The barons were Václav Dubá, Jan Chlum, Jindřich Lacembok, Václav Myška of Hradec, Bohuslav Dúpov, and Bleh of Stradov. The first two were knights who had accompanied Hus to Constance. The text of their letter and its date suggest that there was awareness of Jerome's presence in the area and a willingness on the part of the Czech barons to defend him and advocate for an opportunity for him to clear his reputation and defend his faith against charges of misdoing.[74] The intercession of the Czech barons on Jerome's behalf failed to have any immediate effect, and therefore an impatient or apprehensive Jerome left the Constance-Überlingen area for good either on April 8 or 9. He had been there a scant five days.[75] He did not see Hus. He accomplished nothing.

Shortly thereafter, on April 11 or 12, a very provisional safe conduct was issued to Jerome, to wit, only to the extent that the issuers were capable and only to the extent that the faith allowed.[76] In other words, Jerome was

---

70. F. M. Bartoš, ed., *Listy Bratra Jana a Kronika velmi pěkná o Janu Žižkovi* (Prague: Blahoslav, 1949), p. 36.

71. Brandmüller, *Das Konzil von Konstanz 1414–1418*, vol. 2, p. 119.

72. František Šmahel, "Leben und Werk des Magisters Hieronymus von Prag," *Historica* 13 (1966): 110.

73. Brandmüller, *Das Konzil von Konstanz 1414–1418*, vol. 2, p. 119.

74. Hardt, vol. 4, cols. 685–686. See appendix 6.

75. Hardt, vol. 4, col. 755.

76. Hardt, vol. 4, p. 106, col. 687.

granted permission and protection to come to the city but with no guarantee for departure: *salvum conductum veniendi sed non recedendi* ("a safe conduct to enter the city but not for leaving it").[77] This indicates somewhat persuasively that Council members were aware that Hus's *salvus conductus* contained round-trip protections and guarantees. In formulating a provisionary notice allowing Jerome to come to the city, the Council was taking care to avoid entering into commitments that might later hamper a judicial process. Elsewhere, it is noted that "on Thursday the eleventh of the previously noted month of April, the deputies from the four nations gathered in the German nation's place of meeting. There a safe conduct for Master Jerome of Prague was finalized and signed by the notaries of the Council's nations."[78] If Jerome's request for a safe conduct was curiously combative, official news that he was in the area must have exercised men such as Jean Gerson, Dinkelsbühl, Peter Pulka, and perhaps many others. They must have been exceptionally pleased to think that Jerome was willing to appear voluntarily before the Council. However, when the offered safe conduct was ignored and Jerome did not act on its provisions, the Council at its sixth session, on April 17, issued a formal summons for Jerome to appear at a hearing within fifteen days. The text of the summons exhibits language and imagery that may have caused Jerome to have second thoughts about coming to Constance were he still in the area and amenable to an appearance before the synod.[79] In the formal citation, it is pointed out that the Council has no greater duty than to capture the foxes that seek to destroy the vineyard of the Lord. Under that duty, then, the Council solemnly summoned Jerome to appear as one suspected of teaching error and having rashly advanced those errors, to answer whatever charges might be lodged by any person with respect to the faith. The summons was issued with the "MARS" seal of the presidents of the four nations and signed by Grumpert Faber, the notary of the German nation.

The following day, April 18, a large group of witnesses led by the redoubtable Michael de Causis, appeared before the commission tasked with examining the charges against Jerome. Members of that board of inquiry included the proctors Henry of Piro and John Scribanis of Piacenza. Both men were

---

77. *Passio*, p. 353.

78. Hardt, vol. 4, p. 106, but erroneous, as the phrase "notarios nationum concilii" must surely be wrong.

79. Hardt, vol. 4, p. 119, cols. 686–687; and Mansi, vol. 27, col. 611. See appendix 7.

also involved in the simultaneous procedures lodged against Hus and John XXIII. On the same day, de Causis had the citation read in the presence of the lawyer John of Solichin and several witnesses and thereafter posted the summons in several locations in Constance, including the Church of St. Stephen, the cathedral, and the Franciscan monastery.[80] Other sources note that Jerome's departure from Constance was with the intention of returning to Bohemia in order to strengthen the heresies that existed there. His subsequent capture was said to have been by divine dispensation.[81]

The tradition that faith need not be kept with heretics had currency at Constance. King Ferdinand I (Antequera) of Aragon, in a letter of March 27 to Sigismund, reflected this principle and insisted that if his own wife fell into heresy, he would be the first to light the fire.[82] Martin Porrée, bishop of Arras, opined: "Remember the oath of King Herod which in the end turned out to be an evil one, likewise in the case of a heretic who has a safe conduct, his stubbornness necessitates that the decree be changed because the promise is impious when it is completed with a crime."[83] The summons for Jerome to appear before the Council referred to contumacy and heresy, and there were men at Constance who had previously been in Paris, Cologne, Heidelberg, Vienna, Prague, and Kraków who possessed knowledge of Jerome's activities in those places, not least among them the trial in Vienna, which had been derailed by Jerome's clandestine escape. The matters raised at the several universities and during the legal process in Vienna were now all at issue. Jerome was a suspected heretic and an excommunicate. Surviving manuscript sources sometimes feature voluminous references to the heresy of Jerome.[84]

Despite the fact that Jerome made no reply to these overtures by the Council, and indeed it is unlikely he was even aware of their existence, Henry of Piro and John Scribanis of Piacenza were associated with the

---

80. Hardt, vol. 4, pp. 146–147; and *FRB*, vol. 8, p. 340.

81. Text in *FRB*, vol. 8, pp. 305–330.

82. *Documenta*, pp. 539–540.

83. Louis Ellies du Pin, ed., *Joannis Gersonii, Opera omnia*, 5 vols. (Antwerp: Sumptibus societatis, 1706), vol. 5, col. 572.

84. Šmahel, "The *Acta* of the Constance Trial," p. 333, draws attention to the *Rubrica concilii Constantiensis*, Leipzig, Universitätsbibliothek, MS 1316, fols. 7r–12r, 15r–526r, which constitutes a transcript of the official *Acta*, especially fols. 266v–270v, which feature more than a dozen marginalia about the "heresy" of Jerome. See, for example, fol. 267v and the reference concerning the rise of the heresy ("Unde oriebatur heresis").

commission charged with examining the case against Jerome and were instrumental in the charge of contumacy. These men requested a renewal of the citation against Jerome, and the president of the session Jean-Allarmet de Brogny, the cardinal bishop of Ostia, put the matter into the hands of Henry of Piro.[85] As noted earlier, each of these men played a role in the prosecution of Hus, which was at the same time very much in process. The third citation in the summons of Jerome was displayed on the cathedral doors and also on the Church of St. Stephen on May 4.[86] Hence the three citations were published on April 18, May 2, and May 4. The obligatory *canonica monitio* was issued regularly to fulfill the canonical requirements.[87] According to law, full excommunication could also validly be applied only after three warnings.[88] Once the citation expired and as a result of that process, at the seventh session, proceedings for contumacy were put in motion against Jerome.[89] On the same date, the books and memory of Wyclif were also condemned, and John XXIII was formally cited. In terms of the former, during the eighth session of the Council, "perverse assailants" of the faith, motivated by curiosity to know and understand more than they should, followed the false Christian Wyclif into error.[90]

Arrest and Imprisonment

While all of this was in process, Jerome was making his way across German territory en route to the safety of Czech lands. On either April 24 or 25, he was arrested in Hirschau by the servants of Hanus, son of Clem, and the village magistrate, Mayor Teynsdorfer.[91] Hirschau is situated about 310 kilometers, or 193 miles, from Constance and sits in the Upper Palatinate (Bavaria) about 45 kilometers, or 28 miles, from the Czech border, northwest of Domažlice. Clem was the nickname for Ruprecht of the Palatine

---

85. Hardt, vol. 4, pp. 118–119; and *FRB*, vol. 8, pp. 340–341.

86. Hardt, vol. 4, p. 148.

87. X 2.28.26 *Reprehensibilis*, in Friedberg, vol. 2, col. 418.

88. C.17 q.4 c.21 *Quisquis inventus*, in Friedberg, vol. 1, col. 820.

89. Hardt, vol. 4, p. 142.

90. Hardt, vol. 4, pp. 153–156.

91. Hardt, vol. 4, col. 760. Hanus is a moniker for Duke Johannes of the Palatinate-Neumarkt.

(1352–1410), who had been the German king between 1400 and 1410. The prisoner was brought to Sulzbach by the Bavarian Duke Johannes of the Palatinate-Neumarkt, where he was put into jail. Evidently, suspicion had been aroused when Jerome, who was conversing with the parish priest and other clerics over dinner, referred to the Council of Constance as a "school of Satan" and a "synagogue of unrighteousness." The authorities were alerted to the presence of the outspoken stranger, and the arrest occurred after Jerome apparently made his intemperate public remarks denouncing the Council as a demonic institution and a congregation of gross iniquity.[92]

Back in Constance, a rumor circulated that Jerome had been arrested. In the days immediately following his arrest, letters confirming his capture were presented from Duke Johannes of the Palatinate-Neumarkt. Ostensibly, several letters were found on Jerome's person written by Czech nobles in Latin, German, and Czech, with attached seals. It was later alleged that Jerome had in his possession at the time of arrest a document with seventy seals affirming both his innocence and that of Hus.[93] These developments were reported to Sigismund, who at that moment was in Radolfzell with Albrecht of Nürnberg. Sigismund was pleased at the news and gave his royal ring to Albrecht so that the latter might write under its authority to Duke Johannes requesting that Jerome be brought to Constance to appear before the Council. A similar letter was dispatched to the prisoner.[94] We catch occasional glimpses of Jerome in the regular dispatches Pulka sent to Vienna, though admittedly most of these communiqués consisted of appeals for more financial support.[95]

The news of Jerome's arrest reached Constance by means of a letter from Johannes of Neumarkt, Bavarian duke and palsgrave, dated May 8, which indicated that a man named "Jeronimus," or more accurately "Erronimus," had been taken into custody. The text is a pun, with the

---

92. Buck, *Chronik des Konstanzer Konzils*, pp. 62–63.

93. Buck, *Chronik des Konstanzer Konzils*, p. 63; and see Šmahel, *Život a dílo Jeronýma*, p. 143, n. 322.

94. A letter dated April 27, 1415, from Pulka to the University of Vienna notes these developments. Firnhaber, "Petrus de Pulka," pp. 19–21.

95. Girgensohn, *Peter von Pulka*, p. 54.

reference to "erronimus" meaning the "deluded one."[96] The letter asked what should be done with this detainee.[97] In reply to the letter, and independently of Sigismund, the Council requested that the prisoner be transferred to Constance. The man in charge of these events was Duke Ludwig of the Palatine, son of Ruprecht, the former king of the Romans. So it came to pass that on May 23, Jerome was returned to Constance in chains.[98] Clem's other son, Ludwig III, the Palatine elector, met the entourage from Sulzbach at the city gates and took custody of Jerome from his brother and the assigned guards. Ludwig ordered Jerome to be put in new chains and escorted through the streets of Constance in humiliation to the refectory of the Franciscan monastery. Thus manacled, the prisoner was led at the end of a long clanging chain, "holding in his hands iron fetters and long chain," to the Franciscan refectory, where prelates, princes, and lawyers were gathered.[99] One suspects that Gerson, Dinkelsbühl, Pulka, de Causis, and others eagerly cast their eyes upon the captive. Once inside the monastic refectory, the prisoner was fastened to a pillar before a large gathering.[100] It was Ludwig who would later execute the sentences of the court against both Hus and Jerome.

The appearance of Jerome at Constance, his departure from the city, his subsequent arrest and return to the Council venue, and his additional incarceration formed a chapter in the history of Bohemia. One of the most important chronicles of the period records the events succinctly:

> Then in May [sic], Master Jerome, endowed by God with eloquence, publicly displayed notices in Constance. He attached and nailed them on gate-houses, on the gates of the town, church doors, the doors of houses where the cardinals were and the houses of other distinguished prelates, asking King Sigismund and the council to provide him with a letter of safe conduct in order to give answer

---

96. This appellation is based on Třeboň, Regional State Archives, MS A 11, which has been edited in Augustin Neumann in *Studie a texty* 4 (1925): 149–152.

97. The letter has been preserved in several other manuscripts, including Třeboň, Regional State Archives, MS 16, fol. 204r–v; Vatican Library, Vat Pal., MS 595, fol. 6v–7r; Paris, BN Lat, MS 1508, fols. 23r–25r; and Oxford, New College, MS E 161, fol. 176 (these manuscripts have been identified in Šmahel, *Život a dílo Jeronýma*, p. 145, n. 341).

98. Hardt, vol. 4, pp. 215–218; and *Notae de Concilio Constantiensis, FRB*, vol. 8, p. 320.

99. *Passio*, p. 354.

100. *FRB*, vol. 8, pp. 341–343; and *FRB*, vol. 8, pp. 354–357.

publicly to anyone who would charge him with sin and the shame of heresy and errors, and for defending these matters before the council and that he might then return to Bohemia. But he did not succeed in this. While returning he was captured by officials of Duke Johannes of Bavaria, son of Clem, count of the Palatine, having been betrayed by his enemies in Hirschau, and brought before that duke in Sulzbach. When the Hungarian and Roman King Sigismund and the council learned of it, they sent a message to Duke Johannes asking him to send Master Jerome to Constance in chains. The afore named Johannes complied with their wishes and sent Master Jerome in shackles to Constance together with a letter wherein he encouraged them to turn in Master Jerome and similar people to the destruction of their bodies so that their spirit might be saved. Therefore Master Jerome was brought in chains to Constance and put before the council, where he was harassed by numerous blasphemies and scolding, and then put into a hard jail in a town tower near the cemetery of St. Paul. In this jail he was put in stocks with iron shackles on his hands and feet and he was hung by his hands in this prison for eleven days, receiving only a little food, and he was afflicted with a serious illness almost to the point of death. They allowed him to rest for several days so that his health could improve, hoping that he would assent to the council in everything and would praise their decisions. So they relaxed the conditions of his imprisonment so that he lay in prison bound for one year.[101]

The narrative of Vavřinec of Březová is essentially correct and represents the accounts that were transmitted back in Bohemia, though it is telling that Jerome's arrest is attributed to betrayal. Once he had been returned to Constance in chains, Jerome was taken to the Franciscan convent, where he was essentially arraigned on charges of heresy by means of a public reading of the May 2 citation. Jerome answered the initial allegations.[102] It was here, on the first day in which Jerome appeared before the Council, that his past began to come back to haunt him. Accusations of Trinitarian

---

101. Hussite Chronicle, in *FRB*, vol. 5, p. 336.

102. Hardt, vol. 4, pp. 217–218.

heresy expressed at Heidelberg were raised against the prisoner. The shield of faith was mentioned in a derogatory fashion. Jerome asserted that what he had written and depicted in Heidelberg he was willing to do also in Constance. He declared to his accusers that if he could be shown to be in error, he would recant.

It can be argued there were three types of prosecutorial articles against Jerome. The first consisted of the ones Jerome outrightly denied. These included accusations of blasphemy. The second set of charges was related to his teaching about universals. The controversy over universals may be characterized as the *"causa celebris* of the Czech medieval thought."[103] The third type encompassed those articles that Jerome essentially admitted. Implicit here is the fact that Jerome was accused of holding to ideas that were deemed unacceptable because they amounted to a promulgation of Wyclifite heresy, which had been repeatedly condemned.[104]

Following these preliminary allegations, charges were raised about his conduct in Paris, Cologne, Heidelberg, and various other places. There were calls there and then for Jerome to be burned. Gerson spoke about Paris, Dietrich Kerkering of Münster raised issues dating back to Cologne, and, though it is not entirely certain, it is probable that Master Konrad Koler of Soest spoke about Jerome's controversial stay in Heidelberg.[105] There were many others present in Constance with whom Jerome had previously crossed swords. These included the Silesian doctor of theology Johannes of Münsterberg; the former dean of Prague university Albrecht Varentrapp; Peter Storch of Zwickau, who had formerly taught at Prague; Jan Náz; Nicholas Zeiselmeister, a Prague canon, former official of the Prague diocese, and bitter enemy of Hus; the theologian Ondřej Brod; Štěpán Páleč, and Mařík Rvačka. Gerson, Pulka, Dinkelsbühl, Johannes Lagenator of Frankfurt, and metropolitan/archbishop of Gniezno Mikołaj Trąba should be among that number and in the background, King Sigismund. When calls for Jerome's immolation were raised, with agitated shouts of "Burn him! Burn him!" and the insistent cry that he must be sent to the fire, he replied with remarkable coolness to the effect that if that was the desire of the Council, then he was prepared for death to

103. Noted in Ivan Müller, ed., *Commentarius in I–IX capitula tractatus De universalibus Iohannis Wyclif Stephano de Palecz ascriptus* (Prague: Filosofia, 2009), p. 9.

104. Šmahel, *Život a dílo Jeronýma*, pp. 88–89.

105. Vilém Herold, "Magister Hieronymus von Prag und die Universität Köln," *Miscellanea Medievalia* 20 (1989): p. 261.

come for him in the name of God. However, Robert Hallum, the bishop of Salisbury, with the agreement of John Stokes, objected, saying that God preferred repentance of the sinner over the penalty of death. There is some confusion around this objection, and it is also possible that this intervention was undertaken by the prince-archbishop of Salzburg, Eberhard III von Neuhaus.[106] There was considerable tumult at this stage, but once order was restored and the examination concluded, Jerome was given over to Johannes von Wallenrode, archbishop of Riga, who, under cover of night, took charge for his incarceration, which was at an unidentified nearby place.

Both the *Passio* and the *Narratio* record the visit of a friend to Jerome, who spoke with him through the window until the conversation was discovered and the man was chased away.[107] This was likely Mladoňovice. Another follower of Hus, Vít of Březina, who had come to Constance with Jan Chlum, later spoke with Jerome through the barred window, but he, too, was detected by the guard. Unlike the first visitor, Vít of Březina was arrested on the spot and taken to the prison. A day later, he was released. However, as a result of these two incidents, Jerome was taken by Wallenrode to a cemetery against the west wall of the city, where he "lies in the tower of St. Paul under the surveillance of citizens."[108] The modern address is 73 Obere Laube. It was in this prison where Jerome was kept for nearly a year. During his first days in prison, as we have seen noted in the chronicle of Vavřinec of Březova, he subsisted on nothing more than bread and water. He was subjected to torture and in his dire condition despaired of life. "They took Master Jerome by his legs and put him in one town tower in a stock, so high above ground that he could not reach it, as he was hanging upside down from the ceiling, he was lying like this many days, having only bread as meal and water as drink. And when he fell ill, he asked for a confessor. And they, after several days, knowing that he was overcome with illness, did not allow him

---

106. Hardt, vol. 4, pp. 215–218. The "Archiepiscopus Salisburgensis" is Hallum (p. 218). The *Passio*, p. 356, claims that it was an English archbishop who addressed Jerome. Šmahel, *Život a dílo Jeronýma*, p. 75, and Šmahel, *Jeroným Pražský*, pp. 157–158 believes the proper identity is Hallum.

107. *FRB*, vol. 8, pp. 342–343, 356.

108. Hardt, vol. 4, pp. 217–218; also Poggio and *Relatio*. On the bishop of Riga, see Bernhart Jähnig, *Johann von Wallenrode O.T., Erzbishof von Riga, Königlicher Rat, Deutschordens Diplomat und Bishof von Lüttich im Zeitalter des Schismas und der Konstanzer Konzils, um 1370–1419* (Bonn: Verlag Wissenschaftliches Archiv, 1970), p. 102.

this, and then they made the prison easier, in which he was seven days less the whole year."[109] Jerome's treatment was illegal. Suspected heretics were legally remanded to prison pending trial or were frequently incarcerated during trial proceedings. However, imprisonment in such circumstances was designed as custodial and was not to be used as a form of punishment.[110] A century earlier, the Council of Vienne had stipulated that individuals held on the criminal charge of heresy "shall not be committed to harsh or close imprisonment which seems more like punishment than custody."[111] This seems quite clear that the medieval judicial doctrine of *peine forte et dure* (severe and hard punishment) was inapplicable. There are other early-fifteenth-century sources that made clear that penal incarceration was illegal.[112] Practices did not often mirror policy. We learn from Archbishop Guillaume of Narbonne in the thirteenth century and Bernard Gui and Jacques Fournier in the fourteenth century that prisons were often used as a means of inducing confession, so in that sense, they did function as a form of punishment in addition to being custodial. Jerome's harsh confinement became known, and Mladoňovice eventually bribed the jailer to allow food to be brought to the prisoner.[113] Other sources say he was remanded to a *sonder gemach* (special chamber) in the Gottlieben Castle.[114] If this were the case, then he would have been imprisoned with Hus for about ten days before the latter was transferred back to Constance for the summation of his legal process. However, the reference to Jerome being imprisoned at Gottlieben is simply an error or a falsehood on the part of the chronicler Ulrich Richental.

---

109. *Passio*, p. 357.

110. Clem. 5.3.1 *Multorum querela*, in Friedberg, vol. 2, col. 1182. On prisons in the Middle Ages, see G. Geltner, *The Medieval Prison: A Social History* (Princeton, N.J.: Princeton University Press, 2008); and Edward M. Peters, "Prison before the Prison: The Ancient and Medieval Worlds," in *The Oxford History of the Prison: The Practice of Punishment in Western Society*, ed. Norval Morris and David J. Rothman (New York: Oxford University Press, 1995), pp. 3–47.

111. Clem. 5.3.1 *Multorum querela*, in Friedberg, vol. 2, cols. 1181–1182.

112. The anonymous *De carceribus*, discussed in Geltner, *The Medieval Prison*, pp. 46–47.

113. *FRB*, vol. 8, p. 357; and Hardt, vol. 4, p. 218.

114. Buck, *Chronik des Konstanzer Konzils*, p. 63.

During the trial of Hus, which reached its final stages not long after Jerome was returned to Constance in chains, Sigismund was unable to remember his name but declared that the matter involving Jerome could be disposed of quickly, since Hus was the master and Jerome but the disciple. That was an uninformed and inaccurate assessment of Jerome. Much later, the great difficulty the Council had in uprooting the "notorious heretic" Jerome was noted.[115] Oblivious to the challenges ahead, the emperor advised the conciliar representatives they should take immediate steps to deal with all of the "secret disciples and followers" of Hus and not to delay, since he had soon to depart from the city. Sigismund then gave explicit instructions that they should "especially deal with that man, that man who is here in prison." When asked if he meant Jerome, the emperor said, "Yes, Jerome. We can end this matter in one day as the case will be easier for Hus is the master and this Jerome is his disciple."[116] There was clear predetermination in the case of Hus, and this likely extends to the matter involving Jerome. Sigismund told the Council authorities on June 8, 1415, that he had no objection to the burning of Hus. However, it would be quite wrong to ascribe too much power over the Council either to Sigismund or to any other secular authority.[117] The sermon of Dinkelsbühl, noted above, should not be taken too literally. Jerome's fate was not placed in the hands of the king.

Shortly after the preliminary hearing during which Jerome was arraigned on charges of heresy and was thereafter remanded into the custody of Wallenrode and locked up in the cemetery tower at St. Paul's, we lose sight of Jerome for a period of some months. The deposition of John XXIII and the trial of Hus preoccupied the Council in May and June. There are a few references to Jerome in Hus's letters. From the Franciscan monastery prison, Hus wrote to some of his friends in Prague on June 7, wondering how "Barbatus Jeronimus" (the bearded Jerome) was doing and ruefully reflecting on how Jerome had ignored the counsel of friends and had placed himself in harm's way by coming to Constance.[118] In another letter to Prague friends dated June

---

115. In a sermon preached by the Dominican Girolamo of Florence on January 6, 1424, before the Council of Pavia-Siena. The text appears in Walter Brandmüller, *Das Konzil von Pavia-Siena 1423–1424*, 2 vols. (Münster: Ashendorff, 1968–1974), vol. 2, pp. 193–199.

116. *Relatio*, p. 110.

117. Hartmut Boockmann, "Zur politischen Geschichte des Konstanzer Konzils," *Zeitschrift für Kirchengeschichte* 85 (1974): 52–53.

118. Novotný, *M. Jana Husi Korespondence a dokumenty*, p. 263.

9, Hus mentioned that he had dreamed about Jerome being in prison and then recalled the words Jerome spoke to him concerning the latter's belief that should Hus venture to Constance, it was likely he would never return.[119] Hus later commented, on June 10, that he had no word about Jerome or the latter's situation: "About Master Jerome, my beloved fellow worker, I have heard nothing, except that he is in a cruel prison, expecting death just as I do, on account of his faith, which he has displayed so bravely to the Czechs. But the Czechs, who are our most ferocious opponents, turned us over to the power of other enemies and into prison."[120] On June 27, Hus wondered why his death and that of Jerome had been delayed. He went on to elaborate that God had given both of them time to reflect:

> The Lord God alone knows why my death has been postponed as well as that of my dear brother Master Jerome, whom I trust will die in holiness, without guilt, and that he conducts himself and suffers more bravely than I, faint-hearted sinner. The Lord God has given to us a long time in order that we might better remember our sins and in good time express sorrow for them. God has granted us time so that this protracted and significant test might remove from us major sin and bring us comfort. God has given us time to remember . . . to meditate . . . and, for that reason, to suffer with even greater joy. Also that we may call to memory . . . that the saints entered the king-dom of heaven by means of numerous sufferings. Some were cut up into pieces, others impaled, others boiled, others roasted, others skinned alive, buried alive, stoned, crucified, crushed between mill-stones, dragged, drowned, burned, hanged, torn into pieces, having been first reviled, put into prison, beaten and chained up. Who is able to describe all of the tortures which these saints . . . suffered on account of the truth of God, especially those who corrected the wicked behavior of priests and preached against it. It would be odd if in these times one would not suffer for taking a courageous stand against such wickedness, particularly that relating to priests, which does not permit itself to be touched.[121]

---

119. Novotný, M. Jana Husi Korespondence a dokumenty, pp. 265–266.

120. Novotný, M. Jana Husi Korespondence a dokumenty, p. 272.

121. Novotný, M. Jana Husi Korespondence a dokumenty, pp. 325–326.

The last reference to Jerome among Hus's letters comes the day before Hus's own execution, wherein he mournfully commented that he suspected Jerome would be put to death and noted that this eventuality had been represented to him by certain delegates of the Council.[122] It is a reflection of the nature of their relationship and Hus's affection for Jerome that he referred to Jerome as his *socius carus* (dear companion) and as his *frater carus* (dear brother).

On July 11, the bishop of Litomyšl, Jan the Iron, wrote to King Václav noting that on the past Saturday, July 6, the Council had condemned Hus and his Wyclifite teaching and that he had been burned to death together with his books. The bishop went on to say that the Council was now preoccupied with the interrogation of Jerome. Bishop Železný ominously stated that it would "not be concealed to Your Grace how this will end."[123] Shortly after Hus's demise, Gerson admitted that some of the theses advanced by Wyclif and Hus might be defensible and might even, in fact, be true. However, the special and unique *modus loquendi* (method of speaking) had been ignored, even if the propositions did not appear to contravene scripture. Therefore, these heretics could be damned. Gerson alluded to the condemnation of Utraquism under this same rubric. Paris University had thus far been spared the ravages of error and heresy by following the simple rule of "demanding and forcing academics" to always adhere to that requirement. According to Gerson, the requirement to adhere to this principle was the bulwark for exterminating both heresy and the heretic. It was nonsense, he argued, for a man such as Hus to claim that unless he could be convicted by the testimony of scripture, he would not recant. Gerson underscored the argument that the sayings of the doctors, canon law, and ecclesiastical decrees were regarded by men such as Hus as lacking authority. Hus wanted to be shown error by means of scripture, and Jerome demanded refutation by means of argument. Jerome definitely regarded truth as the foundation for authority claims, and obedience could be only to the truth.[124] Jerome steadfastly refused to cede to Gerson or anyone else, for that matter, a form of *plenitudo potestatis* authority to issue pronouncements on matters of dogma or truth. Gerson commented on the positions taken by Jerome

---

122. Novotný, *M. Jana Husi Korespondence a dokumenty*, p. 335.

123. *Documenta*, pp. 563–564.

124. Ota Pavlíček, "La figure de l'autorité à travers Jean Hus et Jérôme de Prague," *Revue des sciences religieuses* 85, no. 3 (2011): 371–389.

and Hus and asserted that "there is no one who cannot clearly perceive that such presumption results in error." Gerson went on to lament that if only the same rules practiced at Paris applied elsewhere, errors might be contained.[125] This reveals in concise form the intellectual divide that existed between Jerome and Gerson. This had been the problem for Jerome in Paris in 1406, and it was again the issue he had to confront a decade later at the Council of Constance. At Paris, when it seemed there could be no resolution short of censure and a humiliating retraction, Jerome simply vanished into the night. Things were quite different in Constance. The philosophical dissension that convulsed some academic circles at the end of the Middle Ages lay at the very heart of the dispute between Jerome and the medieval church. After the defection of Štěpán Páleč and Stanislav of Znojmo from the ranks of the reformers in Prague, Hus commented bitterly that they had thrown their previous realism *ad cloacas* (into the toilet).[126] Gerson believed that was the proper place for the assumptions, arguments, and conclusions of Jerome. Páleč and Stanislav had avoided heresy by renouncing their own ideas and adhering to the mainstream of thinking and theology within the Latin church. Hus and Jerome had contumaciously persisted, and Hus had paid with his life for his refusal to abandon Wyclifite thought. Now Jerome lay in prison, awaiting trial and faced with a decision that would dictate the remainder of his life.

Following the execution of Hus, most sympathizers of the Czech reform movement left Constance. Jerome's enemies remained and went to work preparing the case against Jerome, as noted above, which had been reported to the king by the bishop of Litomyšl, Jan Železný.[127] De Causis and his colleagues, with the active assistance of members of Vienna University, continued to build a case against Jerome.[128] On July 19, Jerome appeared in the Church of St. Paul, where he was made to submit an explanation for why he had left Constance in April and further to reply to accusations lodged against him.[129] The extent and detail of this session have been lost, but we know that Jerome defended an orthodox view of the Eucharist. This question continued to swirl around the Council

---

125. "Prosperum iter faciet nobis Deus," in Glorieux, vol. 5, pp. 476–477.

126. *Contra Stephanum Palecz*, in *MIHO*, vol. 22, p. 252.

127. *Documenta*, pp. 563–566.

128. Mansi, vol. 27, col. 628.

129. Hardt, vol. 4, cols. 634–646.

of Constance and figured into practically every discussion of the reform movement in Bohemia and throughout Hussite history. Hus was suspected of holding Wyclifite views on the sacrament, and it was assumed that Jerome was similarly inclined. The assumptions were without merit. Jerome admitted that he loved Hus when charged with being Hus's best friend. Jerome said Hus was a good man, that he did not run around with women, and that Jerome had never heard anything heretical from him.[130] In the *Passio* of Mladoňovice, Hus was described as Jerome's "very dear inseparable friend." That bond between the two men was also a liability for Jerome at his trial. Being intimately connected to a convicted and executed heretic made one a suspect. It was classic guilt by association rhetoric, but in this case, there was sufficient evidence to bring Jerome into formal examination quite apart from his friendship with Hus.

While the case against Jerome was building toward an actual legal process, a bull of August 31 issued by the Council of Constance gave the bishop of Litomyšl, Jan Železný, the power and authority to proceed against heresy in the Bohemian and Moravian provinces. The bull designated him a special legate to use all powers at his disposal to cite, issue interdict, excommunicate, and otherwise root out all heresy in those jurisdictions.[131] Immediately thereafter, the Council specifically requested that Jan of Jindřichův Hradec, the priests of Prague, and the entire diocese assist Železný in fulfilling his mandate.[132] Bishop Jan the Iron was selected for this formidable task because of his personal connections to the Czech lands but, more important, because of his reputation as an "obedient son" and a "brave and prudent athlete of Christ." Hence, the "athlete of Christ," Železný, was pitted against the "athlete of Antichrist," Jerome. The bishop was the steward of truth, while the peripatetic philosopher was designated as the enemy of God. Železný was born in 1360 and entered the Order of the Canons Regular of Prémontré (Premonstratensians) at the abbey of Strahov in Prague. He came to prominence as the bishop of Litomyšl between 1392 and 1418. However, Dietrich Niem tells us that Železný felt so threatened by the hostile environment in Bohemia after the deaths of Hus

---

130. *FRB*, vol. 8, p. 290.

131. The bull is *Postquam superna providencia* and appears in Jaroslav Eršil, *Acta summorum pontificum res gestas Bohemicas aevi praehussitici et hussitici illustrantia*, pt. 2 (Prague: Academia, 1980), pp. 611–612.

132. Eršil, *Acta summorum pontificum*, p. 613.

and Jerome that he lived in fear for his life and stayed indoors.[133] He was thereafter bishop of Olomouc from 1418 until 1430. During that tenure, he was made cardinal in 1426 and was appointed apostolic administrator of Vás in Hungary between 1429 and 1430. He was thrice unsuccessful in securing the see of Prague, though he greatly desired the appointment. He died at Ezstergom on October 9, 1430, having lived long enough to see the almost complete failure of the Western church at putting down the Hussite heresy generated and facilitated by Hus and Jerome, men he had personally encountered and opposed at the Council of Constance.[134]

Meanwhile, back at Constance, by early September, numerous Czech barons signed a letter to the Council protesting the treatment of Hus and Jerome. The barons informed the Council that the execution of Hus "had the same effect in Bohemia as oil has when thrown into a quick fire." The letter went on to comment about the case of Jerome. "You have unmercifully imprisoned and possibly already put to death Master Jerome of Prague, who certainly was a stream of eloquence. He was a master of the seven liberal sciences and a very capable philosopher. You have condemned him without having seen him, without having convicted him, and have done so upon the false testimony of his and our perfidious accusers."[135] The assumption about the fate of Jerome was premature, but the testimony to his erudition is both instructive and corroborative. It should be pointed out that leading men of the Council such as Pierre d'Ailly and Francesco Zabarella worked very hard in an effort to secure a recantation from Jerome. On the part of these men, there was very much reluctance to see another execution. D'Ailly has been characterized as the "stern prosecutor" of Hus and Jerome, but it appears his tact was somewhat different in the case of Jerome.[136] There is some possibility that d'Ailly and Zabarella were supported in their initiative by Cardinals Giordano Orsini and Antonio Panciera.[137] Pulka wrote a letter to the University of Vienna on

133. *De vita ac fatis Constantiensibus Johannis Papae XXIII*, bk. 3, chap. 3, in Hardt, vol. 2, cols. 425–426.

134. Zdenka Hledlíková and Stepán Kohout, "Johann der Eiserne (de Bucca)," in *Die Bischöfe des Heiligen Römischen Reiches, 1198 bis 1448: Ein biographisches Lexikon*, ed. Erwin Gatz and Clemens Brodkorb (Berlin: Duncker and Humblot, 2001), pp. 596–598.

135. *Documenta*, p. 582.

136. Agnes E. Roberts, "Pierre d'Ailly and the Council of Constance," *Transactions of the Royal Historical Society*, 4th series, 18 (1935): 133.

137. Šmahel, *Život a dílo Jeronýma*, p. 77; and *FRB*, vol. 8, p. 345.

July 24, 1415, noting that members of the Council hoped to induce Jerome to recant.[138] This was an intentional strategy on the part of some Council delegates. There were men at the Council who testified that no effort was spared in the effort to secure Jerome's retraction.[139] It is fair to say that Jerome was doubtless shaken by Hus's fate and perhaps was more amenable to considering reconciliation with the church by means of revocation than Hus had been.

Recantation

Cardinal Francesco Zabarella was an accomplished extemporaneous speaker and a persuasive orator.[140] At length, Jerome was persuaded to accept Zabarella's advice, and on September 11, 1415, he wrote a formal recantation, which he then read out in the Church of St. Paul. A number of versions or records of this statement have been preserved.[141] Dietrich Niem says the recantation occurred on September 12.[142] It appeared that the dying prayer of Hus about Jerome would be unfulfilled. Hus hoped that his colleague would die in holiness, without guilt, and that he would suffer more bravely than Hus believed he himself would.[143] The retraction was noted or recorded by a number of witnesses, including Dietrich Vrie. He was a German Augustinian monk from Saxony (Osnabrück), who taught theology and wrote a history of the church and a history of the Council.[144] Vrie was also a poet and wrote a work called *De consolatione ecclesiae*, modeled on Gerson's *De consolatione theologiae* and on the works of Boethius. Although he was a firm conciliarist and stridently opposed to clerical corruption, he was unremittingly negative toward the Hussites and wrote a hostile account of Jerome's death.[145] His perspective is worth

---

138. Firnhaber, "Petrus de Pulka," p. 24.

139. Dietrich Vrie, *Historia concilii constantiensis*, in Hardt, vol. 1, col. 170.

140. Paul Arendt, *Die Predigten des Konstanzer Konzils: Ein Beitrag zur Predigt-und Kirchengeschichte des ausgehenden Mittelalters* (Freiburg im Breisgau: Herder, 1933), pp. 28–29.

141. Quoted in Vrie, Hardt, vol. 1, cols. 171–174; *Documenta*, pp. 596–597; and Hardt, vol. 4, cols. 688–689. It is misdated in Šmahel/Silagi, p. 223.

142. Hardt, vol. 4, p. 498.

143. Novotný, *M. Jana Husi Korespondence a dokumenty*, pp. 325–326.

144. *Historie concilii Constantiensi*, in Hardt, vol. 1, cols. 1–221. His vita follows on pp. 222–227.

145. Hardt, vol. 1, col. 202.

noting. Setting aside the question of motivation for the time being, Jerome's recantation is worth reviewing in detail.

Jerome acknowledged the authority of the church and confessed the apostolic faith. He announced that he was prepared to denounce every heresy. His opening statements were precisely what the Council wanted to hear: "I, Jerome of Prague ... do anathematize and renounce all heresies especially those with which I have been accused and which in times past were held and taught by John Wyclif and Jan Hus in their works, books and sermons." Jerome said the two were convicted of heresy on the basis of erroneous teachings that had been condemned by the Council of Constance. Jerome then turned his address to specific matters, such as "the keys, sacraments, orders, offices, and ecclesiastical censures, indulgences, relics of the saints," and agreed that he was not opposed to such things. Jerome consented to the articles of accusation lodged against the heretics prosecuted by the Council as "notoriously heretical, blasphemous, erroneous, offensive, rash, and seditious." Jerome then denounced his use of the contentious and controversial shield of faith, which had been employed in many places in an effort to teach. Jerome declared that he had neither drawn the shield of faith nor named it. Turning to Hus, Jerome told his listeners that he believed Hus had been a good man and that he had often heard him preach and had never heard anything that could be construed as an attack on the teaching of the church. However, Jerome said that after he came to Constance, he was informed about the nature of Hus's objectionable theology. At first, Jerome did not believe the allegations to be true. However, he was persuaded by "certain eminent doctors" that these were articles held and taught by Hus. Evidently, Jerome was shown manuscript copies of Hus's work that he recognized as being in the handwriting of Hus, being as familiar with Hus's hand as with his own, as he testified. Faced with such unassailable evidence, Jerome felt that he had to acknowledge the manifest errors and heresies of his former colleague. Based on this evidence, Jerome declared that Hus and his doctrine were rightly and justly condemned by the synod as both "heretical and insane." Persuaded by the force of argument and presented with unimpeachable proof, Jerome concluded that "the sentences and judgments pronounced by the sacred council against the doctrine of the said John Wyclif and Jan Hus, and against their persons" were not incorrect, and Jerome concluded that he "most humbly consented and agreed" with the judgment against those heretics. In terms of everything he may have taught previously, Jerome asserted his complete willingness to subject all of his ideas to the authority and judgment of the church and was prepared ever after to submit to that determination. "Moreover, I swear both by the holy Trinity and also by the most holy gospel, that I will forever abide without doubt in the truth of the catholic church." Jerome went further and stated his support for the eternal damnation of anyone who otherwise disagreed. The declaration concluded with Jerome affirming his own fidelity to the church and his willingness to accept any further penalty for divergence. "If I myself at any time (God forbid that I do) should ever presume to think or preach anything to the contrary, I will submit myself to the severity of the canons and shall be liable to eternal pain and punishment." Jerome confirmed that the statement he had just made was his own confession, which he freely and voluntarily had written personally and presented to the Council.[146]

The Czech perspective on all of this was recorded by Vavřinec of Březová for posterity. He placed a nuance on Jerome's retraction:

He was kept in chains for a long time and then brought before the council. Being threatened by the death of Master Jan Hus, he was forced to say that the council sentenced him justly, and he recanted before the council according to the letter presented to him. He was put into prison again, but to a lighter one this time, and was guarded by armed men. Then some Carmelite brothers, arrived from Prague with new lies, attempting to take his life, and trying to get him to the stake. The same judges of his, cardinals, noting the anger of those . . . instigators, Cambrai [Pierre d'Ailly], Jordan [Giordano Orsini], Antonius of Aquileia [Antonio Panciera or Antonio Caetani], Francesco Zabarella, realized that injustice was done to Jerome, worked before the council for his release. But Germans and Czechs, some enemies of his, resisted it strongly, saying that he should, under no circumstances, be released. Doctor Náz gave strong and murderous speeches to the cardinals, advising that he be put to death, accusing him and other disciples of Hus of heresy. Then Jerome was given a hearing, which will be dealt with later in more detail.[147]

---

146. Mansi, vol. 27, cols. 791–793; Hardt, vol. 4, p. 499, col. 506.

147. Hussite Chronicle, in *FRB*, vol. 8, p. 340.

This suggests that the recantation was coerced and that Jerome consented to it on account of fear. In his retraction, Jerome explained how he was forced under the weight of evidence to admit that not only the forty-five articles of Wyclif's (if they were really his) but also the thirty articles of Hus were rightly condemned by the Council. No matter how he used to be Hus's devoted friend and defender of his honor, he did not now wish to be a defender of his errors.[148] There was some uproar in St. Paul's Church after Jerome read his confession, and he was pressed to recant more and essentially declare that he supported whatever the Council might further or thereafter condemn and to confirm that resolve under oath.[149]

It is altogether legitimate to question Jerome's sincerity in confirming his rejection of Hus and Wyclif and placing himself perpetually under a vow of obedience to adhere without failing to the dictates of the church. There is nothing in Jerome's past or personality to suggest that he was naturally inclined to adopt such positions. In fact, there is considerable evidence for arguing quite the contrary. Be that as it may, there must have been lingering doubt among some members of the Council along these lines, for the next day, Jerome was compelled to agree to write letters to King Václav, Queen Žofie, Prague University, and others, stating and affirming his recantation. Whether these letters were actually written and dispatched cannot be adjudicated. However, there is a single surviving letter that appears to have fulfilled his obligation. The letter was discovered in the Carthusian monastery at Dolany in Moravia in the nineteenth century by the Czech philologist and historian Josef Dobrovský. On October 12, Jerome wrote a letter to Lord Lacek of Kravář.[150] In this missive, Jerome informed Lacek that he was alive and well in Constance, noting that he was aware of the "great storm" that the execution of Hus had caused in Bohemia and Moravia on the assumption that Hus had been unjustly condemned and illegally burned. Jerome says the presumption is wrong and nothing improper had been done. Jerome admits that initially he thought the Hus process was flawed, but after examining the articles against Hus with several experts, he had concluded that some of these articles were heretical, others were erroneous, and

---

148. Vrie, in Hardt, vol. 1, cols. 171–174; and Šmahel/Silagi, pp. 223–229.

149. *FRB*, vol. 8, p. 345.

150. The text has been published in *Documenta*, pp. 598–599, and in Šmahel/Silagi, pp. 257–259. See appendix 9.

still more were offensive and harmful. Jerome tells Lacek he assumed the articles had been taken out of context. However, having been shown Hus's books, he had to admit that Hus had indeed proclaimed the errors and heresies he was accused of. Jerome admitted to having been Hus's longtime friend and had previously defended him. Now he had been persuaded by the force of argument and evidence that he had been mistaken. Unwilling to continue to defend falsehood, Jerome told Lacek, he had willingly renounced all of Hus's heresies openly and in detail before the entire Council. The document is a faithful summary of the recantation. Some consider this letter prima facie evidence of Jerome's duplicity and indication of his true character, which had been explicated as "dishonorable."[151]

Despite these public declarations and private letters, not all were satisfied that the matter of Jerome had been properly and completely addressed. At the nineteenth session, on September 23, Jerome came under renewed fire. He was permitted to speak from the official rostrum in the Church of St. Paul. He was again forced to read his revocation during the Council proceedings. He embellished his recantation, adding to it a formal renunciation of the shield of faith, and pledged obedience to the church.[152] Addressing the savage divisions and controversies over philosophical distinctions, Jerome withdrew his previous conviction that in the absence of the doctrine of *de universalibus realibus*, it was impossible to defend the Christian faith. In other words, the real general ideas were not necessary. There were severe insistence and pressure on Jerome to stand down from this conviction. As noted already, there was a reference to the shield of faith in the context of the controversy at Heidelberg.[153] There are some disagreements about the Council's view with respect to his views of the Trinity. Jerome attempted to explain those views with reference to the "shield of faith." Jan Sedlák has suggested that the Council simply rejected Jerome's understanding of the Trinity as erroneous.[154] Ota Pavlíček disagrees and suggests that the Council had reservations about the attempt by Jerome

---

151. Count [František] Lützow, *The Life and Times of Master John Hus* (London: Dent, 1909), pp. 328–329, 333–334.

152. Hardt, vol. 4, cols. 499–514; Fillastre, pp. 50–51. See appendix 8.

153. *FRB*, vol. 8, pp. 355–356.

154. Jan Sedlák, "Nauka o sv. Trojici za Husa," *ST*, 1, (1919), pp. 9–10.

to explain the structure of the created world on the basis of the Trinity.[155] The distinction may be subtle, but it is significant. Jerome's shield of faith was an object of suspicion during the Council.[156] The matter was raised formally at least three times. On May 23, 1415, it came up when Jerome was returned to Constance and an unnamed master accused the prisoner of speaking errors about the Trinity and using a drawing of a shield in so doing.[157] The second occasion came during the formal revocation offered by Jerome on September 23, 1415.[158] It was raised again thereafter and is included among the articles of April 27, 1416, that were submitted to the Council.[159] Though they were controversial, it is possible that the Council was not objecting to the Trinitarian analogies advanced and utilized by Jerome but was instead objecting to the insistence on real universals.[160] The murky waters of philosophical debate shroud the case against Jerome and cloud the charges of heresy.

Gerson, Bishop Giacomo Balardi, and perhaps others took the view that Jerome had failed to maintain a proper distinction between theological and philosophical methodology.[161] Gerson made the point repeatedly. On December 3, Gerson again voiced his conviction that scripture could not and should not be exegetically guided by the facility of logic or dialectic. Those who insisted on doing so only deceived themselves. According to Gerson, "Scripture has its own logic and grammar."[162] Bishop Giacomo said that Jerome had inflicted six disasters upon himself and by failing to distinguish between logic and rhetoric had indicted himself and brought himself into a fatal "labyrinth of errors." The bishop declared the matter so serious that it might have been better for the entire kingdom of Bohemia had Jerome not been born. "O Kingdom of Bohemia happy if that man

---

155. Pavlíček, "Two Philosophical Texts of Jerome of Prague and His Alleged Designation of Opponents of Real Universals as Diabolic Heretics." *BRRP* 8 (2009): 96.

156. See Pavlíček, "Two Philosophical Texts," pp. 87–96.

157. *FRB*, vol. 8, p. 342.

158. Šmahel/Silagi, pp. 235–241. See appendix 8.

159. Mansi, vol. 27, col. 847.

160. Pavlíček, "Two Philosophical Texts," p. 92.

161. Pavlíček, "Two Philosophical Texts," pp. 94–96, covers this succinctly. See appendix 10.

162. "Résponse à la consultation des maîtres," in Glorieux, vol. 10, p. 241.

[Jerome] had never been born" (*O beatum regnum Bohemie, si natus non fuisset homo iste!*).[163]

Jerome also explained why he had taken the side of Hus, proceeded to renounce Hus's heresy, and declared that he accepted the verdict of the Council.[164] The events of September around Jerome's efforts to explain himself, resulting in a recantation along with its reiteration, amounted to a performance that only harmed Jerome further.[165] These acts of recantation and the embellishment thereof caused Jerome to be the disgraced martyr. His recantation (and subsequent revocation of that) has a parallel with Thomas Cranmer 140 years later.[166] Jerome would later withdraw these remarks and say that the worst thing he had done in his entire life was to agree with the condemnation of Hus. In the end, Jerome would reverse himself and affirm that he had always believed Hus to be a holy man.[167] But the months of imprisonment in a harsh medieval tower were sufficient to induce Jerome to recant.

Having succeeded with Jerome where efforts with Hus had resulted only in failure, the Council considered the vanquishing of Jerome a major triumph. His recantation, the so-called *Revocatio errorum et heresum magistri Hieronymi*, was distributed across Europe and survives in numerous manuscripts.[168] It may be noted that Jerome read his recantation from the pulpit where the decrees of the Council were normally announced. This gave his recantation an official stamp. On the same day, a new commission was formed with the brief to investigate heresy. This was coordinated by Jean Rochetaillée (John of Rupescissa), patriarch of Constantinople, and Jean d'Achéry, the bishop of Senlis.[169] They were especially delegated

---

163. *FRB*, vol. 8, p. 497.

164. Šmahel/Silagi, pp. 231–241.

165. Šmahel, *Život a dílo Jeronýma*, p. 80.

166. Diarmaid MacCulloch, *Thomas Cranmer: A Life* (New Haven, Conn.: Yale University Press, 1996), pp. 600–603.

167. Hardt, vol. 4, col. 768.

168. See František M. Bartoš and Pavel Spunar, *Soupis pramenů k literární činnosti M. Jana Husa a M. Jeronýma Pražského* (Prague: Historický ústav ČSAV, 1965), pp. 283–284, which notes a total of eleven manuscripts, with additional manuscripts noted in the *Repertorium fontium hussiticarum*. More recent research has increased the number of surviving manuscripts containing the revocation to twenty-one. See Šmahel/Silagi, pp. 233–234.

169. Hardt, vol. 4, cols. 528–529, cols. 561–562.

to investigate allegations of adherence to Hus. They were to hear, decide, and adjudicate such matters and inquire among all ranks, and no one was exempt from their authority. They were specifically empowered to proceed to a definitive sentence.

Session nineteen was presided over by Jean-Allarmet de Brogny, along with nine cardinals, priests, and six cardinal deacons. Only Zabarella was missing of the four-member commission. Following a sung Mass, d'Ailly announced that Jerome had abjured all of his heresies and errors and had been returned to the fold of the church. This seemed to suggest the case was closed.[170] Jerome was then taken back to the tower in St. Paul's cemetery and guarded by armed men. D'Ailly's announcement was received with some suspicion by certain members of the Council. It appeared that Zabarella and d'Ailly had been thwarted in their efforts to relieve Jerome by the intervention of de Causis and Páleč.[171] These two men, who had worked so ardently at securing the condemnation of Hus, now worked with great zeal to see Jerome convicted of serious crimes. They prevailed upon Gerson to exert more energy in securing Jerome's condemnation. Gerson's hostility to Jerome may be attributed in large measure to the *odium philosophicum* in which Jerome had been involved from one end of Europe to the other over many years.[172] Despite the revocation of previously held controversial ideas and a firm declaration that he would thereafter adhere assiduously to official church teachings, Jerome's situation remained largely unchanged. It was not just the sustained opposition of de Causis and Páleč but also the arrival of reinforcements from Prague, prepared to submit new and additional evidence to the Council to aid in the continued prosecution of Jerome, that provided the hinge on which the fate of Jerome would turn.

Debates about the Dissenter

The matter of Jerome's revocation was regarded in some quarters with abiding suspicion, and there were others who believed that even though his recantation may have been genuine, there were still serious concerns.

---

170. Hardt, vol. 4, cols. 499–502.

171. *FRB*, vol. 8, p. 345.

172. Hardt, vol. 4, p. 533.

One of those who remained unsettled was Gerson. He had been a key factor in the prosecution of Hus earlier in the year. Gerson later admitted that he had labored as diligently as anyone at the Council to secure the heresy conviction of Hus.[173] On October 19, 1415, Gerson lectured publicly on the idea of recantation with some pointed remarks under the title "On Recantation in the Matters of Faith." Several crucial points can be found in this address. According to Gerson, recantation does not eliminate the serious stain and guilt of heresy, and therefore even heretics who repent must be perpetually locked up.[174] In other words, confession of faith is insufficient and in any event cannot remove suspicion of heresy. The whole point of Gerson's lecture appeared to call into question Jerome's recantation and draw it under a renewed cloud of suspicion. Regardless of how the revocation was viewed, in Gerson's mind, it could not be grounds for release of the prisoner. Freedom was not an option. This opinion must have come as a devastating blow to Jerome, who doubtless believed that his recantation would provide both grounds and justification for parole.

Perhaps motivated by Gerson's remarks, on December 19, the German nation at the Council urged that the case of Jerome be reopened.[175] One must wonder on which legal or procedural grounds a repentant heresy suspect could be returned to an inquisitorial fray. Jan Náz spoke on behalf of the Germans, referring to Jerome as the "suspected heretic." Náz was president of the German nation. On this same date, Náz reminded everyone that Sigismund had more than once called for the case of Jerome to be concluded.[176] Náz was even more pointed in his remarks, which he advanced with some force. "The council convened for three principal reasons: to put an end to the schism, to condemn heresies, and to reform the church in head and members. Jan Hus has already been most justly condemned, and John XXIII has been deposed." Náz went on to say that he had no faith whatever in the sincerity of Jerome's recantation.[177] This

---

173. *Dialogus apologeticus*, in du Pin, *Joannis Gersonii*, vol. 2, p. 387; Glorieux, vol. 6, pp. 296–304. The statement was made at the end of the Council in September 1418.

174. Hardt, vol. 3, cols. 39–53; and Gerson, *Iudicium de protestatione et revocatione in negotio fidei*, in Glorieux, vol. 6, pp. 155–165.

175. Hardt, vol. 4, col. 556. For the renewed judicial proceedings, see Šmahel, *Jeroným Pražsky*, pp. 173–175.

176. Hardt, vol. 4, cols. 556–557.

177. Hardt, vol. 4, col. 556.

was the crux of the matter. The character of Jerome was well known, and a recantation probably surprised most of those active in the case. They were stunned initially by the fulsome intellectual surrender, but that astonishment soon gave way to suspicion. The papal notary Giacomo Cerretano tells us that both Gerson and Jean Mauroux, the patriarch of Antioch, were dissatisfied with Jerome's recantation. Interestingly, Mauroux was described by d'Ailly as a "snake in the grass."[178] Despite these reservations, the continued incarceration of Jerome prompted a formal protest, and on December 30, a letter bearing the signatures of 452 Czech barons reached Constance. It was read to the Council after the new year. The contents did not motivate any particular change to the Council's view of Jerome, and he continued to languish in the tower of St. Paul in the cemetery against the west wall of the city.[179]

The previously mentioned reinforcements who joined the prosecution against Jerome were Carmelite friars. They arrived at Constance from Prague during the winter, armed with "evidence" and allegations of Jerome's incitement to iconoclastic activities, which were noted earlier as having occurred in 1412 and 1414.[180] These monks joined forces with de Causis. The Carmelite accusations were direct: "This same Jerome is a sacrilegious man and a robber of churches and of God's priests. On the year and month already named, he violently robbed the said monastery and with many armed men burst into it and injured some monks, and captured one preacher who especially preached against Wyclif's heresies and held him many days as his prisoner in a special jail and caused him a lot of injustice."[181] It was also alleged that in August 1411, Jerome had caused the arrest of "the honest man A. a cutler," an inhabitant of Prague, who hated the false teaching of Wyclif and Hus and who said it was heretical. This man was placed in a harsh prison and was treated very badly. He was put in a pillory, and Jerome, possibly along with others instigated by Jerome, allegedly abused the poor man by throwing gourds at him. After several

---

178. Noted in Louise R. Loomis, "Nationality at the Council of Constance," *American Historical Review* 44, no. 3 (1939): 515.

179. *Documenta*, pp. 580–584. The 452 nobles were later formally summoned to appear before the Council. Hardt, vol. 4, cols. 839–852.

180. *FRB*, vol. 8, p. 345.

181. *FRB*, vol. 8, p. 288.

days of abuse, the man died.[182] Meanwhile, these additional deponents testified that in St. Vitus's Cathedral, Jerome apparently had declared that the relics of the Virgin Mary, "the veil and gown of the glorious Virgin," had no greater value than the skin of the ass upon which Christ sat. At the Church of St. Mary of the Snows on September 28, 1412, Jerome was alleged to have incited the people to smash a reliquary and to trample relics underfoot.[183] The acts of iconoclasm, especially those in 1412, were presented with the important caveat of characterizing Jerome as perpetrating such wickedness on account of having been "seized by a diabolic spirit" that prompted him to declare that the pope was a "liar, heretic, and usurer."[184] This testimony must have given pause to those initially satisfied with the September revocation.

All of these events were summarized and preserved in Czech sources. According to the *Passio*,

in the following year 1416, the arch enemies from Bohemia, the unfaithful and renegade Michael [de Causis], parish priest of Smradař, Dr. Páleč, with monks from the Mother of God of the Snows in Prague brought new charges against Jerome. But the cardinals, recognizing the anger of those inciters, Czechs and Germans, and that injustice would be done to Master Jerome, diligently worked before that council to secure his freedom. But his enemies were trying to stop it shouting that he should not be freed, saying: "It is not proper for you to plead for such a heretic, from whom not only we with all students in Bohemia suffered a great deal of evil, but I am afraid that your honesty will also suffer. Because if you care about him this means that you are doing it because of gifts." The cardinals, hearing this, ceased to advocate for him and got rid of the position of the judge, and in their places were, by instigation of his enemies, appointed others, who had also sentenced Master Jan Hus to death.[185]

---

182. *FRB*, vol. 8, p. 296; and Hardt, vol. 4, col. 666.

183. Hardt, vol. 4, cols. 674–675.

184. *FRB*, vol. 8, p. 298, with additional details and commentary on the various acts of iconoclasm on pp. 300–301.

185. *FRB*, vol. 8, p. 358.

In other words, Mladoňovice believed the judges in the case against Jerome were both biased and bribed. It is also significant to note a thinly veiled reference to the aftermath of the 1409 Decree of Kutná Hora.

There was some justification for the suspicion. Náz represented one point of view to the Jerome commission, and to those members who desired to see Jerome released. "We are very surprised, most reverend fathers, to find you making intercession for such a wicked heretic, for whose sake we in Bohemia, with the whole clergy, have suffered much trouble and mischief. Is it possible that you have been bribed either by the King of Bohemia, or by some of these heretics? Is it possible they have secured from you the freedom of this fellow?"[186] This was not the first assumption or presence of bribery in legal proceedings at Constance.

At length, the original Jerome commission was disbanded and replaced. D'Ailly and Zabarella were dismissed, and the new members were vested with collecting evidence. These new members included the Frenchman Jean Rochetaillée (John of Rupescissa), canon lawyer and since 1412 the titular patriarch of Constantinople, and the theologian Dinkelsbühl from Vienna.[187] It is altogether possible that Páleč and de Causis, along with Náz, worked to secure the condemnation of Jerome, and these men may be seen as constituting a driving force in the change of personnel on the commission.[188] The original commission had voiced concerns about the process against Jerome, and men such as d'Ailly and Zabarella had been only recently involved in the Hus case. Moreover, Zabarella was a canon lawyer of some renown. Some scholars have suggested that bribery may have motivated Rochetaillée and Dinkelsbühl.[189] To what extent issues such as bribery or genuine concern for legal procedure motivated the change cannot be determined. Nonetheless, the new commission became dominated by men eager to secure an irrevocable judgment against the defendant.

If not the memory of Hus, then the ghost of Wyclif continued to lurk throughout the trial of Jerome. Indeed, sworn enemies of Wyclif's, such as Thomas Netter were unprepared to allow his memory to fade. At one

---

186. *Narratio de Magistro Hieronymo*, p. 345.

187. *FRB*, vol. 8, p. 283; and Hardt, vol. 4, cols. 615–616.

188. Matthew Spinka, *John Hus: A Biography* (Princeton, NJ: Princeton University Press, 1968), p. 294.

189. Brandmüller, *Das Konzil von Konstanz 1414–1418*, vol. 2, p. 126.

stage in the proceedings, Jerome was accused of having a painting of Wyclif, depicted as the prince of philosophers wearing a halo, in his room at Prague.[190] Jerome admitted that he had a painting but denied that Wyclif was featured wearing a halo.[191] Evidently, it was common knowledge in Prague that there were portraits of great philosophers at the place where Jerome lived. The accusations of heresy lodged against Jerome went further in alleging that the defendant considered the same condemned Wyclif to be a holy man, and in the house in Prague where he resided, he had ordered that in one room Wyclif should be painted in the same way as the saints were depicted. This was done, and thereafter, Jerome revered and worshipped the picture. In this manner, Jerome was characterized as having committed the sin of idolatry and manifest heresy in these acts. The accusations against Jerome included the claim that the offensive painting could be seen to the present day.[192] The suggestion also reveals the nature and extent of the toleration of heresy supposed to persist in Prague.

By February 12, 1416, during a Council session "in a bigger church of Constance," the procurator Henry of Piro announced that many people had been and were defaming the Council, especially in the Czech lands, and were following up such activities by sending out sealed letters defending Hus against the charges laid against him and against his conviction for heresy, saying that he had been unjustly burned, that his condemnation and execution were an affront to truth. Instead of being a heretic, Hus was promoted and defended as a holy man, who had been condemned on account of "the fat clergy." The last phrase functioned as derogatory shorthand for corrupt clerics. Henry called for such people who had written against the Council to be summoned as "slanderers and friends of heresy."[193] A relevant citation was then issued for these pernicious "Hussite"

---

190. Hardt, vol. 4, cols. 654, 751, 764.

191. *FRB*, vol. 8, p. 308.

192. *FRB*, vol. 8, pp. 295, 308. The oldest depictions of Wyclif are likely those contained in manuscripts of Czech provenance. These include Castle Archive, MS C 38, fols. 18v, 119; and NK, MS VIII C 3, fol. 2r. On the accusations of iconoclasm and idolatry (the latter with particular reference to the portrait of Wyclif with a halo) against Jerome at Constance, see Karel Stejskal, "Obvinění mistra Jeronýma Pražského z ikonoklasmu a modlářství na Kostnickém koncilu," *Husitství—reformace—renesance: Sborník k 60. narozeninám Františka Šmahela*, 3 vols., ed. Jaroslav Pánek, Miloslav Polívka, and Noemi Rejchrtová (Prague: Historický ústav, 1994), vol. 1, pp. 369–380.

193. *FRB*, vol. 8, p. 283.

heretics on February 23. The Council cited as heresy suspects each of the 452 Czech barons to appear, and the notices were published that spring in Constance.[194] Unsurprisingly, the barons did not respond. The Council later acted, on September 4, to reissue the citations. This latter action was initiated by de Causis, who had been commissioned to spearhead the Council's policy against the Hussites. He reported his activities to the Council in session, to the end that he had personally cited 424 nobles on account of Hussite beliefs.[195] The text noted that in these last days, Satan had raised up "heresiarchs" and "ministers of damnation" against the church, with the purpose of destroying the faith. Two of these heresiarchs were identified as Wyclif and Hus. Such men had clearly fallen into "damnable error" and had led many astray. The citation was ordered posted on the doors of every church in Constance.[196] While Jerome was not mentioned in the citation, it seems sensible to place him within the thinking of those who promoted it. His trial at Constance was predicated, in part, on his reputation for disseminating errors and heresies. With this renewed assault, Jerome was once again publicly charged with heresy. Henry of Piro read formal accusations against Jerome before the Council.[197] Altogether, there were many people united in accusing Jerome of heresy.[198]

Rochetaillée, the titular patriarch of Constantinople and leading member of the reconstituted commission, was invested on February 24 to examine witnesses in the case against Jerome. The questioning of witnesses, the recording of the depositions, and the work required by the notaries occupied the better part of two months. By April 18, the commission heard a large group of witnesses associated with de Causis. These deponents submitted evidence that Jerome was known to disrupt church services and incite violence among common people, especially in Prague.[199] As noted previously, de Causis and Páleč were the main leaders in the prosecution of Jerome, in much the same way as they had acted in the legal case

---

194. The text of the citations appears in Hardt, vol. 4, cols. 829–852. Briefly noted in *Notae de Concilio Constantiensis, FRB*, vol. 8, p. 321.

195. Buck, *Chronik des Konstanzer Konzils*, p. 80.

196. Text in Jacques Lenfant, *History of the Council of Constance*, 2 vols., trans. Stephen Whatley (London: Rivington, 1730), vol. 1, pp. 562–563.

197. Hardt, vol. 4, cols. 557, 615.

198. Poggio, p. 157.

199. Hardt, vol. 4, pp. 146–150.

involving Hus. Along with Náz and Gerson, these men can be considered the individuals who contributed the most to Jerome's indictment and subsequent conviction.

By April 27, at the twentieth session, the case was declared by the *commisarii deputati* ready to proceed. Jerome was not present at this session, and we cannot be certain that he was aware of the proceedings until after the fact. Dinkelsbühl read out the accusations. The patriarch of Constantinople announced that the accusations had been supported by witnesses, and he delivered "a long and prolix report to the Council of the second proceedings against the said Master Jerome of Prague."[200] By this means, the court established the canonically required *fama publica* (belief by reputable persons that the defendant is guilty). The law mandated that an accusation had to rest on *infama* (infamy or bad reputation). This was to be established either by *clamosa insinuatio* (notorious suspicion) or *fama* (common report).[201] Both requirements were met in the trial procedures involving Jerome.

The Franciscan inquisitor Jean de Rocha (Jean Roques of the brothers Minor) read a series of articles (either thirty-one or forty-five) addressing Jerome's alleged Wyclifism, along with more than one hundred additional articles (numbering either 102 or 104) ranging across his entire career. These voluminous charges were derived from activities purported to have transpired in England, Prague, Paris, Heidelberg, Kraków, Vienna, Russia, and Constance over a thirteen-year period. The Knín *Quodlibet*, the Zbyněk affair, the protests over indulgences in 1412, his activities in Russia, and his alleged heresies with respect to the Trinity, predestination, and the Eucharist were among those matters at issue.[202] Jerome was also accused of breaking his commitment to the Czech king and queen by not confirming his recantation and by affirming Hus. The reading of the articles was prefaced with remarks that the charges had been assembled so that "Your Graces could learn about the heresy and other sins of one Jerome of Prague, very suspect of heresy and prosecuted through this holy congregation of Constance."[203] Rocha requested that Jerome be required

---

200. Cerretano, *Liber gestorum*, in Finke, *Acta*, vol. 2, p. 279.

201. Supported in canon law by X 5.1.21 *Inquisitionis negotium*, in Friedberg, II, col. 742; and C.2 q.3 c.1–6, in Friedberg, I, cols. 451–452.

202. Hardt, vol. 4, cols. 629–631, cols. 633–656; *FRB*, vol. 8, p. 284.

203. *FRB*, vol. 8, p. 284.

to fast on the grounds that the prisoner had indulged in drunkenness and gluttony the whole time he had been incarcerated in the cemetery tower. The request seems unusual and at variance with other accounts of Jerome's imprisonment. Rocha went on to suggest that the prisoner, who persistently went about "dressed as a layman with a big beard," be tortured and that if he refused to simply answer all allegations with a simple yes or no, he should be relaxed to the secular arm for execution of sentence as a contumacious heretic.[204] Rocha's suggestions contravened the due process of medieval heresy proceedings and would have constituted illegal procedure. In any event, the recommendations were not accepted. Further, it does not appear that Jerome was subjected to judicial torture.[205]

Giving aid and comfort to other suspects also considered weak on the message of the true faith featured among the Council's concern about the activities of Jerome. For example, in terms of his extraordinary journey to areas beyond Europe, and in order to impress the Russian schismatics, those leaning toward the Orthodox church, Jerome allegedly took off his cassock and tried to approximate their habits by wearing a long beard and long hair. At Constance, evidence was submitted suggesting that matters were even worse, to wit, that during the welcome of the grand duke in Vitebsk, Jerome caused a public outrage when he preferred the procession of "perverse" schismatics to local brothers and other monks.[206] In the presence of a large crowd, numbering between four thousand and five thousand people, he ostentatiously bowed before icons and, while kneeling, worshipped false relics and in this manner confirmed to the Ruthenians the "perfection" of their faith. He allegedly behaved similarly while he was in Pskov, where he rashly entered the local church of the schismatics during a celebration of the Mass.[207] What is missing in this relatively extensive

---

204. Hardt, vol. 4, cols. 628–691. There is a good summary in Karl Joseph von Hefele and Henri Leclercq, *Histoire des Conciles d'apres les Documents Originaux*, 10 vols. (Paris: Letouzey and Ané, 1907–1952), vol. 3, pt. 2, pp. 377–387, 394–408.

205. Hardt, vol. 3, col. 60.

206. Hardt, vol. 4, cols. 675–680.

207. Along with Novgorod, Pskov was a center in the late fourteenth and early fifteenth century where the Strigolnik heresy flourished. The abbot Iosif of Volokolamsk, writing one hundred years after the time of the Strigolniks, when the Russian church was combating the Judaizer heresy, makes reference to the earlier heresy with some relevant information about the Strigolniks. Iosif Igumen Volotskii, *Prosvetitel' ili oblichenie eresi zhidovstvuiushchikh* (reprinted Farnborough: Gregg International, 1972), Old Church Slavonic text. More

listing of Jerome's transgressions is receiving Orthodox communion in both kinds. The evolving eucharistic practice of receiving communion in both kinds (*sub utraque specie*) has been suggested by some historians as the main reason for Jerome's journey to Orthodox areas.[208] This is a telling omission and presents sound evidence (*a silentio*) for not attributing the practice to Jerome. Be that as it may, information about Jerome's activities in eastern Europe was gleaned from Polish delegates at Constance and from Páleč and Rvačka, who formed close relationships with those men. Mikołaj Trąba (metropolitan/archbishop of Gniezno) was at Constance; Witołd of Lithuania and the bishop of Vilnius Mikołaj Gorzkowski were not in attendance (though the former was represented by George Giedigold). Jerome admitted that he had spoken before Witołd at Vilnius but denied the specific allegations lodged against him.[209]

"The same Jerome being a slanderer and a defamer of others and especially of God's Church and her prelates, wrote many defamatory books against the Pope and against enlightened princes [especially] Ernest the Austrian and Ernest the Bavarian and nailed them on a pillory and ordered them to be nailed. Particularly against lord Zbyněk, the Prague archbishop, he wrote against him and signed it, he nailed up defamatory books at many places. At Bethlehem Chapel he poked his head out of the window when Jan Hus was preaching, and adamantly defamed lord Zbyněk of good memory in front of a large crowd of people and incited the people

---

contemporary documents include the following: a letter written by Patriarch Nilos of Constantinople, ca. 1380; Stephen of Perm, *Instruction*, ca. 1386; Metropolitan Photius, four letters addressed to the city of Pskov, September 23, 1416, 1422–1425, June 22, 1427, and September 23, 1427; and several brief entries in the Nikonian and Novgorodian chronicles. The documents written by Nilos, Stephen of Perm, and Photius have been published in N. A. Kazakova and Ia. S. Lur'e, *Antifeodal'nye ereticheskie dvizheniia na Rusi XIV–nachala XVI veka* (Moscow and Leningrad: Izdatel'stvo Akademii Nauk SSSR, 1955), pp. 230–255. Short studies in English include David M. Goldfrank, "Burn, Baby, Burn: Popular Culture and Heresy in Late Medieval Russia," *Journal of Popular Culture* 31, no. 4 (1998): 17–32; Alexey I. Alexeev, "A Few Notes about the *Strigol'niki* Heresy," *Cahiers du monde russe* 46, nos. 1–2 (2005): 285–296; and Thomas A. Fudge, *Heresy and Hussites in Late Medieval Europe* (Farnham: Ashgate, 2014), II, pp. 217–221.

208. The theory that Jerome brought the idea of Utraquism back to Prague from his trip to Russia (Lithuania and White Russia) has been expounded in F. M. Bartoš, *Čechy v době Husově 1378–1415* (Prague: Jan Laichter, 1947), pp. 395–399. It is true that Jerome had taken some interest in the rites of the Orthodox church. The theory about Utraquism is controversial and has not attracted much support.

209. Šmahel, *Život a dílo Jeronýma*, pp. 66–67.

against him."[210] Jerome later essentially admitted to these allegations, and his statements tend to confirm that he did have personal involvement in these affairs.[211] There is additional reference to the Council at Rome in 1413, where John XXIII burned objectionable books. Jerome's answer was evasive, in that he said that he believed the council took place in Pisa.[212] Wyclif was formally condemned by the papal authority of John XXIII on February 2, 1413, at a Lateran Council, and his books were burned on February 10 in Rome in front of St. Peter's Basilica. The bull of condemnation is extant, and there are also surviving brief notices of the event in manuscript sources.[213]

At Constance, we find reiteration that no proper Christian was permitted to read any of Wyclif's books, to explain their contents, to teach them, to own them, or to mention them whether publicly or privately, under pain of ecclesiastical punishment and suspicion of heresy.[214] Outside these deliberations, Jerome forcefully testified that he had never knowingly taught heresy and, in response to direct questioning, asserted that he had never been expelled from Hungary.[215] None of these details, explanations, or testimony by the defendant appears to have made any difference as the trial proceeded. Instead, Jerome was characterized as "a man of bad reputation and character, a rioter, a follower and teacher of heresy, and he is considered, called and announced like this publicly and in front of everybody."[216] He had a few defenders, but siding with someone under notorious charges of heresy was risky. From the sympathetic point of view, Jerome was considered scholarly and, in the Czech version of the *Passio* written about him by Mladoňovice, "a faithful knight of God."[217]

We also find Jerome accused of denying the doctrine of transubstantiation in much the same fashion as Hus had been accosted with the

---

210. *FRB*, vol. 8, p. 288.

211. Mansi, vol. 27, col. 845.

212. *FRB*, vol. 8, p. 285; and Mansi, vol. 27, cols. 505–506 note the condemnation and burning of the books.

213. *Documenta*, pp. 467–469; and, for example, NK, MS III G 16, fol. 98.

214. *FRB*, vol, 8, p. 285.

215. *FRB*, vol. 8, p. 286.

216. *FRB*, vol. 8, p. 290.

217. *FRB*, vol. 8, p. 351.

same allegation.[218] Many of his responses caused some of his accusers to be ashamed, and others were silenced.[219] It is often difficult to untangle the responses as recorded by different notaries or eyewitnesses. One thing that is constant and undisputed is that Jerome was alleged to have spread Wyclifite heresy in Prague, Vienna, Heidelberg, and Hungary.[220]At Heidelberg, when "the masters of the same Heidelberg University recognized that his ideas were heretical and inconsistent with the Christian faith they did their best to capture him and force him by law to recant those heresies, but he, being warned again, secretly fled."[221] Predictably, Jerome denied many of these accusations, though from time to time, he admitted that some of them were true. His responses are recorded under the proceedings of April 27.[222] The language is strident: Jerome was accused of many heresies and represented as possessing a reputation in most of Christendom that described him as a man of evil reputation, a notorious heresy suspect, rebellious, and even more dangerous to the faith than the errors of Arius.[223] For many years, Jerome had been characterized as a man with a bad reputation and an evil nature, one given to rebelliousness, who followed the pathways of heresy, and he was considered to be an important teacher among the "new suspicious sects." In particular, Jerome was presented as a proponent of the heretical sect of Wyclifite heresy. Jerome's enemies gave witness that this was how he was publicly regarded by practically everyone in the Czech kingdom and in many other countries of the world, indeed almost the whole of Christendom.[224] The hyperbole was typical boilerplate components of medieval heresy trials, which aimed to demonize the defendant and impress upon the court the nefarious influence of the suspect.

The chief prong in the case for the prosecution hinged on the suspicion that both Hus and Jerome were characterized as "sons of iniquity" who had taught heresies. Jerome's response was to argue that the

---

218. *FRB*, vol. 8, p. 291.

219. *Passio*, p. 359.

220. *Documenta*, pp. 416–421.

221. *FRB*, vol. 8, p. 303.

222. Hardt, vol. 4, cols. 633–647.

223. *FRB*, vol. 8, pp. 291–292.

224. *FRB*, vol. 8, p. 293.

assumption was untrue, though he admitted that he had collected the books of Wyclif and brought them to Prague.[225] Jerome replied to the charge: "It is false that I taught heresies and errors from Wyclif's books. But I admit, that when I was a young man and full of zeal for learning I went to England, and hearing the fame of Wyclif, that he was a man of subtle and excellent genius, when I could get hold of copies of his *Dialogus* and *Trialogus* I transcribed them and brought them back with me to Prague." Jerome also alluded to two other unidentified texts on the Eucharist which he obtained in England.[226] It is possible that these books were Wyclif's *De eucharistia* and *De apostasia*, but this is no more than a guess.[227] Others have suggested that these writings may have been Wyclif's *De eucharistia* and *De simonia*.[228] Prosecutors noted that Jerome played a central and essential role in the transmission of heretical literature into Bohemia. "Jerome, going to the land of the kingdom of England, zealously sought out the books of John Wyclif, either himself or by others, and having found them, he copied them with singular delight with his own hand, and having thus copied them he brought and published these works of Wyclif in diverse lands, and especially in the kingdom of Bohemia, asserting in the hearing of different trustworthy witnesses that these books ought to be kept and loved by all those who aspired to true knowledge and understanding."[229]

The trial proceedings alleged that Jerome and his associates had been endangering their own souls and the souls of others by teaching, preaching, receiving, enlarging, and defending the heresies of Wyclif and Hus. The triadic correlation among Wyclif, Hus, and Jerome is almost impossible to avoid.[230] Jerome was accused of infecting many people over many years, seducing them from the true faith and teaching them heresy. Jerome was included with Wyclif, Hus, Křišťan of Prachatice, and Jakoubek Stříbro as

---

225. *FRB*, vol. 8, p. 285.

226. Hardt, vol. 4, cols. 634–635, 649, 651.

227. Anne Hudson, *Studies in the Transmission of Wyclif's Writings* (Aldershot: Ashgate, 2008), II, p. 646.

228. Gordon Leff, *Heresy in the Later Middle Ages: The Relation of Heterodoxy to Dissent c.1250–c.1450* (Manchester: Manchester University Press, 1999), p. 622, but this presents no evidence to support the claim.

229. Hardt, vol. 4, col. 649, from the additional articles of accusation, April 27, 1416.

230. *FRB*, vol. 8, p. 292.

clearly identifiably wicked men.[231] The trial process against Jerome alleged that, along with Hus, he had taught that no one need fear (or pay heed) to papal or episcopal anathemas unless such censures were of God.[232]

With all of this underlying the legal process and motivating the case against Jerome, by April 27, Rochetaillée and Dinkelsbühl were delegated by the commission to present at least 135 articles to Jerome. He rejected most of the propositions initially advanced by the Franciscan inquisitor Rocha and did so in writing.[233] To the larger series of additional articles, *Additationes ad articulos*, Jerome flatly refused to respond, arguing that he should be allowed a public hearing. There was some concern over acceding to this demand, and some members of the Council adamantly opposed it. Nevertheless, at length, it was decided that the prisoner would be allowed a public hearing. This was finally formalized at the twentieth session of the Council on May 9, when on behalf of the commission investigating matters of faith (*in causa fidei*), the patriarch of Constantinople, Rochetaillée, reported to the entire Council, and a public hearing in the matter of Jerome was scheduled. The "athlete of Antichrist" would finally and publicly face an ecumenical council representing the entire church to defend himself on charges of heresy.

---

231. *FRB*, vol. 8, p. 294.
232. *FRB*, vol. 8, p. 298.
233. Hardt, vol. 4, cols. 633–646.

7

Five Days in May

THE BATTLE FOR CONSCIENCE

AFTER MONTHS OF legal wrangling, the case involving Jerome of Prague appeared to culminate. The process may well have concluded in April 1416, had the defendant not insisted on challenging normal procedure. This meant that the trial of Jerome was not quite finished. The defendant had refused to reply to many of the allegations and had demanded a public hearing. By May 9, the process was sufficiently advanced to allow Jean de Rochetaillé, the patriarch of Constantinople, to speak on behalf of the new commission. That body was made up of Bishop Vitalis of Toulon, Abbot Kaspar from St. John in Perugia, Henry of Perugia, Lambert Sluter of Gelderen (Euskirchen), Bishop Thomas of Lubeck, and Bernard de la Planche. None of the previous cardinals who had expressed some sympathy for Jerome remained on the commission. Among the new judges, Jerome was known personally only to Sluter, who had been the assistant judge of the Vienna tribunal, who most likely replaced Nicholas Dinkelsbühl.[1] The bottom line boded badly for Jerome. He insisted on a public hearing. Initially, the request was denied. Jerome protested. Although the idea of a public hearing in a heresy trial was irregular, the request eventually was granted. This is a parallel to the Jan Hus trial. Jerome insisted he was able to articulate the views of Hus and his own in such a manner as to clarify any residual ambiguity. Like Hus, Jerome seems to have approached the hearings at Constance as though they were academic disputations or the kind of university debates to which he was accustomed (i.e., *Quodlibet*).

---

1. Hardt, vol. 4, cols. 732–733.

Eight months earlier, Jerome had recanted all of his objectionable ideas and undertook to avoid any repetition of those errors and heresies. It is likely that he fully expected that his revocation would result in his conditional release from prison. Once that occurred, it is altogether probable that given opportunity, he would have left Constance and returned to Bohemia. That expected release from the confines of the tower in the cemetery near St. Paul's Church did not occur. As noted, powerful men questioned both the sincerity of the recantation and the advisability of releasing a man such as Jerome even if his revocation was sincere. While these matters were being debated in Council chambers, Michael de Causis and Štěpán Páleč worked strenuously to secure a reconsideration of the case against Jerome. Evidently, neither man was satisfied with the immolation of Hus. Additional charges were laid against Jerome, new witnesses arrived, and the prisoner remained incarcerated in the tower along the west wall of the city. By spring, the Council decided to accede to the demands of the defendant and allow a public hearing. Initially, there was a period reserved for the examination of Jerome, which was set from May 18 to 21.[2] Jerome's idea of a public hearing was quite different from that envisioned by the Council.

Public Hearings

The hearings in the case of Jerome before the Council took place on May 23 and 26. Jerome, the "most pugnacious leader of the Wyclifites," was brought to the cathedral.[3] Cardinals Branda di Castiglione, Guillaume Fillastre, and Antonio Chalant sat with four judges on an elevated platform.[4] The general congregation on May 23 in the cathedral was chaired by Jean-Allarmet de Brogny, cardinal bishop of Ostia. The chief accusers included Rochetaillé, representing the French nation; Kaspar, representing the Italian nation; John Welles, prior of St Mary's, in York, who represented the English nation; and Sluter, who represented the German nation. Rochetaillé again spoke on behalf of the examining magistrates

---

2. Hardt, vol. 4, p. 37. Hardt has the wrong dates, as nothing relating to the trial of Jerome transpired on those dates.

3. Howard Kaminsky, *A History of the Hussite Revolution* (Berkeley: University of California Press, 1967), p. 62.

4. Hardt, vol. 4, cols. 748–753.

and summarized the case. Jerome confounded the proceedings by refusing to take an oath, on the grounds that he was not being permitted to speak freely but required only to reply to the charges.[5] He declined the oath, insisting that the new commission was not competent to hear the case and that the new examination demanded by de Causis, Páleč, and their supporters was irregular. Jerome took the view that since there were so many accusers arrayed against him, it was only sensible for him to have opportunity to reply point by point to all of the charges. However, he demanded opportunity to speak in his own defense first and to make an appeal to the Council. In other words, Jerome demanded the chance to speak generally on his own behalf before having to address the particulars of the charges lodged against him. This procedural innovation was denied. Standing in the middle of the cathedral and thus thwarted, Jerome launched into a veritable attack on the court, referring to the several requests he had made in order to secure a hearing and alluding to the reticence of the court to grant that hearing and furthermore to the refusal to allow him to speak in his own defense:

> What an injustice this is! While I was for three hundred and forty days held in a harsh and dark jail, in stench, dirt, in excrement, in chains, in deprivation and want of all things, you in that time always listened to my adversaries and enemies, but you do not want now to listen to me even for one hour! And the consequence of this undoubtedly is that the ears of all of you were open to their slanders and they were denigrating me as a heretic and an enemy of the faith for a long time, so that you have condemned me in your minds as ignoble before you could learn what I really am. But even you are humans and not gods, you do not live for ever, but you are mortal, and therefore even you can stumble into sin, go the wrong way, make mistakes, even you can be deceived and misled as other people. It is said that here are all together the lights of the world and the most prudent men of the entire world. This is all the more reason why you should keep in mind not to do something frivolously, unadvisedly and against justice.[6]

---

5. Hardt, vol. 4, cols. 751, 764–771.

6. Poggio, p. 158.

There was considerable shouting and commotion frequently interrupting Jerome. In sum, he dismissed the broad range of allegations against him as specious and nothing more than the malicious concoctions of his enemies. Voices in the hearing then accused Jerome of attacking the papacy, speaking evil of the pope, caricaturing the cardinals, engaging in the persecution of prelates, and generally hating the priesthood. The rebuttal was one of attributing sustained anticlericalism to the defendant. Jerome's reply was both classic and penetrating. Standing with his arms spread out, he demanded to know that if such things were true, where he was to appeal. He dismissed the option of the Council. Jerome argued that this was impossible, for his detractors had already prejudiced the Council against him. "My enemies have already alienated your minds from any consideration with respect to my well-being. They have presented me as the enemy of everyone who sits in judgment here. There is even the possibility that should the charges against me be considered unsound that your judgment will have already been moved by the notion that I am the enemy and the common adversary of everyone as these people have falsely said about me. If you accept their words, then there is no hope for my life."[7] The words made a powerful impact, and Jerome spoke with an air of unassailability.

The narrative about the one-sided nature of the trial, the filth of the prison, and the darkness of the prison that Jerome was forced to endure are details derived exclusively in the text written by Poggio Bracciolini. Those details aside, it took up the remainder of the day for the promoter to read out the details of the prosecution and to hear Jerome's answers to sixty-five of the 107 articles lodged against him.[8]

Among the central issues on which Jerome was examined was the question of the Eucharist, which remained a perennial concern. When asked by one of the Council delegates to express opinion on the Eucharist, Jerome said that prior to consecration, it was bread and wine, but following consecration, it was the true body and blood of Christ. Jerome was then challenged by another unnamed member of the Council, who stood up and said, "Jerome, it is known about you that your opinion is that the bread also remains at the altar." This, of course, was a comment in support of the allegation that Jerome had adopted John Wyclif's position on

---

7. Poggio, p. 159.

8. *FRB*, vol. 8, p. 346.

the sacrament. The defendant deflected the statement by deftly answering that "my opinion is that the bread is only in the baker's shop and not in the Eucharist." The eyewitness Poggio effectively said that Jerome acquitted himself on charges of remanentism by quipping that "the bread does remain at the baker's," though Poggio erred in assuming that Hus followed Wyclif into eucharistic error. Fillastre agreed that Jerome departed from Wyclif and Hus on the sacrament.[9] Tempers flared, and there were exchanges that were little short of incendiary. During the interrogation, Jerome was interrupted by a Dominican, and the defendant retorted with the stinging comment, "shut up, you hypocritical monk."[10] To another who claimed that he accused Jerome according to his own conscience, Jerome replied that such a declaration was a good way to deceive. A third detractor Jerome simply dismissed with the caustic conclusion that the man was an ass and apparently refused to dignify the man by calling him by name but only referred to him consistently as "dog" or "ass." Jerome's unflinchingly direct rhetoric won him few friends.

At the same hearing, the Council clearly wished to obtain responses from the defendant concerning the 107 additional articles he had not previously addressed. Poggio, a papal secretary and a *scriptor* in the Poenitentieria, the office of the Curia that issued indulgences, provides a good summary of the session. He referred to Jerome as a man of considerable eloquence and learning. "I have never seen anyone who argued a case, especially in a capital case where one's life was at stake, with eloquence as near to that of the ancient writers whom we so greatly admire."[11] Poggio went on to remark that it was a great shame that a man with such an astute mind had strayed into heresy. He hastened to add the caveat that he wondered if in fact the charges against Jerome were accurate and true. In his narrative account of the hearing, Poggio pointed out that the skill and erudition exhibited by Jerome as he replied to charges and defended himself were

---

9. Fillastre, p. 61; and Hardt, vol. 4, cols. 752–762, for Jerome's speech on May 26. On Hus and the Eucharist, see Paul de Vooght, "Jean Huss et ses juges," in *Das Konzil von Konstanz—Beiträge zu seiner Geschichte und Theologie: Festschrift unter dem Protektorat seiner Exzellenz des Hochwürdigsten Herrn Erzbischofs Dr. Hermann Schäufele*, ed. August Franzen and Wolfgang Müller (Freiburg: Herder, 1964), p. 160, where he is completely and quite rightly absolved of error with respect to the sacrament.

10. Poggio, p. 159; also *Passio*, pp. 359–360.

11. Poggio, p. 157. See appendix 12.

remarkable. He declared that unless Jerome had engaged in duplicity or falsehood, there was no cause for a sentence of death to be pronounced.

Not to be denied, Jean Gerson spoke up, reproaching Jerome for causing outrage at Paris with his comments about universals and ideas: "When you were in Paris, Jerome, you thought you were an angel from heaven with all your eloquence, and you disturbed the entire university by stating many erroneous conclusions in the schools, along with their correlates, especially on the subject of universals, on ideas, and on other matters still more controversial."[12] At the Council of Constance, it was Gerson who took the lead in deducing that there was potential for heresy in Jerome's understanding of universals.[13] The main point of Jerome's philosophy was considered at best a convenient fiction and at worst an unverifiable hypothesis that threatened the fabric of theology. The trial at Constance had underscored those more controversial matters, and Gerson was as determined as de Causis and Páleč that Jerome should not escape by any means. He was simply too dangerous. Jerome acquitted himself and declared that the accusations had been brought falsely by those who hated him. Several years earlier, Jerome noted, one preacher in Prague, "prattling on about the book of Revelation," claimed that the apocalyptic dragon whose tail swept down a third of the stars from heaven was "John Wyclif who allegedly had turned to his heretical faith more than one third of the church militant."[14] Jerome was now being characterized as a threat of similar proportions.

It is arguable that Gerson and others among Jerome's opponents deliberately or in ignorance convoluted philosophical issues and theological considerations. Jerome scrupulously distinguished between the two. Of course, as noted previously, Jerome did not recognize any incumbent pressure to keep the two disciplines separate. Nevertheless, as a quadruple university master, Jerome insisted he had dealt with, and argued, philosophical propositions that had not touched on doctrine or the articles of Christian faith. The conflict over ideas and universals remained at the core of the case against Jerome at Constance, the point of view taken on such matters played a major role in the

---

12. Hardt, vol. 4, p. 217; and *FRB*, vol. 8, p. 342.

13. Zénon Kaluza, *Les querelles doctrinales à Paris: Nominalistes et réalistes aux confins du XIVe et du XVe siècles* (Bergamo: Lubrina, 1988), pp. 22, 61.

14. *Recommendatio artium liberalium*, in Šmahel/Silagi, p. 217.

eventual condemnation of Jerome, and this conflict goes some distance toward explaining why the defendant was convicted.[15] It seems apparent that Gerson's methodology consisted of looking critically at theses that seemed problematic to him, then drawing out from them the theological implications that he thought were questionable or dangerous and then assigning these to the author. This is how he proceeded with respect to Jerome.[16] Even before he had encountered Jerome, Gerson was concerned with eliminating what he considered worthless teachings that were utterly useless for faith. Theological reform required the eradication of useless pseudo-theologizing, which only confused and detracted from what was essential for salvation. Such inquiries were vain and corrupted proper theology, led to the ridicule of theologians, and essentially degraded the gospel. That was Gerson's view in April 1400.[17] Six years later, he encountered Jerome at Paris and a decade thereafter crossed paths again with him at Constance. Nothing during those sixteen years caused Gerson to change his mind on this matter one iota. In fact, the ideas and arguments of Jerome only confirmed Gerson in his point of view:

> In the year of our Lord 1416, on the Saturday before the day of the Ascension of the Lord Christ, on the 25th day [sic] of the month of May, Master Jerome was brought to a hearing again. Once again on this occasion, before the entire council, 107 articles were presented against him so that he could not escape the snares of death. During this hearing, held from the morning until midday, he gave answers to all forty articles, which had been written falsely, and he did not admit his guilt, saying that the false witnesses, his enemies, had written them against him, and he was given a deadline until the 28th [sic] day of the month of May to make a reply to the other articles.[18]

---

15. See Vilém Herold, "Der Streit zwischen Hieronymus von Prag und Johann Gerson—eine spätmittelalterliche Diskussion mit tragischen Folgen," in *Société et Eglise: Texts et discussions dans les universités d'Europe centrale pendant le moyen âge tardif*, ed. Sophie Włodek (Turnhout: Brepols, 1995), pp. 77–89.

16. Kaluza, *Les querelles doctrinales à Paris*, p. 22.

17. Letter to Pierre d'Ailly, in Glorieux, vol. 2, pp. 26–27.

18. Hussite Chronicle, in *FRB*, vol. 5, p. 343.

We catch a glimpse of de Causis, who was involved again at the end of the hearing on May 23.[19] The complexity of the charges, the prolixity of the replies, and the nature of the trial procedures made it necessary for an adjournment. It was decided that the hearing should be recessed and reconvened three days later. It cannot be determined with any sense of accuracy what transpired during those days. One can only suspect that Jerome spent them in the tower in the cemetery of St. Paul's, preparing himself mentally for his appearance before the Council. It is most unfortunate that we have no prison letters from the pen of Jerome to rival those written by Hus. It is possible that the Council took specific care to make sure that Jerome was unable to engage in this type of contraband and, like Hus, smuggle letters and other documents in and out of the prison. We cannot possibly know what his thoughts were during these long, dreary months, nor can we be certain that he planned to say what he did on May 26 or if, seized by the moment, he simply launched into an impromptu, intellectually extemporaneous speech that revealed the testimony of conscience. Either way, the trial of Jerome was approaching its conclusion.

At the continuation of the hearing on May 26, Rochetaillé spoke again, and as before, Jerome once more refused the oath. Notwithstanding, the remaining articles were read out by Abbot Kaspar. Jerome provided replies to the articles and also addressed the audience at the invitation of the patriarch of Constantinople.[20] The anonymous chronicler has Jerome declaring that the articles were prejudicial to him and that he would swear nothing but would reply as he had previously. He denied having been involved with respect to the three young men killed over indulgences in 1412, and especially with respect to a procession and the singing of *Isti sunt sancti*. During this session, Jerome was asked about his perspective on indulgences. His answer could hardly be impugned. He replied that papal indulgences issued by the church were lawful and might legitimately be given. However, buying an indulgence was an abuse and therefore illicit. In other words, the economic dimensions of the indulgences trade were at issue, but the concept and theology of indulgences were not objectionable.[21] The incident concerning the public protest against indulgences and

---

19. *FRB*, vol. 8, p. 314.

20. Poggio, pp. 157–163; and the official version of the speech in Hardt, vol. 4, cols. 752–762; see also Niem, in Hardt, vol. 2, cols. 449–454.

21. Hardt, vol. 4, cols. 752–753, 755–773; and *FRB*, vol. 8, pp. 311–314.

a procession through the streets of Prague involving one or more contrived whores and the abusive denunciation of indulgences, those who
sold them and the papacy, was raised, and it was noted that the blasphemous affair included the burning of papal bulls and indulgences. The
articles before the Council claimed that Jerome was the chief instigator,
but at this hearing, Jerome declared that it was not he who had burned
the bull.[22] The reply might be taken as an astute response, and perhaps
Jerome had not, as he testified, actually committed any document to the
fire in the New Town square. However, his denial is a very limited one
and may be considered evasive and equivocal. After all, he had answered
the questions around the matter of Pope John XXIII burning objectionable books in Rome in 1413, and he had evaded the question by asserting
that he believed the Council had taken place in Pisa. Rochetaillé summed
up the charges and Jerome's replies and declared that Jerome stood "convicted as a four-fold heretic" and had been convicted on the basis of his
"own worthless talk."[23] In response, Jerome called on God, the Blessed
Virgin Mary, and the saints in prayer, asking that his mind and intellect
might be enlightened to avoid saying anything that might damn his soul.
Jerome insisted on being heard, on the grounds that since the Council had
evidently listened with much patience over a long period of time to his
enemies, it was only reasonable that he should be allowed equal consideration. There were many strenuous voices opposing this suggestion, but
the Council agreed to allow him to speak. Jerome mentioned many others throughout history who had been falsely convicted and said it would
not be a surprise if he, too, were consigned to the flames because of such
vindictive men, who were also liars. He referred to the original commission, in which Francesco Zabarella and Pierre d'Ailly had been members,
being replaced by a prejudicial one including men such as Rochetaillé and
Dinkelsbühl. Jerome stated that he did not recognize their authority and
did not acknowledge their right to be judges in his case, for they were not
objective. The defendant claimed that he had been disadvantaged by his
Czech enemies and by "certain Germans who hated him."

Jerome defended the Decree of Kutná Hora. He asserted that had he
encouraged Hus to take a stand against German domination. If accurate,
this underscores an assumption expressed earlier that Jerome played a

---

22. Hardt, vol. 4, cols. 672, 753.

23. *FRB*, vol. 8, p. 311; Hardt, vol. 4, col. 756.

considerable role in events in Prague in 1409 and thereafter. We are not informed about how this may have happened, but it appears that Jerome and Hus prevailed upon King Václav to intervene in the Prague town councils and change the balance of the constituency to reflect a Czech majority.[24] Jerome went on to speak at some length about the enmity that existed between Czechs and Germans at Prague on account of the way the university was structured. The anonymous account of the Jerome process indicates that about half of Jerome's speech was devoted to the political struggle between Czechs and Germans.[25] The following extract underscores and highlights that component of the trial:

> I am condemned by none but my fellow Bohemians, the German Bohemians; the reason for their hatred is this: the Czechs are descended from the Greeks, and as there is hatred between the Greeks and the Teutons, so it continued until the kingdom came into the hands of the emperor Charles IV. This same Charles, being king of Bohemia, saw that it was a rich country, not lacking in food, gold or silver, but only in educated men, and that his subjects had to go outside the realm to acquire learning, to Paris and other places to get the degree of master or doctor. Therefore the lord Charles, wishing to endow the kingdom of Bohemia and the city of Prague, founded and built a university there. In that university many Germans secured prebends and fellowships, so that the Czechs had nothing. And when a Czech had graduated in arts, if he had no other means of livelihood, he had to go to the towns and villages and earn his living by teaching in some private school. The Germans were in complete control of the university of Prague and all of its benefices; they held the seal of the foundation and all the insignia. Also they had three votes in the University, namely the Bavarian and the Saxon and more than half the Polish vote, for the Silesians, who were reckoned among the Polish nation, were all Germans, so that the true Poles were only a minority therein. Whatever the Germans wanted in the university was as good as done. The Bohemians could do nothing.[26]

---

24. Mansi, vol. 27, col. 892.

25. Hardt, vol. 4, cols. 755–773.

26. Hardt, vol. 4, cols. 757–758.

In addition to these remarks, Jerome related his own journey to Constance and how he stayed in a castle nearby, which was identified by the chronicler Petr Mladoňovice as Überlingen. He admitted nailing up notices in Constance about Hus. It should be pointed out that Jerome had testified earlier that he had arranged for the notices to be posted in the city. The official *Acta* seem to convey the sense that Jerome was heretical despite his repeated denials. It is thought that Dietrich Niem participated in this general congregation on May 26.[27]

Jerome then reached a crucial turning point in his address to the Council. The entire case against him hinged on the testimony of witnesses. Unlike Hus, Jerome had written very little, and even less of what he had written had to do with theology. Texts by Jerome that did exist were confined largely to *quaestiones* from university disputations. While the possibility cannot be excluded, I have been unable to find any evidence that Jerome was read during his lifetime. Therefore, allegations of heresy were almost completely hearsay. In 1415, the books of Hus had been examined. The Council found therein evidence to support allegations. A year later, there was no corpus of written material for the delegates of the Jerome commission to examine. Recognizing the hearsay testimony of witnesses spanning a decade or more, Jerome put forth an argument for why no one should trust such witnesses, who, in his opinion, had come to Constance not in search of truth but because they desired to obtain a platform from which to vent their hatred and spite. Jerome went on to delineate the nature and foundations of the hatred that had coalesced around him, resulting in a trial for heresy before an ecumenical council. Poggio observed that Jerome's argument was so profound and convincing that practically everyone was inclined to err on the side of mercy and perhaps vote to acquit the defendant. This must be doubted if we consider men such as Gerson, de Causis, Páleč, Niem, Dinkelsbühl, and others who had crossed paths with Jerome in Paris, Cologne, Heidelberg, Buda, Vienna, Prague, and elsewhere. Now face to face with their nemesis, Jerome's enemies gathered from all over Europe and were able to see through the wandering scholar's practices.[28] Poggio's assertion can only be taken as rhetorical flourish and

---

27. Šmahel, *Život a dílo Jeronýma*, p. 111.

28. František Šmahel, "Poggio und Hieronymus von Prag: Zur Frage des hussitischen Humanismus," in *Studien zum Humanismus in den böhmischen Ländern*, ed. Hans Bernd Harder and Hans Rothe (Cologne: Böhlau, 1988), p. 80.

hyperbole. Jerome further pointed out that he had come to Constance voluntarily hoping to clear his name of the opprobrious reputation that had been unfairly attached to him. Tellingly, the defendant argued that differences of opinion were not necessarily harmful or fatal. After all, disagreements had transpired between the saints and the holy men of antiquity, and by means of such discourse they were able to arrive at truth. There was little that could be disputed in Jerome's comments. However persuasive his speech was, and despite the force of argument and compelling prose, one of the persistent concerns for the Council was the threat Jerome had posed to the church on account of his incessant traveling and propensity for discourse and disputation. This can be summarized with a single reference. Štěpán Dolany, the abbot of a Carthusian house in Moravia, did not attend the Council, but he surely had Jerome firmly in mind when he complained of suspicious wanderers, who went into one country after the other, causing trouble and disseminating heresies. Dolany noted that this had occurred especially in Bohemia and Moravia, but these missionaries of heresy went into the courts and residences of secular princes, shamelessly appeared in churches and cathedrals, boldly visited convents, and even attempted to infiltrate his own Carthusian order, their nefarious influences turning up in Carthusian cells. Such individuals solicited both men and women and especially targeted university students.[29] From Oxford to Kraków, Jerome had represented Wyclifite philosophy in academic forums. He was also skilled in diplomatic circumstances, and he promoted agitation against the church in courtly circles and even ventured beyond the crowned heads of state.[30] Gerson, de Causis, Páleč, Niem, Dinkelsbühl, Peter Pulka, Jan Náz, Dietrich Vrie, Dietrich Kerkering, Konrad of Soest, Johannes Lagenator, Mikołaj Trąba, and many others who had previously crossed paths with Jerome in places as far afield as Paris, Cologne, Heidelberg, Buda, Vienna, Kraków, and Prague were aware of his activities and could testify to the validity of the complaint published by Dolany. It is certain that the suspicion lingering in the minds of these men was not pacified. Indeed, their hesitation was soon confirmed.

---

29. *Antiwikleffus*, in *Thesaurus anecdotorum novissimus seu veterum monumentorum*, 6 vols., ed. Bernard Pez (Augsburg: Philippi, Martini, & Joannis Veith fratrum, 1721–1729), vol. 4, cols. 157–158.

30. Astutely pointed out by Ferdinand Seibt, *Hussitica. Zur Struktur einer Revolution* (Cologne: Böhlau, 1965), p. 78.

Revoking the Recantation

What happened next was decisive. It is difficult to determine if the nature of the resumed hearing came as a surprise to anyone. Certainly, men such as Gerson must have felt vindicated. Gerson did not flinch from boasting thereafter that he supported the condemnation of Jerome with all his strength. He later went on record as late as September 1418 with the proud declaration that he had labored as diligently as anyone at the Council to secure the heresy conviction of Hus.[31] It is said that Jerome spoke as an experienced orator, without fear and in a voice that was pleasing and dignified.[32] As shocking as it must have seemed to many members of the Council, Jerome retracted his recantation from the previous autumn, claiming he had agreed to a revocation only from fear. He announced to the congregation that he had harmed his conscience and therefore without delay retracted all negative statements he had previously made concerning Hus and Wyclif. Later sources suggest that Jerome's retraction of his recantation was inspired by the Holy Spirit.[33] As noted earlier, it is possible that Jerome thought in September 1415 that his recantation might secure his release. A month after the case had concluded, the Czech noble Jindřich Lacembok (Chlum) was accused of heresy. However, he was freed when he swore that he was not a Hussite and denounced both Hus and Jerome. He left Constance on July 1 and returned to Bohemia; he died at Grätz adhering to the Hussite faith.[34] The previous autumn, Cardinals Zabarella and d'Ailly had been in favor of Jerome being released. When that did not happen, and after an additional eight months of imprisonment, Jerome now "fell to praising Jan Hus ... praising Jan Hus."[35] The

---

31. His boast about Jerome can be found in *Contra vanam curiositatem studentium*, in Glorieux, vol. 3, pp. 243, 246. Noted also in Kaluza, *Les querelles*, p. 33. His remark about the Hus trial is in *Dialogus apologeticus*, in *Joannis Gersonii, Opera omnia*, 5 vols., ed. Louis Ellies du Pin (Antwerp: Sumptibus societatis, 1706), vol. 2, p. 387; and Glorieux, vol. 6, pp. 296–304.

32. Poggio, p. 157.

33. *FRB*, vol. 8, p. 444.

34. Thomas Martin Buck, ed., *Chronik des Konstanzer Konzils 1414–1418 von Ulrich Richental* (Ostfildern: Jan Thorbecke Verlag, 2010), pp. 79–80; Hardt, vol. 4, col. 796; and *Notae de Concilio Constantiensis*, in *FRB*, vol. 8, pp. 321–322.

35. Poggio, p. 161; also *FRB*, vol. 8, p. 312.

place Jerome now found himself in was an effect of his past and the cause of his future.

Jerome referred to the fact that many Christian martyrs, and also heathen ones, and holy prophets, all of whom had to die for the truth, were tortured by various means. He referred to Socrates, Plato, Virgil, Seneca, Boethius, Moses, Elijah, Samuel, Susannah, John the Baptist, Stephen, and the apostles, many of whom were "put to death by a college of priests." The speech was a dazzling display of eloquence. The prose penetrated the minds of the congregation like a high-powered drill. Jerome then proceeded to deliver what amounted to a speech about Hus. He said he had known Hus since his youth. As far as Jerome was concerned, Hus was a "brave, just, and pious man," who was upright and devout, one who never deviated from the truth. Jerome asserted that the bulk of the opposition to Hus was on account of the fact that Hus confronted the irregularities of the priests. This resulted in those same clerics, "driven by spite against the teaching of Master Jan Hus and the hate for him which they fostered," appointing de Causis to represent them at the Curia for the purpose of having Hus cited there. Jerome noted that de Causis was German, a Teutonicus and not a Bohemus.[36] He argued that Hus was a good man, that he had not been a fornicator, had not been greedy, was not a drunkard, and had not been contaminated by other obvious sins, as Jerome implied his enemies had. Jerome defended Hus as a humble, honest, and modest man who was extraordinarily diligent in learning and reading. According to Jerome, Hus was a righteous and faithful preacher, and Jerome went so far as to declare that Hus was a saint. He then went on the offensive. He declared that whatever Hus and Wyclif had preached against sinfulness, pride, anger, brutality, and the greed of the clergy, he also desired to profess and to do so until his death. As far as other articles of the Christian faith were concerned, Jerome confessed agreement with everything and believed according to the common Christian Church and asserted that he did not agree with any heresy. The speech ended with Jerome stoutly declaring that he was revoking the recantation he had made on the "cursed chair," which he had only made because of his fear of death, noting that his conscience did not bother him as much for all his own sins as for the sin he committed against the holy and good Master Jan Hus, when he, during his recantation, spoke against him, especially when he agreed with

---

36. Hardt, vol. 4, col. 759.

his unjust vilification.[37] Among Jerome's remarks is the declaration: "I do not believe that Jan Hus was justly condemned. Previously when I admitted that he had been I acted contrary to conscience. His teaching was holy and right. So was his life. I will hold to him and do so firmly. I confirm this here and I revoke the letter which I sent to Prague wherein I denounced the views and teaching of Jan Hus. With respect to the books and doctrines of Wyclif, I have never known anyone who wrote as well or as profoundly. When I condemned the teaching of Jan Hus this was not because I wished to cease from such teaching but I recanted out of fear because I was afraid of the fire." Jerome's statements were an effort to qualify his previous recantation and to attribute that action solely to terror and fear. His revocation, he now argued, was nothing other than an example of human frailty and a confession of cowardice. He fired yet another salvo with the declaration that he did not suppose for a moment that he would be the last victim of the cunning wickedness of evil priests. Turning once more to his judges, Jerome declared that the day would come when those same judges would see him preceding them to the judgment seat of God and indeed summoning each of them to judgment, where they would be made to render an account to God for their unfair and wrongful treatment of him.[38] Unsurprisingly, once the speech concluded, many were angry, and Jerome was taken back to prison, "with heavy chains around his legs, hands, and around his chest."[39] Eyewitnesses noted that Jerome presented himself as a man worthy of remembering, whose knowledge was outstanding, whose learning was prodigious, whose eloquence and skill were admirable. Nevertheless, the powerful speech of Jerome attracted the comment

---

37. *Passio*, p. 361.

38. There are confusion and chronological challenges in comparing the texts of the *Acta* and the account prepared by Mladoňovice on this point. It appears that the remarks made by Jerome have been convoluted. The *Acta*, which I have followed here (Hardt, vol. 4, col. 757), have Jerome making these comments at the end of his speech on May 26. By contrast, the narrative by Mladoňovice has Jerome saying something very similar to this on May 30 (*FRB*, vol. 8, p. 347). There is some preference for the account contained in the *Acta*. The thread of argument in the speech version in the *Acta* appears to fit more properly. For example, Jerome's words in the *Acta* are conveyed as "Quod una vice post hanc vitam haberent videre Hieronymum eos praecedere et eos omnes ad judicium vocare." The text in Mladoňovice assumes a rather different perspective: "Et cito vos omnes, ut respondeatis mihi coram altissimo iudice infra centum annos." In the Mladoňovice version, the completely indefinite phrase "una vice" becomes a rather definite "one hundred years" in the future, which is both unnecessary and puzzling. It works well in hindsight from a Protestant point of view but suggests textual emendation. The account in the Acta is preferred.

39. *FRB*, vol. 8, p. 362; and Hussite Chronicle, in *FRB*, vol. 5, p. 343.

that his agile intellectual skills and rhetorical gifts were also possibly his own worst enemy.[40] Once back in prison, Jerome was given two days to reconsider his position and offer appropriate repentance. Despite the fact that a number of eminent men of the Council came to the prison tower to see Jerome, among them especially Cardinal Zabarella, who tried to get the prisoner to change his views, there is no evidence that Jerome wavered or even considered a second revocation. Zabarella's efforts failed.[41]

The battle for conscience was waged singly by Jerome in the darkness of a prison tower over the course of many months in the winter of 1415–1416. In the absence of documents from his hand during the period of his confinement, such as we do have from Hus, who managed to have letters smuggled in and out of the Dominican and Franciscan prisons, we have no way of knowing how Jerome fought that battle of conscience. Our information is limited to his disclosures the following spring. A millennium before Jerome, Augustine had finally gotten around to writing his *Retractiones* (Reconsiderations), a project he had been considering for about fifteen years.[42] The "reconsiderations" are especially valuable for pointing out how Augustine's mind had changed on issues throughout his long and productive life. They correct previous errors and misunderstandings, while enlarging his own theology. Some scholars regard them as a "long and detailed examination of conscience."[43] Unlike Augustine, Jerome wrote nothing on the matter of his reconsideration of his autumn recantation. But like the bishop of Hippo, Jerome engaged in a long and careful examination of conscience. In the end, that battle was one for conscience, and the struggle in the tower of the cemetery of St. Paul against the western walls of Constance prompted the prisoner to withdraw his revocation, to choose the more difficult path, and to publicly and dramatically set the record straight. In many ways, Jerome's performance was not unusual, if his oratorical repertoire and curriculum vitae are taken into account. An analysis of surviving university polemics and formal *quaestiones* of Prague provenance provide sound evidence to support Jerome's

---

40. Poggio, p. 163.

41. *FRB*, vol. 8, p. 336; and Poggio, p. 163.

42. A. Mutzenbecher, ed., *Sancti Aurelii Augustini Retractationum libri II*, Corpus Christianorum Series Latina, vol. 57 (Turnhout: Brepols, 2003).

43. Agostino Trapè, "Saint Augustine," in *Patrology*, ed. Angelo di Berardino, trans. Placid Solari (Westminster, Md.: Christian Classics, 1995), vol. 4, p. 345.

reputation as a first-rate philosopher.[44] The quality of mind and sweeping intellectual abilities were on display in Constance.

Poggio was both impressed and appalled. He wrote that many of those who heard Jerome were filled with grief. According to Poggio, many were eager to see Jerome avoid a capital conviction, mainly because they were impressed with his outstanding intellectual capacities. But Jerome appeared intent on his own destruction and seemed not to care that death might take him as a result of his rash declarations. The central issue was his unmitigated praise of Hus, wherein he defended the latter against the charges lodged and sustained against him. Jerome attempted to instruct the Council that they had erred in condemning Hus. The unjustly burned heretic had not attacked the church at all. Instead, his focus was solely on the abuses and irregularities of the priesthood and the prelates. The church was supposed to provide aid to the poor and afflicted and tend to the cure of souls. Hus opposed the practice of spending church resources on whores, sumptuous feasts, games, rich clothing, and gaining wealth. All of this, Jerome declared, was in opposition to the true religion of Christ.[45] These words cut many to the heart and were deliberately inflammatory.

With respect to his disavowing of Hus and Wyclif, there is corroboration from other witnesses, especially around Jerome's defense of Hus and the explanation for why Jerome had originally agreed with the execution of Hus and made a comprehensive recantation. "He had made that confession and abjuration and had assented to and approved those verdicts wickedly and falsely, in foolish terror of an imaginary fire."[46] The defense by Jerome made a great and wide impression. While there is only a short entry in Fillastre's diary, it appears that the notaries recorded Jerome's performance faithfully.[47] There is an anonymous account delineating the last days of Jerome that refers to his stand at the Council.[48] As previously noted, Poggio remarked that during Jerome's formal addresses to the Council, his use of wit and sarcasm evoked laughter, and he was persuasive. This is

---

44. See František Šmahel, *Die Prager Universität im Mittelalter* (Leiden: Brill, 2007), p. 579, and also the larger context on pp. 539–580.

45. Poggio, pp. 161–162.

46. Fillastre, p. 61.

47. Finke, *Acta*, vol. 3, pp. 60–61.

48. *Vita*, in *FRB*, vol. 8, pp. 335–338.

not to imply that all were impressed with the speech. For example, Niem savagely assailed Jerome, alleging that he insulted Germans and misrepresented them, noting that Jerome had returned to his original theology and that appropriate punishment for that offense was entirely deserved.[49] Poggio makes no mention of Jerome's September recantation at all. Vrie notes succinctly that Jerome "revoked his heresy as elegantly as he had propounded it."[50]

During the recess on May 27, Fillastre made a special note in his diary that Jerome's public hearing had been ordered at the request of the defendant. Fillastre characterized Jerome's address as a great speech (meaning long) in which he endeavored to persuade the congregation that his conviction had been achieved by means of perjured testimony, falsehood, and malice. Fillastre also noted that Jerome had retracted his agreement with the condemnation of Hus and Wyclif. This, of course, was the crucial declaration. An additional comment recorded both by Fillastre and by the anonymous notary, pointed out that Jerome distanced himself from Wyclif and Hus on the matter of the Eucharist. This is confirmed also in the anonymous account.[51] This is either a curious annotation by Fillastre or an error on the part of Jerome. Wyclif's eucharistic doctrine was well known and had been condemned inasmuch as it advanced a theory of remanence and denied the church doctrine of transubstantiation. Hus was accused of adhering to Wyclif on numerous points of theology, but it was quite incorrect to assume or argue that Hus followed Wyclif in the matter of the sacrament. To the very end, Hus remained utterly orthodox in his eucharistic theology, and it is not persuasive to accept the argument that Jerome's statements were accurate because he was intimately familiar with Hus's ideas and therefore revealed the truth that Hus withheld.[52]

The words of Vrie on Jerome's lengthy and passionate address before the Council on May 26, that he "revoked his heresy as elegantly as he had propounded it," are both apt and important. It is impossible to delineate

---

49. Hardt, vol. 2, cols. 449–454.

50. Vrie, in Hardt, vol. 1, col. 202.

51. Fillastre, p. 61; and Hardt, vol. 4, cols. 755–757.

52. See the analysis in Thomas A. Fudge, *Jan Hus: Religious Reform and Social Revolution in Bohemia* (London: I. B. Tauris, 2010), pp. 49–54. For the counter position, see Walter Brandmüller, "Hus před koncilem," in *Jan Hus mezi epochami, národy a konfesemi*, ed. Jan Blahoslav Lášek (Prague: Česká Křesťanská Akademie: Husitská Teologická Univerzity Karlovy, 1995), p. 216.

what happened in Jerome's thinking over the course of eight months as he lay chained in prison.[53] We learn details from Poggio that are neither confirmed nor refuted by other sources and may contain sufficient truth. For 340 days, the prisoner languished in a filthy dungeon where there was little or no light.[54] Evidently, Jerome could neither see well nor read. There is further the question of the psychological trauma that must have attended those long months in the cemetery tower. Poggio alludes, without expansion, to the "anxiety of mind which must have tormented him daily and which could very well have erased memory" and driven Jerome to madness.[55] Did Jerome despair of release? Had he denounced Hus and Wyclif only as a ploy to gain his freedom? Why did he reverse himself so dramatically in May, when he might well have gained freedom had he continued to agree with the decisions of the Council on the matter of heresy? As he pointed out so eloquently, the case against him was circumstantial, predicated on memory and testimony that was hardly unimpeachable. Solid prima facie evidence was lacking.

There are two schools thought on Jerome's revocation. The first is that he was forced to undertake it. The second is that he embarked on that morally perilous journey in an effort to escape captivity and gain his freedom. I do not think that Jerome was forced to do anything, though it would be unwise to fail to take into account the circumstances of Jerome's incarceration and the psychological effect it may have had on him. That said, I believe the second option is closer to the truth. After all, Jerome had absconded from Vienna after giving his word that he would remain in the city until the conclusion of the trial. He later defended his volte-face by appealing to factors that suggest a bit less than complete honesty or integrity. Jerome was also a gifted equivocator. Still, it is too easy to condemn a man who had to endure the rigors of a medieval prison as Jerome did. If he was able to flee from Vienna in good conscience, then it is likely that he was able to arrive at a suitable justification for agreeing with a decision after the fact, only to reverse himself later. There is nothing to suggest that Jerome truly agreed with the censure or condemnation of either Wyclif or Hus. Jerome quite honestly revealed that he had betrayed

---

53. On medieval prisons, see G. Geltner, *The Medieval Prison: A Social History* (Princeton, N.J.: Princeton University Press, 2008).

54. Hardt, vol. 3, col. 69, says 360 days, but this is surely a typographical error, where CCCXL should properly be CCCLX.

55. Poggio, p. 162.

his own conscience in agreeing with their condemnations and had done so out of fear. The long winter months allowed him ample opportunity to review his situation. Once the opportunity for public hearings became a reality, Jerome was faced with the same dilemma he had wrestled with the previous year. A battle for conscience ensued. Once he had retracted his revocation, he had five days in which to ponder the outcome. On May 26, Jerome committed himself to a fate that entailed following the path of Hus to Brüel Field and to the stake beyond the city walls. He had five days in which to contemplate that outcome. After his dramatic reversal in the cathedral, he was taken back to the tower in chains. Five days later, he would return to the cathedral for the last time. On the fifth day, he would have one final opportunity to abjure Hus, along with any errors and heresies that were outstanding against him. At this stage, it was highly unlikely that he would be released, even with a comprehensive recantation. Jerome chose to take a stand on conscience and relieve himself of the guilt that had accumulated over the past months. Life, for Jerome, required perpetual falsehood, and that was a price he was not prepared to pay. Honesty meant a cruel death. The battle for conscience resulted in a decision for the latter. We cannot know what thoughts the prisoner entertained as he reviewed his predicament but he was aware that on the fifth day, he would face the world again in the final chapter of the battle for conscience.

8

Heretic and Hero at the Stake

ONE YEAR AFTER the trial of Jerome of Prague concluded, priests in Prague pulpits preached vivid sermons to their congregations, summarizing and detailing the events that had engulfed Jerome during the Council of Constance. One example is the sermon preached in 1416 in Jan Hus's Bethlehem Chapel in Prague by his friend and successor Jakoubek Stříbro:

Master Jerome was imprisoned for over one year in very cruel jails in heavy chains, his legs and hands were in the stocks or fettered. On one occasion, in a tower, he was hanging head down for over eleven days from a joist with holes so tight and sharp that his legs started to rot as the skin and flesh were torn. On top of this he was tortured with hunger and thirst as well as other sufferings. This hanging was so cruel and so long that he almost died because of it. They also fabricated articles against him, with which they provoked and tried him. They attempted especially to get him to abandon the teaching of Master Jan Hus and John Wyclif and to agree with the condemnation of them. And though at the beginning he seemingly and partially agreed with them, later, when they submitted to him one hundred and seven articles he was supposed to answer, he proclaimed during the public hearing that many of these articles were advanced and fabricated by dishonorable false witnesses. Later, again during the public hearing, he praised the holy life of Master Jan Hus, saying that he had known him from his early days, and that he was neither a fornicator nor a drunkard nor a criminal, but a pure and sober man, a saint and a righteous preacher of the Holy Scriptures. And whatever Jan Hus and Wyclif advocated, whatever they have written against the wrongdoings and pretentious arrogance of prelates, he himself wished to advocate until his death, because they were holy men. And he said that in all the articles of the faith his beliefs were in agreement with the Roman Church. And if he partially and formally agreed with the condemnation of Master Jan Hus previously, he took it back publicly, proclaiming that he did injustice to the holy man and his teaching.[1]

Definite interpretive bias can be detected in this narrative. Jakoubek's claim that Jerome "seemingly and partially agreed" with the Council on the condemnation of Hus is not based on any close reading of Jerome's revocation, and the conclusion that Jerome "partially" agreed with the decisions made by the Council in the Hus matter lacks historical credibility. Jerome's recantation does not contain the qualifiers Jakoubek later communicated to his congregation.

The Last Day

On Saturday, May 30, after Ascension Day, "at the third hour of the day" (nine A.M.), the final chapter in the trial of Jerome began in the cathedral of Constance.[2] The prisoner was brought to the church "with a number of armed men."[3] The twenty-first session was chaired by the cardinal-bishop of Ostia, Jean-Allarmet de Brogny. Thirteen other cardinals were present, wearing miters and copes indicating their senior ecclesiastical rank. The presence of these cardinals should be taken as a reflection of the importance the Council attached to the session and to the proceedings. In addition to the cardinals, there were also many international ambassadors, prelates, representatives of universities, envoys, and other dignitaries from places as far afield as Norway, Poland, Dacia, Sweden, Naples, France, Cyprus, and Aragon.[4] This congregation was altogether appropriate, given Jerome's many years of travel around Europe and his international reputation. Notably absent were King Sigismund and his

---

1. NK, MSS VIII E 3, VIII G 13; *FRB*, vol. 8, pp. 231–243; and Bohuslav Havránek, ed., *Výbor z české literatury husitské doby*, 2 vols. (Prague: Československá akademie věd, 1963–1964), vol. 1, pp. 234–238.

2. Hardt, vol. 4, col. 465.

3. Hussite Chronicle, in *FRB*, vol. 5, p. 341.

4. Hardt, vol. 4, cols. 764–765.

deputy Palsgrave Ludwig. Sigismund had left Constance earlier on his way to Spain in an effort to secure the formal abdication of Benedict XIII, who had been deposed by the Council along with John XXIII a year earlier.[5] Mass was said, and Jerome, like his predecessor Hus, was made to wait outside the church. Once the Mass had ended, the defendant was led into the cathedral to hear the sermon against heresy that normally came at the end of heresy trials. The sermon (*sermo generalis*) was delivered by the Dominican bishop of Lodi, Giacomo Balardi Arrigoni, the same man who had preached against Hus a year earlier.[6]

Preaching against Heresy

The general sermon was predicated on the conviction that heretics should be answered neither lightly nor with soft language but rather ought to be confronted with harshness. Correction that is mild is often not taken seriously and may even be ignored. Therefore, more severe measures are likely to attract more attention. If a wound cannot be healed by means of a gentle treatment, then the infected parts must be cut off, even if that inflicts great distress. The sermon's declared intention was not to stir up a fire, but rather it was delivered in mercy, with charitable motivations. The sermon underscored the fact that heresy was a result of contumacy, and the character of the defendant revealed that his was a full-formed identity that had evolved into monstrous proportions over many years.[7] Unbelief can be corrected and thereafter pardoned. Contumacious heretics can only be exterminated. The sermon characterized the defendant as perpetrating a labyrinth of error and heresy which entrapped many of the faithful. The judges had been kind to the suspect, but this had been rebuffed with arrogance and a refusal to take any note of sound advice. Therefore, "it is not another's shit [*stercus*] that I throw in your face, but your own, that you may see and repent of your crimes." The preacher expressed his own

---

5. *Notae de Concilio Constantiensis*, in *FRB*, vol. 8, p. 321, notes that Sigismund was absent from July 18, 1415, until January 27, 1417.

6. The text of the sermon appears in *FRB*, vol. 8, pp. 494–500. See appendix 10. There is an analysis of the sermon in Thomas A. Fudge, *Jan Hus Between Time and Eternity: Reconsidering a Medieval Heretic* (Lanham, MD: Lexington, 2016), pp. 99–116.

7. In the Middle Ages, a heretic was one who, being familiar with established evidence, insisted on holding another view with respect to matters of the faith. Annelise Maier, *Ausgehendes Mitteralter. Gesammelte Aufsätze zur Geistesgeschichte*, 3 vols. (Rome: Storia e letteratura, 1964–1977), vol. 2, pp. 59–81.

opinion, in concert with that expressed earlier by the Franciscan inquisitor Jean de Rocha, that the accused should have been subjected to judicial torture. Further, the public hearings that had been granted were regrettable, for they had only afforded the defendant opportunity to disseminate even more heresies and errors and had produced no salutary outcome. The sermon included a plea for the prisoner to repent but noted that the Council was obligated to move to summary judgment in the case.

Six times in the sermon, the bishop referred to Jerome by name. This contrasts with the sermon he preached against Hus, in which he never referred to that defendant by name.[8] The sermon on this occasion was based on the text "he found fault with their unbelief and hardness of heart" (Mark 16:14). The bishop said that the more serious the disease, the more rigorous was the treatment required. Jerome was singled out for stubbornness bordering on blockheadedness. Hus and John Wyclif were described as "treacherous men" who demonstrated "presumptuous temerity" in their wickedness. Jerome had been complicit, and the offenses he had been involved with were both numerous and wide-sweeping. According to the bishop, Jerome had worked to

> stir up the entire noble kingdom of Bohemia, to incite the barons and princes to strife and schism, to call out the soldiers, to overturn ancient and worthy governments, to call up armies, divide peoples, foment bitter dissension among the citizens, lead gangs, keep henchmen, keep men in arms, commit murders or have them committed, plunder churches and profane altars. Oh happy kingdom of Bohemia, had that man not been born! How utterly detestable it is that men of the church, under some pretext of sanctity, who should be devoted to God, who should pray day and night, pray for the sins of the people whose goods they consume, spend all their time in prayer—do not shrink to vex the courts of kings, princes and barons, to stir up disputes, to overturn the decrees of the kingdoms at will, to devote themselves to quarrels. Oh how great evils was the presumption of those two uncouth provincials the root! How many have been killed on either side, how many duly ordained clergy have been forced out, how many exiled, how many driven away with violence, how many robbed, how many beaten, how many killed, how

---

8. The text of the sermon preached against Hus is in *FRB*, vol. 8, pp. 489–493.

many buried, how many churches laid waste, how many altars profaned, how many monasteries destroyed?

Jerome was nominated as the most egregious heretic ever, surpassing even Arius, Sabellius, Fautus, Nestorius, and all the other notorious enemies of the faith. Michael de Causis had previously described Hus as the scion of all heretics and the most dangerous one in a thousand years.[9] The bishop of Lodi seemed to present Jerome as an even more dire threat to the faith than Hus had been. This resonated with Jean Gerson's assessment that Jerome perpetrated "matters still more controversial" and Gerson made much of his conviction that both Jerome and Hus had blundered into theological error.[10] Adopting this perspective, the sermon suggested that Jerome's heresy had penetrated all of Bohemia, France, Hungary, Poland, Lithuania, Russia, Italy, and Germany. The sermon went on to delineate six self-inflicted "mischiefs," which coalesced to bring Jerome to ruin and condemnation. First, he dismissed those who tried to defend him. Second, he did not deny many of the serious charges. Third, he endeavored to prove that his detractors were liars. Fourth, he failed to understand the difference between logic and rhetoric in the matter of proofs. Fifth, he persisted in praising Hus. The bishop described Hus as "a rebel and a heretic," going on to excoriate him on the grounds that "there is no worse fornication than that which he practiced against the Catholic faith." Sixth, Jerome's own testimony was cited as an example that "proved you a liar, a perjurer, no, a madman and a relapsed heretic, in that you repudiated the holy oath you had sworn and so fell into worse and more serious error."

The sermon may be read as an "enlightening illustration of the attitude of the fifteenth-century church towards heresy and the heretic; it is a scholarly, eloquent, logical, bitter and merciless exposition of the thesis that the 'more pestilent the disease, the more violent must be the remedy.'"[11] Guillaume Fillastre said it was a "fine sermon."[12] Ulrich Richental, in yet

---

9. *Documenta*, p. 196.

10. Glorieux, vol. 9, p. 639.

11. R. R. Betts, *Essays in Czech History* (London: Athlone, 1969), p. 231. In general, on the subject of heresy in sermons preached at Constance, see Paul Arendt, *Die Predigten des Konstanzer Konzils: Ein Beitrag zur Predigt-und Kirchengeschichte des ausgehenden Mittelalters* (Freiburg im Breisgau: Herder, 1933), pp. 156–168.

12. Fillastre, p. 61.

another error of detail, claimed the sermon was delivered by "a master of theology from England."[13] It was a dark sermon calling for penance.[14]

Jerome Responds

Contrary to established practice, following the sermon, Jerome addressed the judges.[15] The defendant stood in the middle of the cathedral, perhaps on "an elevated bench" so that he could be seen and heard by everyone present. We are told that he spoke in a clear voice, but his face was pale, and he wore a long beard. He addressed the cardinals, patriarchs, archbishops, bishops, doctors, masters, and the entire congregation. He asserted that he had no idea by what spirit Bishop Giacomo had delivered his sermon. "This lord Jacob the preacher, I do not know by what spirit he was speaking," because in everything he said he twisted the intended message into something quite different. Jerome implored all those in the cathedral, "through the blood of Jesus Christ, by which we have all been redeemed, not to think in this manner about me." He denounced the emphasis and intent of the preacher when Bishop Giacomo had asserted that Jerome scorned churchmen, declaring the allegation was false. Jerome absolutely denied the suggestion that he had brought Bohemia into disrepute, arguing that quite contrary to that charge, he had always kept the best interests of the country in mind. His conduct in the schools and during university disputations was never directed or intended to the disparagement of his country. His enemies were explaining events in a false and contrary way. His opponents were wicked and perverse men, and they ought to be recognized as such. Jerome affirmed that he was a Christian and that such false speech as uttered by the bishop could be used to vilify and misrepresent anyone and ought not to be taken seriously. Jerome declared that the sermon was an exercise in malice and an affront to God.

Moving away from the sermon specifically, Jerome addressed the accusations of heresy lodged against him. He expressed gratitude to Cardinal

---

13. Thomas Martin Buck, ed., *Chronik des Konstanzer Konzils 1414–1418 von Ulrich Richental* (Ostfildern: Jan Thorbecke Verlag, 2010), p. 67. See appendix 11.

14. Arendt, *Die Predigten des Konstanzer Konzils*, p. 57.

15. Jerome's response to the sermon was recorded by Dietrich Vrie, in Hardt, vol. 1, pt. 1, cols. 201–202; Hardt, vol. 4, cols. 766–768; and *FRB*, vol. 8, pp. 314–315. See also comments in Walter Brandmüller, *Das Konzil von Konstanz 1414–1418*, 2 vols. (Paderborn: Ferdinand Schöningh, 1991–1997), vol. 2, p. 134.

Francesco Zabarella for his instruction and patience. But he also noted
the changes that took place in the commission that had been assembled
to investigate his case, expressing his concern over this and explaining
that his refusal to take an oath during the hearings the previous week was
on account of the politics that constituted that new commission. Jerome
expressed his desire that everyone might know what he truly believed. He
said that the articles noted against him were not read by custodians elected
for that purpose, and he appealed to God, stating that he had not affirmed
those things alleged against him. Such affirmations would confirm stubbornness, and Jerome was unwilling to be thus classified. He went on
to point out that he was willing to suffer even though he professed one
holy catholic church, which, he insisted, was made up of all those who
had been redeemed. He then affirmed his belief in the church. He did
not reject the church hierarchy, as long as those prelates taught the law of
God. However, he confessed that he did reject those churchmen who had
apostasized from the faith. Jerome affirmed that he held and professed the
articles of the faith of the church. He confirmed the validity of the Mass
and the liturgical aspects of the faith. However, he affirmed that there were
at times disagreeable elements among the priests and that these were to
be rejected. Jerome went on to explain that he would never consent to the
loftiness and excess by which some clerics changed the proper heritage
of Christ to suit their own pride and interests. For example, he rejected
their use of alms, which he said they used to have their horses cleaned
and to purchase and maintain houses, courts, and expensive and beautiful
clothes. Instead of giving the donations to the poor, wicked priests misap-
propriated these resources for their own interests, which included cavort-
ing with whores.

He reiterated his disavowal of the letter he had written to Lord Lacek of
Kravář in Prague the previous October, affirming his recantation, which had
included an admission that he had preached heretically against the faith.
Contrary to that declaration, Jerome admitted that he had contributed to
great iniquity when he approved the condemnation of Hus. He confessed
that he had spoken badly and never worse in his entire life and had acted
against his conscience when he condemned Hus. Jerome expressed regret
for his actions. He reaffirmed his statements five days earlier and confessed that his recantation the previous September was solely "because he
feared the fire and the cruelty of its heat." At that stage, Jerome was interrupted by Jean Rochetaillée, the patriarch of Constantinople, who ordered
that the letter written by the defendant to Lord Lacek be "read word by

word publicly with a strong voice," and Jerome's signature was shown. The defendant admitted that he had written and signed the letter only from fear but now rejected it unconditionally, noting, "I have failed like a lunatic and I regret it very much especially when I recanted the teaching of Jan Hus and John Wyclif, and when I agreed with the condemnation of Jan Hus because I believe him to be a just and holy man and I have done this most wrongly."[16] During the discourse, there was a unique and interesting exchange between Jerome and Fillastre, the cardinal of St. Mark. Jerome had asserted that Hus had been condemned because he withstood the wickedness of priests. The rejoinder from Fillastre was that Jerome was wrong to invent such grounds for Hus's condemnation. The Council was well aware of irregularities within the priesthood and had gathered to address and correct these.[17] In his several addresses to the Council, Jerome did labor to cast doubt on the findings of the commission and to discredit its witnesses. Did he naively believe he might sway the Council to overturn the findings of its own commission and declare him innocent? Whatever pause or ambiguity Jerome's impassioned speech may have aroused was quickly resolved. The defense of Hus, of course, sealed his fate.

Sentence of the Court

When this procedural interlude concluded and once Jerome had finished his final address to the Council, proctor Henry of Piro asked for the definitive sentence to be passed on Jerome. The patriarch of Constantinople read the sentence.[18] Rochetaillée began with reference to the words of Christ in John 15:6, where it is written that if anyone did not abide in

---

16. This summary chiefly follows the Czech *Acta*, pp. 314–315, but also takes into account the anonymous account in Hardt, vol. 4, cols. 766–768, and Vrie's account in Hardt, vol. 1, cols. 201–202.

17. Fillastre, pp. 60–62. See appendix 11. "Official" versions of Jerome's speeches on May 23, 26, and 30 appear in Hardt, vol. 4, cols. 755–773. Petr Mladoňovice's account is in *FRB*, vol. 8, pp. 339–350. Mladoňovice was there for some of the early events, and for the latter he obtained an account from a sworn eyewitness. The records are essentially objective, with the caveat that the lion's share of attention ignores the defense aspects of the trial. Karl August Fink, "Zu den Quellen für die Geschichte des Konstanzer Konzils," in *Das Konzil von Konstanz—Beiträge zu seiner Geschichte und Theologie: Festschrift unter dem Protektorat seiner Exzellenz des Hochwürdigsten Herrn Erzbischofs Dr. Hermann Schäufele*, ed. August Franzen and Wolfgang Müller (Freiburg: Herder, 1964), p. 472.

18. Hardt, vol. 4, cols. 768–771. There is a translation in Norman P. Tanner, ed., *Decrees of the Ecumenical Councils*, 2 vols. (London: Sheed & Ward, 1990), vol. 1, pp. 433–434.

Christ, they were to be cast out for destruction, and such people were to be gathered, thrown into the fire, and burned. The sentence noted that the layman Jerome had been subjected to a trial following inquisitorial procedure and that the trial had been conducted on the basis of report, public infamy, and testimony of witnesses. The process revealed that the defendant held, maintained, and taught many erroneous and heretical articles, despite being rebuked and instructed by the holy fathers, and had been duly warned that the articles in question were "blasphemous, offensive to the ears of the godly, were seditious," and were in many respects the same heresies proclaimed by Wyclif and Hus, who were "men of the most damnable memory" and who had been condemned by this same synod for heresy. It was noted that Jerome had once agreed with that decision. Moreover, the same Jerome had undertaken to avoid heresy, to ignore the errors of Wyclif and Hus, and to follow ever after the way of truth as determined by the church. Had not Jerome affirmed that should he at some future time deviate from the faith, he was liable to eternal punishment? Having made such confession, many days later, the sentence read, it was noted with disdain that Jerome was like a dog returning to its own vomit with the intention that he might vomit forth the deadly poison that had lurked in his heart and which he had for a long time kept secretly hidden within.[19] With that evil intent prompting him, the defendant had demanded a hearing before the Council wherein he might disseminate that poison publicly. Given that opportunity, he admitted that he had shamefully lied when he denounced Hus. The recitation of the sentence pointed out that Jerome was not ashamed to admit that he had lied. It was manifestly evident to the Council that Jerome had "diligently read, studied, and declared" the ideas of Wyclif and Hus, and the Council pointed out that in earlier sessions, it had definitively identified the numerous errors and heresies contained in those books. "Therefore it is obvious from the matters written above that the same Jerome holds on to the disgraced Wyclif and Hus and their heresies and that he was their friend and still is. For this reason the same holy and sacred congregation has determined that the said Master Jerome is a rotten, dried out, withered branch, no longer growing on the vine, and has decided that he be cut off and cast out. The said synod also announces, declares, and condemns him as a heretic who has fallen into all kinds of heresy, and is therefore excommunicated and damned." The

---

19. *FRB*, vol. 8, p. 316; and *Passio*, p. 364.

Council declared that the prisoner should be relaxed to the secular authority to receive the just and proper punishment commensurate with "such a great offense." Nevertheless, the Council of Constance would beg the secular judges to "moderate the sentence without peril of death."[20] This request for mercy was a procedural commonplace in heresy trials. When a convicted heretic was handed over to the secular authorities for fulfillment of the sentence decreed by the court, a boilerplate formality was often included that asked for mercy for the condemned and begged the secular powers not to harm the prisoner in the course of fulfilling its duties.

The deputies or presidents of the nations were asked to vote on the matter. As noted previously, we have evidence that the nations at Constance voted in a similar fashion to university faculties.[21] Antonio da Ponte, bishop of Concordia, for the Italians; Nicholas Lubich, bishop of Merseburg, for the Germans; Vitalis Valentini, bishop of Toulon, for the French; Patrick Foxe, bishop of Cork, for the English; and Jean-Allarmet de Brogny for the cardinals answered *placet*, or "it is agreed." A close reading of the protocol for session 21 does allow for a strict conclusion that twelve out of the thirteen cardinals who were present did not express any personal opinion and that only de Brogny said *placet* for himself.[22] Even if the other cardinals did not vote, their silence does not mean that they abstained on account of holding doubts about the verdict against Jerome. If there were no objections expressed by the cardinals, we have some evidence that not everyone in the cathedral was in agreement. Kaspar Schlick, a secretary in the chancery of Sigismund (having joined in 1416 at the young age of sixteen or seventeen), protested before the entire Council in the name of Sigismund against the condemnation and sentence of Jerome. When he found no support, he left the assembly in anger, and the chronicler remarked that the "chancellor withdrew without having gained anything."[23] The appeal in the name of

---

20. *FRB*, vol. 8, pp. 316–317. The reference to the proceedings against Jerome as inquisitorial can be found in Hardt, vol. 4, col. 766.

21. Peter Pulka to the University of Vienna, February 7, 1415, in Friedrich Firnhaber, "Petrus de Pulka, Abgesabdter der Wiener universität am Concilium zu Constanz," *Archiv für österreichische Geschichte* 15 (1856): 14.

22. Hardt, vol. 4, col. 769.

23. Hardt, vol. 4, col. 765. On Schlick, see the three-part study by Petr Elbel and Andreas Zajic, "Die zwei Körper des Kanzlers? Die 'reale' und die 'virtuelle' Karriere Kaspar Schlicks unter König und Kaiser Sigismund—Epilogomena zu einem alten Forschungsthema," *Mediaevalia Historica Bohemica* 15, no. 2 (2012): 47–143; 16, no. 1 (2013): 55–212; and 16, no. 2 (2013): 73–157.

Sigismund was specious. There is no evidence from before, during, or after the trial that the king had any hesitation about the condemnation of Jerome.

With these procedural steps completed, the Council relaxed the convicted heretic to the secular authorities for execution of sentence. Count Eberhard of Kellenburg and Count Hans of Lupfen represented the Council. The city council was represented by two burgomasters, Konrad Mangold and Henry Guntersschweiter.[24] Richental insisted that Sigismund's delegate as chief guardian of the Council, Ludwig III, received Jerome from the Council and ordered him turned over to the secular authorities.[25] In similar fashion to what was done with Hus, a miter with red devils was placed on Jerome's head.[26] Petr Mladoňovice recorded the action succinctly: "Following his conviction, they brought before Master Jerome a large tall crown with red demons painted all around so that he might go to his death wearing it."[27] Later sermons drew correlations with Hus. "Then they put a paper cap on his head with pictures of red devils, just as they had done to Master Jan of blessed memory, and they led him out to execution."[28] The headgear with demons was also noted by Fillastre. The miter is mentioned by almost all the records. "They put a tall paper crown with red devils painted on it on his head, and took him out of town."[29] One source asserts that Jerome placed the miter on his head with his own hand after flinging his own hat at the prelates.[30] At the moment of degradation and infamy, Jerome compared himself to Christ: "Our Lord Jesus Christ, my master, was crowned for me when he was about to die, with a crown of thorns. In place of such a crown, I will gladly wear this crown out of love for him."[31] Jerome also affirmed

---

24. Karl Joseph von Hefele and Henri Leclercq, *Histoire des Conciles d'apres les Documents Originaux*, 10 vols. (Paris: Letouzey and Ané, 1907–1952), vol. 7, pt. 1, p. 278.

25. Buck, *Chronik des Konstanzer Konzils*, pp. 67–68. Ludwig was, in fact, away from Constance in the entourage of Sigismund.

26. Hardt, vol. 4, cols. 766–768.

27. *FRB*, vol. 8, p. 365.

28. NK, MSS VIII E 3, VIII G 13; *FRB*, vol. 8, pp. 231–243; and Havránek, *Výbor z české literatury*, vol. 1, pp. 234–238.

29. Hussite Chronicle, in *FRB*, vol. 5, p. 344.

30. Vrie, in Hardt, vol. 1, col. 202.

31. Vrie, in Hardt, vol. 1, col. 202; Hardt, vol. 4, col. 765; Fillastre, pp. 61–62; and *FRB*, vol. 8, p. 365.

that he would not act against conscience.[32] One must question whether this Christ-consciousness was truly expressed by Jerome or if the attributions are the work and interpretations of those later writing accounts of the final events in the life of Jerome.

The verdict of the Council included the decision that the church was removing Jerome from the tree of life because he was a rotten branch, corrupted by heresy and contumacy, and had become a "damned and confounded heretic." Before he was taken from the cathedral, Jerome is reported to have spoken one last time, addressing his tormenters and those who had advocated for his execution: "You have resolved to condemn me maliciously and unjustly, without having convicted me of any crime; but after my death I will leave a sting in your conscience and a worm that shall never die. I make my appeal from this place to the most just judge of all the earth, in whose presence you shall appear to answer to me a hundred years from now."[33] This saying, coupled with remarks made by Hus at the time of his execution, formed the basis for the legend that out of the ashes of the stake at Constance would emerge a swan that would vindicate the deaths of these martyrs and whose reforms could not be impeded. The legend of the Czech goose and the German swan served theological and propagandist purposes in the sixteenth century, and while the idea reflected hagiographical significance, it lacks historical meaning.[34] It is notable that none of the sources mentions the presence of anyone who might be construed as a friend to Jerome. Jan Chlum, Václav Dubá, and Mladoňovice are not recorded as having been in Constance on May 30, 1416, as they had been on July 6, 1415, when Hus was executed. Unlike Hus, Jerome seems not to have had the immediate moral support of friends.

---

32. *Passio*, p. 363.

33. *Passio*, pp. 364–365; Hefele and Leclercq, *Histoire des Conciles*, vol. 7, p. 213; *Documenta*, p. 135; and Hardt, vol. 4, col. 757. See Jiří Kejř, *Husovo odvolání od soudu papežova k soudu Kristovu* (Prague: Albis International, 1999), p. 45, n. 143, for the citation. The historicity of the comment, especially the reference to the passage of a hundred years, has been questioned. Jacques Lenfant, *History of the Council of Constance*, 2 vols., trans. Stephen Whatley (London: Rivington, 1730), vol. 1, p. 590. The text diverges in both time and language from the *Acta*; Hardt, vol. 4, col. 757, as noted previously.

34. See Adolf Hauffen, "Husz eine Gans—Luther ein Schwan," *Prager Deutschen Studien* 9 (1908): 1–28; Gerhard Seib, ed., *Luther mit dem Schwan* (Wittenberg: Schelzky and Jeep, 1996); and Thomas A. Fudge, *Jan Hus: Religious Reform and Social Revolution in Bohemia* (London: I. B. Tauris, 2010), pp. 195–203.

To the Stake

A large crowd followed the death march to the place of execution. Sources report that Jerome sang as he walked to his death, that he was taken to execution "merrily singing in a loud voice."[35] Some specifically say that he began to sing as soon as he left the cathedral, while others note that the singing began as he passed through the Gelting Gate in the city walls, leading into Brüel Field and beyond to the Gottlieben Fortress. Jerome is said to have sung the Marian song *Felix namque es sacra Virgo*, the *Credo*, and other liturgical texts, and he may have sung the entire liturgy if eyewitness accounts are to be taken literally. Some sources note that Jerome sang the entire time from the city until he arrived at the stake. From the cathedral to the traditional execution site required at least fifteen minutes. Reaching the end of his earthly pilgrimage, at the place where a year before they had burned Hus to death, the condemned man knelt next to the stake and prayed very humbly at some length. Then the executioners, perhaps impatient with the long prayer, lifted him and removed his clothes until he was naked. He was made to wear "an ugly canvas" in order to cover his loins. Dietrich Vrie characterized Jerome as a miserable man about to endure his final agony; he was a pitiful spectacle to all, except himself. Jerome displayed no pity, shame, or sorrow for what had befallen him.[36]

Accounts of martyrdoms are particularly suspect when it comes to recording details, especially when those details purport to be verbatim accounts of speeches or other oral texts. With that qualification, it should be noted that an entire prayer text, ostensibly uttered by Jerome, has been preserved in one manuscript:

> Lord God, grant freedom to all who love you
> and profess your truth everywhere, no matter where they are
> after Christianity.
> Give us your grace,
> our Lord Jesus,
> grant that we will come to the eternal realm,
> where you reign with all power
> with your chosen ones.

---

35. *Passio*, p. 365.

36. Vrie, in Hardt, vol. 1, col. 202. See appendix 11.

Holy Spirit
visit us sinning Christians,
help us to know the right way
to reject heresies,
and to be in the truth.
May we be informed
by the word of God
and by eternal things.
Anything that is different
and fallible
take away from us
and grant us grace.
Let us ask, all of us, the one
who would be announced to us
God the Father, Son and Holy Spirit
saying together Amen. Amen. Amen.[37]

Immediately thereafter, he was tied "ruthlessly with ropes and iron chains to the stake driven into the ground." When they began to put wood and straw around him, he sang the Easter hymn *Salve festa dies*, emphasizing the words of the refrain, "hail happy day and always be adored, when hell was conquered by heaven's great lord," and further, "be greeted most glorious day, in reverence above all other times, in which the Lord God defeated hell and the devil and reigns in heaven," and he sang this song until the end. Jerome then also chanted the *Credo in unum Deum*, declaring that he did believe in one God.[38] Having confessed the common faith, he lifted his voice to the people who had gathered and were standing around. He addressed the crowd in the German language: "Dear people! You should believe just as I sang now. This is what I believe and not otherwise. You should also hold to the other articles of the faith as every Christian should believe. But I must die now, because I would not agree with this congregation of priests with respect to the condemnation and humiliation of Master Jan Hus that it was as true and just. Because I knew the Master from a young age and knew that he was virtuous man of integrity, and a preacher

37. *FRB*, vol. 8, p. 367.

38. Hardt, vol. 4, col. 769; *FRB*, vol. 8, p. 337; Buck, *Chronik des Konstanzer Konzils*, p. 68; and Hardt, vol. 4, cols. 772–773.

of the faith concerning the law of God and of our Lord Jesus Christ." At this stage, the executioners had surrounded him with wood and piled it up until it had reached the top of his head. They put his clothes on the pile of wood. One source adds the detail that when the executioner began to light the pyre behind Jerome, the condemned man told him to light the fire in front of him, saying that if he feared the fire, he would never have come to this place. With a torch, the pile of wood surrounding Jerome was set ablaze. As the flames billowed up, the condemned heretic was heard to sing again in a strong voice and to say, "Lord God, I commend my soul into your hands." When the fierceness of the flames overcame his strength, he cried out in the Czech language: "Almighty God, have mercy on me. Forgive me my sins! You know that I loved your holy truth." As he recited *redemisti nos* ("you have redeemed me"), the smoke and fire prevented him from speaking further, and it appeared that he prayed for a while until he passed away in the fire. Reports indicate that Jerome, unlike Hus, suffered for a long time in the blaze of the stake because he was a strong man, and he lingered alive in the flames for about the interval of time required to walk from St. Clement's Church in Prague across the Charles Bridge to St. Mary the Virgin, perhaps fifteen minutes. This fortitude might be reckoned to Jerome's superior physical strength; he was described as "a stout, strong man, with a large, thick, black beard." Some accounts report that he died screaming, and many people felt pity for Jerome because he was more learned than Hus.[39] Others said that Jerome embraced the fire.[40] An anonymous writer (perhaps Mladoňovice) reported that blisters the size of eggs appeared on Jerome's body during the burning. The officials had ordered that Jerome's bed, his blanket, his clothing, and all personal items were to be burned along with him.[41] After it appeared that he had expired, they brought his straw bed, bedclothes, hood, boots, and other personal items he had in the tower prison in the cemetery of St. Paul and burned them to ashes. Once the fire had burned itself out, the ashes and remains were loaded onto a cart and the contents thrown into the Rhine.[42] This

---

39. Buck, *Chronik des Konstanzer Konzils*, p. 68. See appendix 11.

40. Poggio, p. 163.

41. Hardt, vol. 4, col. 771.

42. It has often been said that the place of execution was near the Rhine, where the ashes of both Hus and Jerome were dumped. In fact, the traditional site is at least a brisk ten-minute walk from the river, which means it would have taken somewhat longer to push a wheelbarrow there. For reasons not entirely clear, one source records that three and a half weeks

was done "so that nothing was left of his memory."[43] "Thus was destroyed by unfaithful clergy a faithful and true Czech, whose steadfastness and faithfulness should be remembered by faithful Czechs. It can be assumed that he went to the Lord God almighty, who grants to those who suffer for justice the Kingdom of Heaven. Amen."[44]

Mladoňovice, the chronicler of the last days of Jerome, insisted that he had seen and heard everything he recorded and that his testimony was true. He insisted that should other vastly different accounts of these events emerge in the future or if others gave contrary testimony, they were not to be trusted. Jerome's initial arrival in Constance and his return when he entered the city in chains were events the writer claimed to have personally observed and not predicated on hearsay or second-hand accounts. The chronicle set down for posterity what had been recorded as a perpetual memorial. The author claimed not to have altered or falsified any detail and appealed to God as witness to that statement. The author admitted his lack of style and the appearance of ignorance in his writing, which he accepted in deference to a truthful testimony that he insisted was preferable to eloquent style and pleasing narrative but could not be utilized at the risk of "swerving from or going astray from the truth of this story."[45]

One source notes that while Jerome was at the stake, his famous and notorious beard, which seemed to offend so many, was on fire.[46] The several references to Jerome's beard suggest that it was peculiar or notable. The German papal official Dietrich Niem noted that Jerome persisted to the end in his obstinacy for as long as he could open his mouth, and in death he behaved as he had in life, confirming his diabolical and damnable opinions.[47] Vrie confirms details recorded elsewhere when he tells us that Jerome sang parts of the liturgy at the stake, including the *Credo*, and other hymns. Vrie's account includes references to the crown of thorns,

---

lapsed between the burning of Hus and the destruction of his clothes. Between the hours of six and seven (*inter primam et secundam horam*) in the morning of July 30, 1415, his robe, hood, and hat (*palium, capucium et biretum*) were burned near the sewer drain (*circa cloacam*) in the churchyard. *Notae de Concilio Constantiensis*, in *FRB*, vol. 8, p. 321. See also appendix 11.

43. Hussite Chronicle, in *FRB*, vol. 5, p. 344.

44. *Passio*, p. 366. There is no record that Jerome had a confessor before his death. Šmahel, *Život a dílo Jeronýma*, p. 88, with comment on p. 50, n. 418.

45. *Narratio de Magistro Hieronymo*, p. 350.

46. Hardt, vol. 4, cols. 770–771.

47. Hardt, vol. 2, col. 454.

the choice of hymns, and the fact that Jerome sang a great deal during the last period of his life, but it also points out his appalling lack of repentance and draws attention to the steadfastness in belief exhibited by Jerome, which confirmed his self-assurance. Vrie tells us that the crowd was generally hostile to Jerome.[48] Vrie says that the execution was fitting, because Jerome's revocation of his recantation was a "frivolous . . . and contumacious act," and therefore the Council had no other option but to determine that he was a "dreadfully rotten limb" (*palmitem putridum et aridum*) and therefore had to be cut off from the body of Christ. At the end of the judicial process, there was a decisive sentence leveled against him. Vrie means that the decision was unanimous. He refers to the opprobriously decorated crown, characterizing it as "a crown of disgrace, a crown of horror, a crown of depravity." Vrie claims that Jerome referred to the miter with demons as similar in nature to the crown of thorns that Christ was made to wear. This accords with other eyewitnesses. Vrie ends his account with the caustic remark: "that miserable heretic yielded up his wretched soul to the abyss and submitted it to be burned forever."[49] There were objections to this representation. "They lit the fire and burned him, because he did not want to renounce the truth of the gospel. Because he confessed the truth in front of all the people while exposed to such humiliation and defamatory death, he was raised after his death to God."[50] This was the fervent description and interpretation found in a sermon preached in Bethlehem Chapel in Prague by the Hussite priest Jakoubek in 1416. Based on Matthew 5:10, "blessed are those who are persecuted for righteousness's sake, for theirs is the kingdom of heaven," the sermon was the first in a long series of homilies in the Bohemian province on the theme of martyrdom, extolling the faithfulness, righteousness, and sacrifice of the steadfast martyrs who laid down their lives in dungeons, in the fires of the stake, and at sword point in defense of the Hussite faith. The most prominent of those who suffered for the faith were Hus and Jerome. The sermon was preached on the eve of the promulgation of a crusade bull against the Hussite heretics in Bohemia, and the memory of Jerome became one of the motivational factors in early Hussite history.

---

48. *Narratio de Magistro Hieronymo*, p. 349; Hussite Chronicle, in *FRB*, vol. 8, p. 343; and the *De Vita Magistri Ieronomi*, in *FRB*, vol. 8, p. 337.

49. Hardt, vol. 1, col. 202.

50. NK, MSS VIII E 3, VIII G 13; *FRB*, vol. 8, pp. 231–243; and Havránek, *Výbor z české literatury*, vol. 1, pp. 234–238.

In the Shadow of the Stake

The legality of the trial of Jerome has been questioned along the same lines as for the process of Hus.[51] Did the condemnation of Jerome have later papal approbation inasmuch as it was carried out *sede vacante* and on the basis of *Haec sancta?* There was no pope in office, and the Council had declared itself to be the highest authority in Christendom. During the final session of the Council, when a Polish delegate asked Martin V about the case of the Dominican Johannes von Falkenberg, the pope made this rejoinder: "The pope approves everything which has been done in a conciliar fashion. He ratifies everything that has been dealt with by the council in a conciliar manner with respect to matters of faith. Whatever has been done in this way and not in another fashion, is approved."[52] Pursuant to *sede vacante*, when the papacy is vacant, jurisdiction is delegated to the power of the chapter, and the church through its bishops retains the authority to judge people in matters of heresy.[53] Heresy is a matter of the faith, and therefore Martin V did not question the legality of the trial of Jerome.

Jerome presented the late medieval church with a crisis. He represented a threat to the tranquility of Latin Christendom and posed a danger to the reform efforts and the campaign to eliminate heresy from the Western church. His detractors supposed that should he be released following his initial recantation, he would doubtless precipitate disaster in the Bohemian province. The risk was too great. He remained in the tower in the cemetery of St. Paul. The Council's action against Jerome in 1415 and 1416 indicated that the Latin church was serious about heresy and prepared to deal with it. The action aimed at Jerome was further intended to signal a warning. The conviction and execution of the defendant created impact and immediate fallout. Gerson, de Causis, Nicholas Dinkelsbühl, and their supporters must have felt satisfaction and vindication. Many people in Prague were dismayed, outraged, possibly shocked. Out of the collision between a would-be reformer and an institution that had little interest in taking cues from outsiders, several reactions fomented and formed. The immediate

---

51. Thomas A. Fudge, *The Trial of Jan Hus: Medieval Heresy and Criminal Procedure.* (New York: Oxford University Press, 2013), pp. 19–20, 29–30.

52. Walter Brandmüller, "Besitzt das Konstanzer Dekret *Haec Sancta* dogmatische Verbindlichkeit," *Annuarium historiae conciliorum* 1 (1969): 112.

53. X 3.9.1–3, *Ne sede vacante*, in Friedberg, vol. 2, cols. 500–501.

threat had been eliminated. The heretic Jerome was burned alive, consumed in the flames, and obliterated from the church. Ecclesiastical authority was reestablished, and the Council appeared to be in control. With the posthumous condemnation of Wyclif and the elimination of Hus and Jerome, the conciliar delegates must have felt a sense of accomplishment in having achieved one of the main goals of the Council, which was to eliminate heresy. With the removal of Jerome, the last component in the heresy threat appeared to have been identified and contained. The Latin church had taken a significant step toward returning to normal conditions. The threat was met, and the vulnerable faithful had been saved from the danger of heresy. In the Czech lands, a different forward pathway was beginning to take shape. The conciliar-driven Western church and a revolutionary breakaway faction in Bohemia both began adopting medium- to long-range responses and strategies aimed at rebuilding damaged communities. Those strategies would lead to even more serious collisions and confrontations. The life and death of Jerome played a significant part in the religious history of later medieval Europe.

The verdict at Constance and the death of Jerome at the stake did not conclude the matter, even if the newly elected pontiff agreed with the proceedings and the condemnation of Jerome. A tradition that sprang up in Bohemia, fueled in large measure by the deaths of Hus and Jerome, was energized by those tragedies, and chroniclers drew correlations. "Then in the year of our Lord 1418 on the day of the Holy Spirit, the Council of Constance, after making certain conclusions and after unjustly vilifying and burning for the holy truth the excellent Christian men Master Jan Hus and Master Jerome, and having elected a new pope, was dissolved and dispersed. But they had to settle accounts for the unjust vilification of the Utraquist communion of the body and blood of the Lord Christ and of the aforementioned masters Hus and Jerome before the most righteous judge, the almighty God."[54] This was a reference to the unrest in Bohemia that started to brew in the wake of the executions of Hus and Jerome. That unrest escalated into rebellion, which resulted in religious wars, crusades, a revolution unparalleled in the Middle Ages, and the establishment of reformed religious practice in the Bohemian province. Among the heroes and influences undergirding these momentous developments was Jerome, at once to some a Christian martyr and to others the

---

54. Hussite Chronicle, in *FRB*, vol. 5, pp. 341–344.

"athlete of Antichrist." His body perished at the stake in Constance, and he was claimed by the kingdom of the dead. But his spirit persisted among Hussites everywhere, and his memory was added to a new and emerging pantheon of saints that gradually informed the ethos of Christian faith and identity in the Czech lands, producing a unique chapter in the religious history of Europe.

9

Jerome Remembered

LITURGY, REVOLUTION, COMMEMORATION

THE EXPANSE OF six hundred years since the time of the Council of Constance has not dented the impressions of Jerome of Prague, which remain vividly embedded in the surviving records. These reveal a man who was reckless and romantic, daring, egotistical, impulsive and exaggerated, fearless and violent, in both language and action. He was a man who possessed keen intellect, deep erudition, and a persuasive voice, one filled with energy, enthusiasm, and outspoken zeal. Boundless drive took this intellectual outlaw from one end of Europe to the other, and he seems never to have wearied of challenge, debate, disputation, and argument. While all of this is true, there is a sense in which Jerome has been lost. "The seed sown by Hus was not lost. But the memory of Jerome was lost. In the course of time the two figures were merged into one . . . At last there was only the one figure bearing the name of Hus."[1] This book has endeavored to recover the lost memory of Jerome.

The execution of Jerome (like that of Jan Hus) was largely a result of the political struggle that had engulfed the late medieval church. It is not persuasive to argue that Jerome's execution amounted to judicial murder. This is confirmed by other scholars.[2] Not everything that is permitted or legal is honest or right.[3] However the case of Jerome is adjudicated, he

---

1. Paul Roubiczek and Joseph Kalmer, *Warrior of God: The Life and Death of John Hus*, trans. Ruby Hobling (London: Nicholson and Watson, 1947), p. 264.

2. See, for example, Walter Brandmüller, *Das Konzil von Konstanz 1414–1418*, 2 vols. (Paderborn: Ferdinand Schöningh, 1991–1997), vol. 2, pp. 116, 137–140.

3. "Non omne quod licet honestum est." D 50.17.144 (Paulus).

was not the subject of a lynch mob or of a kangaroo court or the victim of provincial minds. Hus and Jerome were burned by learned professors and brilliant intellectuals. From the year of his death, Jerome assumed a place in the pantheon of Czech heroes, and his name became inextricably linked with the violence of religious discourse and practice in the later Middle Ages. To his detractors, he was the "athlete of Antichrist," who disturbed the tranquility of the faith and perpetrated grievous errors and heresies that according to Jean Gerson resulted in "matters still more controversial."[4] Poggio Bracciolini disagreed, hailing Jerome as a man worthy of being remembered.[5] By the time the Council of Constance convened, Jerome's name was known across Europe. By the time the Council disbanded, he was both a revered martyr and a notorious heretic. The execution of Hus had injured Czech sensibilities and inflamed a nation. The destruction of Jerome added insult to injury. By September 1415, with Hus reduced to ashes and Jerome in chains within the gloomy confines of the cemetery tower of St. Paul in Constance, 452 Bohemian and Moravian nobles addressed the Council. The barons declared that the death of Hus, "our dearly beloved friend of good memory," had brought eternal shame and great infamy to Bohemia and Moravia. The nobles went on to accuse the Council of the cruel murder of Jerome, a man characterized as both eloquent and famous but maligned by false and sinister accusations conjured by men who could only be described as betrayers.[6] The Czech nobles were misinformed. Jerome was not dead, though he was hanging upside down in a dark and squalid prison. Nevertheless, his eventual execution was perennially noted with outrage in Czech sources.[7]

Many learned men were grieved at the death of Jerome because he was a far greater scholar than Hus.[8] Others were no less moved by the plight of the erudite intellectual with the great beard. "One might well grieve to see so lofty an intellect and such outstanding gifts put to the service of heretical studies; if, indeed, the charges brought against him

---

4. Hardt, vol. 4, p. 217; and *FRB*, vol. 8, p. 342.

5. Poggio, p. 162.

6. *Documenta*, p. 582, dated September 2, 1415.

7. See, for example, the "Kronika velmi pěkná o Janovi Žižkovi," in František M. Bartoš, ed., *Listy bratra Jana a kronika velmi pěkna o Janu Žižkovi* (Prague: Blahoslav, 1949), pp. 36–37.

8. Thomas Martin Buck, ed., *Chronik des Konstanzer Konzils 1414–1418 von Ulrich Richental* (Ostfildern: Jan Thorbecke Verlag, 2010), p. 68.

were true."[9] After listening to Jerome, Poggio concluded that there was no heresy in Jerome's speech, though he also declared that he was unqualified to judge theological guilt or innocence but that Jerome's claims of false, biased, and fabricated evidence lodged against him were convincing. Some say Poggio's letter amounted to a defense of a heretic: "It was a defense, barely within the bounds of the permitted, of a heretic."[10] The reluctance expressed by many at Constance at the thought of Jerome's execution extended to the higher echelons of the late medieval intellectual world.[11] Nevertheless, four days after the burning of Jerome, the Council appointed four judges to investigate the prelates and ecclesiastical authorities in Bohemia and Moravia on suspicion of gross negligence in dealing with the heresies that had been adjudicated at Constance.[12] The Council was serious about the problem of heresy, and in addition to common men and women, priests, scholars, kings, and bishops came under scrutiny. The prelates at Constance were determined to find out why men such as Jerome had been able to flourish for so long with impunity.

In a sweeping display of retrospective rule-making, practically everything that Hus and Jerome stood for and taught was suspect, and those who defended them or appeared sympathetic to their cause were viewed with suspicion. There appeared to be a climate of resistance in the Czech lands to this ethos, leading to disobedience and rebellion. In the face of papal schism, latitudinarianism had little appeal within the later medieval church. Jerome appeared to defend toleration, declaring that diversity of beliefs may be maintained "not in order to harm the faith, but in order to find out the truth."[13] That attitude and approach presented as many problems for Jerome in the fifteenth century as they had in the twelfth century for Peter Abelard. The church declared his intellectual imprint suspect and undesirable. Shortly after Jerome's execution, the Council ordered the University of Vienna to take steps against heretics in the city. This was a reference to the lingering influence of Jerome, who had apparently created

---

9. Poggio, p. 157.

10. Renee Neu Watkins, "The Death of Jerome of Prague: Divergent Views," *Speculum* 42 (January 1967): 113.

11. Brandmüller, *Das Konzil von Konstanz*, vol. 2, p. 116.

12. Fillastre, p. 62.

13. Poggio, p. 161.

a considerable storm there in 1410, which the verdict of excommunication handed down by the Grillenberg-Gwerleich court had not eradicated.

Reports of Jerome's death reflect divergent points of view. These range from the expansive and expressive panegyric of Poggio to the muted perfunctory ecclesiastical accounts.[14] The core of the story is agreed on and corroborated by the surviving witnesses, and I have attempted to outline that story in chapters 5, 6, and 7, relying on those accounts. Details vary, of course, from text to text, but there are few serious divergences. There are glaring errors or misrepresentations, but most of these are superficial rather than substantial. Of course, there are unique observations and records that have been preserved, and these are valuable for the nuances they bring to the overall story. Some of these reflect the authorial perspective. The exchange between Jerome and Guillaume Fillastre on May 30 following the general sermon by the bishop of Lodi was not noted by any of the others who wrote accounts of the last days of Jerome, but Fillastre wrote it down, probably because he was involved in the exchange. All in all, there are few accounts that go beyond a basic narrative of events. By contrast, Poggio attempted to determine what sort of man Jerome was. Several main areas of agreement can be identified from the main sources extracted from points made by Jerome. These included the allegation that the judges in the trial of Jerome were unfair and that many people throughout history had been unjustly condemned, including Socrates, Boethius, Maro (probably Soranus), Seneca, Plato, Anaxagoras, Zeno, and Rutilius, along with Saint Jerome, Elijah, Daniel, numerous prophets of the biblical narratives, Susannah, and many others.[15] A third major point was the thesis that the witnesses arrayed against Jerome had perjured themselves. In other words, the witnesses lied, and there were compelling reasons for this. Jerome also argued that he was not a heretic, that Hus was not a heretic, but instead that Hus was a good man who had focused chiefly on reforming abuses within the church. By implication, Jerome considered himself a good man who was also not opposed to the true or real church but was interested in seeing irregularities corrected. Many of the extant sources, especially from Constance, tend to reflect these convictions and assumptions, even if they do not necessarily agree with them. All of this raises the question about truth and reliability. The letter by Poggio has

---

14. *Notae de Concilio Constantiensis*, in *FRB*, vol. 8, p. 320, is just as brief.

15. From the anonymous chronicle in Hardt, vol. 4, cols. 755–773.

been described as an excellent example of humanist writing but also as a "text of perpetual truth."[16] The assumption must be contested. It seems more prudent to conclude that in the hands of Poggio, the historical Jerome has been replaced by a philosophically ideal Jerome who endured myriad tribulations, including being burned alive with an air of calm and resolute constancy.[17]

Liturgical Commemoration

Among liturgical compositions from the fifteenth and early sixteenth centuries is a song about Jerome. There are no extant manuscripts, and the earliest printed text dates to 1522, but it is likely that it was composed prior to 1482.[18] The song describes the fate of Jerome. There is nothing new in the text beyond what we already know from the various accounts of his death. What is significant is its inclusion and delineation within the corpus of Czech liturgical history. Jerome's designation as a holy man is significant

About Master Jerome of Prague

The holy Jerome
was quickly captured
in the place called Sulzbach,
when from fear he hoped to escape death.

He was captured and tied,
bound with chains,
delivered into Ludwig's hands
and marched down the streets to be ridiculed.

He was handed over to the council
and was accused
by fierce enemies,
by hypocritical clergy and doctors.

---

16. Milada Nedvědová, *Hus a Jeronym v Kostnici* (Prague: St. nakl. Krásné lit., hudby a uměni, 1953), p. 269.

17. Watkins, "The Death of Jerome of Prague," p. 119.

18. The opinion of Novotný, in *FRB*, vol. 8, p. cxxxv.

They did not rest,
But tied him up like a dog,
escorted him to a jail,
chained him in a cruel stock.

He could not sit,
he had to hang,
and touch the floor with his head,
thus hanging he was close to death.

He asked for a priest;
being in such desire
he wanted to confess,
but he did not receive this from them.

They tortured him so much
while he was hanging,
then they made it easier for him
and they left him only in chains.

They brought him before the council,
they did him much injustice,
with false accusations,
scheming about him.

They plotted together
and said,
asking him to approve
that the council had properly burned Hus to death.

He obeyed them
because he wanted to tame their ruse
and so escape death;
he started to torment himself.

So changing his mind,
He asked to be heard,
Changed his first speech
as the Holy Spirit taught him.

And he said: "What I have said
I said because you wanted so,
I regret it
and I reject it."

And now all from the council
did him injustice,
sentenced him to death,
prepared a paper crown,

and on it
were painted devils
like elongated greyhounds,
hairy, gingery and red.

He put it on himself
and said
that Jesus, the master of heaven,
bore a heavier crown when he was put to death.

Tied by the executioners,
by fathers and prelates,
he was escorted to the execution,
his head covered by the mocking crown.

Immediately with joy
he sang "Faith" bravely,
and other good songs,
being quickly escorted to the execution.

He, kneeling with humbleness,
prayed, but was quiet,
tied to the stake,
being ridiculed by many, also by the executioners.

The Master manfully
said bravely that he had faith,
"I do not suffer for heresies,
but for the limbs of Antichrist."

Already surrounded with
wood, led by the spirit,
he began loudly
to sing about that celebration.

He was burned quickly,
he left here the reputation
of God's martyrs,
commending his soul to His hands.

And so he gave his life,
he was sitting a whole year save seven days,
in jail in prison,
for Christ's profession of faith.

Therefore all of us,
professing the truth
of the chalice, let us ask Jesus Christ
to come to the Judgment sooner,

so that his faithful
under various suffering
do not become snared on account of faintness and fragility
in the trap of Antichrist,

but so that they are firm
in your faith. Oh King
Christ, also give to us by your grace,
following death, eternal joy in heaven. Amen.[19]

There is nothing unique or particularly controversial in the song, though several points might be noted. The text declares that Jerome recanted because he feared death but also suggests that he did so as a ruse, which would then serve to facilitate his escape from the clutches of his enemies. In a curious turn, the song text points out correctly that Jerome withdrew his revocation and thereafter the Council dealt with him unjustly

---

19. *FRB*, vol. 8, pp. 443–444.

and sentenced him to death. From a legal point of view, executing relapsed heretics was not viewed as unjust. Finally, the song notes that Jerome died quickly once the fire was lit. This contrasts with other testimonies, including that of Petr Mladoňovice.

The liturgical remembrance of Hus and Jerome has vivid testimony in the Czech lands. "Two lamps arose . . . and through bitter martyrdom crossed over into heaven." While the Council of the wicked in Constance crowned Hus with flames, the army of heaven interceded to transport the righteous man to heaven.[20] One line in this song implores God to "grant that their merits might benefit us by means of our heavenly songs."[21] Jerome and Hus are added to the historic and noble army of apostles and martyrs, and when compared to the men and women who had previously laid down their lives in the cause of Christ, they are given the highest accolades. They are the "steadfast warriors, firm adherents of the law of Christ, zealous until death, condemned by the reprobate court in Constance. O happy Constance to whom with excellent parts as well the Czech nation grant grace for the benefit of the Church and for our comfort. Having suffered many things for the name of Christ, having washed their robes in blood they possess the joy of eternal life in the court of heaven."[22] Jerome is a lamp of truth and inspiration who becomes an intercessor for all the faithful on earth and heir of eternal life. Jerome came to occupy a central place in the memory of all faithful Czechs who suffered for Christ.[23]

---

20. The simultaneous burning of Hus and his conveyance to heaven have been effectively depicted in iconography. Litoměřice Gradual, Lovosice, Regional State Archives of Litoměřice, MS IV C 1, fol. 244v.

21. Esztergom, Főszékesegyházi könyvtär (Bib. Metropolitana Strigoniensis), MS I. 313, pp. 501–511, which dates from the second half of the fifteenth century. The complete text of the liturgy for the feast of Hus was printed fifty years ago. František Fišer, "Hodinkové oficium svátku Mistra Jana Husa," *Časopis národního muzea* 135, no. 2 (1966): pp. 81–98.

22. This liturgical segment can be found in numerous Hussite sources, including the Smiškovský Kancionál, ÖNB, MS 15492. Details on the codex are in Barry Frederic Hunter Graham, *Bohemian and Moravian Graduals 1420–1620* (Turnhout: Brepols, 2006), pp. 561–568. The prosae have been collated in David R. Holeton, "'O felix Bohemia—O felix Constantia': The Liturgical Celebration of Saint Jan Hus," in Ferdinand Seibt, ed., *Jan Hus: Zwischen Zeiten, Völkern, Konfessionen* (Munich: Oldenbourg, 1997), pp. 399–400, with reference to a number of liturgical sources.

23. For example, the song "Mučedlníkův českých připomínáme" ("We commemorate the Czech martyrs"), in Václav Novotný, *Husitský zpěvník: Nábožné písně a Mistru Janovi Husovi a Mistru Jeronymovi* (Prague: Reichel, 1930), pp. 45–47.

Jerome Excluded

It is regrettable that the iconography of the fifteenth and sixteenth centuries reflecting the progress of reform and its several iterations frequently omits Jerome. For example, in the Malostranská gradual of the Lesser Town of Prague, we find a full page devoted to Hus. The folio is headlined "O Swatem Mistru Janowi Husy" ("Concerning Holy Master Jan Hus"), and the accompanying song is in Czech. An illumination in a capital letter reveals John the Baptist about to be decapitated. The bottom quarter of the page depicts Hus at the stake. The right margin shows three figures. These may be identified as John Wyclif rubbing two stones together striking a spark, Hus below him holding a small candle, followed by Martin Luther brandishing aloft a flaming torch.[24] Accordingly, it appears that the conviction expressed in the image is that three of the most visible reformers (or notorious heretics) at the end of the Middle Ages are connected in some way. Hus was certainly accused of advocating Wyclifite tenets, and Luther was later charged with imbibing the ideas of Hus. Sixteenth-century Protestants depicted Hus and Jerome in woodcuts and pamphlets in a deliberate effort to incorporate them into the pantheon of heroes of the true faith and thereby protestantize their memory.[25]

The same idea set forth in the Prague gradual was visualized even more clearly elsewhere in a Czech broadsheet. The same three men this time are portrayed as actively engaging in the initiation and transmission of the fire of reform (or heresy). On the left, a kneeling Wyclif can be seen kindling a spark inside a tinder box. He looks up at Hus, who is bending over. In his right hand, Hus holds a small taper with which he captures the spark created by Wyclif. In his left hand, Hus holds a glowing candle. Luther extends a larger stick, which catches fire from Hus's candle. In Luther's left hand, he holds upright a large torch. Luther looks to his left, where he observes a newcomer to the motif. The flame is joined by Philip Melanchthon, who receives the torch from Luther and holds an even larger light. All of this takes place under the inspiration of the Holy Spirit, symbolized by the dove overhead. The four men are named "Ian Wiklef, M. Ian

---

24. Malostranská Gradual, NK, MS XVII A 3, fol. 363r.

25. Siegfried Hoyer, "Jan Hus und der Hussitismus in den Flugschriften des ersten Jahrzehnts der Reformation," in *Flugschriften als Massenmedium der Reformationszeit*, ed. Hans-Joachim Köhler (Stuttgart: Klett-Cotta, 1981), pp. 291–307.

Hvs, D.M. Lvther, F. Melant," eliminating any residual ambiguity present in the Malostranská gradual.[26] The message of the broadsheet is unmistakable: the progression of the heretics provides light (perhaps an allusion to the light of the world motif in the New Testament), posits an understanding of the origins of reform, and outlines a type of apostolic succession, which encompasses both the heretics of the later medieval period and the leading personalities of the German Reformation. Jerome belongs here, too. He died as a condemned heretic but also as a martyr to reform.[27]

Jerome in Art

There were other kinds of ecclesiastical reform in the latter Middle Ages, and the legal procedures against Hus and Jerome at Constance may be understood as addressing irreconcilable differences between the varieties of reform.[28] Though frequently overlooked and never portrayed as often as Hus, there are a number of representations of Jerome. The most frequent depictions are of Jerome at the stake or arriving at the place of death. (See figure 9.1.) These are to be found mainly among the colored drawings in the pages of the *Chronicle of the Council of Constance* by Ulrich Richental, which survive in several editions.[29] The bearded Jerome is shown led to the stake by armed men. In some of the depictions, the condemned is escorted by a large crowd; in others, he is led by as few as two men. The guards are sometimes heavily armored, with banners and weapons held aloft. Jerome wears a black or brown frock. In one representation (the Prague version), his hands are bound, but many of the other depictions do not reflect manacles. In every image, his head is covered either with a hat

---

26. Berlin, Staatsbibliothek, Preussischer Kulturbesitz, Handschriftenabteilung, YA 872, reproduced in Thomas A. Fudge, *The Magnificent Ride: The First Reformation in Hussite Bohemia* (Aldershot, U.K.: Ashgate, 1998), plate 3.3, p. 133.

27. Šmahel/Silagi, pp. CXXVII–CXXVIII.

28. See Jürgen Miethke, "Die Prozesse in Konstanz gegen Jan Hus und Hieronymus von Prag—ein Konflikt unter Kirchenreformern?" in *Häresie und vorzeitige Reformation und Spätmittelalter*, ed. František Šmahel (Munich: Oldenbourg, 1998), pp. 147–167.

29. Illustrated manuscripts include NK, MSS XVI A 17, VII A 18 (the latter formerly in St. Petersburg); New York Public Library, Spencer Collection, MS 32 (Aulendorf); Constance, Rosgartenmuseum, Inv. Hs.1; ÖNB, MS 3044; Karlsruhe, Badische Landesbibliothek, Codex St. Georgen 63 and Codex Ettenheim-Münster 11. There are at least nine other manuscripts in Stuttgart, Wolfenbüttel, St. Gallen, Innsbruck, Zurich, Winterthur, and Lindau. See Buck, *Chronik des Konstanzer Konzils*, pp. LVIII–LIX.

FIGURE 9.1 Jerome at the stake, 1460. *The Chronicle of Ulrich Richental* (Aulendorf).
© New York Public Library, Spencer Collection, Astor, Lenox, and Tilden Foundations.
Used by permission.

or with the paper miter decorated with images of demons that we know
he received in the cathedral. The miter can be seen particularly in the
Karlsruhe and Prague editions of Richental. In the latter, a single demon
appears to be dancing on the top of the opprobrious headgear.[30] In both
cases, the miter is annotated with the word *Eresiarcha*, drawing attention

30. NK, MS XVI A 17, fol. 124r.

to the assumption that Jerome was a leader of heretics and in that sense was every bit as much of a heresiarch as Hus. Additionally, the Karlsruhe and Prague editions of the Richental chronicle appear to emphasize the great and controversial beard worn by the condemned heretic.[31] There are two depictions of Jerome in the famous and important Jena Codex. In the first, a full-page illumination, the bearded Jerome wears a miter featuring three demons and is clad in a white gown and chained to the stake. Religious and secular men have gathered. In the other, a small woodcut, Jerome is clean-shaved, and his miter features only one demon, but he is shown with a halo.[32] These are pro forma depictions hardly distinguishable from those of Hus.[33]

In the sixteenth century, we find several images of Jerome. A woodcut by the artist M.S, which appeared in the collection of documents attributed to Hus and Jerome anonymously edited by Flacius, shows Jerome at the stake surrounded by flaming faggots. Jerome is chained to the stake with fetters around his waist and neck, and his hands are behind his back and appear to be fastened to the stake. His beard is featured, and he wears a short gown and the paper miter on which two demons have been drawn. A Latin epitaph appears below the image, reflecting on the holy martyr Jerome of Prague.[34] Jerome also appears in the grand martyrology of John Foxe. Armed men stoke the fire on either side of the stake, while a naked Jerome, bound with chains but with his hands free, appears to gesture. The faggots have been stacked to a height commensurate with the condemned. He is bareheaded but wears a large bushy beard. (See figure 9.2.)[35]

The former Franciscan church of St. Ulrich in Braunschweig (Brüdernkirche) has sixteenth-century choir stalls (oil on panels) that recognize the progression of witnesses to the faith (forty-eight full-length portraits in all), forming a visual genealogy. These stretch from

---

31. Karlsruhe, Badische Landesbibliothek, Codex St. Georgen 63 (Pap. Germ.), Bl. 20; and NK, MS XVI A 17, fol. 124r.

32. Jena Codex, KNM, MS IV B 24, fols. 38v, 48r.

33. Jena Codex, KNM, MS IV B 24, fols. 38r, 41v.

34. *HM*, vol. 2, fol. 348b, p. 521.

35. Jerome is shown at the stake in all four sixteenth-century editions. The online critical edition of Foxe has been used inasmuch as it supersedes all previous printed editions. *The*

FIGURE 9.2 The burning of Jerome. John Foxe, *Acts and Monuments*, 1563, bk. 5, p. 301.

second-century figures such as Ignatius and Polycarp to sixteenth-century personalities. Most of those included would have been of unimpeachable orthodoxy to the medieval church: Irenaeus, Cyprian, Athanasius, Saint Jerome, Augustine, Gregory the Great, Anselm, Bernard of Clairvaux, Bonaventure, and Gerson. However, as the choir-stall depictions reach the end of the Middle Ages, the designer incorporated other figures that could not possibly be included among faithful Christians. After Gerson, the choir stalls feature Hus and Jerome. (See figure 9.3.) The bearded "Iohannes Hvss," clad in black cap and gown, has turned away from the viewer to his left and gestures with his left hand while holding a scroll in his right hand. This may be a subtle indication that Hus is directing his

---

Unabridged Acts and Monuments Online or *TAMO*, HRI Online Publications, Sheffield, 2011, www.johnfoxe.org. *Acts and Monuments*, 1563, bk. 5, p. 301; 1570, bk. 5, p. 775; 1576, bk. 5, p. 637; and 1583, bk. 5, p. 660. From the second edition on, a woodcut medal depiction appeared, featuring both Jerome and Hus: 1570, bk. 6, p. 933; 1576, bk. 6, p. 769; and 1583, bk. 6, p. 794. Both illustrations carried captions alluding to the alleged prophecies made at the stake of how the persecutors would be called to judgment within a century.

FIGURE 9.3 Jerome as witness to the faith. Sixteenth-century choir stalls (oil on panels). Franciscan church of St. Ulrich in Braunschweig (Brüdernkirche).

message and influence toward those who follow him. A goose hovers at his feet. "Hieronimvs Prage" faces outward and, like Hus, wears a black cap and a gown that reaches nearly to his ankles. He gestures with his right hand and holds a book with a red cover in his left. At his feet, fittingly enough, are several large books. The Czech heretics Hus and Jerome are prominently featured in the Braunschweig Brüdernkirche and are linked to movements of Protestant Christianity represented by Luther who is shown next to Jerome with the visual suggestion that the ideas of Hus and Jerome are somehow connected to those of Luther.[36]

Two other images of Jerome do not show him at the stake and are worth noting. The first is an intriguing feature embedded in an enamel-on-copper art form. This is Counter-Reformation art. The orthodox Christian faith is shown as having triumphantly defeated all her enemies.

36. Robert Kolb, *For all the Saints: Changing Perceptions of Martyrdom and Sainthood in the Lutheran Reformation* (Macon, Ga.: Mercer University Press, 1987), pp. 146–147; additional information in Joseph Leo Koerner, *The Reformation of the Image* (Chicago: University of Chicago Press, 2004), p. 388.

FIGURE 9.4 *The Triumph of the Eucharist and the Catholic Faith.* Léonard Limousin, 1561–1562. © The Frick Collection, New York. Used by permission.

(See figure 9.4.) The "Triumph of the Faith" is depicted as a woman (Antoinette de Bourbon) holding aloft symbols of the faith, a eucharistic chalice and host in her left hand and a cross in her right, seated in a chariot that rides triumphantly across the landscape (characteristic of the Fontainebleau School), featuring members of the House of Guise. The chariot runs roughshod over the bodies of at least twenty heretics, and these have been crushed by the chariot of "the faith." Originally, these vanquished heretics were identified by gilt inscriptions over or near their heads. The gold, applied after the firing of the enamel, is now almost completely obliterated. The heretics may be identified as Iehan Hvs (Jan Hus), Donatuvus (Donatus), Beze (Theodore Beza), Adamite (a sub-Hussite group), Fraticelli (a designation applied to a heretical branch of the Franciscan order), a beardless Prage (Jerome of Prague), Arius, Calvin, Anabaptiste (Anabaptists), Vabapt (possibly another reference to the Anabaptists), and a fragment that ends with the letters VS. The presence of a Turkish turbaned head lends support to the idea that this might represent Aenobarbus, the Latinized name of the sixteenth-century Turkish admiral often referred to as Barbarossa.[37]

Two slightly different seventeenth-century Dutch engravings feature a candlestick symbolizing the light of the gospel. (See figure 9.5.)[38] The "light of the gospel [has been] rekindled by reformers." Seated around the table are sixteen reformers, including Wyclif, Jerome, and Hus. Wyclif (labeled A) is looking away and writes in a book. He may be distracted by the hand of Matthias Flacius Illyricus (M) on his shoulder. Hus (B) is wearing a cap and holding a book to his chest. Jerome (C) sits between Luther (E) and Phillip Melanchthon (I), bearded and wearing a hat but otherwise undistinguished. Of the sixteen reformers, only Luther, Melanchthon, Martin Bucer (G), and William Perkins (Q) are bareheaded. On the wall behind the table are portraits of more reformers and their supporters.

Jerome also appears in recent religious iconography. A Czech Orthodox icon featuring the "holy martyrs of Constance" presents "Jeroným" and "Jan" as full-length figures, wearing halos and holding small crosses, on either side of a figure in the flames of the stake (Hus) who is also represented

---

37. Léonard Limousin (ca. 1505–1575/77), *The Triumph of the Eucharist and the Catholic Faith*, 1561–1562. Painted enamel on copper, partly gilded. 7.75 × 10 in. (19.7 × 25.4 cm). Henry Clay Frick Bequest. Accession number 1916.4.22. Frick Collection, New York. Andrew Carnduff Ritchie, "Léonard Limosin's Triumph of the Faith, with Portraits of the House of Guise," *Art Bulletin* 21, no. 3 (1939): 238–250, has deciphered the faint lettering in the lower left of the image.

38. Anonymous copper engraving, 40.5 cm × 53 cm, after 1640, Amsterdam, Rijksmuseum, RP-P-OB-78.421; the other, also anonymous and dating to ca.1650, is oil on canvas 96 cm × 126 cm, at the Museum Catharijneconvent in Utrecht, Inv. No. RMCC s10. There are several other iterations of the motif, chiefly of British provenance. These include the anonymous "Protestant Reformers," after 1660, oil on canvas 95.3 cm × 177.8 cm, Society of Antiquaries, Burlington House, London, LDSAL 1300; Scharf LXXXI; a line engraving, 25.7 cm × 37.2 cm, published by John Garrett, mid-17th century, National Portrait Gallery, London; an etching ca. 1640, 26 cm × 37.3 cm, published by Thomas Jenner, British Museum, 1907, 0326.31; another etching dating to the later 17th century, 12.6 cm × 9.9 cm, British Museum, 1877, 1208.325 (which includes Jerome but not Hus); and an English School engraving by Lodge, now held in a private collection. Other variations include "Martin Luther in the Circle of Reformers," German School, 1625–1650, oil on wood, 67.5 cm × 90 cm, Deutsches Historisches Museum, Berlin, Inv. Nr. Gm 97/24; a "Group Portrait of Reformers," Anglo-Dutch School, oil on canvas, 104.1 cm × 126.7 cm, formerly in the possession of William Bull, minister of Newport Pagnell Congregational Church, 1749–1814; and lastly the etching "Effigies praecipuorum illustrium atque praestantium aliquot theologorum," by the painter and engraver Hans Schwyzer (1625–1670), executed around 1650, 87 cm × 47.6 cm, Zentralbibliothek, Zurich. Among the more than forty "illustrious theologians" we find along the rear wall, buttressing four pillars, Savonarola, Wyclif, Hus and Jerome.

FIGURE 9.5 *t'Licht is op den kandelaer gestalt.* Anonymous copper engraving, after 1640. Amsterdam, Rijksmuseum, RP-P-OB-78.421. Used by permission.

FIGURE 9.6 Jerome of Prague and Jan Hus as the holy martyrs of Constance. Jana Baudišová, 2009. Icon, tempera on panel. Private collection at Saints Wenceslas and Ludmila Orthodox Church, Jihlava, Czech Republic. Used by permission.

with a nimbus. (See figure 9.6.) Behind these figures, one can see the walls and spires of the city of Constance, the Bodensee, and the Rhine. Christ presides over the scene of the *svatí mučedníci kostničtí* and provides witness to the declaration written on parchment that Hus displays in his left hand: *braň pravdu až do smrti* (defend the truth until death).[39]

---

39. The 2009 icon, executed in the Russian style in tempera on panel, 34 x 39 cm, is the work of Jana Baudišová. Formerly at the Dormition of the Blessed Mother of God Monastery

FIGURE 9.7 Jerome and the Bohemian saints. Altar predella, late fifteenth century. Church of the Holy Cross, Chrudim, Czech Republic. Chrudim, Regional Museum, inv. no. U-46. Used by permission.

Jerome does appear in other visual art and at times is shown as a saint. For example, Hus and perhaps Jerome are depicted in the company of the Czech patron saints Wenceslas and Prokop on the altar predella from Chrudim, which may be dated to the end of the fifteenth century. (See figure 9.7.) The altarpiece, originally in the Church of the Holy Cross (a local funerary church), depicts the resurrected Christ in the center of the piece and presents Mary and John the Baptist as intercessors (*Deisis*). The Bohemian saints—Hus, Wenceslas, Jerome, and Prokop—are shown as assistants at the Last Judgment, each featuring a gold nimbus.[40] At the left end of the predella, a white-surpliced Hus holds a large gold chalice in his left hand, while his right hand is raised in the manner of consecration. At the right end, a black-robed Prokop holds a crozier in his left hand, and with his right he strangles a small demon. Both Hus and Prokop are tonsured. The long-haired and bearded Wenceslas wears a red gown, a red and white hat, and holds what appears to be a scepter. Jerome stands right of center, beardless, sartorially represented as a secular intellectual wearing a green gown, red chaperon, and possibly holding a book. The large space in the middle of the predella is where the altar was formerly attached, partially obscuring the figures of Wenceslas and Jerome. This visual depiction expresses well the sentiment embedded in various liturgical texts where Jerome and Hus, along with traditional Czech saints, have become intercessors. These visual and textual portrayals troubled the Latin church.

---

in the village of Vilémov just west of Olomouc, Czech Republic, it is now in a private collection at Saints Wenceslas and Ludmila Orthodox Church, Jihlava, Czech Republic.

40. Chrudim, Regional Museum (Czech Republic), inv. no. U-46. There is additional information about the altarpiece in Kateřina Horníčková and Michal Šroněk, eds., *Umění české reformace (1380–1620)* (Prague: Academia, 2010), pp. 139 and 141.

The Posthumous Jerome

Even while the Council was still in session, there were formal complaints about the active continuation of the memory of Hus and Jerome among those who followed their teachings. There are many allusions, and among these, we find a letter of December 1416 from the canons of the cathedral chapter in Olomouc to the Council.[41] The letter asserts that the spread of Hussite religion had gained active support from many barons, knights, and common people. As a result, the traditional Christian faith was under serious threat. The sacerdotal system of the late medieval church was now the object of derision on account of these renegade "Wyclifites and Hussites." The canons declared that the church in Olomouc was suffering under grievous oppression. The Council of Constance was being held in contempt, and the church and proper religious practice were imperiled. The letter expressed both rage and fear. The letter of the Moravian canons makes reference to special services in which many people venerated Hus and Jerome. The canons pointed out the obvious and objectionable fact that the two being venerated were publicly condemned heretics, yet they were scandalously celebrated as though they were saints and martyrs. The Olomouc canons suggested that Hus and Jerome were being favorably compared to Laurence and Stephen in terms of merits and suffering, and it appeared that Christians in the Czech lands gave these new saints priority even over Peter and other traditional saints. The letter stated that these "true disciples of Belial and followers of John Wyclif, Jan Hus and Jerome, had been condemned by the holy synod, were painted in the temples of God and worshiped as citizens of heaven and of the household of God." Jan Železný was confirmed as bishop of Olomouc on December 14, 1416, and this letter represents his point of view. Železný, of course, had been appointed by the Council to act against heresy in the Czech lands. An early-seventeenth-century report noted that both Hus and Jerome were depicted on the Bethlehem Chapel pulpit burning at the stake.[42] There are other examples of the veneration of Jerome in liturgical or quasi-liturgical

---

41. Johann Loserth, "Beiträge zur Geschichte der Hussitischen Bewegung," *Archiv für öster-reichische Geschichte* 82 (1895): 386–391.

42. Fr. Táborský, František M. Bartoš, Ferdinand Hrejsa, Karel Guth, and Václav Novotný, *Betlémská kaple. O jejích dějinách a zachovaných zbytcích* (Prague: Grafické závody V & A Janata v Novém Bydžove, 1923), p. 61.

contexts. An incomplete judicial citation traced to the chancellery of Pope Martin V in 1418 refers to the celebration of Mass in the vernacular in places other than churches (noting villages, barns, and ordinary rooms), where once again we encounter the allegation that Hus and Jerome were venerated as saints.[43] A Hussite liturgical book from the early 1450s drew Jerome and Hus into chants for the Mass where the word *constancia* functioned as a pun underscoring both their place of execution and their fortitude in death. The prominent Hussite leader Jan Rokycana reinforced July 6 as the feast day for the martyrs, and that commemoration did not ignore Jerome.[44] There is a wealth of evidence indicating that Hus and Jerome were regarded in Bohemia as martyrs and were in some cases painted as saints on church walls and that in a Hussite liturgy of 1491 they were placed alongside Saints Laurence and Stephen. Hymnody also referred to these martyrs. One example is "A Song about Hus and about Communion in Both Kinds" (*Píseň o Husovi a o přijímání pod obojí*), which claimed that Hus and Jerome were executed because they opposed sin.[45]

Jerome and the Wyclifite Mass

In liturgical parodies, Jerome also appears, but predictably he is cast in a negative light. In the "Book of the Generations" of heretics within a parody of the Mass known as the "Wyclifite Mass," Jerome is designated the "athlete of Antichrist." "The Book of the Generations of All the Accursed Sons of the Heretic" begins with Wyclif, who is nominated as the son of the devil. The parody attempts to link the notorious villains who were held responsible for the heresies that convulsed the Bohemian church. Wyclif begat Swevia, possibly Petr of Znojmo; Swevia begat Stanislav of Znojmo; Stanislav begat Hus; Hus begat Marek of Hradec Králové, who lectured at Prague from 1399; Marek begat Zdeněk of Labouň, who was chancellor of the university according to the new statutes of 1409 and a consistent supporter of King Václav against Archbishop Zbyněk; Zdeněk begat Šimon

---

43. Josef Macek, "K počátkům táborství v Písku," *Jihočeský sborník historický* 22 (1953): 119–124. The text is extant only in a single manuscript preserved in the holdings of the Prague Cathedral Chapter library. Castle Archive, MS XXVII, fol. 5v.

44. Thomas J. Talley, "A Hussite Latin Gradual of the XV Century," *Bulletin of the General Theological Seminary* 48, no. 5 (1962): 10–11.

45. Jiří Daňhelka, ed., *Husitské pisne* (Prague: Československý Spisovatel, 1952), p. 140.

of Tišnov; Šimon begat Petr of Koněprusy, who was the dean of the faculty and in the Wyclifite Mass is called a "fivefold wicked rogue." He begat "Michalec," who should probably be understood as Křišťan of Prachatice, the rector at St. Michael's Church in the Old Town. He begat Matěj Knín, the father of all evil, who gained notoriety in 1408 and 1409 in a heresy trial and during a fractious university *Quodlibet*. Knín begat Jerome, the athlete of Antichrist. In turn, Jerome begat Jan Jesenice before the implications of the Decree of Kutná Hora took effect, and after those events Jesenice begat Zdislav Zvířetice, "the Leper," who gained notoriety for appealing from the archbishop to the pope in 1410 on behalf of Hus. The blasphemous Mass declared that the resulting "contagion infected many people to the extent that in these last days these fantastic Wyclifite errors persisted not only among the learned, but lay people in general and all people." In the third stanza of the *Prosa*, it is noted that Hus and his accomplices had erred. Knín, Šimon of Tišnov, and Jesenice followed in these errors, and Jerome was among them.[46] This a satirical genealogy and an anti-Hussite parody of the alleged heretics in Bohemia based on the schema outlined in the gospel of Matthew 1. The analysis of the Wyclifite Mass reveals that it is anonymous but may have been composed by students. Hus supposed that Germans were responsible for its composition.[47] There seem to be two versions of the "Mass." The parody has an opening verse, an epistle, a gradual, the *Allelujah*, a *prosa*, and, after the sequence, the "Book of the Generations," which is where we find Jerome characterized as the "athlete of Antichrist."

The second version of the Mass appears to be directed at the Táborites after 1419 but is modeled on the 1410 version. It has the same introit, collects, epistle, gradual, *Credo*, offertory, and other liturgical components. The *prosa* is missing. There is a note that explains the absence of the *Kyrie* and the *Gloria*. That note says that the absences are apparent on account of the fact that all of the "Hussites" are excluded from the highest realm of the angels.[48] The "Book of the Generations" is also different.

---

46. Fudge, *The Magnificent Ride* p. 194, with reference to the "Missa Wiklefistarum," ÖNB MS 4941, fols. 262r–263v. Text in Paul Lehmann, *Die Parodie im Mittelalter*, 2nd ed. (Stuttgart: Hiersemann, 1963), pp. 217–223; and *UB*, vol. 2, pp. 521–522. Analysis in Zdeněk Nejedlý, *Dějiny husitského zpěvu*, 6 vols. (Prague: Československá akademie věd, 1954–1956), vol. 3, pp. 369–375, who dates part of it to 1410 and the other part to 1419.

47. *Contra Palecz*, in *MIHO*, vol. 22, p. 235.

48. Třeboň, MS A 17, fol. 64r, noted in Nejedlý, *Dějiny husitského zpěvu*, vol. 3, p. 374. These texts are treated in larger context in Thomas A. Fudge, *Jan Hus Between Time and Eternity: Reconsidering a Medieval Heretic* (Lanham, MD: Lexington, 2016), pp. 187–210.

Here we find that Wyclif begat Hus, Hus begat Václav Koranda, Koranda begat Jan Čapek, Čapek begat Olešák, Olešák begat Jan Sádlo and Petr Zmrzlík, Zmrzlík begat Jerome, Jerome begat Šimon Tišnov, Tišnov begat Jakoubek Stříbro, Jakoubek begat Křišťan of Prachatice, Křišťan begat Simon Rokycana, Simon begat Marek of Hradec Králové, Marek begat Jan Jesenice, and Jesenice begat Zdislav of Zvířetice. The sum and substance of this text with respect to Jerome are that he is numbered among the dangerous enemies of the faith and a man responsible for the subversion of pure Christianity.

Complaints

If complaints were being filed with the Council of Constance, that synod also had cause for alarm and grievance. By late 1416, members of the Council complained to Sigismund that admirers of Hus and Jerome in Bohemia were treating the memory of these heretics as though they were saints, referring to them in sermons, incorporating them into prayers, and saying Masses for martyrs and including them among that august number. The letter warned of the danger of scandals, errors, and heresy. "The disciples and followers of Wyclif, Jan Hus, and Jerome, are abounding in wickedness and perfidy and they do not hesitate to proceed against sacred truth. All were condemned as heretics by this sacred synod. Yet now they are depicted in churches, and venerated as though they were saints. Masses are said for them as though they were martyrs. Moreover, their perverse teachings are being promoted so much so that the souls of simple people are being trapped in snares of eternal death. Even the learned and intelligent of both sexes have been drawn into the perfidy, fraud, deception, and those seduced thereto are many."[49] There were even allegations that images of Hus and Jerome were publicly displayed in Prague and carried through the streets in processions. The Council implored the king to take action and rectify the situation. Affairs in Bohemia had been exacerbated by the troubling indifference shown toward heresy by the royal administration of King Václav. The Council advised the king that the cult of Jerome and Hus had to be stopped. Certain heretics connected to the University of Prague, infected with the errors of men such as Wyclif, Hus, and Jerome, continued to disseminate heresies, and certain barons and

---

49. *Documenta*, pp. 647–651.

nobles of the kingdom of Bohemia favored them, offered them protection, and defended them. These same barons declared their adherence to this evil by affixing their seals of authentication and boldly made this known to the Council. It appeared that burning heretics created martyrs which thereafter resulted in the formation of cults devoted to the memory of holy men who had suffered unjustly for truth.

Mladoňovice, who had been a staunch defender of Hus, likewise esteemed "the excellent man" Jerome as a prophetic figure. Just as Elijah had been transported in a chariot of fire from doubt to the joy of paradise, so now Jerome, "fearless and zealous for the truth of the gospel" on account of his faith and martyrdom, had been transformed into "an example and mirror of perseverance" in witness of the power of truth.[50] In the hands of sixteenth-century thinkers, ideas such as prophets, witnesses of divine triumph in history, and the eschatological reemergence of mythical figures such as Elijah and Enoch were all applied to Jerome in a dramatic memento mori.

For example, in the century after his demise at Constance, Jerome was heralded as the undefeated athlete of Christ.[51] Along with Hus, Jerome was considered a figure of apocalyptic significance at the apex of history. In the book of Revelation (11:4), the two witnesses are called olive trees and lamp stands who had been ordained of God to bear light. John Foxe offered a striking interpretation of that passage. At the Council of Constance, Hus and Jerome were left in "a difficult place, on the dunghill, in mourning, in darkness, in the harshest fetters, cruelly separated and in need of everything. These are the two olive trees and the two candlesticks."[52] In this exegetical tradition, forces of wickedness and worldly powers overcame the faith temporarily, and the eschatological "Enoch and Elijah" (in the persons of Jerome and Hus) were executed. The Council judged them as heretics rather than prophets, with the result that the Czech scholars experienced the same fate as Christ, Stephen, and other apostles.[53] The massive collection *The History and Monuments of Jan Hus and Jerome of*

50. *Narratio de Magistro Hieronymo Pragensi*, p. 339.

51. John Foxe, *Eicasmi sev meditationes in sacram apocalypsin* (London: George Byshop, 1587), p. 177.

52. Foxe, *Eicasmi sev meditationes*, p. 180.

53. Foxe, *Eicasmi sev meditationes*, p. 178. For a broader treatment, though with particular emphasis on Hus, see Thomas A. Fudge, "Jan Hus as the Apocalyptic Witness in John Foxe's History," *CV* 56, no. 2 (2014): 136–168.

Prague, Confessors of Christ (*HM*), which appeared in 1558, underscored a broad swath of opinion on Jerome's role in the religious history of the later Middle Ages. In his commentary on the Apocalypse, Foxe presented a summary of the trial of Jerome up to his condemnation and burning.[54] Part of that commentary included an extended effort to identify the two witnesses in the Apocalypse as Jerome and Hus.[55] After the tragedy of the Council of Constance, "a memorable history of the Bohemiãs" followed, consisting of numerous "vexations and conflictes," which the Hussites "hadde for the relygion of Ihon Hus and Ierome of Prage, and of their victories."[56] The renewed time of troubles for the church had been exacerbated by the Council of Constance, while Jerome and Hus emerged as the two witnesses mentioned in the Apocalypse during the harrowing history of persecution. This climate persisted in Bohemia, and during the heady days of the Hussite revolution, Jerome of Prague was both the witness and the undefeated athlete of Christ.[57]

Somewhere between the spring of 1416 and the autumn of 1417, an anonymous submission was received by the Council of Constance with the incipit "a complaint against the sly King Vaclav."[58] The text suggested that because the heresies and errors of Wyclif and Hus were being tolerated and defended by the Czech king, who was himself a notorious suspect, Jerome and others were allowed to be venerated. In the aftermath of the judicial procedures against Hus and Jerome, there was a backlash in Prague against those who were seen as their persecutors. One example is the case of a Dominican monk who flourished in Prague between 1414 and 1417. Petr Uničov had gone around Constance declaring that he was Hus's main enemy and greatest opponent. It is reported that Petr took great pleasure in the reputation.[59] Once back in Bohemia, he discovered an abrupt change of climate and overt

---

54. Foxe, *Eicasmi sev meditationes*, pp. 168–172.

55. Foxe, *Eicasmi sev meditationes*, pp. 173–185.

56. John Foxe, *Acts and Monuments*, 1563, bk. 2, p. 302.

57. See Amedeo Molnár, "Eschatologická naděje české reformace," in J. B. Souček et al., eds., *Od reformace k zítřku* (Prague: Kalich, 1956), pp. 21–58; and Thomas A. Fudge, *Heresy and Hussites in Late Medieval Europe* (Farnham: Ashgate, 2014), V, pp. 33–45.

58. *Documenta*, pp. 638–642.

59. Hus, letter of June 23, 1415, in Václav Novotný, ed., *M. Jana Husi Korespondence a dokumenty* (Prague: Nákladem komise pro vydávání pramenů náboženského hnutí českého, 1920), p. 300; and *Relatio*, p. 41.

hostility to his point of view. On March 13, 1417, he was forced to recant and in the course of that retraction declared that both Hus and Jerome were free of error.[60] The revocation and statements of affirmation were coerced and cannot be regarded as sincere in any sense of the word. In the same year, in May, Charles University issued a eulogy of Hus and Jerome, praising the quality of their lives and their devotion to the faith and insisting that neither was heretical.[61] These were building blocks in the formation of a new culture and the foundations of a new religious practice. The early song *Tvórče milý zžel sě tobě* ("Dear Creator Have Mercy"), from 1417 or 1418, notes: "Already two years have passed since the priests started the Council of Constance, they have accomplished nothing salutary save that they killed two masters: Master Jan and Jerome. . . . Amen, amen, amen, amen, amen, let all of us say Amen. Master Hus lived in justice, fought sins and praised virtues, taught the commandments of God and gave his life for this."[62] Hus consistently takes precedence over Jerome in both Hussite art and literature, but it would be a mistake not to note the significance of Jerome in the memory of religious practice in the Bohemian province.

By February 1418, with the conciliar sessions coming to an end but with sustained challenges to the official church persisting in Bohemia, the Council of Constance published twenty-four resolutions against what was now coalescing into a movement known as the Hussites. The seventeenth resolution forbade all songs that lauded Hus and Jerome, "the condemned heretics," while the twenty-third resolution mandated that all who continued to violate that order would themselves be punished as heretics.[63] Rumor and practice must have been substantial in order for the Council to issue such directives. Such laws had no force whatever in Bohemia, and the veneration of the cult of Hus and Jerome continued to grow. On February 22, Pope Martin V issued the bull *Inter cunctus*, which ratified the acts of the Council with respect to Hus and Jerome. The document aimed at providing a theoretical basis on which to punish heretics and was addressed

---

60. The retraction has survived in three languages. The Latin appears in NK, MS III G 16, fol. 73; the Czech in MS XI E 3, fols. 96r–97v; and the German in MS XI E 3, fols. 98r–99v. The most accessible printed Latin version is Johann Loserth, *Wiclif and Hus*, trans. M. J. Evans (London: Hodder and Stoughton, 1884, 2nd ed. 1925), pp. 343–347.

61. *HM*, vol. 1, pp. 103–104.

62. *FRB*, vol. 8, pp. 429–430.

63. Höfler, pp. 240–243; Thomas A. Fudge, *The Crusade against Heretics in Bohemia, 1418–1437: Sources and Documents for the Hussite Crusades* (Aldershot: Ashgate, 2002), p. 19.

to the prelates and inquisitors in Bohemia, Moravia, Austria, Germany, Silesia, and Poland. This papal pronouncement identified "Jerome of Prague of damnable memory," who was mentioned together with Wyclif and Hus, and characterized the triumvirate as a menace who "had gathered together no small number of unfaithful [causing] ruin and misery."[64] The bull declared that the three men had been cast out of the house of God and had suffered "wretched destruction." The three were referred to as "heresiarchs" and "damned men." Together with depictions of Jerome at the stake wearing the miter of the heretic inscribed with the word *Eresiarch*, this refutes claims that Jerome was never characterized as a heresiarch.[65] *Inter cunctus* included a questionnaire of sorts aimed at detecting heresy among followers of men such as Wyclif, Hus, and Jerome. The context is very much preoccupied with the theological errors of Jerome and his predecessors. The tenor of *Inter cunctus* is rigid. Heresy suspects are ordered to be investigated concerning whether they believe that the acts of the Council with respect to the faith, especially in affirming and condemning what it has decreed, are good, right, and proper. Essentially, *Inter cunctus* requires a profession of faith in the integrity of the Council in its doctrinal rulings. Jerome, having perpetrated "matters still more controversial," is presented and regarded as a nemesis of the goals of the Council. In response to the bull, the archbishop of Salzburg, Eberhard III von Neuhaus, who had been at Constance during the trial of Jerome, issued an ordinance to the priests in Salzburg that forbade the teaching of Hussite or Wyclifite doctrine and called on all bishops to enforce the prohibition. We may suspect limited success, as the decree was reissued in 1420.[66] It is apparent that Jerome was seldom mentioned apart from reference to Wyclif and/or Hus. There is no doubt that he has been overshadowed by these men from 1415 to the present. His recantation hurt him immeasurably and sullied his posthumous reputation. He also had the misfortune of having to follow and therefore in some sense to remain in the shadows of the others, especially Hus. That reality must not distract us from recognizing the independence of Jerome and the stature of his presence in the late medieval world.

---

64. Mansi, vol. 27, cols. 1204–1215.

65. David S. Schaff, "Jerome of Prague and the Five Hundredth Anniversary of His Death," *Bibliotheca sacra* 73 (April 1916): 193.

66. Paul P. Bernard, "Jerome of Prague, Austria and the Hussites," *Church History* 27 (1958): 14–15.

Jerome in the Hussite Ethos

Despite the best efforts of the Latin church to suppress the memory of Jerome and his heretical colleagues, he remained a presence in the evolving ethos of reformed religious practice in the Czech lands. For example, the radical Hussite priest Jan Želivský referred to martyrs in a sermon on November 19, 1418, and again on July 23, 1419, drawing attention to several cases of Hussite martyrdom which included Hus and Jerome in Constance and the deaths of the laymen in the Old Town of Prague in 1412, as suggested earlier. This latter event may have been a result of instigation on the part of Jerome, inspiring the three young men to undertake their fateful public demonstrations.[67] A satirical letter ascribed to King Sigismund also appeared, in which the memory of Jerome was noted as playing a role in the reformed religious practices in Bohemia. "You have entered into the list of saints Jan Hus and Jerome and some laypeople, murdered, as you insist, for Christ's law, and you celebrate ostentatiously their day, neglecting the days of other saints. Driven by the desire to similarly achieve the crown of the martyrs, you have certainly welcomed with grateful minds the infallible preachers of wisdom of both genders, something never before even heard of."[68] In Hussite propaganda, Sigismund instantly became the target of Czech outrage because of the atrocities perpetrated against Hus and Jerome at the Council of Constance. In 1420, Vavřinec of Březová, better known for his valuable chronicle of Hussite history from 1414 to 1422, composed satirical complaints and accusations against both Sigismund and the Council of Constance.[69] These texts were motivated by a strident political and nationalistic agenda. Sigismund is characterized as the enemy of Czechs and the wicked persecutor of Hus and Jerome:

> He lured to Constance,
> The perpetrator of evil things,
> By his letters of safe conduct
> —I can say they were devious—
> My virtuous son Jan,
> A priest valuable for you,
> Hus, the devotee of your truth

---

67. NK, MS V G 3, fols. 218r, fol. 19v.

68. The text is in *UB*, vol. 2, pp. 523–525.

69. The texts appear in Jiří Daňhelka, ed., *Husitské skladby budyšínského rukopisu* (Prague: Orbis, 1952). See also John Klassen, "Images of Anti-Majesty in Hussite Literature," *Bohemia* 33, no. 2 (1992): 267–281.

And permanent preacher of your truth,
Imprisoned him and ordered him burned to death
And to throw his ashes in the water.
Then he burned to death
As an evil man and stubborn heretic
A learned man,
More eloquent than any other,
Jerome, the honest master
Born in Prague,
For professing your truth
For announcing sins of the clergy,
To vituperate me
And to disfigure my glory.[70]

Here we see Jerome presented as an intellectual without peer who was persecuted and executed for no other reason than that he professed the truth. A similar claim is advanced in a separate text, with the repeated declaration that the deaths of Hus and Jerome were disgraceful and were a result of Sigismund's duplicity:

Under his letter of safe conduct, under his faith,
I can say under non-faith,
He captured my virtuous son,
Hus, the pious master Jan,
He imprisoned him in Constance,
Held him there for a long time, then eradicated him by fire,
Then master Jerome.
And the only guilt of both was
That they professed the truth
And announced the evil done by priests.
Here he put new shame
Never before heard of
Upon my Czechs, upon my country—
God is my witness that without any guilt.[71]

---

70. Accusation of the Czech crown in verse, in Daňhelka, *Husitské skladby budyšínského rukopisu*, p. 46.

71. Complaint of the Czech crown, in Daňhelka, *Husitské skladby budyšínského rukopisu*, p. 64.

The uses of Jerome's memory were not simply nationalist or political. These were elements in the Hussite movement, but at its core, the reforms facilitated by Hus and Jerome generated a religious movement that was motivated by religious conviction and concern. The life and witness of Jerome were nominated among the factors that facilitated reformed religious practice. In the kingdom of Bohemia and in the margraviate of Moravia, many sincere disciples were attracted to the new religious practices and were thus brought to righteousness through the perseverance of Hus and Jerome together with divine guidance.[72]

The two reformers and martyrs were almost always linked, but both were rightly characterized as leaders. "Master Jan Hus and Jerome and other masters had those books among them and liked to learn from them. . . . Then canons and parish priests gathered and had consultations. They . . . denounced [Hus] . . . they expelled him . . . they burned him. . . . They did the same to Master Jerome a year later."[73] According to the early histories of the Hussite movement, "the people of Prague . . . lamented the unjust sentencing of Master Jan and Master Jerome by the Council of Constance."[74] They were champions of the faith and heroes of the Czech nation. Such sentiment was not simply evident among the common people but is expressed also at the national level. During the Diet at Čáslav in 1421, the sentiment was reflected, and once again we find Sigismund held responsible for the deaths of righteous men. "All apostates from the Holy Church and dishonored heretics had a free hand in the Council of Constance, and Your Grace, always augmenting the shame of the Czechs, allowed the burning to death of another master, Master Jerome, in spite of a papal and your [own] letter of safe conduct."[75] This is a frequent theme in Hussite literature. Jerome and Hus were innocent victims, and the man most responsible for their tragic deaths was Sigismund.

The king predictably denied culpability and resisted the insinuations that he had acted contrary to the best interests of Bohemia. His response

72. Mikuláš Pelhřimov, in Höfler, pt. 2 [FRA, vol. 6], pp. 475–820; see pp. 477–478.

73. František Svejkovský, ed., Veršované Skladby doby Husitské (Prague: ČSAV, 1963), pp. 156–163.

74. Hussite Chronicle, in FRB, vol. 5, p. 353.

75. Hussite Chronicle, in FRB, vol. 5, p. 489. The Diet was convened between June 3 and 7 at Čáslav, a town about forty-five miles southeast of Prague. It should be noted that Jerome had neither a papal nor an imperial safe conduct.

is one of measured indignation but also couched in careful political rhetoric: "We Sigismund, by the favor of God etc., announce to all lords, knights, pages, people of Prague and municipalities of our Czech kingdom: You accuse us of many items and namely of the burning to death of Master Jan Hus and Jerome, and you also mention heresy, defamation and the dishonoring of the Czech land. But we are not guilty of this, because we were never interested and are not in anything that would cause the shame of our Czech crown, and it is well known that we have faithfully and bravely argued in the name of our brother of blessed memory before the Council of Constance, and therefore we have been exposed to great tribulation and vilification in Constance."[76] The allusion to defending his half brother Václav, the late Bohemian king, is political grandstanding, and his expression of brave and faithful defense of Czech interests is little more than self-serving rhetoric.

By August of the same year, the Bohemian Diet issued its demands to Sigismund, noting that Hus and Jerome were not censured by anyone in the land.[77] It would appear that the political climate in Bohemia in the aftermath of the Council of Constance was incapable of evolution or progress without reference to Hus and Jerome. When efforts to quell an uprising in Bohemia failed, the church and the empire agreed to address the Hussite problem by means of a formally constituted crusade. To that end, the crusade bull *Omnium plasmatoris domini* was issued on March 1, 1420. Once again, the church felt obligated to announce that Hus and Jerome had been justly condemned by the Council of Constance.[78] That being the case, it was quite improper for Czechs to continue protesting and using that disagreement to thwart the progress of official religion. The Latin church was so committed to that perspective that it was prepared to go to war.

Neither ecclesiastical nor civil authorities in Bohemia took any note of that position and gave no indication that they were persuaded by the force of such argument. On July 10, 1420, a formal letter from Prague officials to the Doge and Council of Venice included reference to Jerome in which he

---

76. Hussite Chronicle, in *FRB*, vol. 5, p. 492.

77. František Palacký, ed., *Archiv český čili staré písemné památky české i moravské*, 6 vols. (Prague: Kronberg and Riwnáče, 1840–1872), vol. 3, pp. 206–208.

78. *UB*, vol. 1, pp. 17–20.

was characterized as "an admirable university master and philosopher."[79] That was the official position within the Czech lands. In religious circles, he continued to be viewed as a martyr and a holy man, held in esteem not unlike that in which Hus was held. Moreover, his influence persisted. It was noted previously that shortly after Jerome's execution, the Council of Constance issued a directive to the University of Vienna to deal with resid- ual heresy in the city. Whatever actions may have been undertaken do not appear to have met with much success, and obviously *Inter cunctus* had not sufficiently motivated bishops and inquisitors to take the necessary steps to stamp out heresies. In 1424, a full eight years later, Jerome's old neme- sis from trial procedures in Vienna and Constance, Nicholas Dinkelsbühl, wrote a tract addressing the grim fact that Hussite heresy continued to be openly proclaimed by some professors in Vienna.[80] It must have seemed to the church that the baleful ghost of Jerome continued to haunt the Austrian province. Around the same time, a sermon preached before the Council of Pavia-Siena on January 6, 1424, by the Dominican Girolamo of Florence noted the difficulty the Council of Constance had encountered in its efforts to "condemn, burn, and uproot the two notorious heretics, Jan Hus and Jerome."[81] The situation in Austria and in Bohemia appeared to validate that observation.

In 1426, a full decade after the immolation of Jerome, Gerson wrote a letter to an unnamed Franciscan in which he referred to Hus and Jerome as among those whose thinking became enmeshed in error and who fol- lowed a path to insanity.[82] The insanity Gerson referred to persisted, and the memory of Jerome in liturgy and in the Hussite uprising and revolu- tion gave ongoing testimony to an insanity that the church struggled to contain by means of crusade, which it preached and conducted over the course of two decades.[83] A 1430 manifesto published in the name of the Táborite captains noted that the church persisted in claiming that Hus and Jerome were found to be in manifest error by not only the pope but the

---

79. *UB*, vol. 1, pp. 39–43.

80. *Quaestio de heresibus et hereticis ac de veritatibus katholicis*, ÖNB, MS 4384, fols. 1a–15b.

81. Text is in Walter Brandmüller, *Das Konzil von Pavia-Siena, 1423–1424* (Münster: Aschendorff, 1974), vol. 2, pp. 193–199.

82. Glorieux, vol. 2, pp. 277–278; he also refers to them in the same year as examples of theological error, vol. 9, p. 636.

83. Fudge, *The Crusade against Heretics*.

entire Council at Constance and that therefore they were burned at the stake as incorrigible heretics. The military commanders declared that their active opposition to the crusade was predicated partly on the belief that neither Hus nor Jerome was actively convicted of any error, and this was manifestly obvious when examined against the criteria of holy scripture. Instead, their executions were carried out on the basis of nothing more than the trifling violence of dishonest witnesses. In opposing the crusade with military might, the Táborites declared that the men at Constance who had taken such action against Hus and Jerome and who were culpable in their deaths could expect to merit the severity of divine punishment.[84] A subsequent manifesto of 1431, issued under the aegis of the entire Czech land, again pointed out that Hus and Jerome "were not convicted by Holy Scripture but by wanton and unrighteous violence and God will punish all who assented to this through counsel or assistance."[85] It is fair to maintain that the opposition to the crusade preached against the Hussites was carried out on a platform that included resistance to the position that Jerome was a heretic and deserved capital punishment. The willingness on the part of Czechs to go to war was also part of a commitment to the propagation and defense of the memory of Jerome.

Hussites at Basel

Seventeen years after Jerome perished in the flames of the stake at Constance and after more than a dozen years of crusade futility, the Latin church reluctantly invited Hussite heretics to attend the ecumenical Council of Basel in an effort to resolve the problem of heresy in the Bohemian province by means of diplomacy.[86] After protracted negotiations, representatives of the Hussite faith appeared at the synod. During the Council of Basel, on January 21, 1433, the outspoken bishop of the Táborites, Mikuláš Pelhřimov, also known as Biskupec, defended Jerome before the conciliar delegates with a bold declaration: "Master Jerome was irreligiously annihilated by fire, because he refused to confirm that

---

84. Amedeo Molnár, ed., *Husitský manifesty* (Prague: Odeon, 1986), pp. 156–170.

85. *MC*, vol. 1, pp. 153–170.

86. Most recently, see Thomas A. Fudge, "The Hussites and the Council," in *A Companion to the Council of Basel*, ed. Michiel Decaluwé, Gerald Christianson, and Thomas Izbicki (Leiden: Brill, in press).

this was just, and did not want to agree with the condemnation of John Wyclif." When Bishop Mikuláš mentioned Jerome and went on to claim that both he and Hus were innocent, the reaction was palpable. "Hearing this explanation, which was very hateful for the council, some laughed, others gnashed their teeth, the rest muttered. But the legate clasped his hands and looked up to the skies." The loud, scornful laughter and Cardinal Guiliano Cesarini rolling his eyes made it quite clear that the Council of Basel was no more ready to reconsider the matter of Jerome than the Council of Constance had been seventeen years earlier to dismiss the charges against him. [87] A month later, on February 17, Gilles Charlier, the dean of Cambrai, took up the matter of Jerome. Charlier asserted that Jerome was a wicked man because he had dared to mention Hus in his speeches and responses at Constance, and numerous heretical articles were advanced against him during the Council. There, Charlier insisted, "because he thought that he could not err in the faith, he was, as I am convinced according to the faith, justly sentenced." According to Charlier, Wyclif had been condemned long ago for holding to "Arian unbelief" and because he was guilty of many other errors and heresies which he dis-seminated in his books. Charlier attacked Jerome as conceited and told the Council that when he was at the University of Paris, he had absconded "without the permission of his host." We have already seen that Jerome was at the University of Paris from 1404 to 1406 and became master of arts, but his commitment to Wyclifite thought brought him into sharp contention with other thinkers at Paris, and he came under suspicion of heresy. In 1406, it was rumored that Gerson, chancellor of the university, was about to take action on behalf of the "zealots for the faith" against the heresy suspect Jerome, but being warned, Jerome covertly left Paris.[88] Charlier wanted the delegates at Basel to be familiar with the nature and reputation of the man that Mikuláš had so ardently defended. Biskupec's reply to Charlier again drew attention to the innocence of Hus and Jerome and to common Hussite opinion that their executions were wrong: "We do not consider them to have been legitimately condemned." This decla-ration was met with jeers, shouts of protest, and considerable agitation. Thereafter, on March 4, Jan Rokycana spoke highly about Hus and praised Jakoubek, but the chronicler noted that he was completely silent about

---

87. *MC*, vol. 1, pp. 268–294.

88. These details emerged during his trial. Hardt, vol. 4, col. 681.

Jerome.[89] A few years after the appearance at Basel, Mikuláš began his chronicle of the history of the Táborite communities within the Hussite movement. The narrative is predicated on theological assumptions and convictions. Mikuláš understood history as the story of how God intervened in time with the help of ordinary people to revitalize the Christian faith. The Táborite priests were the guardians of the law of God. The "story containing the cause of the Táborite priests" concentrates on theology as the foundation for the reform of religious affairs in the Bohemian province. The chronicle of Mikuláš aimed to establish a testimony for posterity.[90] This was a deliberate construction of *memoria*. The Táborite bishop considered Hus, and by extension Jerome, the direct inspiration for the radical communities and believed that constructive reform was effected in the Czech lands by means of the perseverance of Hus and Jerome aided by divine visitation.[91]

The perspective reflected by Mikuláš became part of the collective ethos around the memory of Jerome. It was hotly contested by those who opposed the Hussites. In 1451, the humanist Aeneas Sylvius Piccolomini, while debating with Táborites, emphatically declared that the inordinate allegiance to Hus and Jerome was at the root of the Bohemian problem. "The whole of Christendom is against you and still you do not recede from your opinion, which if it is true means that all of your forefathers who had no part in the chalice burn with the Devil and his angels. For before the instruction of Jan Hus and Jerome, this kingdom always took communion in accordance with the rite of the Apostolic See."[92] Such admonitions fell on deaf ears. It is noteworthy that Aeneas attributed to Jerome a specific pedagogical role in the promotion of Utraquism. Elsewhere, an inquisition in 1458 discovered recalcitrant heretics in Pomerania and Brandenburg who

---

89. *MC*, vol. 1, p. 320.

90. *Chronicon causam sacerdotum thaboritorum continens*, in Höfler, vol. 2, p. 730.

91. *Chronicon causam sacerdotum thaboritorum continens*, in Höfler, vol. 2, pp. 475–820. The chronicle was written between 1435 and 1444.

92. The letter of August 21 was addressed to Juan Carvajal, the cardinal of San Angelo. The text has been translated from the edition found in Rudolf Wolkan, ed., *Der Briefwechsel des Eneas Silvius Piccolomini*, in *FA* II, vol. 68, pp. 22–57. Aeneas Sylvius Piccolomini (1405–1464), from 1458 Pope Pius II, visited Tábor twice in the summer of 1451. His account is significant for its witness to persistent heresy in Bohemia and the failure of the repeated crusades to eradicate it.

venerated Wyclif, Hus, and Jerome as saints in heaven.[93] One might expect that the narratives prepared by Czechs would be sympathetic to Jerome, and this assumption is borne out entirely by two anonymous texts and an account attributed to Mladoňovice.[94] The perspective of the Mladoňovice text is revealed in the title, which purports to delineate a "narrative of Master Jerome of Prague who died for the name of Christ at Constance." These texts were heavily influential in Bohemia, especially among the communities of Hussites. Outside the purview of historical writings in Bohemia, we have the *Acta* of the Council of Constance with respect to the trial of Jerome. It will be useful to summarize this perspective, as it reflects the official view of the church on the matter. Beyond this, there are two enduring portraits of Jerome that were rendered to posterity by Italians who wrote vivid and moving accounts of the man who became known as the "athlete of Antichrist." The first was written by Poggio immediately after the trial concluded, while the other was set down forty years later by Aeneas Sylvius. In the same year in which the second account appeared, its author was elected to the papacy and took the name Pope Pius II.

Questioning the Eyewitnesses

Before turning to these records, it is important to consider the reliability of historical accounts, particularly those written from an eyewitness perspective. It is often taken for granted that eyewitness accounts are generally thought to be accurate. But is this assumption warranted? Psychological research has suggested a number of important qualifications. Bearing in mind that late medieval Europe represents a different cultural context from the twenty-first century and that it is folly to transfer contemporary theory into the distant past, and accepting that cultural context and literacy levels do have an impact on the process of memory, it is worthwhile to consider the accuracy of eyewitness testimony. Personality, interest, or a priori assumptions will determine to some extent what people see and how they understand or interpret what they experience. Such factors will also unconsciously influence what an eyewitness may find interesting,

---

93. Wilhelm Wattenbach, "Über die Inquisition gegen die Waldenser in Pommern und der Mark Brandenburg," *Philosophische und historische Abhandlungen der königlichen Akademie der Wissenschaft zu Berlin* 3 (1886): 79–80.

94. *Notae de Concilio Constantiensis*, in *FRB*, vol. 8, pp. 319–322; *De Vita Magistri Ieronomi*, in *FRB*, vol. 8, pp. 335–338; and *Narratio de Magistro Hieronymo*.

noteworthy, important, or memorable, and two or more eyewitnesses may on that basis produce two very different but honest accounts of the same event. Compelling factors based on these criteria may, in fact, explain why certain elements of the event are elaborated on while other components are dismissed, distorted, or glossed over. The time lapse between the event and the recording of one's recollection of the event implies the likelihood that memory is subject to deterioration, despite the fact that the eyewitness may insist and be certain that his or her memory is accurate. Moreover, eyewitness recollections develop over time, and this is subject to formation by accessing other points of view by means of discussion, reflection, or reading other points of view on the event. Group memory is thought to be more stable over time than individual memory, but group memory is a social construct. While this may be true, there is also the possibility that errors or misunderstandings may become locked into memory and into the narratives that are produced. After the passage of sufficient time, it is no longer possible to amend the original account. Even if an alternative narrative is located, the dilemmas facing the first text can hardly be excluded from the second or subsequent text, though any number of variables may cause a reader to believe that one account is more accurate or reliable than another. Modern psychological research around the topic of memory or remembering stories consistently shows that trustworthy verbatim repetition is unusual and rarely accurate. An exception might involve specific rituals. If the story is told and retold often, a stereotype emerges that may unwittingly diverge from the event it reflects. Consequently, a falsehood repeated a thousand times becomes truth.[95] In the recording of the last days in the life of Jerome, the historian must come to terms with the fact that Mladoňovice and Poggio, along with the anonymous notaries and chroniclers who recorded specific accounts, operated not just as reporters but as interpreters of history. Mladoňovice, Poggio, and the anonymous notary compiling the semiofficial account of the hearings in May 1416 doubtless were selective, and in the case of Mladoňovice and Poggio predicated that selectivity on existing historical, theological, or ideological perspectives aimed at facilitating predetermined purposes. This factor is present in every historical record, and it is questionable to assert that oral transmission in the later Middle Ages was measurably more accurate than

95. "If you repeat a lie a thousand times, it becomes truth" is an apocryphal statement frequently, but unverifiably, attributed to Joseph Goebbels.

it is today. In sum, eyewitnesses are both interpreters and sources of history. It is necessary for the historian to rely on the existing sources, or eyewitness testimony, but none of these sources should be taken absolutely literally or accepted uncritically.[96] With those caveats in mind, we turn our attention now to the narratives written about the death of Jerome.

Official Views of Jerome

We have previously discussed the absence of official *Acta* for the Council of Constance. I regard the anonymous semiofficial account of the hearings in the case of Jerome from May 23, 26, and 30, 1416, as the best formal account resembling a transcription recorded by a notary.[97] The record favors the prosecution rather than the defense and allows far more space to delineating the case against Jerome than it does to allowing the defendant to respond to the accusations. Though unbalanced in coverage, there is no compelling reason to question its basic objectivity in reporting. This record provides a more fulsome account of Jerome's hearings than does Fillastre, Dietrich Vrie, or Dietrich Niem or indeed any of the other pro-church narratives. The account delineates the charges Jerome faced when he was brought to trial, and these were read to the entire Council. The commission that had investigated Jerome concluded he was a heretic, while noting that the defendant steadfastly denied this. Jerome argued strenuously for a public hearing in which he might be permitted to defend himself. The notary records that Jerome declared that he had been unfairly treated, that his judges were biased, and that many of the witnesses brought against him were dishonest and unreliable. Jerome argued that there was nothing particularly unusual about this and went on to recite a litany of unjust condemnations endured by good people throughout history, with a primary focus on the classical and biblical worlds. Jerome seems to have anticipated his own demise and marshaled a series of prior cases, apparently to illuminate his own. He denied that he was heretical and defended the late Hus against similar charges. This account devotes an inordinate amount

---

96. Rather than voluminous reference to modern psychological literature, I cite Judith C. S. Redman, "How Accurate Are Eyewitnesses? Bauckham and the Eyewitnesses in the Light of Psychological Research," *Journal of Biblical Literature* 129, no. 1 (2010): 177–197, which has references to a considerable body of that literature.

97. Hardt, vol. 4, cols. 755–773.

of space to the arguments mounted by Jerome concerning the clashes between Czechs and Germans. The rhetoric of the anonymous account is unvarnished and direct and functions more as straight reporting than annotated explanations or interpretations. There is no particular literary flair and little effort to do more than report the proceedings. Nevertheless, selection criteria also prevailed in the composition of the record.

The anonymous chronicle reports that it was decided that Jerome should be permitted to speak in his own defense as a strategy for allowing the defendant to "be convicted by his own worthless chatter." During his formal addresses to the Council, it was noted that the defendant faced a hostile audience. The narrative is unencumbered and appears to summarize the facts and proceedings we have enumerated earlier. The chronicler notes that once Jerome finished his speech, the fathers of the Council declared that a definitive sentence would be handed down on the next Saturday and would be "inscribed on iron and announced." The record refers to Jerome as a "son of iniquity," as a "slanderer and defamer of others," a "seducer," and a wicked heretic. All of these prejudicial phrases, however, are simply a selection of language extracted from articles of accusation lodged against Jerome and cannot be understood as necessarily reflecting the anonymous writer's point of view.

The semiofficial account only blandly reports the death of Jerome. The text notes that he was handed over to the secular arm. Jerome commended his soul to God and sang to the end. He was manacled and marched through the streets of Constance to the place of execution, where they burned him to death. The deposition and sentence are appended to the narrative, and herein we find references to the dog that returns to its own vomit, to Jerome as a withered and rotten branch that must be destroyed, and to the defendant as a definite heretic. But once again, this is mainly reporting as opposed to commenting. The anonymous *Acta* are therefore strikingly neutral when compared with Mladoňovice, Vrie, or most of the other sources, including Poggio and Aeneas Sylvius. That does not mean, however, that the narrative is entirely free from bias or perspective.

Poggio Bracciolini

Poggio witnessed the death of Jerome and his speeches when he was arraigned before the Council, which he characterized as an epic performance for the ages. So laudatory was Poggio's account that he was warned by a colleague. Leonardo Bruni Aretini feared that Poggio had revealed altogether too much regard for a man who was a convicted heretic, and he suggested that Poggio should write a bit more cautiously about such matters.[98] If Jerome was excoriated on account of his defense of Hus and loyalty to a man already sent to the pyre, then Leonardo Bruni may have feared that his friend Poggio exhibited altogether too much favor for Jerome and might also find himself in some difficulty should his views be brought to the attention of Council officials. The account of the death of Jerome by Poggio took the form of a letter, which he wrote to Leonardo Bruni on the same day Jerome was sent to the stake.[99]

Poggio admits that he cannot write a detailed account of the case but has chosen instead to present an edited version of what transpired. Though Jerome was accused and publicly arraigned on charges of heresy, Poggio admires the eloquence and the persona exhibited by the defendant. Whether or not the defendant had actually placed his remarkable skills in the service of "heretical studies," Poggio is not prepared to adjudicate, admitting that such determinations lie outside his purview and beyond his expertise. Jerome's impertinence, his charisma, and his reckless daring were all on display but cloaked in astonishing eloquence. The man on trial for his life exhibits no fear but trembles only at the thought that a congregation of such wise men could blunder so badly into returning an unjust and unjustifiable verdict and thereby create a terrible and dangerous precedent. When onlookers tried to shout him down or officials attempted to force him to observe another protocol in his replies, Poggio noted that Jerome handled all of it with panache and amazing fortitude. Jerome defended himself manfully, undercut the integrity of the case presented against him, called into question the veracity of those who had submitted sworn testimony against him, and did not speak a single word that could possibly be considered unworthy or heretical. With the use of wit and sarcasm and the force of argument, Poggio asserted, Jerome persuaded many onlookers to his point of view. When interrupted by hostile detractors, the defendant simply dismissed the interruption with the curt admonition to shut up.

Even though there was considerable opposition to allowing Jerome to speak at length to the court, he proceeded with aplomb. He called to

---

98. Leonardo Bruni Aretini, *Epistolarum Libri VIII* (Hamburg: Theod. Christoph. Felginer, 1724), bk. 4, letter 7, p. 129–130.

99. Poggio, pp. 157–163. This supersedes Tomaso de Tonneli, ed., *Poggii Epistolae*, 3 vols. (Florence: L. Marchini, 1832–1861), vol. 1, pp. 11–20.

his side a veritable litany of venerable figures from classical and biblical narratives. The skill with which Jerome lectured his hearers made a deep and lasting impression on Poggio. Hyperbolically, Poggio submitted that Jerome had waxed so eloquent that everyone now hoped that he might acquit himself by retracting whatever objections had been assigned to him, present himself in submission to the authority of the church, ask forgiveness, and pledge fidelity to a purer form of the faith. Poggio tells us that instead of this penitential posture, Jerome "fell to praising Jan Hus." This created an uproar. Jerome was repeatedly interrupted by protests and noise. He remained undeterred. Going on the offensive, the large man with the big beard caused all of his detractors to fall back in silence at his eloquence. When the crowd swelled against him, he shouted out and prevailed. He refused to back down or modify his language. In everything, Jerome stood firm, displaying an absolutely courageous and fearless spirit. Poggio marveled at the legendary memory displayed by the defendant. A year in prison bereft of books and even the light of day had neither dulled his recall nor clouded his mind. His resolute stand courted death. As far as Poggio was concerned, "this was a man to remember."

At length, when the Council was unable to prevail upon Jerome to repent, change his mind, turn from heresy, and seek sanctuary in the safety of the church, he was condemned and relaxed to the secular authorities and consigned to the fire. He was unshakable and went to his death with a cheerful countenance. According to Poggio, "no Stoic ever displayed such a steadfast mind when death struck him down." He was a wonderful man, in every respect, save for his alleged heretical ideas, and it was a shame that he had to perish. Nevertheless, his death was the sort of passage one might find described in a book of philosophy from the ancient histories. Gaius Mucius Scaevola did not offer his hand to be burned nor did Socrates drink the hemlock more willingly than did Jerome present his entire body to be burned.[100] The letter detailing the death of Jerome is a panegyric reminiscent of the "tranquil Socrates" and the "imperturbable Cato."[101] It had nothing in common with Richental's later insistence

---

100. The reference to Gaius Mucius is an allusion to a sixth-century BCE story told in the monumental history of Rome by Livy, *Ab Urbe Condita Libri*, bk. 2, 12–13. B. O. Foster, trans., *Livy, History of Rome, books 1–2*, Loeb Classical Library, no. 114 (Cambridge, MA: Harvard University Press, 1919).

101. Watkins, "The Death of Jerome of Prague," p. 120.

that Jerome died screaming.[102] Jerome was the eloquent philosopher who persevered to the end and willingly gave up his life for truth and justice. This is what Poggio thought Jerome should be like, a contrast to the conservative, reactionary baroque mentality of the Council. In the hands of Mladoňovice, the image of Hus was as a medieval Jesus, the suffering servant, a martyr of Christ-like quality. In the hands of Poggio, by contrast, Jerome's image was less that of a Christ figure than that of an exemplar of the ideal philosopher. It is possible to regard Poggio's letter as a carefully contrived account of courtroom drama and capital-punishment horror, but that would miss an important point.

Poggio created an ideal man who faced death fortified in his own faith and convictions. Unvarnished virtue becomes the main component in the narrative and functions as a template for reading and understanding the death of Jerome as narrated by Poggio.[103] Poggio downplays any factor that might suggest heresy on the part of the defendant, and apart from the unrestrained affirmation of the righteousness of Hus, Jerome is a titan of integrity and fortitude. Heresy is not a problem that Poggio can cognitively incorporate into his depiction of Jerome, nor does he display any realistic appreciation of the legal aspects of the trial, to wit, expressing the hope that the defendant might either clear himself of all suspicion of heresy or otherwise persuade the court to dismiss the case without prejudice. Earlier interpreters of Poggio suggest that he was dismissive of the theological subtleties that preoccupied the Council delegates and was perhaps silently contemptuous of the arcane debates and possibly ridiculed with suppressed laughter the intricate and irrelevant proceedings involving the suspected heretics Hus and Jerome.[104] If so, that cynicism vanished in late May 1416, when Jerome reached the climax of his trial. Here, at last, was a glimmer of daring discourse and intellectual excitement in a world of regressive insecurity. In seeking to present that point of view, Poggio shaped the historical narrative of what actually happened, though it would be too strident to conclude that he distorted history into an unrecognizable caricature. Certainly, he redacted the story of Jerome to construct an interpretation, and his letter to Leonardo Bruni must be read as an interpretive version

---

102. Buck, *Chronik des Konstanzer Konzils*, p. 68. See appendix 11.

103. Summarized in Watkins, "The Death of Jerome of Prague," pp. 120–121.

104. Georg Voigt, *Wiederbelebung des classischen Alterthums oder das erste Jahrhundert des Humanismus*, 3rd ed., 2 vols. (Berlin: Georg Reimer, 1893), vol. 1, p. 235.

of truth, fact, and history but one that can be accepted as a useful and corroborative source.[105] Rather than simply reporting events and outcomes, it is apparent that Poggio sought, for his own purposes, to discover what sort of man Jerome really was and to discover why he refused to submit to the Council of Constance and further to arrive at understanding what motivated Jerome to embrace the stake as a means of eternal life rather than clinging to mortal life.[106] Poggio may have chafed at the pedantic proceedings of the Council, but he was esteemed. When Cardinal Francesco Zabarella died on September 26, 1417, it was Poggio who delivered the funeral oration.[107]

I think it is altogether compelling to accept the observation that the standard accounts of the case of Jerome at Constance, such as the anonymous *Acta*, are more objective and more strictly historically accurate than the rendition provided by Poggio. However, they are also less critical about the assumptions that underlay the legal process and also more likely to accept the ethos that pervaded the Council. Gerson, Dinkelsbühl, Štěpán Páleč, and Michael de Causis believed they saw in the face of men such as Jerome a reflection of the devil. Peering back across the cathedral precincts, Jerome saw in those same men the forces of evil that he and Hus alone were willing to oppose. They defended truth and justice, and that cause was the true church of God, not the community of popes and prelates. Poggio approached Jerome from an altogether different point of view from that of the other chroniclers and notaries. He interpreted Jerome from the perspective of the moral tradition of the classical philosophers in which eloquence was not merely the ability to speak in charming prose but was instead a reflection of justice itself with a firm commitment to ideas such as perseverance, truth, and dignity.[108] This is what caused Poggio to present Jerome as a hero worthy of admiration.

Aeneas Sylvius

Forty years later, in 1458, Aeneas Sylvius wrote his history of Bohemia. Unlike the anonymous chronicler and Poggio, Aeneas Sylvius was not an

---

105. Šmahel, *Život a dílo Jeronýma*, p. 83.

106. Watkins, "The Death of Jerome of Prague," pp. 113–121, is a useful and commendable interpretation of Poggio.

107. Hardt, vol. 1, pt. 9, pp. 537–546.

108. Watkins, "The Death of Jerome of Prague," p. 120.

eyewitness. He had interacted with Hussites in situ at Tábor in 1451, but his knowledge of Jerome and the Council of Constance was derivative. He had read both the semiofficial account and Poggio. He referred to some of the heroes of the Hussite revolution, such as Jan Žižka and Jan Čapek, whom the Czechs remembered with satisfaction as powerful leaders who had won so many battles. Václav Koranda and Jakoubek Stříbro were among those leaders whom the people listened to carefully, "as though they were apostles or angels sent from heaven." Among these false apostles and mistaken heavenly angels were also Hus and Jerome. They had been sentenced by the great Council of Constance to be burned to death. They had suffered and would continue to suffer forever in hell for contaminating the true faith.[109] While Aeneas admired the account of Jerome's death as written by Poggio, he was disinclined to follow the same trajectory of interpretation. Rather than focusing on the famed eloquence of Jerome or on the ideal philosopher whom Poggio found so appealing, Aeneas referred to Jerome as "unreasonable," and this led him into the perilous posture of contumacy, which is what caused him to become responsible for the contamination of pure religion.[110] The *Historia bohemica* delineated the fate of Hus and Jerome as two sides of the same story, and the compelling narrative served as a template for many readers thereafter. The "Czech matters caused immense worries to the fathers when they were thinking about how the country might be cured." The way forward was decided upon by bringing the main protagonists to Constance. These two were considered the more learned, the recognized leaders, and the main advocates of heresy. Both of them appeared before the Council, "ready not so much to humbly learn about the opinions of others but rather to shamelessly push their opinions, wishing rather to instruct than to learn, and eager for appeal to the people." In other words, they were more eager to teach than to be taught: *docendi quippe quam discendi cupidiores.* "Hus was considered older and more respectable, Jerome more scholarly and more outspoken." After much disputation, the ideas of Jerome and Hus were proven to conflict with the law of God and led only to ruin. Though recognizing that these were intelligent men, the Council concluded that both had been corrupted by a "Wyclifite delusion." The "obdurate Czechs" could not be persuaded

---

109. Aeneae Silvii, *Historia bohemica*, ed. Dana Martínková, Alena Hadravová, and Jiří Matl (Prague: Koniasch Latin, 1998), p. 4.

110. Aeneae Silvii, *Historia bohemica*, chap. 36, pp. 98–102.

and stubbornly held to their opinions. When the Council "recognized the intractability and inflexibility of these cursed fellows," they concluded that they were rotted limbs of the church, which had to be cut off for the sake of the vine. Aeneas employs the same metaphor as the Council. "Both of them endured death with resolute and unwavering mind and rushed to the stake as if they had been invited to a feast, not even making a sound, which could be taken as a sign of regret. When the flames took hold of them they sang hymns which the flames and the crackling of fire could hardly deafen. None of the philosophers is said to have gone through death so bravely like these men endured burning to death."[111] In this description, Aeneas seems very close to the language of Poggio. Aeneas noted with regret that their destruction by fire did not eliminate their memory or influence from the earth. Ruefully, the *Historia bohemica* records that both men "enjoyed reverence as martyrs and were considered not less important than Peter and Paul to the Romans." When these things were reported in Prague, Aeneas wrote, a cult of remembrance sprang up around the deceased, and the disobedient initiated annual celebrations. This led to unrest, uprisings, and the widespread destruction of the official church.[112] The history of the crusades against the heretical Czechs, fought on Bohemian soil, is a grim witness to that savage memory.

Jerome and Radical Hussitism

Remembering Jerome in the days following the Council of Constance can be traced in the surviving records of religious practice in the Hussite era within the Bohemian province. Liturgical texts do tend to favor Hus, and we find no trace of an office for the feast of Saint Jerome of Prague as we do for Hus. Still, Jerome is here and there in the liturgical texts of the later Middle Ages, invariably connected to Hus but nevertheless a figure of significance in his own right, adorned with a nimbus, regarded as a holy martyr, and referred to as a saint. The revolution that sprang from the ashes of two convicted heretics at Constance bore the name of Hus, not Jerome. That said, Jerome cannot be excluded from the ethos of the revolution, and indeed the nature of some of its iterations reflects more broadly and more accurately the personality of Jerome than it does that of Hus. For all of his

---

111. Aeneas Sylvius, *Historica bohemica*, p. 100.

112. Aeneas Sylvius, *Historica bohemica*, chap. 36, pp. 100–102.

salutary qualities, the priest Hus was not as well suited to lead a popular revolution as was the wandering scholar Jerome. The latter was an individual of enormous intellect and reckless daring, who has been described by those who knew him at the height of his powers as a large man with a big, bushy black beard, whose oratory commanded the attention of all the sage men of European Christendom. It was he, obscured by the glory ascribed to Hus, who was the face and the force of the radical Hussite history.

Jerome, The Shield of the Christian Faith, 1406

Snow, ice, rain—three names, but in spite of this only one thing: so also God is in three persons but only one, he is the Father with the Son and the Spirit who is breathed forth by them at the same time.

It is necessary to know that the aforementioned differ from each other, but also concur with each other. They differ in this way. Because in the nature of God the Father is to give birth to the Son, while the Son only has the possibility of being born. The Father is not identical with the Son. Also it is the nature of the Holy Spirit to proceed from both. Therefore God the Son is not the Holy Spirit. Similarly, the nature of the Father is not to proceed from both persons. Therefore, God the Father is not the Holy Spirit. Also, the nature of God the Father is to engender actively, which the Holy Spirit cannot. Therefore, the Holy Spirit is not God the Father, and God the Father is not the Holy Spirit, and so on.

However, they concur in one thing, in essence, which is in divinity. Because the Father is God, the Son is God, the Holy Spirit is God, and thus they concur in one essence, which is common to all three persons. Thus Christ correctly says: I and the Father are one, which is to say [one] in essence. He does not say "we are one" in person, because the persons are different.

Similarly, memory is not reason and so on, because memory is the capacity to memorize, reason is the capability of thinking and the will is the capacity of wanting. However, the capability of memorizing is not thinking or wanting and by this they differ from each other. However, they concur in one essence, namely in the soul, which is common to all of them, because reason is soul, memory is soul, and the will is also soul.

In the same way, ice is not rain and rain is not snow and snow is not ice and so on. However, they concur not because their essence is water, but because water is the common nature of these concurring things. And so, in spite of the fact that all these things differ from each other, they concur in one essence.

In the same manner, creatures concur in something common, and though they differ from each other in many ways, for example a human and a donkey, they are the same thing, not in one particular thing, but in one common thing, which is as a creature. The limitation of the species can be defined by the statement, a human is a soulful substance capable of sensory perception, a donkey is a substance, and so on.

Similarly, Ambrose, Jerome, and Augustine differ, because Ambrose is not Jerome, etc., but they concur in the common essence. Because it is correct to say that Jerome is human and the same about the others and that a human is a mortal creature endowed with reason, and so on. It is the common unity, because if it were a numerical unity, then Jerome would be Ambrose and so forth. But because they do not differ by number, though Jerome and Augustine are the same thing, because one and the other is a creature endowed with reason, it is possible to admit that Augustine, Ambrose, and Jerome are three human beings, as far as the persons are concerned, but not three humans as far as essence is concerned, that is to say, that there are three human natures. From this arises that there are three divine persons, but not so far as essence is concerned, which means that there are three divine essences.

The Trinity made the uncreated Trinity in its own image and likeness.

ST, vol. 3, pp. 21–23; and Šmahel/Silagi, pp. 195–197.

Jerome, In Praise of the Liberal Arts, 1409

Jerome of Prague's speech at the 1409 annual Charles University academic disputation (*Quodlibet*) reflects his keen awareness of university politics, his commitment to Czech identity, his nationalist fervor, and the value he placed on the liberal arts. In the first half of his speech, which has not been included here, Jerome delineates the nature and value of the seven liberal arts, personifying them as virgins who serve the goddess of philosophy. In the first half of the speech, he draws heavily on the *Anticlaudianus* of Alain of Lille, which is a twelfth-century *summa* of the seven liberal arts.[1] In the second half of the speech (translated below), Jerome extols the virtues of the annual Charles University *Quodlibet*, vilifies the German masters who refused to participate in the 1409 event, praises the city officials who supported King Václav, and then launches into an impassioned appeal for the superiority of Czechs over foreigners in their own country. He defines a pure Czech in terms of homeland (*patria*), language (*lingua*), parental origin (*sanguis*), and proper faith (*fides*). Jerome insists that no real Czech had ever been convicted of heresy. He defends the use of John Wyclif's books and lauds the leader of the *Quodlibet*, Matěj Knín (referred to as the *quodlibetarius*), as a servant of God. Having taken Horace literally, *nec verbum verbo curabis reddere fidus interpres*, the text that follows is, in part, a sum-and-substance paraphrase rather than a strict word-for-word translation.[2]

Because our gracious virgins, the "seven free arts," along with philosophy, their queen mother, took part and are participating in the respectable dance of

---

1. Robert Bossuat, ed., *Alain de Lille, Anticlaudianus. Texte critique avec une introduction et des tables* (Paris: J. Vrin, 1955).

2. Horace, *Ars Poetica*, 132–134. *Horace. Satires, Epistles, Art of Poetry*, trans., H. R. Fairclough [Loeb Classical Library, vol. 194] (Cambridge, Mass.: Harvard University Press, 1926), p. 460.

this *Quodlibet*, all those clerics and masters who sophistically show their love for these admirable girls, but did not even dare to appear at their celebration in spite of the fact that they were invited, should be ashamed. In so doing, they offended our mother, the faculty of free arts, in the worst possible way. Caught off guard by their own intrigues, did they not tumble down to the chasm of shame, though they thought that they hatched a conspiracy against the gravity of our mother University and her excellent son, the honorable master *quodlibetarius*? The *Quodlibet* is a tournament of the strength of the knights of erudition, where masters one after the other undergo a test by the swords of their arguments and for their efforts achieve fame as an appropriate reward. The many masters who shamelessly refused to participate in this celebration should be embarrassed. By this action they have impaired the natural benefit of learning—which is the purpose of such gatherings—which all the unfortunate students vainly expected. Failing to appear when summoned, even if it were a matter of life, is regarded as shameless by secular knights and simple fighters. Dear students, you are rightly obliged to those masters, as a group and individually, who took part at this *Quodlibet* celebration as a tournament, because it is inappropriate not to remember the benefit. But to the others you should render thanks as they deserve it, as cowardly knights. This is what I wanted to say to the praise, honor, and celebration of the beautiful virgins, the free arts, and those who profess them together with the queen, philosophy, their honorable mother.

Following this tribute which we paid to our mother, let us now proceed at least in the main features to the praise of her son—without embellishment and without exaggeration. According to divine and human laws, it is proper to praise only those who seek after both rational and moral virtues which is confirmed by the philosopher in the fourth book of Ethics.[3] If we did not pay tribute and honor to those who deserve it, the virtue would fade away by regret that she did not receive the necessary reward. In order not to cause with harmful silence, even unintentional harm, but to the contrary in order that you harvest the fruit of your long and exhausting efforts, I think it is now suitable to offer something of a kind of libation of praise and honor, in your presence, even though it is not unknown to me the utterance of Aristotle from his second book of Rhetoric, where he says that to praise the present is a sign of flattery.[4] Your praise is not based on short-lived matters as is sometimes in the case of others. But these "rejoice when they have committed

---

3. Jacqueline Hamesse, ed., *Les Auctoritates Aristotelis. Un florilège médiéval, Étude historique et édition critique* (Louvain: Peeters, 1974), pp. 12, 69.

4. Hamesse, *Les Auctoritates Aristotelis*, pp. 16, 43.

something bad, and praise every bad thing. Their acts are atrocious and their steps have bad reputation." "Carousing without shame they feast at banquets, they only look after themselves. They are clouds without water, carried along by the wind, they are trees in autumn without fruit, totally dead, uprooted, wild waves of the sea tossing away their shame like foam, wandering stars, for whom gloomy darkness is prepared for ever" (Jude 12). Disregard well-fed horses and take beautiful clothes and the fur of dead animals away from them—and you instantly take their virtue from them. In their hearts they are full of filth, extravagance, simony, injustice, and deception. They steal from the poor and commit sacrilege. Similarly, they are whitened graves full of dead bones. Outwardly they threw over themselves pride, pomposity, abusiveness, lies, and other crimes like a disgraceful coat. In this way they seek to cover their own shame and the disgraceful slander of magnanimous persons who are beneficial for the entire community of our honorable town. Even though by their lives and morals they are heretics, they ceaselessly and falsely refer to the orthodox members of our sacrosanct Czech nation as heretics. However, there is an ancient saying that no pure Czech can be a heretic, and events from time immemorial up to now prove its veracity. If according to Solomon a good name is more valuable than expensive ointments,[5] I will implore immortal God that each and every one of you who love the honor of our most glorious prince King Václav, the Roman and Czech king, and this kingdom, and who candidly love the good reputation of our most holy city of Prague, to endeavor collectively and individually by all means available to preserve the good, yes the most excellent name, which we have up to now in all countries. Do not believe cunning liars, who are attempting to denigrate this good name and disparage the representative of our holy Czech nation.

I especially address you, prudent aldermen and illustrious burghers, who were given such great honor from the serene ruler Václav, Roman and Czech king, not to anyone else, but precisely to you. On account of your vision he confidently entrusted the management and protection of his most majestic and dearest treasure, the community of all people of this holy town of Prague. I therefore admonish and beseech you to be diligent, and using all possible means, to maintain this holy Czech town in devotion to its king without fear and using all means to limit the defamation of perverse liars. Should anyone announce that any pure Czech was or is a heretic—from king to knight, from knight to yeoman, from yeoman to peasant, from archbishop to canon, from canon to the last priest, from burgomaster of the town to alderman and burgher, from burgher to any tradesman—I must answer on behalf of everyone

---

5. Ecclesiastes 7:1.

with my whole heart and my full voice, without fear, that he is lying and does not deserve to be believed. I will stand behind this statement now and always.

I have no doubt that you can prove from living memory that many times numerous people were brought here from foreign nations and that in this holy town they were convicted according to the law as heretics and were burned to death. But you have never heard, neither your fathers, nor the fathers of your fathers, that a single pure Czech has ever been burned for heresy. Many foreign liars are trying cunningly and falsely to place that degrading coat marked with a gray cross on the most loyal men of our holy nation, in order to conceal their own disgrace and shame. If I am attributing to my homeland necessary honor, and if I defend her with all my ability against liars, no one on this account should consider me an unreasonable daredevil and reckless man. Even many writers from antiquity demonstrate that the love of homeland should be above everything to such an extent that we should fight for our homeland not only with words but also with acts. Cato says "fight for your homeland."[6] Cassiodorus, in the twentieth letter of his first book says, "to everyone his homeland should be dearest."[7] He also writes in the thirty-eighth letter, that "the most noble-minded are those who consider the flourishing of their homeland."[8] According to Horatius in his book of poems it is even "sweet and noble to die for one's country."[9] Unfortunately, the love of the homeland has already disappeared from many, especially in this town. They care little or not at all that this holy community and its useful members are dishonestly and falsely stained. To tell the truth, which community in the world would tolerate such humiliation if it could defend itself? Is it not known to everyone that half-educated priests, not having any high title, have falsely in vernacular sermons blathered that in this town there are many heretics, whom they call Wyclifites? As far as I am concerned, I proclaim before all of you that I have read and examined the books of Master John Wyclif, just as I have the books of other teachers, and I admit that I have learned much good from them. But God forbid, I do not wish to be so foolish and espouse everything as faith which I have read in his books or in the books of any another Church teacher. I will be obedient only to the Gospel. If the Gospel says that it is so, then it is truth.

---

6. *Catonis Disticha Monostica* 30 and *Disticha Catonis, Sententiola* 23, in *Disticha Catonis*, ed. Marcus Boas (Amsterdam: North-Holland, 1952), p. 19.

7. *Cassiodorus, Variae* I, *recte* 21, 1, in *Magni Aurelii Cassiodori Variarum libri XII* (CCSL, vol. 96), ed. A. J. Fridh (Turnhout: Brepols, 1973), p. 30

8. *Cassiodorus, Variae* I, *recte* 3, 10, 1, in *Magni Aurelii Cassiodori* , p. 105.

9. *Horatius, Carmina* III, 2, 13, in *Horace Odes and Epodes* (Loeb Classical Library, vol. 33), ed. Niall Rudd (Cambridge, Mass.: Harvard University Press, 2004), p. 144.

If already since our youth we have read with much effort and studied with the greatest care the heathen Aristotle along with other heathen philosophers, in whose books are numerous heresies rejecting the Catholic faith, and no one prevents us from keeping the clear truths which they contain, why then should we not read the books of Wyclif, when they have excellently stored in them many holy truths, even if they agitate both the haughty priests and the laity? There is nothing strange if the same clear light pleases the eyes of a man who can see clearly but harms rheumy eyes. The stupid half-learned should understand that silver, gold, and precious stones are usually buried in foul earth, and whoever does not know this fails to value them more than ordinary soil. But those who master this art do not despise gold or pearls because they appear covered with mud, but quite the contrary, using their art they separate the gold from the mud in kilns. Young men, who can prevent you from learning and recognizing the vein of truth in Wyclif's books? As far as I am concerned, I encourage you with the greatest urgency to often read and diligently study his books, especially the philosophical ones. And if you find in them something that you, because of your young age, are unable to understand properly, postpone it until you reach a more mature age. If there is something in them which seems to disagree with the faith, do not defend it, and do not profess it, but rather be obedient to the faith.

Even the blessed Jerome, who rebuked Origen as a heretic, reminded himself that he had read some three thousand volumes of this writer, and somewhere he says "if only I could have the books of all heretics! I would copy from them what is true and leave what is bad."[10] The half-learned, however, will object. "A bit of yeast will work its way through the entire bread dough" (1 Corinthians 5), so also a piece of nontruth or heresy will spoil the truths contained in some book. But to those I answer: the fools should understand that stable and permanent things have a different nature from things transitory and fluid. The yeast which is temporal and changing, however, permeates transitory and temporal dough, but no untruth or heresy, no matter how large, can corrupt even a small truth, because truth is firm and a lie cannot penetrate it, because during mutual penetration of things it is necessary that one thing makes way for the other. The truth never gives way and will not give way for a lie, because the truth triumphs over everything. Therefore, in the future, never give way, as deceitful people wish, from the glorious truths contained in the aforementioned books and do not be afraid to study these books. It is not proper, of course, that the wise adapt truth to people, but rather people to the truth. Therefore, never in the future hand over books of the aforementioned master

---

10. Jerome, Letter 61, *Ad Vigilantium*, in *PL*, vol. 22, col. 602.

to people who do not understand them at all, who ridicule the truths before they can understand at least their parts. Do you not know the admonition of the highest master who said, "do not throw pearls in front of swine" (Matthew 7), these are longing to lie in manure rather than in the most pleasant smell? From long ago it has been known that goldsmiths test their creative works by careful examination in order to distinguish brightness from odor. Lift up your hearts, brave men! You are supposed to be admirers of the truth and therefore do not bend your neck before deceitful people. Remember that it is just as equally depraved to lie as it is not to bravely resist liars who are attempting to suppress the truth.

To all of you who are young, I am putting before your eyes as an example the beautiful Joseph, whom you resemble by your age and of whom it is written that he was the only one among his brothers who showed constancy, so only he received the long coat of many colors. Because what else does it mean for Joseph's coat to come to the ankles if not the perfect act? Just as a loosely falling coat covers the ankles and arms with permanency, so is the one who does not retreat from established truth. And for you, old doctors of learning, I am placing before your eyes the old man Moses, the legislative doctor of the scriptures of the old covenant, who ordered that at the altar there should be sacrificed with fire an offering which also included the whole tail. This means that for us we should all perfect study and all truth to completion, which we began to teach and not become frightened and begin to go backward like a crayfish. It really is better not to recognize the truth than to abandon with shame the recognized truth because of narrow-mindedness and so entangle also students, who, because of immature thinking, are unable to extricate themselves from it.

Towns support masters and doctors in order that they correct, according to the scriptures, every deviation from the faith or aberration in the faith so that they may face liars and, yes, prove they are liars. But in this town—as is known—many half-educated [preachers] spread lies before people in sermons. I know one who, rather than preaching to the people, prattled on about the book of Revelation. Among other things he was talking about a dragon whose tail pulled a third of the stars down from the sky, and he insisted word by word that this dragon was Master John Wyclif, who allegedly turned more than one third of the Church militant to his heretical faith.

But consider, learned men, if this half-learned man could find it in the text of the scriptures or in the Glossa, or he did not even discover it in the books of ecclesiastical law! Or is he such that we will, because of his pleasing eyes, believe him no matter what he says? We know that the Church entrusted to the doctors of the holy scriptures, time-tested by long study, the task of explaining the sense of the scriptures. They are permitted to utter statements as the intellect of each can understand. But these half-learned priests are not permitted to preach freely from their own heads, but to explain before people clearly limited scriptures without their own additions. I say this in order that the next time you will not believe such half-learned liars.

Though for the moment I do not regard it as my task to patronize the learned Minerva, or to instruct half-learned masters, all of you should not consider only what I am saying, but with what intention I am saying it. In order that what I have in my heart might come to my lips, I will utter a few more words. If you, doctors, whose task it is to rectify liars, do not tame the half-learned priests, who in their sermons before people falsely stain and assign heresy to our sacrosanct Czech community, it will be necessary to conclude that you sanction the false slandering of our community. I am not saying this to put you to shame, or because I would see in the shame of others my own glory, but in order to properly encourage you, learned men, against false preachers. I know that the sound of bugles or a trumpet does not add any strength to horses, but that through it some kind of excitement awakens bravery dormant within them. Similarly, I have no intention of instructing you by my words—you have been instructed long ago—but to encourage you against the spreading of lies, so that the entire community of this honorable Czech town might pay the required and deserved tribute to you. But if you permit liars to falsely defame the faithful community of people, from whom you have accepted dignity, neither clergy, nor burghers, nor working people, will be obliged to respect you. If someone objects that I should not vilify God's priest or revile him, I will answer that I do not revile God's priest, but I am reprimanding the false priest because of his horrible lie. Many half-learned priests should blush with embarrassment because of such a shameless lie!

But let me cease to occupy myself with those hypocritical priests, and address my speech to you who are directing the *Quodlibet*, you truthful man. You deserve the more praise the more bravely you have resisted liars. Even if for you your praiseworthy cautiousness with renowned titles that decorate you is enough, and does not require my eulogizing, we cannot and must not be silent about what we believe speaks in your favor and is to your honor. You deserve more praise then others, the more you have come to the fore above others at such a young age because of your intellectual capability. You did not take this very heavy load of directing the *Quodlibet* upon yourself as others because of the ancient habit or because of fearing some trifling harm. While others in the past declined the proffered honor, you presented yourself, or to say it more truthfully, you accepted the honorable task, offered to you by the dean of the faculty of free arts and the honorable master. You have acted like a learned and prudent man according to the principle "in order that you would not give to others your honor"; you not only made this principle yours, but fulfilled it with action and you also deserve praise for this.

Praise, however, belongs only to virtuous and assiduous men and the qualities of both are deeply rooted in you. It proved your knowledge of various sciences, which at this celebration poured out of you to the benefit of all listeners. If it is necessary to praise doctors of theology because they speak truthfully about God, you deserve praise with them, because you spoke about God not only truthfully but also intelligently like doctors of both laws. No one can take this praise and deserved honor from you, because you will be forever lauded by everyone. If someone gets rich, he should give thanks to fortune. If he is of high birth, the laud for it does not belong to him but to his parents. If he is beautiful and charming, wait for a while when, with the arrival of old age, beauty disappears. But if somebody is learned and wise, he deserves true acclaim for it. Because your acts reflect your laudable qualities, everyone will celebrate you rather than all the wealthy, high born, beautiful, and brave.

Because human acclaim grows from suffering, it is necessary to remember for augmenting your praise, beloved brother, some of your past sufferings. Who would doubt that God handed you over to the hands of diabolical people?[11] They seized you in order to destroy you and uproot your honor. But God delivered you into their power in order to refine you and through various suffering to decorate you even more and prepare you for future excellent honor which we are witnessing today. But we ask why did God wish to leave you at the mercy of insensitive and cruel people, like lions, when your behavior since a very young age up to the present has proven to be salutary? I respond to this in the name of the Lord answering that God did it because you had many gifts from God, but you did not have one thing and this was to be able to thank God even in suffering. Without it your virtue was not yet perfect. It was therefore good that you were firmly tested as to whether you would remain, in suffering, what you were before. Suffering asks everyone if they really love God.

Did not those who joined against you and tested your soul seek to overcome you by superior force or frighten you with confusion when they could not defeat you with reasonable argument? What else was their aim, except to cause you to despair, when they directly attacked you with defamatory words

---

11. *Documenta*, pp. 338–340; and Chronicle of the University of Prague, in *FRB*, vol. 5, p. 570.

and cunningly derisive reproaches? If the mind is internally chained by hopelessness and suffering, and is tormented by defamation which attacks it from outside, an arrow of despair penetrates easily. Where could you concentrate your trust at that time when your adversaries, yearning for your death, opened their mouths at you like lions, shaking their heads and blinking their eyes? If you had looked back, how many stork bills would you see opened above your distress? Were you not abandoned by all or almost all? But it was God who took care of you, who elevates the suppressed and frees the captive. The next time no one should despise you, because, abandoned by individuals, you were not standing upright under a heavy load as was appropriate. Even the righteous one falls seven times a day, but then stands up again, but the godless, if he falls once, will not stand up.[12] Therefore all together those individuals who were attacking your soul and tormenting you by all means should blush and feel ashamed, and let all those who wept because of you in sorrow during the time of your greatest tribulations, now rejoice when they see you with their own eyes purified in great honor.

You, beloved students, do you not accept in your hearts all these words of mine as if I were a direct participant in all of this? Did not many faces turn pale with disgust during that storm of oppression? Was the air then not filled with sighs over the inhuman wrongdoings to which you were exposed? But the burning outrage during the time of yearning for fulfillment cannot even imagine what will be the end of everything. Who would dare, during such a storm, even to think that you would reach the very peak of virtue, where, in the end, all of us can clearly see you? What a great outrage erupted against you, which did not help even the faithful statement of your leader, who publicly announced that he did not find any heresy in you. Let all those who love your honor be happy with you in their spirit, but let all those who previously condemned you falsely, and threatened others, and proclaimed your tribulation as a deterrent, be ashamed.

Do not blame me for verbosity because of such a long speech; I know well this saying in verses:

When shameful rumor blackens someone with disgusting dirt, only great streams of water can make him clean.[13]

---

12. Proverbs 24:16.

13. Henricus Septimellensis, *Elegia*, vide Enrico da Settimello, *Elegia*, in *Enrico da Settimello, Elegia*, ed. Giovanni Cremaschi (Bergamo: Istituto Italiano Edizioni Atlas, 1949), p. 26.

But before I finish shortly, I address all of you, individually and collectively. Listen to me more attentively as we come to the conclusion. Have you not heard and have you not read about Job that he was covered with sores from the soles of his feet to the crown of his head? Have you not learned that in the end he was cured and brought back to his original condition? Have you not heard and have you not learned that this honorable man who directed the *Quodlibet* became the subject of slander and reproach not long ago? Do you not see him now in front of you healed, returned to his original condition and completely purified? It is the same as you know about Job that everything has been returned to him twofold. You can see our master endowed with abundant virtue. Do you not know from holy biblical events that Joseph, the son of Rachel, was handed over by his brothers to the people of Ishmael and dragged to Egypt, and that he was tormented by various tribulations? Even though he was innocent, was he not arrested by the other sons of his own mother and turned over to foreigners? From the same scripture you can learn how Joseph was saved by God and spared for a leading position, so that he could later feed his countrymen and foreigners. Do you not see clearly that our master was also taken away from all past confusions to become at this *Quodlibet* the leader of a fighting formation like a prince? God preserved him to feed the community of our University and the faculty of free arts the rich crop of knowledge with the bread of wisdom and the water of learning.

On account of a multitude of virtues and erudition, with which you are filled, I do not succeed, as I would like, to be your eulogist. Therefore I am gloriously leaving to all to praise you, and I am only adding the request that the one who would next time curse you would be himself cursed by God and whoever would bless you would be blessed by God. For this our thanks should be given to him, the supreme master, to whom injustice is done to his faithful. Because of his holy truths he organizes at the same time law and judgment. And this is as much as should be said in the presence of you all.

Šmahel/Silagi, pp. 211–222.

Letter from Jerome to Andreas Grillenberg, Canon and Official of the Passau Consistory, September 12, 1410

I am sending to you, dignified father, master and lord, in your service and with good wishes for your health. You should know that I am already in Bítov Castle, healthy and merry with many friends who are at your service in all things. I have no doubt that you have excused my involuntary promise, if you wish to take into consideration that it has been done under pressure. We do not despise the law, which we always respect and before which we are always ready to stand. But you would not advise me to stand alone before so many hundred enemies if you love me. "Because my adversaries forged on my back, they postponed injustice for themselves." "But my soul has escaped like a sparrow from the net of the fowlers, the snare has been destroyed, and we have been freed." I thank you sincerely and will always thank you. Send all of my enemies to Prague with the witnesses. I want to be judged with them there in a fair debate. If you prefer, we will go to the papal court, where I am just as well known as they are. I am also pleased to inform you that I have recently been in your church in the city of Laa and there I have invited myself to a discussion with the schoolmaster and the town notary, remembering your favor. I will be of service to you and your people wherever I go. Keep yourself well.

Written in Bítov on the Friday after the birth of the blessed Mary.

Yours always, Master Jerome of Prague

Klicman, pp. 34–35; Hardt, vol. 4, col. 683; *Documenta*, p. 416; and Šmahel/Silagi, pp. 248–249.

APPENDIX 4

Letter from Albert (Wojciech Jastrzębiec), Bishop of Kraków, to Václav Kráĺk of Buřenice, Titular Patriarch of Antioch and Chancellor of the Bishopric of Olomouc, April 2, 1413

Esteemed reverend lord and father. Jerome of Prachatice, as he himself said, was invited here by our lord the king and his brother Duke Witołd (our pious and devout king being ignorant of who he really was). He came here in person and on the first day he appeared with a beard. On the second day he again appeared, without a beard, wearing a red tunic and a gray fur-lined hood. He ostentatiously showed himself to the king, the queen, a gathering of princes, barons, and nobles. Even though he remained only a few days he created the greatest excitement [commotion or ruckus] among both clergy and people than has ever previously occurred in the diocese in human memory. When he came to be examined before me, the ordinary of the locale, in the presence of the provincial metropolitan and the reverend father Bernard, bishop of Castello, who was nuncio of the Apostolic See, along with a large congregation of doctors of canon law, masters of sacred theology, and masters of liberal arts, there followed numerous and various arguments [disputations]. When I interrogated him about the articles of the damned Wyclif he answered in the negative to each and every one of them. He execrated them and affirmed the catholic faith in everything. After this, he was returned to his own native country where he was to work and till the ground in his own place, because here in our country the earth is too dry to be able to receive his seed and produce a crop. This is on account of the fact that the common people are not able to understand the tenets of such a great philosopher, much less the lands of Lithuania and Russia. Further, our serene and gracious lord and king is already travelling.

Dated at Kraków, on the day of the Lord, April 2, 1413.

Albert, by the grace of God, bishop of Kraków, chancellor of the Polish kingdom.

Documenta, pp. 506–507.

APPENDIX 5

Letter from Jerome to King Sigismund, Written at Überlingen, April 7, 1415

To his Serene Highness and master, lord Sigismund, by the grace of God the Roman and Hungarian etc. king, ever Augustus, and also to the entire common council. I, Master Jerome of Prague, master of seven arts of common universities, which is of Paris, Cologne, Heidelberg, and Prague, am announcing with this letter, and as far as I am concerned am announcing to everyone that for cunning slanderers, defamers, and detractors of our kingdom I am prepared voluntarily and freely to come to Constance [to defend] the purity of my Christian faith and innocence, not hiding in corners or before private persons, but publicly prove before the whole council. Therefore it does not matter of what nation or status my slanderers are, whoever wishes to accuse me of any sin or heresy, should accuse me in their own name publicly before the entire council. And I, according to my innocence, am ready before the whole council to answer and prove the genuineness of my Christian faith. And should I be found to be a heretic, I do not object to being punished as is suitable for a heretic. For this cause I am asking for safe and free access. Should I be touched while arriving and submitting to such high justice before any guilt should be proven to me, by an obligation, arrest, or force, then the whole world would learn that this common council does not judge according to justice and pure faith, if they would—while I arrived voluntarily—chase me away by any means from so high and steadfast justice. From which, I think, such a holy and wise council is far from.

FRB, vol. 8, pp. 319–320; Hardt, vol. v, p. 103; and Šmahel/Silagi, pp. 253–254.

Public Letter from the Czech Barons on Behalf of Jerome, April 9, 1415

We Václav Dubá, otherwise of Leštno, Jindřich Chlum called Lacembok, Jan Chlum and at Svojkov, Václav Hrádek called Myška, Bohuslav Dúpov, Bleh Stradov announce publicly with this letter before everyone, wherever it might be read or heard, that the respectable man, Master Jerome of Prague, sent a message by letters and his communication to his Serene Highness and master Sigismund, Roman and Hungarian etc. king, the master most merciful, asking and begging His Grace for a letter of safe conduct and safe arrival to Constance, so that he could announce there his true Christian faith and innocence against his slanderers before the entire common congregation or council in a public hearing. He also asked for a letter of safe conduct and for a public hearing by the whole common council, and for receiving such letter of safe conduct and for the further announcement of his public notice he nailed his notices written in Czech, German, and Latin on the doors of churches, monasteries, and the town hall of the city of Constance, as well as on the houses of cardinals and bishops, as the writing above shows it more clearly and in greater detail. This notice, we, mentioned above, have seen and heard read. However, he was unable to obtain this letter of safe conduct and public hearing from them despite pleas. For which obvious certainty of these matters we have written this letter and put on it for confirmation and for our conscience our seals. Given in Constance on Tuesday after the octave of the resurrection of the Lord in the year 1415.

Hardt, vol. 4, cols. 685–686.

APPENDIX 7

Citation of Jerome to the Council of Constance, April 17, 1415

The most sacred and holy synod and general council of Constance, gathered in faith and congregated in the Holy Spirit, and representing the universal church on earth, to Jerome of Prague, who represents himself as a master of arts of many universities, and supposes to know things which are the purview of the modest and sober, but who knows nothing more than he should. Be aware that a certain document has come to our attention and knowledge, which was set up, in a manner of speaking, by you, upon the gates of the city and the door of churches in Constance, on the Sunday when the *Quasi modo geniti* was sung in the church. In this document you affirm that you are willing to openly answer any who accuse or slander you, objecting to any crime, error, or heresy lodged against you. Of these things you are greatly defamed and accused before us, particularly with respect to the doctrine of Wyclif along with other teachings which are in opposition to the catholic faith and on this account you have desired a safe conduct to come. However, as it is our task to principally and mainly provide oversight and to look into these crafty foxes who go about seeking to destroy the Lord's vineyard, we therefore do cite by the tone of these representations, and summon you who are manifestly defamed and held suspect for this rash affirmation and for the teaching of definite errors. Within the space of fifteen days from the time to be calculated from the date of this document, five days are designated for the first term, five for the second, and the other five for the third, we mandate and determine according to canonical admonition and due warning that you must appear in the public sessions of the holy synod should one be convened on that day and if there is not then you must appear on the first day thereafter when a session is convened. According to the representations of your own writing, you shall answer to those things which any person or persons might object to or bring against you in the cause of the faith and you shall have and receive that which is required by justice. To the extent that lies within our ability, and as the catholic faith requires, we offer to you and declare a safe conduct against any violence (with the exception of justice itself). We declare that whether you appear or not, the process has been established and shall proceed against you by this sacred council either by its representative or representatives, and all things must be observed and maintained without consideration to contumacy or stubbornness on your part.

Given during the sixth session of the general council, on April 17, under the seal of the presidents of the four nations.

Grumpert Faber, notary of the German nation.

Hardt, vol. 4, p. 119 and cols. 686–687; and Mansi, vol. 27, col. 611.

Revocation of Jerome, Constance, September 23, 1415

I, Jerome of Prague, master of arts, knowing and certainly understanding the Catholic church and the Apostolic faith, do curse and renounce every heresy and especially with respect to that which I have previously been accused and defamed, and which in the past Jan Hus and John Wyclif held and taught in their works, treatises, and sermons to the people and clergy. For this cause the said Wyclif and Hus, along with their doctrines and errors, were condemned by this synod of Constance as heretics, and all of the said doctrine was condemned, especially particular articles expressed in the sentences and judgments passed against them by this sacred council.

Also I further give assent and agree with the holy Roman Church, with the Apostolic See, and with this sacred council. With my mouth and heart I profess in all respects, and all things, particularly with respect to the keys, sacraments, orders, offices, ecclesiastical censures, pardons, relics of the saints, ecclesiastical liberty, ceremonies, and everything else pertaining to the Christian religion, as the Roman Church, the Apostolic See, and this sacred council do profess. I especially hold that many of the said articles are notoriously heretical and have been condemned for a long time by the holy fathers. Some of them are blasphemous, others erroneous, some are offensive to the ears of the godly, and many of them are rash and seditious. As such, the aforesaid articles have recently been condemned by this sacred council. All Catholics have been forbidden hereafter to preach, teach, hold, or maintain any of the said articles under pain of anathema.

Moreover, I, the said Master Jerome, inasmuch as I have endeavored by means of the scholastic arts to persuade opinion concerning realities and universals, that one substance of the same species might signify many things subject under the same, and every one of them, as did Saints Ambrose, Jerome, Augustine, and likewise others, for the teaching thereof by a plain example, I described, as it were a certain triangular figure, which was called the Shield of Faith. Therefore to prevent any erroneous and wicked understanding which some might possibly gather thereof, I do say, affirm, and declare, that I did not make the said figure, neither did I name it the Shield of Faith, with the intent or purpose that I would extol or prefer the opinion of universals above the opposite opinion in such a manner that the Shield of Faith or an affirmation of it, was necessary in order for the Catholic faith to be defended or maintained. I would not personally or obstinately adhere to it. But the reason I referred to that figure by that name was to put forth an example, in the description of the triangle, that the divine essence consisted in three different persons, that is to say, the Father, the Son, and the Holy Ghost. I considered this article of the Trinity to be the main shield of faith and the foundation of Catholic truth.

Furthermore, so that it might be evident to everyone the causes for which I was reputed and thought to adhere to and approve of the said Jan Hus, I make it known to everyone by this representation, that when I heard him many times in his sermons and also in the schools, I believed that he was a very good man, and that he did not in any point contradict the traditions of our holy mother church or holy doctors. Inasmuch as when I was lately here in this city and the articles which I affirmed were shown to me, which had been condemned by the sacred council, at the first sight of them, I did not believe that they were his, or at the least not in that form. When I was told by certain famous doctors and masters of divinity that they were his articles, I demanded additional information and asked to have the books in his own handwriting shown to me wherein such things were said and where those articles were contained. When these books were shown to me, written in his own hand, which I knew as well as my own, I found that all of those articles were written in the same form in which they were condemned. Therefore, I do not unworthily judge or think of him and his doctrine along with those who adhere to them to be condemned by this sacred council as heretical and insane. All of this, on the basis of a pure mind and conscience, I do here pronounce and speak, being now fully and sufficiently informed of the previous sentences and judgments given by the sacred council against the doctrines of the said late John Wyclif and Jan Hus, and against their own persons, as a devout Catholic in all things, and by all things I do most humbly consent and agree.

Also I, the same aforesaid Jerome, having previously before the reverend fathers and lord Cardinals and reverend lord prelates and doctors and other venerable persons of this sacred council in this same place, freely and willingly declare and expound my intent and purpose among other things, speaking of the church, I made a threefold distinction. As I later perceived, it was understood by some, that I implied faith in the church triumphant. I do firmly believe that there is a blessed vision of God which excludes doubtful understanding and knowledge. And now I also do state, affirm, and declare, that it was never my intention to prove that there should be faith in this or knowledge far exceeding faith. And generally whatsoever I have said, either there or at any time before, I now most humbly submit myself to the determination of this sacred Council of Constance.

Moreover I do swear both by the holy Trinity and also by the most holy gospel that I will forever remain and persevere without doubt in the truth of the Catholic Church. I declare that whoever by their doctrine and teaching, contravenes this faith together with their teachings, shall be judged worthy of eternal damnation. If I myself at any time (God forbid that I should) presume to preach or teach contrary thereunto, I will submit myself to the severity of the canons, and be delivered to eternal pain and punishment. Whereupon I deliver up this confession and profession willingly before this sacred general council and have subscribed and written all these things with my own hand.

Mansi, vol. 27, fols. 791–793; Hardt, vol. 4, cols. 501–506; and Šmahel/Silagi, pp. 237–241.

Letter from Jerome to Lacek of Kravář, October 12, 1415

My services to you, first of all, dear noble lord and my special benefactor. I wish to inform you that I am alive and healthy in Constance. I hear that there is much excitement [a big storm] in Bohemia and Moravia because of the death of Master Hus, on the assumption that he was unjustly sentenced and brutally burned to death. Therefore I am writing this of my own free will as to my lord, so that you might know what to do. I beg by means of this letter, so that you may know that it is not as though somebody tried mightily to cause injustice to him. By my conscience what has been done to him is what had to be done. Do not think, my lord, that I write this because I am in trouble, forced by necessity, or that I have deserted him out of fear. I have been held in a rough prison and many great scholars have worked with me and they could not change my opinion. I did believe that injustice had been done to him. But when the articles were given to me for examination, for which he was vilified, I examined them very carefully and discussed them not just with one master. I came to the conclusion from those articles that some were heretical, some false, others prone to scandal and harm. But I also doubted that those articles were of the deceased, and I came to the conclusion that they were fragmentary and had been taken out of context and thereby the intended meaning had been changed. Since I was interested in his own books, the council gave me some books written in his own hand to examine. Together with the masters of the scriptures, I compared the articles for which he was burned to death with the books written in his own hand, and I found all of those articles to be in his books in that sense. Therefore I have to say justly that the decedent wrote many heretical and false things. And I, who was his friend and with my mouth had defended him everywhere, having found this out, not wanting to be the defender of these heresies, willingly rejected them as I have admitted before the entire council in more words. And now having too much to do, I could not write in more detail, but I think that hopefully with God's assistance I will soon write about everything concerning events with regard to myself and I will send this to Your Grace. And with this I am sending my compliments to your love. Written by my own hand, in Constance on the Thursday after the birth of the Mother of God.

Documenta, pp. 598–599; and Šmahel/Silagi, pp. 257–259.

Giacomo Balardi, Bishop of Lodi, Sermon against Jerome, Constance, May 30, 1416

Invoking the name of the Supreme Trinity, I came upon a text deserving to be expounded for the present purpose, namely: "He upbraided them with their unbelief and hardness of heart," in the last chapter of Mark and the gospel of the current octave.[1]

Most reverend fathers, orthodox lords, and other faithful Catholics. Since, in the words of Aurelius Augustinus, perverse and obstinate men are not to be met with light words but rather with harsh ones, as it often happens that when mild correction is ignored, a severe or bitter blow commands more attention: so he who is not convinced by kind words must be confuted more vigorously.[2] Wounds that cannot be healed by mild remedies must be cut away with pain, says Isidore in *De summo bono*.[3] Indeed we see that the toughest knot in wood can only be forced out with the toughest tool, says Ambrose.[4] The more pestilential the disease, the stronger the treatment that must be administered, and the deeper the wound, the more skillfully it must be bandaged. And as

---

1. Mark 16:14. Misprints: *incredulitarem* > *incredulitatem, occurentis* > *occurrentis*.

2. Not identified.

3. Isidore, *Sententiae* (*De summo bono*) 3:46:11, in *PL*, vol. 83, col. 716.

4. Ambrose on Matthew 21. I cannot identify the exact tool referred to, though the name *oppressorium* and the context indicate that it is one by which pressure or force is applied to a knot.

long as the hard iron does not readily conform to the mold, it is proper to subject it to fiercer fire and heavier hammer blows.

Therefore, Jerome, after seeing your enduring obstinacy, after noting your persistent defiance and hearing your last shameless reply, I certainly can say to you what is written in Isaiah 47: "I knew that thou art obstinate, and thy neck is an iron sinew, and thy brow brass."[5] But take heed that "An obstinate heart shall be laden with sorrows at the last" (Eccl. 3).[6]

Consider too, that though my reproof may sound dreadful to the ear, yet a charitable delight in mercy dwells within it, and as I may not spare you by the words of my mouth, so I intend to rebuke your faults with goodwill and gentle charity. By no means should one assent to evils, that they be approved, nor ignore them, that they remain hidden. So do not think that I wish to heap affliction upon one who is already afflicted or to stir up the fire with the sword. My purpose is not to goad a second time him who kicks back, or to crush the unbeliever, or to confute the stubborn, but that you may more clearly recognize the charity with which you are rebuked, the love with which you are censured, the long-suffering and gentle kindness with which you have been and will be exhorted and desired to see reason,[7] for this reason I have selected my text which I repeat in the same words: "He upbraided them with their unbelief and hardness of heart," as above.

As this holy Council has rebuked[8] the unbelief of those treacherous men, namely John Wyclif and Jan Hus and their followers, so it rebukes your own unbelief and hardness of heart. Your unbelief is bad, as it has nourished heresy and perfidy. But far worse is your hardness of heart, as it demonstrates your obstinacy and stubbornness. Error reveals the unbeliever, but obstinacy convicts the heretic, for those who defend their opinion, false though it be, without stubbornness or obstinacy and are prepared to mend their ways are in no way to be counted heretics; only those who, despising the opinions of the fathers of old, contend that they can fully defend the perfidy of their errors, prepared to die rather than be corrected, these are called heretics. The words are those of Augustine against Faustus. Nobody is named merely from a tendency, but according to their fully formed character. Hence not every

---

5. Isaiah 48:4.

6. Ecclesiasticus 3:27.

7. *recipisceres* > *resipisceres* (misprint).

8. *exprobavit* > *exprobravit* (misprint).

unbeliever is a heretic, but only he who errs obstinately, since error in reason is the beginning of heresy, but obstinacy and willful hardness of heart are its fulfillment. To err and to deceive are the condition of human frailty. Hence we see that those who possess, I do not say a better or more healthy, but a more acute intelligence are quicker than others to fall into foolishness, since our intelligence by nature is not idle, and so when it strays from the path of truth it plunges into the labyrinth of error. To understand otherwise than is the case is human temptation. But to be excessively enamored of one's own opinion, despising the decisions of the sacred fathers and ending up in the sacrilege of heresy, is the obstinacy of the devil, says Augustine against the Donatists.[9]

Thus error and unbelief are alike to be reproved, but hardness of heart is to be more severely condemned. He who pardons present guilt bequeaths vice to the future, and he harms the good who spares the bad, says Seneca the moralist.[10] Human wickedness would spread without limit, leading to our destruction, like putrefaction, unless dried up by medical intervention. So evil continues growing as long as it lasts, and prompt correction of sin is the healing good, says the blessed Gregory. Sin unless washed away by penitence will drag us into greater sin by its own weight.

Evil must be confronted, that which leads others to sin[11] must be confronted, that wickedness unpunished should not thrive with the passage of time, and iniquity should not gain strength in secret, but rather that ignorance should be instructed by due correction and obstinacy and hardness of heart be quelled by severe discipline. Manifest crimes are not to be expiated by secret correction, but public sinners must be openly convicted, so that as they are brought to reason by public reprimand, those who have erred by imitating them may be corrected. By rebuking one, many are corrected. And it is better that one guilty one be punished for the good of many, than that many be endangered by the impunity of one, as Gregory says (*Registrum*) and Isidore (*De summo bono*, III).

Therefore heretics are to be publicly extirpated, lest they bring others to ruin by their evil example, false doctrine, and pernicious influence. If they despise faith, the purifier of hearts, what can unbelievers do with their understanding of the subtlest arguments about the nature of our mind, except be damned by

---

9. Augustine, *De Baptismo contra Donatistas*, Lib. II Cap. 5, in *PL*, vol. 43, cols. 129–130.

10. Though widely quoted in the form *bonis nocet quisquis malis pepercit*, I have been unable to substantiate the attribution to Seneca.

11. The phrase appears to refer to the biblical "stumbling block," i.e., the σκάνδαλον.

the witness of their own understanding? There are those, says Gregory, who discovering more by thought than they can comprehend, burst out in wrong-headed dogmas, and forgetting to be humble followers of the truth become teachers of error. So just as true and learned simplicity is to be approved, so cunningly concocted falsehood must be rebuked, which entangles men in its errors and lays snares of deception by ornate language.

While every unbeliever must be deservedly rebuked for his perfidy, yet it is most important to consider in what matters and how far he has strayed and how easily he is corrected, or how obstinately he seeks to defend his error. Unbelief, when it accepts correction, deserves to be pardoned. But stubbornness and obstinacy can only be punished by utter extermination. Let no one then be presumptuously stubborn and contumacious in his heart, let no one be confident in his own vain fancy. That obstinacy is of the Devil which commits its own life for a certainty, and that hope is deceptive which hopes to be saved amid the fuel of sin. Victory is doubtful, fighting amid enemy arms, and salvation is impossible, surrounded by flames yet not to be burnt.

He is over hasty who rushes in where he has seen others fall, and reckless who is not struck with fear when others perish. A fault defended is doubled. And he piles sin on sin, who shamelessly and obstinately defends misdeeds. Hardness of heart is therefore to be detested, above all when it is not healed by contrition, nor softened by devotion, nor moved by prayer, which resists threats and is strengthened by blows. Hence he is inexcusably guilty and fatally criminal who refuses the remedy of repentance and will not reject his pride.[12]

Among human errors there are two which are too hard to be tolerated: presumption before the truth is known, and once it is known, presumptuous defense of falsehood. As unbelief is born of pride, so hardness of heart is nourished by its own presumption. No presumptuous man will confess his fault, because he does not believe himself guilty. Even if he sees it, he will not suffer it to be thought or shown that he has erred. Most damnable, therefore, is a presumptuous pride and a proud presumption: where it is, justice is not, for it will arrogate to itself a fictitious justice and will not cease to be proud of its knowledge.

---

12. *Praesumptio, superbia, cupiditas,* and *sciendi* were intellectual sins recognized by mainstream medieval thought. See Edward Peters, "*Libertas inquirendi* and the *vitium curiositatis* in Medieval Thought," in *La Notion de liberté au moyen âge. Islam, Byzance, Occident,* ed. George Makdisi, Dominique Sourdel, and Janine Sourdel-Thomine (Paris: Les belles lettres, 1985), pp. 91–98.

Jerome, I fear lest that great presumption and that high opinion which you entertain of yourself be the cause of your utter ruin. Here is the hidden precipice, here is your labyrinth of error, these things will procure the doom of your obstinacy. Though you are a learned man and have been a teacher, yet I think you have been deceived by your excessive presumption. Your error has prepared a multifarious stairway to error.

I have purposed to smite you, Jerome, on both cheeks, though always with that fitting charity which heals while it wounds and soothes while it pierces. Therefore, do not turn your face toward me like a flinty rock, but rather in accord with the teaching of the gospel: whoever shall smite you on one cheek, turn to him the other also. I will smite you, therefore, and would that I might heal you. You ought to be softened by the recollection of the crimes you have committed or by the sight of such kindness on the part of your judges.

In the first place, it is not another's shit that I cast in your face, but your own, that you may see and repent of your crimes. Would that your obstinacy could so be mollified.

Mark, I pray you, my Catholic lords, how great was the presumptuous temerity of these men, I speak of Jan Hus and Jerome, that such mean, plebeian, low men of unknown birth should dare to stir up all the noble kingdom of Bohemia, to incite the barons and princes to strife and schism, call out the soldiers, overturn ancient and worthy governments, call up armies, divide peoples, foment bitter dissension among the citizens, lead gangs, keep henchmen, keep men in arms, commit murders or have them committed, plunder churches and profane altars. Oh happy kingdom of Bohemia, had that man not been born! How utterly detestable it is that men of the church, under some pretext of sanctity, who should be devoted to God, who should pray day and night, pray for the sins of the people whose goods they consume, spend all their time in prayer, do not shrink to vex the courts of kings, princes, and barons, to stir up disputes, to overturn the decrees of the kingdoms at will, to devote themselves to quarrels.

Of how great evils was the presumption of those two uncouth provincials the root! How many have been killed on either side, how many duly ordained clergy have been forced out, how many exiled, how many driven away with violence, how many robbed, how many beaten, how many killed, how many buried, how many churches laid waste, how many altars profaned, how many monasteries destroyed?

Even if you wished to pursue bad clergy, Jerome, then why did you afflict the good? The example you quoted yesterday, Jerome, I would pray you repeat today and say, "Woe is me, my mother, that thou hast born me a man of strife and a man of contention to the whole earth!"[13] May you not recall with revulsion those holy Carthusians of Prague, whose prior you caused to be driven out and monastery plundered, to the ruin of your souls?[14]

I have smitten you on one cheek, turn to me the other, and mark well the gentleness of the lords your judges. Some if not all men know, and I too should know, the rigorous method that should be observed in relation to those convincingly reported to be heretics. They are to be diligently sought out, arrested, and committed to close prison. Second, accusations are to be received against them and the testimony of any witnesses admitted against them, even that of infamous persons such as usurers, bawds, and public prostitutes. They are to be sworn on oath to tell the truth. Should they fail to do so, they are to be tortured on the rack[15] and other instruments of torture. None may be admitted to see them except in extraordinary circumstances, and they should not be heard in public. If they renounce, they are to be mercifully pardoned. But if they persist, they are to be condemned and handed over to the secular arm.

You have certainly not been treated with such rigor as this, though universally notorious for your heresies. Not Arius, not Sabellius, not Faustus, not Nestorius, not any other heretic was ever so notorious during his lifetime as you were. The infamy of your heresy has spread through England, all Bohemia, France, Hungary, Poland, Lithuania, Russia, Italy, and all of Germany. You were arrested, as such men should be, and brought before the Council, and through urgent necessity alone imprisoned. In regard to this imprisonment my most reverend in Christ fathers and lords cardinals of Ursinis, Aquileia, Cambrai, and Florence personally inquired whether you could be accommodated more comfortably elsewhere. And had they not feared you would escape, for you have done so more than once, any one of them would have willingly received you not only in his home, but at his table and in his chamber.

None but respectable witnesses were admitted to testify against you, masters of sacred theology, doctors of canon law, numerous bachelors, curates of

---

13. Jeremiah 15:10.

14. The first reference to "you" in this sentence is singular, while the second "you" is plural.

15. Suspected misprint: *aculeo > eculeo*. Otherwise, *aculeo* is "with a spike."

great churches and other venerable men, who gave sworn testimony in your presence, and you found no fault with any of them. Most of the accusations brought against you were proven to be true.

You were not tortured. Would that you had been, for had you been so humbled you might have rejected your errors, the pain would have opened your eyes which your guilt had closed. Whoever wished to come and console you, all were allowed. Remember how kindly,[16] how gently the most reverend lords cardinals and many others exhorted you, pitying you from their hearts. How many times did they implore you to come to your senses?

Several public hearings were granted to you at your own wish. Would that they had been refused! I fear those hearings rendered you excessively audacious.

By those hearings six mischiefs were inflicted on you by yourself. In the first place, you stopped the mouths of all those who kindly wished to excuse you, who said in your defense,[17] moved by affection, that you were deranged, demented, foolish, or crazy. But, pray, who but a madman would call you crazy or deranged, a man who could plead with such elegance and speak with such precision? Those who excused you had better keep silent now and say no more, for your speech betrays you.[18]

The second mischief that you did yourself in your hearings was that you did not deny that you are guilty of rebellion and have brought about murders.

The third was that you attempted to prove that those who bore witness against you in many narratives and lengthy examples had lied, yet the uniqueness of your own testimony proves that what they said against you was the veriest truth.

The fourth was this, that by claiming that the testimony brought against you did not amount to demonstrative proof, you showed that you cannot distinguish between logic and rhetoric. You must know that demonstration in logic differs in its nature from demonstration in rhetoric. Logic demonstrates by absolute propositions and expository syllogisms, rhetoric by praise and invective. A natural philosopher demonstrates by other means than an ethical and moral philosopher. Hence a canon or civil lawyer demonstrates by pleadings

---

16. Misprint: *benique* > *benigne*.

17. Misprint: *de defenderent* > *te defenderent*.

18. Matthew 26:73.

and proofs alone. Thus the case against you is demonstrated by legal, proven pleadings fully adequate to establish the truth. I ask you, who could demonstrate more against you than you have demonstrated against yourself! You alone are your enemy, you alone are your adversary, you alone are in conflict with yourself. We all pity you, you alone are fully proved cruel to yourself. All good men stand by you, you alone are turned against yourself.

The fifth was that you did not shrink from praising Jan Hus after having previously anathematized him under oath. I ask you, what impudence, what audacity, what shamelessness could induce you to raise up this man who was a rebel and a heretic and who brought about murders?

I remember you once saying that he was neither a drunkard nor a fornicator. But what is the use, my godly lords, of abstaining from drink and being intoxicated with wrath, pride, and contention? What is the use of fasting with the guts and wallowing in hunting? Abstaining from food and straying in sin? (86. dist. 12; *Quid prodest*).[19] What is it to save the wine and not shrink from shedding blood?

What is it to avoid getting drunk on wine but to spatter blood shed with the teeth, to pointlessly tear the flesh of one's neighbors and destroy them by ceaseless persecution?

You said he was not a fornicator. You might as well have said he was not a heretic. There is no worse fornication than that which he practiced against the Catholic faith.

The sixth and last was that in this public hearing you condemned yourself by your own testimony. Would that you had kept silent! What could tell more forcibly against you than your own testimony, which proved you a liar, a perjurer, nay, a madman and a relapsed heretic, in that you repudiated the holy oath you had sworn and so fell into worse and more serious error?

Wherefore this holy Council, on which all earthly authority is conferred, will judge you according to your ways (Ezekiel 7), even though he who does not believe is condemned already (John 3). In judgment or rebuke, as Seneca says (*De clemencia ad Neronem*), the law has three objects which the ruler or judge should aim at: the correction of him who is punished, or the deterrence of others by his punishment, or the safety of others through the evil being removed.

---

19. D.86 c.12, *Quid prodest*, in Friedberg, vol. 1, col. 300.

Therefore this holy Council proposes now to pass judgment upon you. Would that you would renounce your folly and quell the stubbornness of your heart! But you will be judged according to the rules of equity and the sanctions of the sacred canons. And although you should refuse, far be it!, to be converted, yet the Council must render judgment so as to convert the unbelieving to wisdom, that is, to prepare a people perfect for God through the holy knowledge of faith. Which may he happily grant to this holy Council who is the just judge of the living and the dead, Jesus Christ, blessed forever. Amen.

FRB, vol. 8, pp. 494–500.

APPENDIX II

Accounts of Jerome's Death

On Saturday following the ascension of the Lord, May 30, the Council convened a solemn session, with miters and copes, and Mass was said. The lord Cardinal-Bishop of Ostia presided over the condemnation of Jerome. Following Mass and the usual prayers, the previously mentioned Bishop of Lodi preached a fine sermon, using the text from the Gospel of the Lord's ascension: "he rebuked them for unbelief and their hardness of heart." He spoke with much eloquence urging Jerome to repent and thereby save his soul. After the sermon, the patriarch of Constantinople read out Jerome's declaration which he had made before the Council on September 23 of the previous year. He said that Jerome had later revoked the statement and had relapsed into heresy. With a loud voice, Jerome admitted that he had revoked it, just as he had the previous Wednesday. He went on to make many allegations, arguing as he had before, that he had been defeated by false witnesses, hatred, and lies. He advanced Paul and Christ as examples who had been similarly overcome by the Jews. At length he generally confessed the Catholic faith and refused to recant anything. He asserted that Hus had been called a heretic because he preached against the pride of the priesthood. The cardinal of St. Mark answered that he should not make up such basis for the condemnation of Hus. . . . The patriarch of Constantinople read the sentence against Jerome. . . . Following the reading of the sentence, a paper crown on which were painted demons was given to Jerome, who received it with boldness and put it on his head, announcing that "Christ wore a crown of thorns." He was then turned over to the secular authorities, taken to the fire, and burned.

Fillastre, pp. 61–62.

On Sunday prior to the day of the Holy Cross, 1416, a great session of spiritual people and men of learning convened with the whole Council. Duke Ludwig of Bavaria and Heidelberg participated as our lord King had entrusted to him the business of the Council. After the ringing of the bells, initially following Matins and then again early before Mass, and again following Mass, they sang the solemn Mass of the Holy Trinity. After this, Jerome the heretic [*Jeronimus der kätzer*] was brought in and an English master of theology preached. Following the sermon, the masters of theology demonstrated that Jerome had preached and taught errors and had refused to renounce those errors and would not write a letter to Bohemia. In consequence he was condemned as a heretic and handed over to Duke Ludwig of Bavaria who ordered that he be taken out and burned. So they led him out, as they did Hus, but not as many armed men accompanied them because a majority of the Czechs and laity who had been at Constance had already departed with the lord King, and others had already gone home. As he was led out of the city, he recited the creed and once outside the city he sang the liturgy and then said the creed again. He was burned on the same spot where Hus was and just as had been the case with Hus, no one heard his confession. He endured considerably longer in the fire than Hus because he was a larger and stronger man—He also wore a large, thick, black beard. He screamed horribly, and after he was burned, they threw the ashes along with everything else into the Rhine. Many educated men were sad that he had to die for he was a greater scholar than Hus. He was a master of arts in Prague, in the city of London in England, at Cologne, and in Erfurt.

Thomas Martin Buck, ed., *Chronik des Konstanzer Konzils 1414–1418 von Ulrich Richental* (Ostfildern: Jan Thorbecke Verlag, 2010), pp. 67–68.

[Jerome] was led from the cathedral to execution and death. As he passed through the door of the church he started to sing. In a loud voice with great joy he lifted his eyes to heaven and sang "I believe in one God" in the manner that it is sung in church. As he went on his way he sang the entire litany. At the city gate which leads to the Gottlieben he sang "You are happy, o holy virgin." When that song was finished and he had reached the place of execution where previously Master Jan Hus had suffered death, he knelt before the stake which had been made ready for Jerome in the same manner as that for Master Jan Hus. He said a sorrowful prayer at some length. The executioner lifted him from the ground before he had finished praying and removed all of his clothes until he was naked. They placed a cloth of linen around his loins and tied him to the stake. The stake was a thick post which had been planted in the ground. Standing on the ground, he was fastened to the stake with ropes and iron chains. As they piled the wood around him, he began to sing "Hail, festive day." When he had finished that hymn he loudly chanted the creed (*Credo in unum deum*) to the end. Then he addressed the people in the German language saying, "Dear children, as I have just now sung this is what I believe and not anything else. The creed is what I believe. I shall die now because I refused to agree with the synod that Master Jan Hus was properly and justly condemned by the Council. I know very well that he was a true preacher of the gospel of Jesus Christ." They piled the wood up to the top of his head and placed his clothing on the pile. With a torch the wood was set on fire. As it began to burn he sang in a loud voice "Into your hands O Lord, I commend my spirit." When that was finished and the fire was blazing fiercely he spoke in the Czech language, saying, "Lord God, Father Almighty, have mercy on me and pardon my sin. You know how much I loved your truth." Then his voice was silenced by the fierce flames and thereafter he could not be heard even though his mouth and lips continued to move quickly as though he were praying or speaking to himself. When his body was burning, as well as his beard, on account of the great heat, a large blister about the size of an egg appeared on his body. He remained on fire, alive, suffering martyrdom, for about as long as it takes to walk slowly from St. Clement's across the bridge to St. Mary the Virgin. This was on account of his superior strength. After he died in the ferocious fire, they brought his bed, blankets, clothes, hood, and other belongings from the prison and burned them to ashes in the fire. After the fire burned out, they took the ashes in a wagon to the Rhine River which was flowing nearby and threw them in.

Anonymous, in Hardt, vol. 4, cols. 770–771.

After his revocation and some public penance which was appropriate, [Jerome] relapsed. On account of this silly and, I might say, stubborn act, the holy synod condemned him having decided to cut him off from the body of the holy Christian religion as a dreadful and rotten limb. Hence, the sentence was passed against him. He placed a disgraceful crown, a horrible crown, a depraved crown, upon his own head. He then cried out, "My God, Christ, was made to wear a crown of thorns for me. I am willing to wear this crown for his glory." After this, he knelt for a time and then rose up chanting "I believe in one God" to the end. As he was led to the stake, he walked to this ordeal singing all along the way, "Mother of Christ and sweet virgin" [*Christi [mater et] virgo dulcissima*]. During his last agony, this miserable man was pitiful to all because of his downfall but he did not have pity for himself. He was led to the place where the flames would be started. He was stripped of his clothing and the fire was lit. As he stood naked within the flames and as the fire grew hot he started to sing "Into your hands Lord, I commend my spirit." While he recited "You have redeemed me" the smoke and the fire took his unhappy soul away. In this manner that miserable heretic yielded up his wretched soul to the abyss and submitted it to be burned forever.

Dietrich Vrie, *Historia concilii constantiensis*, in Hardt, vol. 1, fol. 202.

Letter from Poggio Bracciolini to Leonardo Bruni, Constance, May 30, 1416

Poggio to his Leonardo Aretino sends greetings. While I was spending some days at the baths, I wrote a letter from there to our friend Nicolas, which, I imagine, you have read. A few days after my return from there to Constance, there was the trial of Jerome, a man accused and publicly arraigned for heresy. I have undertaken to give you a report of it here, both because of its intrinsic interest and, even more, because of the eloquence and learning of the man. I must confess that I have never seen anyone who argued a case, especially one where his life was at stake, with eloquence as near to that of the ancient writers whom we so greatly admire. It was astonishing to hear his diction and style and logic, to see his countenance and expression and the confidence he showed in answering his opponents. Indeed, the way he managed his whole defense was such that one might well grieve to see so lofty an intellect and such outstanding gifts put to the service of heretical studies, if, indeed, the charges brought against him were true. But it is not for me to decide so grave a question. I submit to the judgment of those who are considered wiser. Do not suppose, however, that in describing the conduct of the orator, I am also going to relate the case to you in detail; that would be a long task and would take days. I shall just describe certain striking points by which you may see the great learning of this man.

Since there were many persons united in accusing Jerome of heresy, it was demanded that he should publicly reply to their various accusations one by one. He had been brought into the meeting, but, when he was told to answer, he refused for a long time to do so, claiming he should first be allowed to speak generally in his own defense, before replying to the evil spoken of him by his enemies. They should, he said, first listen properly to him plead his case, and then he would come to the testimony gathered against him by his rivals. But when this condition was denied to him, he rose up in the midst of the assembly: "What outrage is this," he said, "that you, have listened steadily for three hundred and fifty days to my enemies and accusers while I lay in dreadful prisons, in dirt and filth and excrement, in shackles, in dire want of everything, should now refuse even to listen to me for one hour? In effect, your ears have been open to them alone, and while they have had a long time to persuade you that I am a heretic, an enemy of the faith of God, a persecutor of churchmen, no opportunity has been given me to defend my cause, so that you have prejudged me in your own minds as a wicked man, before you could know what kind of man I am. Yet," as he continued, "you are men, not gods; not eternal, but mortal, you are liable to err, to make mistakes, to be led astray, to be lured into evil. Wise men are called the light of this world, of this earth. Most surely, then, you ought to take all possible pains and to fear nothing in order to be sure you don't do some foolish thing or something not just. I am only a little man, myself, whose life is here at stake, but I do not speak for myself alone, well knowing I am only mortal; the truly terrible thing to me is that men of your great wisdom should proceed against me in a manner outside the bounds of equity, this is terrible not because of my particular case so much as because of the danger in such a precedent."

As he was skillfully expounding these and other points, the shouting and murmuring of many people interrupted his speech, for the decree ran that he should first reply to the charges of error made against him, and then be given the opportunity to speak as long as he liked. The individual accusations were read from the chair, therefore, and he was then asked whether he could refute the charges confirmed by the testimony of many witnesses. He responded with amazing coolness, and defended himself. He set forth not one idea unworthy of a good man; indeed, if he thought as he spoke, not only was there no just cause for putting him to death, but he had not given the slightest offense. He said the charges were all false, all wickedly trumped up by his enemies. When they said, among other things, that he spoke evil of the Apostolic See, opposed the Roman pope, stood against the cardinals, persecuted the prelates, and hated the clergy of the Christian religion, he arose and said in a voice of prayer with his arms outstretched: "Where, then, shall I turn, fathers of the Council? Whose help shall I implore? To whom shall I offer my pleas for mercy? To whom shall I present my testimony? To you? But these, my persecutors, have already alienated your minds from any concern for my welfare, for they have made me out to be the enemy of all who are judges here. It has been supposed, in fact, that if the charges against me should seem unsound, your judgment will still be swayed by the idea that, as they lyingly say of me, I am the adversary and common enemy of all. If you believe their words, therefore, there is no hope of my life."

He persuaded many people by his wit, for he used sarcasm, and he often made them laugh in the midst of this sad occasion by his mocking of their reproofs. When he was asked what he thought of the sacrament, he replied, "Before consecration, bread; in and after consecration, the true body of Christ; and the rest according to faith." Then they said, "But they say you have asserted that bread remains even after consecration." Then he said, "Bread does remain— at the baker's." A certain member of the order of Preachers bitterly inveighed against him. "Silence," he said, "you hypocrite." Another said he would swear against Jerome by his conscience, and to him, he answered, "There is the safest way to lie."

Since it was impossible, because of the multitude of the charges and the gravity of the matter, to dispose of the whole case in one day, it was postponed to the day after next; then, after the list with each single crime was read and many witnesses had sworn to them, he arose: "Since you have so carefully heard out my adversaries, it is only reasonable that you should hear me and what I have to say with like patience." In spite of the opposition of many persons, he was then given an opportunity to speak, and he first addressed himself to God and prayed that he might be given such thoughts and such powers of speech as would conduce to his welfare and the salvation of his soul.

"I know," he proceeded then to say, "that learned scholars, and excellent men as well, have often been persecuted for their virtues, hounded by false witnesses, and condemned by wicked judges." He then began with Socrates, unjustly condemned by his contemporaries, yet a man who, when he could have escaped from prison, did not wish to do so, for he had mastered the fear of the two things that most terrify men, imprisonment and death. He called to mind also the imprisonment of Plato, the torments of Anaxagoras and Zeno, and the wicked condemnation of many other pagans; Rutilius's banishment, Boethius's death likewise, and others whom Boethius mentions and who were wrongfully put to death. After this he turned to Hebrew examples, and first pointed out that Moses, the liberator of his people, the giver of the laws, had often been calumniated by his followers, who called him a seducer and an enemy of the people; Joseph, before this, was sold by his brothers out of envy; afterward, on a groundless suspicion, he was thrown into prison. He also enumerated Isaiah, Daniel, and almost all the prophets, besieged by wicked judgments made upon them and treated both as rebels against God and as sowers of sedition. He here alluded to the judgment passed on many more who, though most holy persons, were overthrown by unjust sentences and decisions. Coming to John the Baptist and to Our Savior, he said that all are agreed these were condemned by false witnesses and by the false decisions of their judges; later Stephen was killed by the college of priests; all the apostles, too, were condemned to death as being, not the good men they were in fact, but seditious agitators, rebels against the gods and doers of wicked deeds. He said it was evil for a priest unjustly to condemn another, yet it had been done; more evil still for an assembly of priests, but he showed it had happened; most wicked for a council of priests, yet he showed that this too had occurred. These things he expounded with skill, and he aroused great expectations in all of his hearers.

Now, since the whole case hung upon the testimony of witnesses, he fully explained why one should put no faith in these witnesses who spoke, in fact, not for the truth's sake, but to give vent to hate, malevolence, and all kinds of spite. The causes of their hatred he set forth so clearly that there was no need for further explanation. The story seemed so likely that, but for the matter of faith, there was indeed little reason to put any credence in their testimony. The minds of all the hearers were moved, and they were inclined to show mercy. He had brought out in his discourse that he had come to the council of his own free will with the hope of clearing himself. He had set forth the story of his life and his studies, showing that he was responsible and virtuous; he had also asserted that, in matters of faith, the learned and most holy men of ancient times were accustomed to disagree sometimes, not in order to harm the faith, but in order to find out the truth. Thus had [Saints] Augustine and Jerome held, not merely different but directly contradictory views, without any suspicion of heresy.

Everyone was now hoping that he would proceed to clear himself by retracting the objectionable points in his teaching or that he would now ask pardon for his errors, but he would not admit he had erred nor did he wish to disassociate himself from the wicked falsehoods uttered by others, rather he fell to praising John Hus, who had recently been condemned to the stake, and he called that man good, just, and holy, and his death entirely undeserved; he also said he was ready himself to submit to a like punishment with a strong and constant spirit, to yield to his enemies and to the witnesses who had lied shamelessly, who, however, would have to render an account of the things they had said when they came before God and would not be able to deceive Him. Great was the sorrow of the spectators, for they were hoping to see a man of such extraordinary character saved, had he shown good will. Since he insisted, however, on maintaining his opinions, he seemed to be courting death; praising John Hus, he said that he had never held any belief opposed to the Church of God, but had opposed clerical abuses, the pride, luxury, and pomp of the prelates. As the patrimony of the church belonged first to the poor, then to the hospitals, and lastly to the building of churches, it had seemed wrong to that good man that it was spent on prostitutes and companions, on food for horses and dogs, on the cult of fashion, and on other things unworthy of the religion of Christ.

The clearest indication of his gifts was this, however, that even when his speech was interrupted again and again by various voices, and some people opposed him by seizing on various statements of his, he struck back at all alike and made them either blush or fall silent. When the murmurs swelled, he silenced the crowd, sometimes by shouting reproof, and then he would continue his speech, imploring and pleading with them to permit him to speak, when they were not willing to hear any more. He shrank back from none of the attacks, but showed a firm and intrepid spirit. The occasion also exhibited marvelously what a memory he had, for he had been three hundred and forty days in the depths of a filthy dungeon and a dark one, the harshness of which he complained of himself, while declaring that, as becomes a man of fortitude, he complained not of this but of being undeservedly persecuted, and he marveled at men's inhumanity toward himself, for he had been put in a place so dark he could not read or even see. I omit the anxiety of mind by which he must have been tortured every day and which might well have blotted out all his memory; yet the fact is he cited so many learned and most wise authorities in support of his opinions, called on so many doctors of the church in presenting his argument, that it might have been enough and more than enough if he had spent all that time studying works of wisdom in leisure and perfect peace. His voice was mellow, open, and strong, and had a certain dignity; his gestures served to express indignation or to move pity, though he was not trying to ask for or arouse the latter. He stood fearless, intrepid, not merely disdaining death but positively courting it, so that you might have said this is another Cato.

This was a man to remember! I do not praise him for holding some opinions contrary to those the church has established, but I admire his learning, his wide knowledge, his eloquence, the elegance of his speech, and his wit in reply; yet I fear that he was given all these gifts by nature for his own destruction. Since two days were given him to repent, many men of great learning went to him to try to change his mind, among them the cardinal of Florence, who hoped to turn his thoughts to the right way. But as he pertinaciously persisted in his errors, he was condemned by the council and burned in the fire.

He went to his death with a cheerful face and open countenance; he did not fear the fire, either as a torture or as a means of death. No Stoic ever showed so constant a mind when death struck him down as sharply as ever he had courted it eagerly. When he came to the place of execution, he took off his own clothes, then, bowing on bended knees, he adored the stake to which he was to be tied; he was tied naked to the stake with wet ropes and a chain; quite heavy wood mixed with chaff was piled around him up to his chest; then when the flames shot up he began to sing a certain hymn, which smoke and fire hardly interrupted. But one thing most clearly showed his strength of spirit: when the executioner started to light the fire behind him so that he might not see it, he said to him, "Come here, light the fire before my eyes, for had I feared it at all, I would never have arrived at this place, which I had the power to avoid."

Thus perished this man, in all but his faith, a wonderful man. I saw the death and I beheld every action. Whether he acted as he did for treason or from stubbornness, the death of the man you might have described from a text in philosophy. I have told you a long story to describe a swift action, for, as I had nothing to do, I wished to do something and to tell you a story a little like something out of the histories of antiquity. For the great Mutius did not give his hand to be burned so confidently as this man gave his whole body; nor did Socrates drink the poison so willingly as this man underwent burning. But enough of this, put aside my words if I have been rather lengthy. The matter, however, called for a still longer account; yet I do not want to be too wordy. Good-bye, my delightful Leonardo.

Written at Constance on the 30th of May, the day on which Jerome suffered his punishment.

Poggio, vol. 2, pp. 157–163; Tomaso de Tonneli, ed., *Poggii Epistolae*, vol. 1, pp. 11–20; and Renee Neu Watkins, "The Death of Jerome of Prague: Divergent Views," *Speculum* 42 (January 1967): 121–124. Watkins is reproduced here with minor alterations.

Bibliography

WORKS OF JEROME OF PRAGUE

Disputatio Magistri Blasii Lupi [Blažej Vlk] *contra Magistrum Hieronymus de Praga in material universalium realium cum responsionibus eiusdem*, in Šmahel/Silagi, pp. 103–137.

Letter to Andreas Grillenberg (September 12, 1410), in Šmahel/Silagi, p. 249.

Letter to friends living in the college of Jerusalem in Prague (September 6, 1410), in Šmahel/Silagi, pp. 245–246.

Letter to King Sigismund (April 7, 1415), in Šmahel/Silagi, pp. 253–254.

Letter to Lord Lacek of Kravář (October 12, 1415), in Šmahel/Silagi, pp. 257–259.

Obiectiones Magistri Hieronymi de Praga contra quaestionem principalem Magistri Michaeli de Malenicz (1411), in Šmahel/Silagi, p. 192.

Professio Magistri Hieronymi de Praga, (September 11, 1415), in Šmahel/Silagi, pp. 225–229.

Quaestio de convertibilitate et suppositione terminorum, Šmahel/Silagi, pp. 73–82.

Quaestio de mundo archetypo in Šmahel/Silagi, pp. 163–188.

Quaestio de potentia materiae primae, in Šmahel/Silagi, pp. 141–159.

Quaestio de universalibus a parte rei, in Šmahel/Silagi, pp. 85–95.

Scutum fidei christianae, in Šmahel/Silagi, pp. 195–198.

Quaestio de veritatibus generalibus (1406), in Šmahel/Silagi, pp. 3–12.

Quaestio duplex de formis universalibus, in Šmahel/Silagi, pp. 15–51.

Quaestio et de universalibus extra signa, in Šmahel/Silagi, pp. 52–69.

Recommendatio artium liberalium, in Šmahel/Silagi, pp. 201–222.

Revocatio Magistri Hieronymi de Praga facta in concilio Constantiensi cum praeambulo (September 23, 1415), in Šmahel/Silagi, pp. 235–241.

PRIMARY SOURCES WITH A SPECIFIC FOCUS ON JEROME

Balardi, Giacomo. Sermon preached against Jerome, in *FRB*, vol. 8, pp. 494–500.

Czech barons, letter on behalf of Jerome, in Hardt, vol. 4, cols. 685–686.

De Vita Magistri Ieronomi de Praga, in *FRB*, vol. 8, pp. 335–338.

Disputatio anonymi magistri contra duplicem positionem Magistri Hieronymi de Praga, in Šmahel/Silagi, pp. 267–71.

Disputatio anonymi magistri contra positionem Magistri Hieronymi de Praga de universalibus praeter animam, in Šmahel/Silagi, pp. 275–282.

Goll, Jaroslav. *Vypsání o Mistru Jeronymovi z Prahy*. Prague: J. Otto, 1878.

Illyricus, Matthias Flacius, ed. [*HM*]. *Historia et monumenta Ioannis Hus atque Hieronymi Pragensis, confessorum Christi*, 2 vols. Nürnberg: Montanus and Neuberus, 1558, 2nd edition 1715.

Klicman, Ladislav, ed. [Klicman]. *Processus iudiciarius contra Jeronimum de Praga habitus Viennae a. 1410–1412*. Prague: Česká akademie císaře Františka Josefa pro vědy, slovesnost a umění, 1898.

Narratio de Magistro Hieronymo Pragensi, in *FRB*, vol. 8, pp. 339–350 [*Narratio de Magistro Hieronymo*].

Nedvědová, Milada, ed. *Hus a Jeronym v Kostnici*. Prague: St. nakl. Krásné lit., hudby a uměni, 1953.

Notae de concilio Constantiensi, in *FRB*, vol. 8, pp. 319–322.

Passio [of Jerome of Prague]. *FRB*, vol. 8, pp. 351–367.

Positio Magistri Iohannis de Francfordia contra Hieronymum de Praga, in Šmahel/Silagi, pp. 263–4.

Šmahel, František, and Gabriel Silagi, eds. *Magistri Hieronymi de Praga. Quaestiones, Polemica, Epistulae*. [Corpus Christianorum Continuatio Mediaeualis, vol. 222] Turnhout: Brepols, 2010.

Summons to Jerome to appear before the Council of Constance, in Hardt, vol. 4, cols. 686–687.

Vavřinec of Březová, *Historia Hussitica*, in *FRB*, vol. 5, pp. 329–534.

Wojciech Jastrzębiec, letter to Václav Králík, in *Documenta*, pp. 506–507.

MANUSCRIPTS

Basel, Universitätsbibliothek
VIII A 24

Prague, Castle Archive [Castle Archive]
B
C 20
C 38
C 39.4
C 63
C 65
C 66.1
C 66.2
C 106
C 114

D 14.2
D 47
D 48
D 49
D 51
D 53
D 54
D 62
D 74
D 88
D 106
D 109.2
D 112
D 114
E 19
K 7
K 13
N 6
N 12
N 50
N 58
N 59
O 7
O 13
O 17
O 29
O 50

PRAGUE, NATIONAL LIBRARY [NK]

1 B 17
1 C 25
1 E 32
1 F 18
III C 15
III G 9
III G 16
III G 28
IV F 23
IV G 14
IV G 15
IV H 12

IV H 17
V E 14
V E 28
V G 3
VI C 20a
VII A 18
VIII C 3
VIII E 3
VIII E 5
VIII E 7
VIII F 2
VIII G 13
X E 24
XI E 3
XII D 1
XIII E 7
XIV E 31
XVI A 17
XVII A 3
XVII A 5
XVII A 10
XVII A 16
XVII A 34
XVII D 21
XXIII C 124

PRAGUE, NATIONAL MUSEUM LIBRARY [KNM]

1 B a 8
1 B a 10
1 E 6
1 F 14
II B 4
II C 7
III B 10
III E 21
IV B 6
IV B 9
IV B 11
IV B 24
VIII D 35
VIII E 67

VIII G 13
XII D 14
XII D 28
XII F 14
XII F 25
XII F 28
XIII D 25
XIII E 15
XIII F 7
XIII F 23
XIV E 23
XVI C 4
XVIII A 5
XVIII C 73
25 E 17
36 F 19

OXFORD, BODLEIAN LIBRARY

e Musaeo 86

ROME, VATICAN LIBRARY

Ottobonianus 348

VIENNA, ÖSTERREICHISCHE NATIONALBIBLIOTHEK [ÖNB]

1401
3044
3062
4002
4131
4299
4314
4384
4488
4520
4704
4937
4941
5113
15492

PRINTED PRIMARY SOURCES

Aeneae Silvii, *Historia bohemica*, ed. Dana Martínková, Alena Hadravová, and Jiří Matl. Prague: Koniasch Latin, 1998.

Borový, Klement, and Antonín Podlaha, eds. *Libri erectionum Archidioecesis Pragensis saeculo XIV. et XV.*, 6 vols. Prague: Calve, 1875–1927.

Buck, Thomas Martin, ed. *Chronik des Konstanzer Konzils 1414–1418 von Ulrich Richental*. Ostfildern: Jan Thorbecke Verlag, 2010.

Cerretano, Giacomo [Cerretano]. *Liber gestorum*, in Finke, *Acta*, vol. 2, pp. 171–348.

Czech *Acta* of the Council of Constance, in *FRB*, vol. 8, pp. 247–318.

Daňhelka, Jiří, ed. *Husitské skladby budyšínského rukopisu*. Prague: Orbis 1952.

Denifle, Heinrich, and Émile Chatelain, eds. *Auctarium Chartularii Universitatis Parisiensis*, 6 vols. Paris: Didier, 1935–1964.

Dittrich, Anton, ed. *Monumenta historica universitatis Carolo-Ferdinandeae Pragensis*, 3 vols. Prague: Spurny, 1830–1848.

Emler, Josef, and František Tingl, eds. *Libri confirmationum ad beneficia ecclesiastica Pragensem per archidioecesim (1354–1436)*, 10 vols. Prague: Grégerianis, 1865–1889.

Eršil, Jaroslav, ed. *Acta summorum pontificum res gestas Bohemicas aevi praehussitici et hussitici illustranta*, 2 vols. Prague: Academia, 1980.

Fillastre, Guillaume [Fillastre]. *Gesta concilii Constanciensis*. In Finke, *Acta*, vol. 2, pp. 13–170.

Finke, Heinrich, ed. [Finke, *Acta*]. *Acta concilii Constanciensis*, 4 vols. Münster: Druck und Verlag der Regensbergschen Buchhandlung, 1896–1928.

Fojtíková, Jana. "Hudební doklady Husova kultu z 15. a 16. století: Přispěvek ke studiu husitské tradice v době předbělohorské." *Miscellanea Musicologica* 29 (1981): 51–142.

Foxe, John. *The Unabridged Acts and Monuments Online or TAMO*. HRI Online Publications, Sheffield, 2011. www.johnfoxe.org.

Friedberg, Emil, ed. [Friedberg]. *Corpus iuris canonici*, 2 vols. Leipzig: Tauchnitz, 1879–81.

Friedrich, Gustav. "Dekret Kutnohorský. Poměr jeho rukopisných textů." *Český časopis historický* 15 (1909): I–XII.

Glorieux, Palémon, ed. [Glorieux]. *Jean Gerson Oeuvres Complètes*, 10 vols. Tournai: Desclée, 1960–1973.

Goll, Jaroslav, et al., eds. [*FRB*]. *Fontes rerum bohemicarum*, 8 vols. Prague: Nákladem nadání Františka Palackého, 1873–1932.

Hardt, Hermann von der, ed. *Magnum oecumenicum constantiense concilium*, 7 vols. Frankfurt and Leipzig: C. Genschii, Helmestadi, 1699–1742.

Harth, Helene, ed. *Poggio Bracciolini Lettere*, 3 vols. Florence: Leo S. Olschki, 1984–1987.

Havránek, Bohuslav, ed. *Výbor z český literatury husitské doby*, 2 vols. Prague: Československá akademie věd, 1963–1964.

Herold, Vilém, ed. *Stanislai de Znojma De vero et falso*. Prague: Československá akademie věd, 1971.

Höfler, Konstantin von, ed. [Höfler]. *Geschichtschreiber der Husitischen Bewegung in Böhmen*, 3 vols. Vienna: Aus der Kaiserlich-Königlichen Hof- und Staatsdruckerei, 1856–1866.

Janov, Matěj. *Regulae veteris et novi testamenti*, 6 vols., ed. Vlastimil Kybal, Otakar Odložilík and Jana Nechutová. Prague and Innsbruck: Universitního Knihkupectví Wagnerova, 1908–1926; Munich: Oldenbourg, 1993.

Kadlec, Jaroslav, ed. "Synods of Prague and their Statutes 1396–1414." *Apollinaris* 54 (1991): 227–293.

Keussen, Hermann, "Regesten und Auszüge zur Geschichte der Universität Köln 1388–1559." *Mitteilungen aus dem Stadtarchiv von Köln* 15 (1918): 1–546.

Klener, Pavel, ed. *Miscellanea husitica Iohannis Sedlák*. Prague: Katolická teologická fakulta university Karlovy, 1996.

Kybal, Vlastimil. *M. Matěj z Janova. Jeho život, spisy a učení*. Brno: L. Marek, 2000.

Lahey, Stephen E., trans. *Wyclif: Trialogus*. Cambridge: Cambridge University Press, 2013.

Lhotsky, Alphons, and Karl Pivec, eds. *Dietrich von Niehem Viridarium imperatorum et regnum Romanorum*. Stuttgart: Hiersemann, 1956.

Loserth, Johann. "Beiträge zur Geschichte der Hussitischen Bewegung." *Archiv für österreichische Geschichte* 82 (1895): 327–418.

Mansi, Giovanni Domenico, ed. [Mansi]. *Sacrorum conciliorum nova, et amplissima collectio . . .*, 53 vols. Graz: Akademische Druck- u. Verlagsanstalt, 1960.

Migne, Jacques Paul, ed. *Patrologia Latina*, 221 vols. Paris: Migne/Garnier, 1844–1865.

Mladoňovice, Petr. [*Relatio*]. *Relatio de Mag. Joannis Hus causa. FRB*, vol. 8, pp. 25–120.

Müller, Ivan, ed. *Commentarius in I–IX capitula tractatus De universalibus Iohannis Wyclif Stephano de Palecz ascriptus*. Prague: Filosofia, 2009.

———. *Commentarius in De universalibus Iohannis Wyclif Stephano de Palecz ascriptus*. Prague: Filosofia, 2009.

Notae de concilio Constantiensi, in *FRB*, vol. 8, pp. 319–322.

Novotný, Václav, ed. *M. Jana Husi Korespondence a dokumenty*. Prague: Nákladem komise pro vydávání pramenů náboženského hnutí českého, 1920.

Palacký, František, ed. *Archiv český čili staré písemné památky české i moravské*, 6 vols. Prague: Kronberg and Riwnáče, 1840–1872.

———. [*Documenta*]. *Documenta Mag. Joannis Hus vitam, doctrinam, causam in constantiensi concilio actam et controversias de religione in Bohemia annis 1403–1418 motas illustrantia*. Prague: Tempsky, 1869.

———, ed. *Monumenta conciliorum generalium seculi Decimi Quinti*, 2 vols. Vienna: Typis C.R. Officinae Typographicae Aulae et Status, 1857–1873.

———. "Staři letopisové česti od r. 1378 do 1527." In *Scriptores rerum bohemicarum*, vol. 3. Prague: J.S.P., 1829.

————, ed. *Urkundliche Beiträge zur Geschichte des Hussitenkrieges*, 2 vols. Prague: Tempsky, 1873.

Podlaha, Antonín, ed. *Liber ordinationum cleri 1395–1416*, 2 vols. Prague: Pražská kapitula, 1910–1920.

Ryba, Bohumil, ed. *Promoční promluvy mistrů artistické fakulty Mikuláše z Litomyšle a Jana z Mýta na univerzitě Karlově z let 1386 a 1393*. Prague: Česká akademie věd a umění, 1948.

Ryšánek, František, et al., eds. [*MIHO*]. *Magistri Iohannis Hus, Opera Omnia*, 27 vols. Prague: Academia and Turnhout: Brepols, 1959–.

Sedlák, Jan, ed. [*ST*]. *Studie a texty k životopisu Husovu*, 3 vols. Olomouc: Matice Cyrilometodějská, 1914–1925.

Šimek, František, ed. *Staré letopisy české z vratislavského rukopisu novočeským pravopisem*. Prague: Historické spolku a společnosti Husova Musea, 1937.

Šimek, František, and Miloslav Kaňák, eds. *Staré letopisy české z rukopisu křižovnického*. Prague: Státní nakladatelství Krásné Literatury, Hudby a Umění, 1939.

Szyller, Sławomir, ed. "Johannis Buridani, Tractatus de differentia universalis ad individuum." *Przegląd Tomistyczny* 3 (1987): 137–178.

Tadra, Ferdinand, ed. *Soudní akta konsistoře pražské (Acta judiciaria consistorii Pragensis)*, 7 vols. Prague: Česká akademie císaře Františka Josefa, 1893–1901.

Tanner, Norman P., ed. *Decrees of the Ecumenical Councils*, 2 vols. London: Sheed & Ward, 1990.

Uiblein, Paul, ed. *Acta facultatis artium Universitatis Vindobonensis, 1385–1416*. Vienna: Böhlaus, 1968.

————, *Die Akten der Theologischen Fakultät der Universität Wien, 1396–1508*. Vienna: Verbrand der Wissenschaftlichen Gesellschaften Österreichs, 1978.

Walz, Dorothea von, ed. *Johannes von Frankfurt, Zwölf Werke des Heidelberger Theologen und Inquisitors*. Heidelberg: C. Winter Universitätsverlag, 2000.

Wyclif, John. [*JWLW*]. *John Wyclif's Latin Works*, 20 vols, in 33 parts. London: Wyclif Society, 1883–1922.

————. *Tractatus de universalibus*, ed. Ivan J. Mueller. Oxford: Clarendon, 1985.

SECONDARY SOURCES

Arendt, Paul. *Die Predigten des Konstanzer Konzils: Ein Beitrag zur Predigt-und Kirchengeschichte des ausgehenden Mittelalters*. Freiburg im Breisgau: Herder, 1933.

Bakker, J. J. M. Paul. "Réalisme et rémanence. La doctrine eucharistique de Jean Wyclif." In *John Wyclif: Logica, politica, teologia*, ed. Mariateresa Fumagalli Beonio Brocchieri and Stefano Simonetta, pp. 87–112. Florence: Sismel Edizioni del Galluzzo, 2003.

Bartoš, F. M. *Čechy v době Husově 1378–1415*. Prague: Jan Laichter, 1947.

————. "Kostnický proces M. Jeronýma Pražského." *Sborník historický* 4 (1956): 56–64.

————. "M. Jeronym Pražský." *Jihočeský sborník historický* 14 (1941), pp. 41–52.

———. "Několik záhad v životě Prokopa Holého." *Sborník historický* 8 (1961): 167–169.

———. "Paměti M. Jeronýma Pražského." *Lumír* 44 (1916), pp. 289–302.

———. "V předvečer Kutnohorského dekretu." *Časopis českého musea* 102 (1928), pp. 92–123.

———. *Z Husových a Žižkových*. Prague: B. Kočí, 1925.

Bartoš, František M., and Pavel Spunar. *Soupis pramenů k literární činnosti M. Jana Husa a M. Jeronyma Pražského*. Prague: Historický ústav ČSAV, 1965.

Bejczy, István. "*Tolerantia*: A Medieval Concept." *Journal of the History of Ideas* 58, no. 3 (1997): 365–384.

Bernard, Paul P. "Jerome of Prague, Austria and the Hussites." *Church History* 27 (1958): 3–22.

Betts, R. R. *Essays in Czech History*. London: Athlone, 1969.

———. "Jeron9ým Pražský." *Československý časopis historický* 5 (1957): 199–226.

———. "The University of Prague: The First Sixty Years." In *Prague Essays*, ed. R.W. Seton-Watson, pp. 57–66. Oxford: Clarendon, 1949.

Blechner, Gernot. "Wo befand sich die heimliche Herberge des Hieronymus von Prag?" *Konstanzer Almanach* 27 (1981), pp. 61–4.

Blechner, Gernot, ed. *1313–2013: 700 Jahre Haus Zum Delphin*. Constance: Werner C. Schupp, 2013.

Boockmann, Hartmut. "Zur politischen Geschichte des Konstanzer Konzils." *Zeitschrift für Kirchengeschichte* 85 (1974): 45–63.

Brandmüller, Walter. *Das Konzil von Konstanz 1414–1418*, 2 vols. Paderborn: Ferdinand Schöningh, 1991–1997.

Brown, D. Catherine. *Pastor and Laity in the Theology of Jean Gerson*. Cambridge: Cambridge University Press, 1987.

Burrows, Mark S., *Jean Gerson and De Consolatione Theologiae: The Consolation of a Biblical and Reforming Theology for a Disordered Age*. Tübingen: J. C. B. Mohr, 1991.

Catto, Jeremy I. "Wyclif and Wycliffism at Oxford 1356–1430." In *The History of the University of Oxford*, ed. J.I. Catto and T.A.R. Evans, vol. 2, pp. 175–261. Oxford: Oxford University Press, 1992.

Courtenay, William J. *Parisian Scholars in the Early Fourteenth Century: A Social Portrait*. Cambridge: Cambridge University Press, 1999.

Dahmus, Joseph. *The Prosecution of John Wyclif*. New Haven, Conn.: Yale University Press, 1952.

De Vooght, Paul. *L'Hérésie de Jean Huss*, 2nd ed. Louvain: Publications universitaires de Louvain, 1975.

———. "Jean Huss et ses juges." In *Das Konzil von Konstanz—Beiträge zu seiner Geschichte und Theologie: Festschrift unter dem Protektorat seiner Exzellenz des Hochwürdigsten Herrn Erzbischofs Dr. Hermann Schäufele*, ed. August Franzen and Wolfgang Müller, 172–173. Freiburg: Herder, 1964.

———. *Les sources de la doctrine chrétienne d'après les théologiens du XIVe siècle et du début du XVe*. Paris: Desclée de Brouwer, 1954.

Dolejšová, Ivana. "Nominalist and Realist Approaches to the Problem of Authority: Páleč and Hus." *BRRP* 2 (1998): 49–55.

Doležalová, Eva. *Svěcenci pražské diecéze 1395–1416*. Prague: Historický ústav, 2010.

Doležalová, Eva, Jan Hrdina, František Šmahel, and Zdeněk Uhlíř. "The Reception and Criticism of Indulgences in the Late Medieval Czech Lands." In *Promissory Notes on the Treasury of Merits: Indulgences in Late Medieval Europe*, ed. R. N. Swanson, pp. 101–145. Leiden: Brill, 2006.

Elbel, Petr. and Andreas Zajic. "Die zwei Körper des Kanzlers? Die 'reale' und die 'virtuelle' Karriere Kaspar Schlicks unter König und Kaiser Sigismund—Epilogomena zu einem alten Forschungsthema." *Mediaevalia Historica Bohemica* 15, no. 2 (2012): 47–143; 16, no. 1 (2013): 55–212; and 16, no. 2 (2013): 73–157.

Evans, G. R. *John Wyclif: Myth and Reality*. Downers Grove, Ill.: IVP Academic, 2005.

Fink, Karl August. "Zu den Quellen für die Geschichte des Konstanzer Konzils." In *Das Konzil von Konstanz—Beiträge zu seiner Geschichte und Theologie: Festschrift unter dem Protektorat seiner Exzellenz des Hochwürdigsten Herrn Erzbischofs Dr. Hermann Schäufele*, ed. August Franzen and Wolfgang Müller, pp. 471–476. Freiburg: Herder, 1964.

Finke, Heinrich. *Forschungen und Quellen zur Geschichte des Konstanzer Koncils*. Paderborn: F. Schöningh, 1889.

Firnhaber, Friedrich. "Petrus de Pulka, Abgesabdter der Wiener universität am Concilium zu Constanz." *Archiv für österreichische Geschichte* 15 (1856): 1–70.

Fudge, Thomas A. *Heresy and Hussites in Late Medieval Europe*. Farnham: Ashgate, 2014.

———. "Hussite Theology and the Law of God." In *The Cambridge Companion to Reformation Theology*, ed. David Bagchi and David C. Steinmetz, pp. 22–27. Cambridge: Cambridge University Press, 2004.

———. "Jan Hus as the Apocalyptic Witness in John Foxe's History." *CV* 56, no. 2 (2014): 136–168.

———. *Jan Hus Between Time and Eternity: Reconsidering a Medieval Heretic*. Lanham, MD: Lexington, 2016.

———. *Jan Hus: Religious Reform and Social Revolution in Bohemia*. London: I. B. Tauris, 2010.

———. *Living With Jan Hus: A Modern Journey Across a Medieval Landscape*. Portland, OR: Center for Christian Studies, 2015.

———. *The Magnificent Ride: The First Reformation in Hussite Bohemia*. Aldershot, U.K.: Ashgate, 1998.

———. *The Memory and Motivation of Jan Hus, Medieval Priest and Martyr*. Turnhout: Brepols, 2013.

———. *The Trial of Jan Hus: Medieval Heresy and Criminal Procedure*. New York: Oxford University Press, 2013.

Gilson, Étienne. *History of Christian Philosophy in the Middle Ages*. New York: Random House, 1955.

Girgensohn, Dieter. *Peter von Pulka und die Wiedereinführung des Laienkelches.* Göttingen: Vandenhoek & Ruprecht, 1964.

Heimpel, Hermann. *Dietrich von Niem (c. 1340–1418).* Münster: Regensbergische Verlagsbuchhandlung, 1932.

Heller, Ludwig. *Hieronymus von Prag.* Lübeck: Aschenfeldt, 1835.

Herold, Vilém. "Magister Hieronymus von Prag und die Universität Köln." *Miscellanea Medievalia* 20 (1989): 255–273.

———. "Die Philosophie des Hussitismus: Zur Rolle der Ideenlehre Platons." In *Verdrängter Humanismus, Verzögerte Aufklärung: Philosophie in Österreich (1400–1650), Vom Konstanzer Konzil zum Auftreten Luthers,* ed. Michael Benedikt, pp. 101–118. Vienna: Verlag Leben-Kunst-Wissenschaft, 1996.

———. "Platonic Ideas and 'Hussite' Philosophy." *BRRP* 1 (1996): 13–17.

———. *Pražská univerzita a Wyclif: Wyclifovo učení o ideách a geneze husitského revolučního myšlení.* Prague: Univerzita Karlova, 1985.

———. "Štěpán of Páleč and the Archetypal World of Ideas." *BRRP* 5, no. 1 (2004): 77–87.

———. "Der Streit zwischen Hieronymus von Prag und Johann Gerson—eine spätmittelalterliche Diskussion mit tragischen Folgen." In *Société et Eglise: Texts et discussions dans les universités d'Europe centrale pendant le moyen âge tardif,* ed. Sophie Włodek, pp. 77–89. Turnhout: Brepols, 1995.

———. "The University of Paris and the Foundations of the Bohemian Reformation." *Bohemian Reformation and Religious Practice* 3 (2000): 15–24.

———. "Vojtěch Raňkův of Ježov (Adalbertus Rankonis de Ericinio) and the Bohemian Reformation." *Bohemian Reformation and Religious Practice* 7 (2009): 72–79.

———. "Wyclif und Hieronymus von Prag: Zum Versuch einer 'praktischen' Umwandlung in der spätmittelaterlichen Ideenlehre." In *Knowledge and the Sciences in Medieval Philosophy,* 3 vols., ed. Simo Knuuttila, Reijo Työrinoja, and Sten Ebbesen, vol. 3, pp. 212–223. Helsinki: Akateeminen Kirjakauppa, 1990.

Herold, Vilém, and Pavel Spunar, "L'Université de Prague et les rôle des disputations *de quolibet* à sa faculté des Arts à la fin du XIVe et au début du XVe siècle." In *Compte rendu de la 69e Session annuelle du Comité de l'Union Académique Internationale,* pp. 27–39. Brussels: Secretariat administratif de L'U A.I., Palais des Académies, 1996.

Hobbins, Daniel. *Authorship and Publicity Before Print: Jean Gerson and the Transformation of Late Medieval Learning.* Philadelphia: University of Pennsylvania Press, 2009.

Holeton, David R. "The Bohemian Eucharistic Movement in Its European Context." *BRRP* 1 (1996): 23–47.

———. "L'Eschatologie et le mouvement eucharistique en Europe centrale pendant la fin du Moyen-Âge." In *Eschatologie et Liturgie,* ed. A. M. Triacca and E. Pistoia, pp. 115–123. Rome: C.L.V. Edizioni Liturgiche, 1985.

———. "Wyclif's Bohemian Fate." *CV* 32 (Winter 1989): 209–222.

Horníčková, Kateřina, and Michal Šroněk, eds, *Umění české reformace (1380–1620)*. Prague: Academia, 2010.

Hudson, Anne. *The Premature Reformation: Wycliffite Texts and Lollard History*. Oxford: Clarendon, 1988.

———. *Studies in the Transmission of Wyclif's Writings*. Aldershot, U.K.: Ashgate, 2008.

Jähnig, Bernhart. *Johann von Wallenrode O.T., Erzbishof von Riga, Königlicher Rat, Deutschordens Diplomat und Bishof von Lüttich im Zeitalter des Schismas und der Konstanzer Konzils, um 1370–1419*. Bonn: Verlag Wissenschaftliches Archiv, 1970.

Jeauneau, Edouard. "Plato apud Bohemos." *Medieval Studies* 41 (1979): 161–214.

Kalivoda, Robert. *Husitská ideologie*. Prague: Československá akademie věd, 1961.

Kaluza, Zénon. "Le 'De universali realî de Jean De Maisonneuve er les *epicure littera-les*." *Freiburger Zeitschrift für Philosophie und Theologie* 33 (1986): 469–516.

———. *Études doctrinales sur le XIVe siècle: Théologie, Logique, Philosophie*. Paris: Vrin, 2013.

———. *Les querelles doctrinales à Paris: Nominalistes et réalistes aux confins du XIVe et XVe siècles*. Bergamo: Lubrina, 1988.

Kaminsky, Howard. *A History of the Hussite Revolution*. Berkeley: University of California Press, 1967.

———. "From Lateness to Waning to Crisis: The Burden of the Later Middle Ages." *Journal of Early Modern History* 4 (No. 1, 2000), pp. 85–125.

———. "On the Sources of Matthew of Janov's Doctrine." In *Czechoslovakia Past and Present*, 2 vols., ed. Miloslav Rechcigl, vol. 2, pp. 1175–1183. The Hague: Mouton, 1968.

———. "Wyclifism as Ideology of Revolution." *Church History* 32 (March 1963): 57–74.

Kejř, Jiří. *Kvodlibetní disputace na Pražské Universitě*. Prague: Universita Karlova, 1971.

———. "Sporné otázky v bádání o Dekretu kutnohorském." *Acta universitatis caroli-nae, Historia universitatis carolinae Pragensis* 3 (No. 1, 1962), pp. 83–95.

———. "Struktura a průběh disputace de quodlibet na pražské universitě." *Acta uni-versitatis carolinae, Historia universitatis carolinae Pragensis* 1 (1960): 17–42.

Klicman, Ladislaus. "Der Wiener Process gegen Hieronymus von Prag, 1410–1412." *Mitteilungen des Instituts für Oesterreichische Geschichtsforschung* 21, no. 3 (1900): 445–457.

Kořán, Ivo. "Knihovna mistra Jeronýma Pražského." *Český časopis historický* 94 (1996): 590–600.

Lahey, Stephen E. *John Wyclif*. New York: Oxford University Press, 2009.

Lambert, Malcolm. *Medieval Heresy: Popular Movements from the Gregorian Reform to the Reformation*, 3rd ed. Oxford: Blackwell, 2002.

Lehmann, Paul. *Die Parodie im Mittelalter*, 2nd ed. Stuttgart: Hiersemann, 1963.

Lenfant, Jacques. *History of the Council of Constance*, 2 vols., trans. Stephen Whatley. London: Rivington, 1730.

Loserth, Johann. *Wiclif and Hus*, trans. M. J. Evans. London: Hodder and Stoughton, 1884, 2nd ed. 1925.

Luss, Jackie. "Some Examples of the Use Made of the Pseudo-Dionysius by University Teachers in the Later Middle Ages." In *The Universities in the Late Middle Ages*, ed. Josef Ijsewijn and Jacques Paquet, pp. 228–241. Louvain: Leuven University Press, 1978.

Lützow, Count [František]. *The Life and Times of Master John Hus*. London: Dent, 1909.

Madre, Alois. *Nikolaus von Dinkelsbühl. Leben und Schriften*. Münster: Aschendorff, 1965.

Marin, Olivier. *L'archevêque, le maître et le dévot: Genèses du mouvement réformateur pragois années 1360–1419*. Paris: Honoré Champion Éditeur, 2005.

McGuire, Brian Patrick. *Jean Gerson and the Last Medieval Reformation*. University Park: Pennsylvania State University Press, 2005.

Mezník, Jaroslav. *Praha před husitskou revolucí*. Prague: Academia, 1990.

Miethke, Jürgen. "Die Prozesse in Konstanz gegen Jan Hus und Hieronymus von Prag—ein Konflikt unter Kirchenreformern?" In *Häresie und vorzeitige Reformation und Spätmittelalter*, ed. František Šmahel, pp. 147–167. Munich: Oldenbourg, 1998.

Muchelmans, Gabriel. "Stanislaus of Znaim on Truth and Falsity." In *Mediaeval Semantics and Metaphysics: Studies Dedicated to L. M. de Rijk on the Occasion of His 60th Birthday*, ed. E. P. Bos, pp. 313–338. Nijmegen: Brepols, 1985.

Murray, Alexander. *Conscience and Authority in the Medieval Church*. Oxford: Oxford University Press, 2015.

Nejedlý, Zdeněk. *Dějiny husitského zpěvu*, 6 vols. Prague: Československá akademie věd, 1954–1956.

Novotný, Václav. *Husitský zpěvník: Nábožné písně a Mistru Janovi Husovi a Mistru Jeronymovi*. Prague: Reichel, 1930.

Novotný, Václav, and Vlastimil Kybal. *M. Jan Hus: Život a učení*, 5 vols. Prague: Laichter, 1919–1931.

Oberman, Heiko Augustinus. *Contra vanam curiositatem: Ein Kapital der Theologie zwischen Seelenwinkel und Weltall*. Zurich: Theologischer Verlag, 1974.

———. *The Harvest of Medieval Theology: Gabriel Biel and Late Medieval Nominalism*. Grand Rapids, Mich.: Eerdmans, 1967.

Palacký, František. *Dějiny národu českého v Čechách a v Moravě*, 6 vols. Prague: Kvasníčka a Hampl, 1939.

Pavlíček, Ota. "La figure de l'autorité à travers Jean Hus et Jérôme de Prague." *Revue des sciences religieuses* 85, no. 3 (2011): 371–389.

———. "*Scutum fidei christianae*: The Depiction of the Shield of Faith in the Realistic Teaching of Jerome of Prague in the Context of His Interpretation of the Trinity." *BRRP* 9 (2014): 72–97.

———. "Two Philosophical Texts of Jerome of Prague and His Alleged Designation of Opponents of Real Universals as Diabolic Heretics." *BRRP* 8 (2009): 52–76.

Perett, Marcela K. "Vernacular Songs as 'Oral Pamphlets': The Hussites and Their Propaganda Campaign." *Viator* 42, no. 2 (2011): 371–391.

Pilný, Joseph. *Jérôme de Prague: Un orateur progressiste du Moyen Âge.* Geneva: Perret-Gentil, 1974.

Rychterová, Pavlína, and Pavel Soukup, eds. *Heresis seminaria. Pojmy a koncepty v bádání o husitství.* Prague: Filosofia, 2013.

Schaff, David S. "Jerome of Prague and the Five Hundredth Anniversary of His Death." *Bibliotheca sacra* 73 (April 1916): 192–213.

Seibt, Ferdinand. *Hussitica. Zur Struktur einer Revolution.* Cologne: Böhlau, 1965.

Shank, Michael H. *Unless You Believe, You Shall Not Understand: Logic, University, and Society in Late Medieval Vienna.* Princeton, N.J.: Princeton University Press, 1988.

Šmahel, František. "The *Acta* of the Constance Trial of Master Jerome of Prague." In *Text and Controversy from Wyclif to Bale,* ed. Helen Barr and Ann M. Hutchison, pp. 323–334. Turnhout: Brepols, 2005.

———. "Doctor evangelicus super omnes evangelistas: Wyclif's Fortune in Hussite Bohemia." *Bulletin of the Institute of Historical Research* 43 (May 1970): 16–34.

———. "Drobné otázky a záhady v studentském životě mistra Jeronýma Pražského." *Český časopis historický* 106, no. 1 (2008): 1–18.

———. "The Hussite Critique of the Clergy's Civil Dominion." In *Anticlericalism in Late Medieval and Early Modern Europe,* ed. Peter A. Dykema and Heiko A. Oberman, pp. 83–90. Leiden: Brill, 1993.

———. *Die Hussitischen Revolution,* trans. Thomas Krzenck, 3 vols. Hannover: Hahnsche, 2002.

———. *Idea národa v husitských Čechách.* Prague: Argo, 2000.

———. *Jeroným Pražsky: Život revolučního intelektuála.* Prague: Svobodné slovo, 1966.

———. "The Kuttenberg Decree and the Withdrawal of the German Students from Prague in 1409: A Discussion." *History of Universities* 4 (1984): 153–166.

———. "Kvodlibetní diskuse ke kvestii principalis mistra Michala z Malenic roku 1412." *Acta universitatis carolinae, Historia universitatis carolinae Pragensis* 21, no. 1 (1981): 27–52.

———. "Leben und Werk des Magisters Hieronymus von Prag." *Historica* 13 (1966): 81–111.

———. "Mistr Jeroným Pražský na soudu dějin." *Husitský tábor,* supp. 1 (2001): 313–323.

———. "Poggio und Hieronymus von Prag: Zur Frage des hussitischen Humanismus." In *Studien zum Humanismus in den böhmischen Ländern,* ed. Hans Bernd Harder and Hans Rothe, pp. 75–91. Cologne: Böhlau, 1988.

———. *Die Prager Universität im Mittelalter.* Leiden: Brill, 2007.

———. "Prolegomena zum Prager Universalienstreit: Zwischenbilanz einer Quellenanalyse." In *The Universities in the Late Middle Ages,* ed. Jozef Ijsewijn and Jacques Paquet, pp. 242–255. Louvain. Leuven University Press, 1978.

———. "Das Scutum fidei christianae magistri Hieronymi Pragensis in der Entwicklung der mittelalterlichen trinitarischen Diagramme." In *Die Bildwelt der Diagramme Joachims von Fiore. Zur Medialität religiös-politischer*

Programme im Mittelalter, ed. Alexander Patschovsky, 185–210. Sigmaringen: J. Thorbecke, 2003.

———. "Univerzitni Kuestie a polemiky mistra Jeronýma Pražského." *Acta universitatis Carolina—Historia universitatis carolinae pragensis* 22, fasc. 2 (1982): 7–41.

———. "Verzeichnis der Quellen zum Prager Universalienstreit 1348–1500." *Mediaevalia Philosophica Polonorum* 25 (1980): 1–189.

———. *Život a dílo Jeronýma Pražského*. Prague: Argo, 2010.

Šmahel, František, and Martin Nodl. "Kutnohorský dekret po 600 letech." *Český časopis historický* 107 (2009): 1–45.

Sommerfeldt, Gustav. "Zwei politische Sermone des Heinrich von Oyta und des Nikolaus von Dinkelsbühl (1388 und 1417)." *Historisches Jahrbuch* 26 (1905): 318–327.

Sousedík, Stanislaw. "M. Hieronymi Pragensis ex Iohanne Scoto Eriugena excerpta." *Listy filologické* 98 (1975): 4–7.

Spěváček, Jiří. *Václav IV. 1361–1419 k předpokladům husitské revoluce*. Prague: Svoboda, 1986.

Stejskal, Karel. "Obvinění mistra Jeronýma Pražského z ikonoklasmu a modlářství na Kostnickém koncilu." In *Husitství—reformace—renesance: Sborník k 60. narozeninám Františka Šmahela*, 3 vols., ed. Jaroslav Pánek, Miloslav Polívka, and Noemi Rejchrtová, vol. 1, pp. 369–380. Prague: Historický ústav, 1994.

Strnad, Alfred A. "Die Zeugen im Wiener Prozess gegen Hieronymus von Prag: Prosopographische Anmerkungen zu einem Inquisitionsverfahren im Vorfelde des Hussitismus." In *Husitství—reformace—renesance: Sborník k 60. narozeninám Františka Šmahela*, 3 vols., ed. Jaroslav Pánek, Miloslav Polívka, and Noemi Rejchrtová, vol. 1, pp. 331–367. Prague: Historický ústav, 1994.

Thomson, Samuel Harrison. "The Philosophical Basis of Wyclif's Theology." *Journal of Religion* 11 (January 1931): 86–116.

Trapp, Damascus. "Clm 27034: Unchristened Nominalism and Wycliffite Realism at Prague in 1381." *Recherches de théologie ancienne et médiévale* 24 (1957): 320–360.

Van Dussen, Michael. *From England to Bohemia: Heresy and Communication in the Later Middle Ages*. Cambridge: Cambridge University Press, 2012.

Vidmanová, Anežka. "K řezenskému dopisu Jeronýma Pražského." *Husitský tábor* 14 (2004): 35–48.

Walsh, Katherine. "Magister Johannes [Siwart] de Septemcastris an der Universität Wien. Versuch eines Gelehrtenprofils aus der Hussitenzeit." In *Ex ipsis rerum Documentis. Beiträge zue Mediävistik: Festschrift für Harald Zimmermann zum 65. Geburtstag*, ed. Klaus Herbers, Hans-Henning Kortüm, and Carol Servatius, 557–569. Sigmaringen: Thorbecke, 1991.

———. "Vom Wegestreit zur Häeresie: Zur Auseinandersetzung um die Lehre John Wyclifs in Wien und Prag an der Wende zum 15. Jahrhundert." *Mittelungen Instituts für Österreichische Geschichtsforschung* 94 (1986): 25–48.

———. "Wyclif's Legacy in Central Europe in the Late Fourteenth and Early Fifteenth Centuries." In *From Ockham to Wyclif*, Studies in Church History, Subsidia 5, ed. Anne Hudson and Michael Wilks, pp. 397–417. Oxford: Blackwell, 1987.

Watkins, Renee Neu, "The Death of Jerome of Prague: Divergent Views." *Speculum* 42 (January 1967), pp. 104–129.

Wei, Ian P. *Intellectual Culture in Medieval Paris: Theologians and the University, c. 1100–1330*. Cambridge: Cambridge University Press, 2012.

Weltsch, Ruben E. *Archbishop John of Jenstein, 1348–1400: Papalism, Humanism and Reform in Pre-Hussite Prague*. The Hague: Mouton, 1968.

Index

Entries for Jerome, Jan Hus, John Wyclif, Jean Gerson, Bohemia, Prague, the Council of Constance, medieval universities, and heresy (laws, trials, and procedures), are selective on account of the fact that these subjects constitute the basic fabric of the book and in consequence are quite numerous. Popes, councils (ecclesiastical synods), and specific churches are listed alphabetically under those headings. Abbeys, convents, cloisters, monasteries, and priories are noted under the heading of religious houses. Unless otherwise noted, the churches and religious houses specifically identified are in Prague or its immediate environs. Medieval people are generally listed under places of origin. Lesser known medieval figures have been identified according to their chief role in connection with the subjects under investigation. Czech proper names have generally been given in their native form. The notable exception is Prague rather than Praha.